Pro Mapping in BizTalk Server 2009

Jim Dawson and John Wainwright

Apress®

Pro Mapping in BizTalk Server 2009

Copyright © 2009 by Jim Dawson, John Wainwright

ISBN-13 (pbk): 978-1-4302-1857-9

ISBN-13 (electronic): 978-1-4302-1858-6

9 8 7 6 5 4 3 2 1

Lead Editors: Mark Beckner, Tony Campbell
Technical Reviewer: Jeff Sanders
Editorial Board: Clay Andres, Steve Anglin, Mark Beckner, Ewan Buckingham, Tony Campbell,
    Gary Cornell, Jonathan Gennick, Jonathan Hassell, Michelle Lowman, Matthew Moodie,
    Duncan Parkes, Jeffrey Pepper, Frank Pohlmann, Ben Renow-Clarke, Dominic Shakeshaft,
    Matt Wade, Tom Welsh
Project Manager: Kylie Johnston
Copy Editor: Heather Lang
Associate Production Director: Kari Brooks-Copony
Production Editor: Laura Cheu
Compositor: Dina Quan
Proofreader: Kim Burton
Indexer: Becky Hornyak
Cover Designer: Kurt Krames
Manufacturing Director: Tom Debolski

Distributed to the book trade worldwide by Springer-Verlag New York, Inc., 233 Spring Street, 6th Floor, New York, NY 10013. Phone 1-800-SPRINGER, fax 201-348-4505, e-mail orders-ny@springer-sbm.com, or visit http://www.springeronline.com.

For information on translations, please contact Apress directly at 2855 Telegraph Avenue, Suite 600, Berkeley, CA 94705. Phone 510-549-5930, fax 510-549-5939, e-mail info@apress.com, or visit http://www.apress.com.

Apress and friends of ED books may be purchased in bulk for academic, corporate, or promotional use. eBook versions and licenses are also available for most titles. For more information, reference our Special Bulk Sales–eBook Licensing web page at http://www.apress.com/info/bulksales.

The source code for this book is available to readers at http://www.apress.com.

Anyone who has spent much time in the IT world knows that success is often due in very large measure to those who came before us who took the time to stop and explain a technique or a method, patiently guided us past our mistakes, or had the grace to let us learn from our failures. While the debt incurred cannot be paid back, it can certainly be acknowledged. So we raise our glasses to the many individuals in our checkered pasts who viewed expertise as something to be shared and not hoarded.

Contents at a Glance

PART 1 ■■■ Basic Concepts of BizTalk Mapping

PART 2 ■■■ Step-by-Step Mapping

PART 3 ■■■ Looping

PART 4 ■ ■ ■ EDI Mapping with BizTalk

PART 5 ■ ■ ■ Advanced Techniques

Contents

PART 1 ■■■ Basic Concepts of BizTalk Mapping

PART 2 ■■■ Step-by-Step Mapping

PART 3 ■■■ Looping

PART 4 ■■■ EDI Mapping with BizTalk

PART 5 ■ ■ ■ Advanced Techniques

About the Authors

JAMES (JIM) LEE DAWSON spent his first life in the U.S. Marine Corps, gaining a number of skills that had no direct applicability to civilian life. He spent a tour in Vietnam as an infantry platoon and company commander and left the Marines in 1978 as a captain.

Since that time, his new life includes more than 25 years' experience in technical environments, including working as a programmer analyst, systems analyst, EDI analyst, BizTalk integrator, team leader, project manager, and departmental director. He has programmed in C, C++, C#, VB, XSLT, PHP, SQL, HTML, FORTRAN, PL1, and Assembly. He has worked with the BizTalk mapping engine for the last six years, concentrating on applying BizTalk to EDI uses as well as creating BizTalk maps.

Jim is currently a managing partner of Second Star Professional Services (SSPS), LLC, a Microsoft Registered Partner that provides expert electronic commerce implementation and integration services. SSPS focuses on BizTalk Server and EDI mapping using Mercator, GXS Application Integrator, and the BizTalk mapper. Jim has extensive experience with the Covast EDI accelerators for BizTalk 2002, 2004, and 2006.

Jim's BA from the University of North Carolina in English enabled him to produce a number of obscure written works, including nonfiction with esoteric titles such as *Mechanized Forces in the Link-up Operation* and *The Soviet Meeting Engagement* and fiction titles like *Black Dugal's Music Shoppe* and *The Sapient Sorcerer*.

Jim currently resides in Siler City, North Carolina.

JOHN D. WAINWRIGHT has over 30 years of experience in various areas of information management, with extensive programming and project management experience in software development. He worked in corporate, manufacturing, and consulting environments on a wide variety of systems, including inventory control, shipping, distribution, cost accounting, shop floor control, and computer-integrated manufacturing control. After 15 years doing software development, John began working as a consultant in EDI, focusing mainly on implementing EDI in supply chain management, transportation, and distribution. John has spent much of the last five years doing BizTalk mapping and claims that he's never seen a purchase order map he doesn't like.

He is currently a managing partner of Second Star Professional Services (SSPS), LLC. John and coauthor Jim Dawson, tired of IT management jobs that weren't any fun, started the company nine years ago so they could get back to doing interesting stuff. They now provide consulting in the EDI integration arena. During that time, John worked primarily with BizTalk mapping, starting out with the Covast EDI accelerator for BizTalk and moving on to work with the R2 product. He's also had extensive mapping experience with Mercator and Application Integrator.

John has an interesting, but not useful, BA in history from Allegheny College. He did graduate work (more interesting and less useful) at Temple University. Fortunately, while learning that an academic career didn't seem too promising, he learned some programming skills as well.

He currently resides in Raleigh, North Carolina.

About the Technical Reviewer

JEFF SANDERS is a 16-year IT industry veteran with extensive experience in solutions architecture, BizTalk, SharePoint, and .NET. Jeff's interests lie in design patterns of message-based architectures and connected systems design, Dublin, WCF, WF, and reducing complexity.

Jeff is a group manager and solutions architect with Avanade Inc., a global IT consultancy specializing in solutions based on the Microsoft enterprise platform that help to achieve profitable growth. He works out of the east region with some of the most talented and customer-obsessed professionals he has ever met.

Jeff also independently consults with DynamicShift and speaks at regional and local user groups on Microsoft technologies and industry-related topics.

With a deep interest in providing better information to business decision makers, event-driven architecture, complex event processing, and business intelligence, Jeff is coauthoring *Pro BAM in BizTalk Server 2009* (Apress, 2009), to be released later this year. You should buy a copy, or five.

Jeff would like to thank Jim Dawson and John Wainwright, Mark Beckner, and Kylie Johnston. Most of all, he would like to thank Lisa, who deserves so much more. Yeah, Beesley, we're in the same time zone, but it does feel far.

Acknowledgments

We'd like to thank the editors and reviewers at Apress and all the clients who allowed us to learn at their expense.

Introduction

When people begin learning Visual Basic, C#, BizTalk, and other technical subjects, they buy how-to books. That is why most technical folk have a reference library close at hand. If they are working with BizTalk, that library contains cookbooks and references on XML, XSLT, and XPATH as well as BizTalk.

The one subject that references fail to cover well is BizTalk mapping. No tips and techniques. No teach yourself books. No mapper's bible. The few BizTalk reference manuals available include limited information on mapping, but these short treatments provide no help in understanding how to overcome minor mapping difficulties, much less help solving complex mapping problems.

As we learned how to adapt BizTalk to X12 and EDIFACT mapping, we wondered if perhaps BizTalk and EDI were not meant to work together in any meaningful way. But as we used brute force to plow our way through EDI maps, we discovered that we could solve any mapping problem without resorting to pre- or post-processing. In fact, we learned that there are often several ways to solve any mapping problem. We've put the most useful of those techniques into this book.

We began with the intent of writing a book with a bunch of sample maps but soon came to the conclusion that such a book is neither possible nor desirable. Why? Because BizTalk mapping is never about solving one large mapping problem. The questions we face every day as mappers are more like "How do I solve this little piece here?" rather than "How do I create this map?" Any mapping project consists of a myriad of small mapping problems, a series of one-percent solutions. Solve the first, test it, and then move on the next. Eventually, all the pieces are solved, and the map is completed.

In that vein, we cover many little mapping solutions in the hope that as you encounter a new type of problem, you can turn to this reference and find a solution or at the least some options that will light the way toward a solution. Anyone who creates maps using the BizTalk Map Editor will benefit from owning this manual.

Who This Book Is For

We include a little something for everyone in this book, and we present a broad range of subjects in the hope that mappers with all levels of skill and experience will find valuable information here. We include basic material to introduce the novice BizTalk mapper to basic mapping techniques. For those BizTalk experts who are not experienced with EDI, we provide a section of the book dedicated to EDI mapping techniques. For advanced BizTalk mappers, we provide examples of how to deal with of more complex mapping topics such as accessing external data or building custom functoids.

How This Book Is Structured

The book is divided into five parts.

Part 1, "Basic Concepts of BizTalk Mapping," consists of four chapters that provide an introductory overview of BizTalk mapping. Since the BizTalk mapper works a bit differently from other mapping engines, Chapter 1, "Creating a Simple Map," introduces those who are new to BizTalk mapping to basic mapping concepts. Chapter 2, "How BizTalk Maps Work," takes a look under the hood to explore how BizTalk maps actually work and focuses on the underlying map code that is generated when you build a map. Chapter 3, "Using Scripting in Maps," looks at how custom scripting can be employed in BizTalk maps. Chapter 4, "Testing BizTalk Maps," concludes the section with an overview of how to test and debug BizTalk maps in the map editor and the development studio using basic testing techniques.

Part 2, "Step-by-Step Mapping," contains six chapters, each of which deals with a specific type of mapping problem: conditionals, numbers, strings, dates and times, collecting and counting, and handling external data.

Part 3, "Looping," contains two chapters that deal exclusively with how to handle the complexities of looping in BizTalk maps.

Part 4, "EDI Mapping with BizTalk," begins with an introduction to EDI and includes subsequent chapters on solving EDI looping problems, using EDI code pairs, and unraveling SDQ segments. This section ends with a chapter devoted exclusively to untangling some of the mysteries of how to map the Advanced Ship Notice.

Part 5, "Advanced Techniques," includes one chapter on constructing external assemblies and custom functoids and a final topic on miscellaneous topics, such as specialized pipeline construction for EDI envelope modification, construction of external XSLT maps, and a section on how to test your custom scripts in the development studio.

Conventions

We use several standard conventions for various types of text in the book. They are presented in a special typeface to bring them to your attention.

Note, Tip, and Caution elements will look like these:

▪**Note** Notes will usually contain information that we think might be worth keeping in mind.

▪**Tip** These are special techniques or methods that might be of help.

▪**Caution** These usually offer a warning to help you avoid a mistake we have made.

Code fragments look like this:

```
public string LoadPO1Table(string inQty, string inPairs)
{
  string pairs = inPairs;
  string pair = "";
// Empty the hash table each time to avoid having residual values
  PO1Table.Clear();
// pairs contains a copy of the input string.  If there is still data in the string
// continue processing through the while loop
  while (pairs != "")
  {
```

We've also included *code comments*: We tried to annotate the code liberally. Some comments are prefixed with a double slash //; others use <!-- to begin and --!> to end a comment. We did not distinguish between script types but generally used the method that made the code easier to read. The // is actually the standard character string for commenting a single line of C# code, while <!-- and --!> are the standard comment strings for enclosing XSLT comments. Please forgive us for this transgression. If you download the code, any comments will be correctly formatted so that the code will compile.

Prerequisites

The book focuses on mapping with the BizTalk Map Editor, a topic that requires a basic knowledge of the support structure for that tool, in particular Microsoft Visual Studio. Basic knowledge of the C# or VB programming languages, BizTalk schemas, XML, and XSLT—all pieces of the BizTalk mapping environment—is also important. A basic understanding of BizTalk port and party configuration in the BizTalk Administration Console helps with testing.

EDI knowledge is not a prerequisite (although it is certainly beneficial), because we realize that most users of the BizTalk mapping engine are not familiar with EDI.

Downloading the Code

All examples in the book—maps, scripts, and test data—are available to readers at www.apress.com, in this book's Downloads section. In most cases in this book, we build a map incrementally and show graphics and code for each step. Generally speaking, the downloadable maps include only the completed map.

The downloadable scripts and maps are arranged as BizTalk projects named for the chapter in which they appear. This method of organization means that some schemas, scripts, maps, and data files may appear in more than one chapter.

The examples in this book may be duplicated on your machine by downloading and unzipping the chapters. With the exception of the Encoding module used in the custom pipeline discussed in Chapter 19, we've included complete code fragments in the text. Aside from that exception, downloading the code is not necessary to understanding the information in this book.

Contacting the Authors

We welcome comments, criticism, corrections, and alternate methods. We also welcome suggestions for examples or areas we've overlooked. Jim and John can be contacted at the following e-mail addresses:

Jim Dawson: jim@sspsi.com
John Wainwright: john@sspsi.com

You can also reach us by snail mail at

Second Star Professional Services, LLC
7008 Robbie Drive
Raleigh, NC 27607

You can visit www.sspsi.com for more information about Second Star Professional Services.

PART 1

∎ ∎ ∎

Basic Concepts of BizTalk Mapping

CHAPTER 1

■■■

Creating a Simple Map

This chapter introduces the basics of mapping with BizTalk, including a high-level overview of the Visual Studio tools with which you will work when creating maps. You will create a simple mapping project in Visual Studio and add to that project a source schema and a target schema. You will then create a map that moves the data from a set of address records in the source schema to the more compact structure of the target document. Finally, you will test the map.

If you are an experienced BizTalk developer, you will already be familiar with the information discussed in this chapter. However, if you are transitioning from other mapping tools to BizTalk and have neither BizTalk nor general development experience, this chapter is for you.

Using the Development Studio

The Visual Studio will be your home for you mapping activities, so as a preface, we'll do a quick tour of the various Visual Studio windows that you will use most frequently. Remember that, in Visual Studio, you can set most windows to float. Alternatively, you can dock them in several optional locations. The positions of the windows in our figures reflect how we happen to like them set up. You should arrange them in the positions that work best for you.

The Mapper Grid

The mapper grid shown in Figure 1-1, which has the Source Schema on the left and the Destination Schema on the right, is the main working window of the map editor. Each map may have up to 20 mapper grids, and each grid has one tab at the bottom. In the figure, there are two tabs, Page 1 and Page 2, thus this map will be spread over two grids.

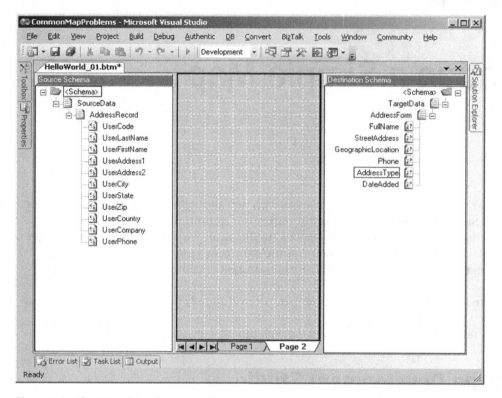

Figure 1-1. *The Visual Studio map editor*

Partitioning the map into grids is especially useful in reducing the clutter. You don't want the map to become so densely populated with functoids and links that you can't distinguish one item from another. By using multiple grids, you split the visual representation of the map onto more than one page. This technique allows you to focus on part of the map without having other parts of the map interfere with your view.

■Note Mapper grids are self-contained when creating a map. For example, a link cannot begin on one grid page and end on another grid page. Thus you can work on only one grid at a time. The grids are invisible to the compiler, so organizing the map into many grids has no impact on how the map functions.

Figure 1-2 shows how to create a new grid. Right-click the existing tab, and click Add Page.

Figure 1-2. *Adding a grid page*

You can rename a new or existing grid tab by right-clicking the tab you wish to rename and replacing the existing text with your own text. Figure 1-3 shows the Rename Page selection.

Figure 1-3. *Renaming a grid page*

Keep in mind that even when you have only one grid page, you still see only a very small percentage of the map. You can right-click the grid and select Grid Preview to see the entire grid for the current tab. Figure 1-4 shows one entire grid in the Grid Preview window.

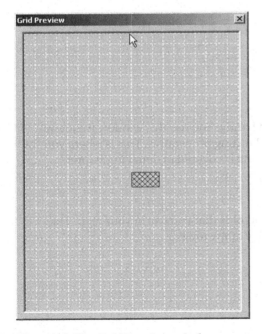

Figure 1-4. *The Grid Preview window*

The cross-hatched rectangle shows the area that will be displayed in the grid window when you close the grid preview. Links are not show in the preview window, but functoids are shown. To change the grid window view to show a particular functoid, drag the green box to the location of the functoid, and close the Grid Preview window. The functoid will now appear in the window.

Tip When you are looking at a mapper grid and the grid appears to be empty, you should check the Grid Preview window to see if there are functoids outside the current viewing area.

The Solution Explorer Window

The Solution Explorer shown in Figure 1-5 contains the current solution on which you are working along with all the projects and project files included in that solution. When working with maps you are mostly concerned with map files and schema files.

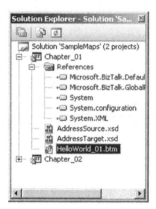

Figure 1-5. *The Solution Explorer window*

The Solution Explorer is a good window to keep handy. You use this window frequently during map development when you use incremental testing procedures. This is where you set parameters for map testing and start a map test. Testing is covered in detail in Chapter 3.

The Toolbox Window

The Toolbox window provides access to all of the functoids that you use in your map. The screen shot in Figure 1-6 shows you a standard display of the toolbar.

Figure 1-6. *The standard Toolbox window*

In BizTalk, you can customize the toolbox. By default, the General tab is empty. We use a subset of all the functoids more often than most and like to have the ones we use frequently in one location. We customize our toolbox by dragging and dropping selected icons into the General tab; our General tab is shown in Figure 1-7.

Figure 1-7. *Our Toolbox window's custom General tab*

You move an icon to a different tab using simple drag and drop. As you see, we selected functoids from the Advanced, Logical, String, and Cumulative Functoids tabs and moved them to the General tab. We also moved the Advanced Functoids menu from the top to the bottom, another drag-and-drop effort.

Tip The bulk of mapping is done with a small selection of the functoids. Moving the ones that you use most into one location, such as the General tab, will lessen the work you have to do to place functoids onto the mapper grid.

The Properties Window

The last menu you use extensively in mapping is the Properties window. Here, you can see the properties of whichever object you have currently highlighted in the mapper grid or in the source or destination schema windows. Figure 1-8 shows the Properties window as it appears when we highlight the root node of our target schema.

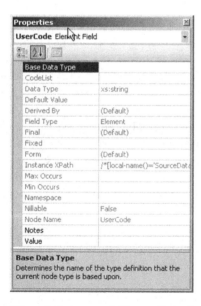

Figure 1-8. *A sample Properties window*

The Working Environment

The working environment for mapping has lots of windows and takes up quite a bit of space on your monitor screen. Figure 1-9 is a screen shot of the way John arranges his windows for optimum use while he maps. This arrangement provides immediate access to all of the principal windows you use when creating maps.

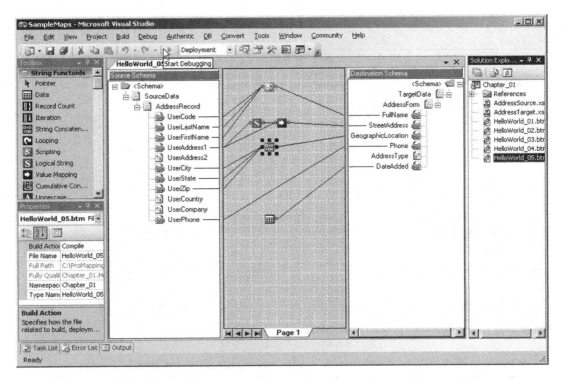

Figure 1-9. *One way to arrange your working screen*

Where John likes to keep his windows visible all the time, Jim uses a different arrangement and prefers to hide windows when the cursor is not over them. You should arrange your screen in the manner that fits your working methods.

Creating the Map

Next, we will build a map from scratch, beginning with the creation of the project and solution. We'll start with a blank slate and go step by step—creating a new project in the development studio, importing schemas into the project, building a map, and testing the map.

Creating a BizTalk Project

Your first step is to open the development studio so that you can create a new BizTalk project. If you want your project to be placed under any particular directory structure, you should create that structure first, but do not create the project directory. The development studio will do that for you when you create your project.

In the development studio, go to the File drop-down, and select New ➤ Project. Fill in the window as shown in Figure 1-10.

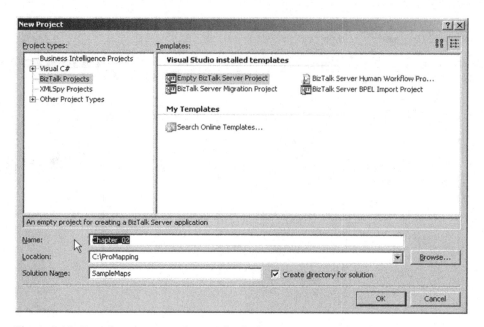

Figure 1-10. *Creating a new project and solution*

When you click OK, the development studio creates the directory tree C:\ProMapping\ SampleMaps\Chapter_01. SampleMaps is the solution directory; Chapter_01 is the project directory. Over the course of the rest of this book, we will build a project for each chapter, and those projects will all fall under this solution.

■**Caution** Don't consider the solution and project structure we use in this book a recommended method. Our standard practices for this are much different. For example, normally, we create a separate project for each map. We've cheerfully violated our normal practices in this book to make loading projects for a specific chapter easier for you.

Once you have created the solution, click the Save All icon to save your work.

Adding a Project File Structure

Your basic mapping project and the default directories are built during the saving process. Inside your Chapter_01 directory, you will find some other default directories created by the development studio. There are two, bin and obj, in the Chapter_01 directory. Each of those has several subdirectories as well, all used by the development studio for building and deploying your project.

We want you to add some folders to the Chapter_01 directory. We use this setup because it works for us in this book. You will develop your own preferences as to how best to organize your folders. Let's add some subdirectories to Chapter_01. You can see them in Figure 1-11.

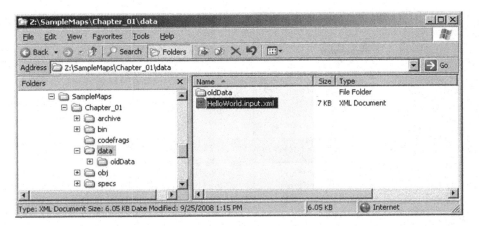

Figure 1-11. *Subdirectories for the project directory*

Create these subdirectories under the Chapter_01 directory:

- archive: We save stages of our maps as we create them. We also go to Windows Explorer and create copies of the saved maps, renaming them to include a sequential number and/or a date time. As we accumulate backup copies, we find it helpful to move them to an archive file, just to reduce the clutter in the project directory.

- codefrags: This is where we keep copies of all the scripts we use in the map. We put details about the scripts in the name of the script. When the map is complete, we copy the scripts into a master library of code fragments. We have found our code fragment library to be a very valuable resource, since we use the same scripts in many maps.

- data *and* oldData: Data files in BizTalk mapping proliferate more rapidly than rabbits. We keep the inputs and associated outputs data files in these directories simply to make finding the correct files easier. Even if there are common data directories, isolating your map test data like this gives you a place where you can modify the data specific to the map if necessary. The oldData directory is where we put old data that has become outdated, perhaps due to a schema change, just in case we need to revert to it.

- specs: This holds any documentation related to the map, such as document specifications, mapping specifications, and notes from discussions about the map.

Creating the Input and Output Schemas

Each map requires a source and a target schema. Sometimes, you will have to create these schemas from scratch, but we have already built them for you for these exercises. For this map, you'll want to add AddressSource.xsd and AddressTarget.xsd. You will find these schemas in the support files that you downloaded for these exercises. Right-click the project name, and select Add ➤ Existing Item, as shown in Figure 1-12.

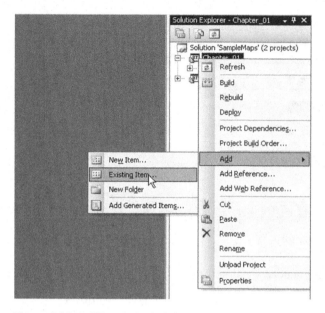

Figure 1-12. *Adding an existing item*

Now, browse to the schema files. Highlight the two schemas, as shown in Figure 1-13, and click the Add button to bring them into your project.

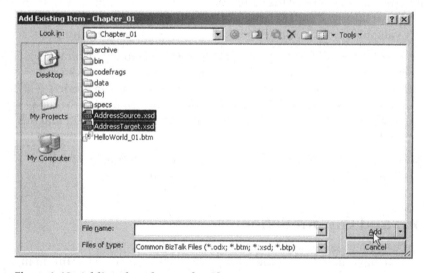

Figure 1-13. *Adding the schemas for Chapter 1*

Now that the schemas are in your project, you can open them in the schema editor. Double-click the schema name AddressSource in your project to open the source schema shown in Figure 1-14.

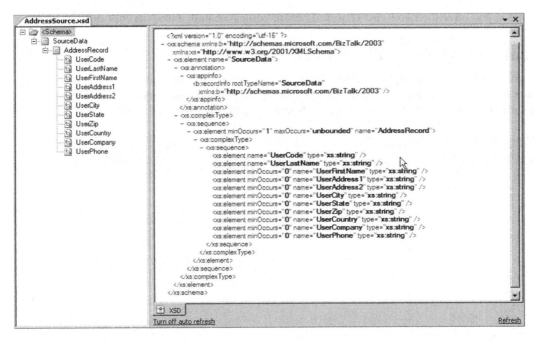

Figure 1-14. *AddressSource.xsd*

The source schema contains an address record. The target schema, shown in Figure 1-15, contains a subset of that information.

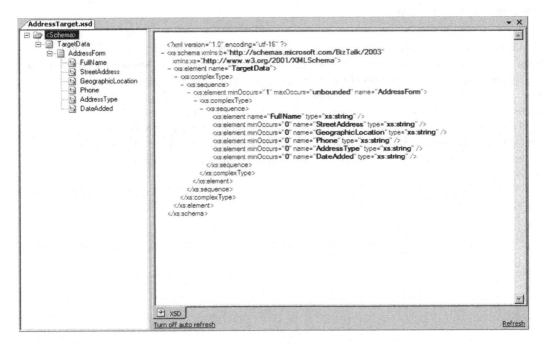

Figure 1-15. *AddressTarget.xsd*

Now, you have the two items required before you can create a map in your project.

Creating a New BizTalk Map File

You create a new map by right-clicking the project name in the Solution Explorer and selecting Add ➤ New Item. The pop-up window shown in Figure 1-16 appears. Select Map Files, then Map, and then type the map name into the Name field. Name the map HelloWorld.btm.

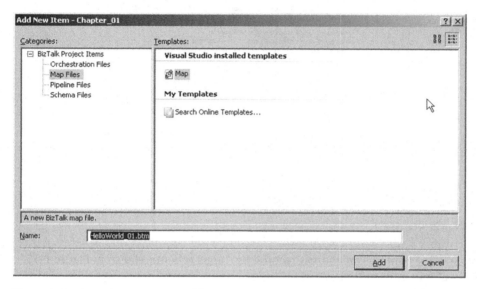

Figure 1-16. *Creating a new map file*

When you click the Add button, the empty map will open automatically to allow you to choose the source and target schemas that you want to use. Figure 1-17 shows the empty map.

Click the Open Source Schema link in the left pane, and you will open the BizTalk Type Picker window shown in Figure 1-17. Expand the Schemas folder, and select Chapter_01. AddressSource. This is the pointer to your source schema AddressSource.xsd.

Your source schema will appear in the left pane. When it does, repeat this process for your target schema. Once both schemas have been opened, your map will look like Figure 1-18.

As you see, all the elements are present for you to begin mapping. Click Save All in the development studio to save your work.

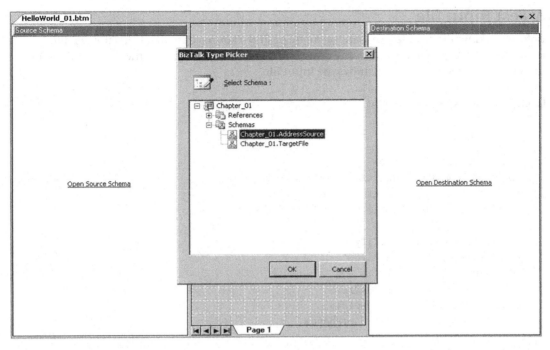

Figure 1-17. *An empty map*

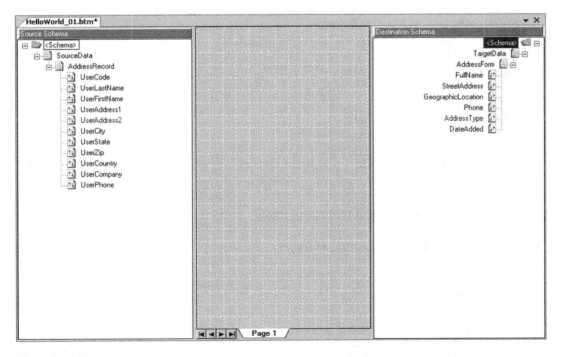

Figure 1-18. *Your new map*

A Test Input file

Before working on the map, we want to create or find a source data file. Copy the test file named HelloWorldInput.xml from the download files for Chapter 1 into the data subdirectory under your project. Listing 1-1 shows the input file.

Listing 1-1. *HelloWorldInput.xml*

```
<SourceData>
  <AddressRecord>
    <UserCode>001</UserCode>
    <UserLastName>Wainwright</UserLastName>
    <UserFirstName>John</UserFirstName>
    <UserAddress1>7008 Robbie Drive</UserAddress1>
    <UserAddress2/>
    <UserCity>Raleigh</UserCity>
    <UserState>NC</UserState>
    <UserZip/>
    <UserCountry>USA</UserCountry>
    <UserCompany>SSPS</UserCompany>
    <UserPhone>555-612-2222</UserPhone>
  </AddressRecord>
  <AddressRecord>
    <UserCode>002</UserCode>
    <UserLastName>Dawson</UserLastName>
    <UserFirstName>Jim</UserFirstName>
    <UserAddress1>230 Shadow Smoke Lane</UserAddress1>
    <UserAddress2/>
    <UserCity>Siler City</UserCity>
    <UserState>NC</UserState>
    <UserZip/>
    <UserCountry>USA</UserCountry>
    <UserCompany>SSPS</UserCompany>
    <UserPhone>555-444-3331</UserPhone>
  </AddressRecord>
  <AddressRecord>
    <UserCode>003</UserCode>
    <UserLastName>Accounts Payable</UserLastName>
    <UserFirstName/>
    <UserAddress1>7008 RedWing</UserAddress1>
    <UserAddress2/>
    <UserCity>Apex</UserCity>
    <UserState>NC</UserState>
    <UserZip/>
    <UserCountry>USA</UserCountry>
    <UserCompany>SSPS</UserCompany>
    <UserPhone>555-876-1234</UserPhone>
  </AddressRecord>
</SourceData>
```

Tip There are many ways that you can open and view data, raw schema, and map files. We rely on two editors that make mapping easier. Altova XMLSpy is an XML editor and development environment that integrates with Visual Studio. IDM Computer Solutions, Inc., provides UltraEdit, a text editor with many features including the capability to view files in binary.

At this point, we have completed all the preliminaries necessary to begin creating the map. We have set up a project in the development studio with the input and output schemas, and we have created a test file.

Building the Map

Finally, we have reached the fun stuff, actually creating a map. The basics of building a map consist either of dragging links from the source window directly to the target window or of dragging links to and from functoids that have been inserted into the mapper grid. You will implement five different processes in this map:

- Simple drag-and-drop
- Concatenation
- Data addition
- Conditional selection
- Custom scripting

Dragging and Dropping Fields

This is the most basic of all mapping steps. We want the map to move the data found in the source node UserPhone into the target node Phone.

1. Click UserPhone in the source schema pane, and hold down the left mouse button.

2. Move the mouse to Phone in the target schema pane. When Phone highlights, release the mouse button.

As you move the mouse from UserPhone to Phone, a line forms behind the mouse. This line represents the link that you are creating between the source and target nodes. When you release the mouse button, the line remains, depicting the completed link, as shown in Figure 1-19.

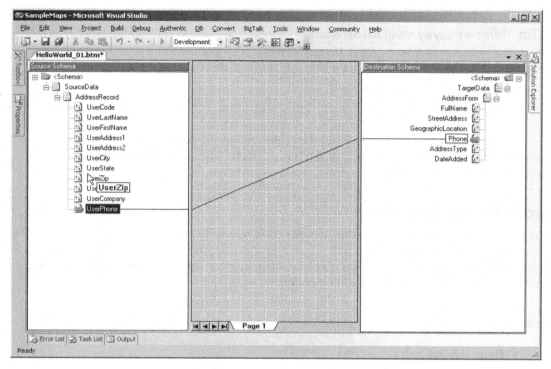

Figure 1-19. *Dragging and dropping a link*

Next, we want to test the link to make sure it does what we expect. Building a map and testing the map in BizTalk are not separate activities. Each change that you make to the map may have an impact on previous work, even to the extent of changing the behavior. This is particularly true when you work with loops.

Tip Testing should be a continuous process as you build your map. Although you don't need to test after every new link, you should test your map as soon as you complete any significant block of work. The drag-and-drop link in this map doesn't warrant testing, but we are inserting a quick overview of testing here to emphasize that it is *never* too early to start testing your map. Of course, the more complex the map, the more important testing becomes.

First, we must set the testing properties for the map. Right-click the map name in the Solution Explorer window, and select Properties. This will bring up the map properties window shown in Figure 1-20.

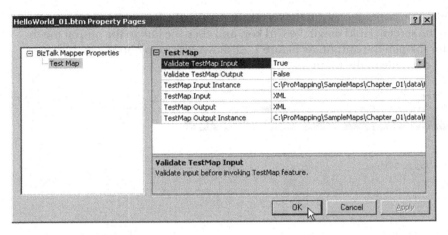

Figure 1-20. *Map properties*

Set the Validate Test Map Output option to False. This allows you to test an incomplete map without the test failing for missing mandatory data. Set the TestMap Input Instance by browsing to your input data file, `HelloWorldInput.xml`. Use the same path for your TestMap Output Instance, changing the file name to `HelloWorldOutput.xml`. This last step is optional but handy because it causes a copy of the output to be produced in your data directory where you can manipulate it if needed. Select OK to test your link.

Execute the test by right-clicking the map name and selecting Test Map, as shown in Figure 1-21.

Figure 1-21. *Executing the test*

The test should run instantaneously. If the test is successful, the output window will pop up at the bottom of the screen. Hold down the Ctrl key, and click the link to the output file to cause the map editor to open the output. As Figure 1-22 shows, the map outputs one Phone node for each UserPhone node in the input file.

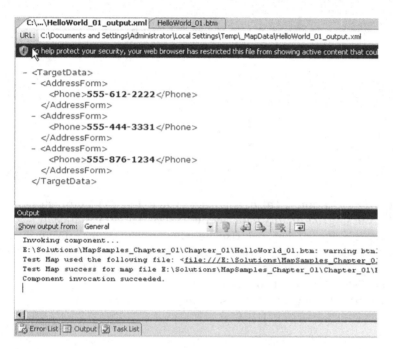

Figure 1-22. *Output from first test*

You can validate this test by comparing the source data with the output, checking the phone numbers to make sure that they were correct and in the correct order.

Concatenating Fields

One common mapping need is to combine two or more strings from the input. The mapping specifications for this map are that the values from three source nodes, UserCity, UserState, and UserZip must be output as one value in the target node GeographicLocation. The mapping specifications also states that the fields must be separated by single spaces. Here are the steps to concatenate fields:

1. Open the Toolbox window, and drag the String Concatenate functoid onto the grid.

2. Drag and drop a link from UserCity to the String Concatenate functoid.

3. Drag and drop a link from UserState to the String Concatenate functoid.

4. Drag and drop a link from UserZip to the String Concatenate functoid.

5. Drag and drop a link from the String Concatenate functoid to GeographicLocation in the target.

The order of the inputs to the functoid is important, since the concatenation will be done in the order that the inputs are received. Your map now looks like Figure 1-23.

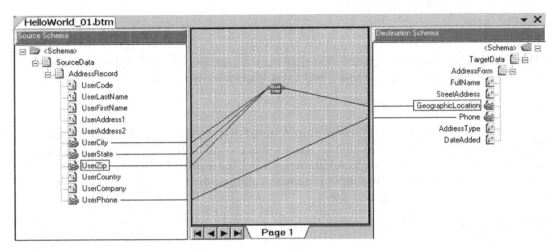

Figure 1-23. *Concatenating UserCity, UserState, and UserZip*

You now must add the spaces to the concatenation. Double-click the String Concatenate functoid to open the Configure Functoid Inputs window shown in Figure 1-24.

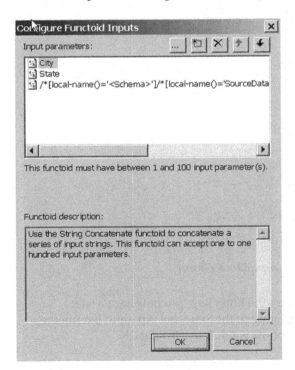

Figure 1-24. *The Configure Functoid Inputs window*

You can see your three inputs in the Input Parameters. We have named two of the links and left the third with the default name to illustrate the difference that naming links can make in understanding which input is which.

Tip You can give a link a name by right-clicking the line in the grid that represents the link and selecting Properties. The Properties window will have a field, Label, in which you type the name.

Remember that the mapping specifications stated that the fields should be separated with single spaces. You now must add the spaces. The second icon at the top of the Configure Functoid Inputs window is Insert New Parameter. Click the input parameter City and then the Insert New Parameter icon. A new input parameter, along with an open text box, will appear following City, as shown in Figure 1-25.

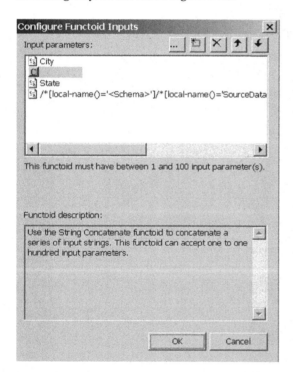

Figure 1-25. *Adding spaces to the String Concatenate functoid's input*

Type a single space into the text box and press the Enter key. You now have a space between the City and State. Next, insert a space between the State and Zip input parameters. When you finish, close the Configure Functoid Inputs window by clicking OK.

Tip If you accidentally enter the new parameter in the wrong location, change the order of the parameters by using the up and down arrow icons to move your input parameters up and down in the list.

Now, you need to make sure that you have set up your concatenation properly. Test your map again by right-clicking the map name in the Solution Explorer window and selecting Test Map.

Your output should look like the output shown in Figure 1-26. Since there are no ZIP codes in the source data, only the city and state appear.

```
  To help protect your security, your web browser has restricted this file from showing active content that could access your computer. Click here for options...    ✕

- <TargetData>
  - <AddressForm>
      <GeographicLocation>Raleigh NC</GeographicLocation>
      <Phone>555-612-2222</Phone>
    </AddressForm>
  - <AddressForm>
      <GeographicLocation>Siler City NC</GeographicLocation>
      <Phone>555-444-3331</Phone>
    </AddressForm>
  - <AddressForm>
      <GeographicLocation>Apex NC</GeographicLocation>
      <Phone>555-876-1234</Phone>
    </AddressForm>
  </TargetData>
```

Figure 1-26. *Output with the String Concatenate functoid in the map*

Adding a System Date

Another common mapping step is adding a system date to the output. In this case, you will put the system date into the DateAdded node. Use the Date functoid from the toolbox as follows to retrieve the current system date:

1. Drag the Date icon from the Toolbox window onto the mapper grid.

2. Drag a link from the Date functoid to the DateAdded node in the target.

The Date functoid does not accept input parameters, as it simply returns the system date in the format YYYY-MM-DD. Your map should look like Figure 1-27 when you've added this mapping rule.

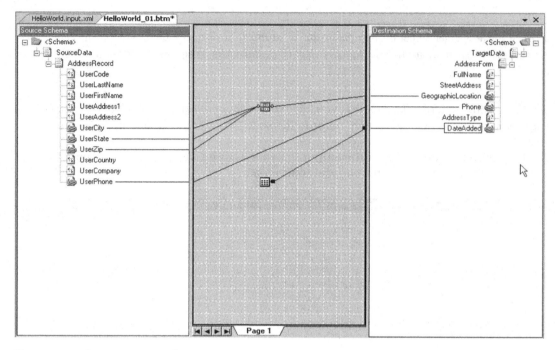

Figure 1-27. *The System Date functoid*

Once again, run a quick test to verify your output; the result should look like Figure 1-28.

Figure 1-28. *Output of map with System Date functoid*

Moving Data Conditionally

You won't always be able to simply move data from source to target. Sometimes, you will need to generate an output node only under certain conditions. We'll use a simple requirement for this map. You are to output the StreetAddress node only if there is data in the UserAddress1 node. As with many map operations, there are multiple ways to achieve the desired result. You should do it this time using the Logical String and Value Mapping functoids.

The Logical String functoid tests one value from the source to see if the value is a string and outputs the result of that test as either true or false. The Value Mapping functoid provides a means for us to control the output of a value from the source using the true/false value received from the Logical String functoid. When the Value Mapper receives true from the Logical String functoid, it outputs the value from the source.

Here are the steps to add these functoids to your map:

1. Drag a Logical String functoid to the grid.

2. Drag a link from UserAddress1 to the Logical String functoid (this is the first input).

3. Drag a Value Mapping functoid to the grid.

4. Drag a link from the Logical String functoid to the Value Mapping functoid.

5. Drag a link from UserAddress1 to the Value Mapping functoid (this is the second input).

6. Drag a link from the Value Mapping functoid to the StreetAddress node.

Your map should now look like Figure 1-29.

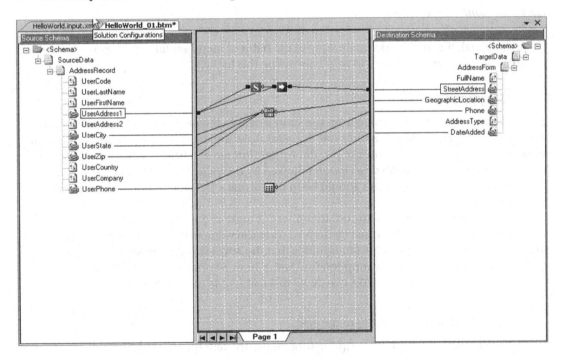

Figure 1-29. *A conditional statement using the Logical String and Value Mapping functoids*

Test your map again to get the output shown in Figure 1-30.

```
C:\...\HelloWorld_04_output.xml    HelloWorld_04.btm
URL: [☞:\Documents and Settings\Administrator\Local Settings\Temp\_MapData\HelloWorld_04_output.xml

 - <TargetData>
   - <AddressForm>
       <StreetAddress>7008 Robbie Drive</StreetAddress>
       <GeographicLocation>Raleigh NC</GeographicLocation>
       <Phone>555-612-2222</Phone>
       <DateAdded>2009-01-09</DateAdded>
     </AddressForm>
   - <AddressForm>
       <StreetAddress>230 Shadow Smoke Lane</StreetAddress>
       <GeographicLocation>Siler City NC</GeographicLocation>
       <Phone>555-444-3331</Phone>
       <DateAdded>2009-01-09</DateAdded>
     </AddressForm>
   - <AddressForm>
       <StreetAddress>7008 RedWing Drive</StreetAddress>
       <GeographicLocation>Apex NC</GeographicLocation>
       <Phone>555-876-1234</Phone>
       <DateAdded>2009-01-09</DateAdded>
     </AddressForm>
   </TargetData>
```

Figure 1-30. *Conditional output*

As expected, the map works again. Stay in the habit of incremental testing as we are doing with this map, though, because you won't always be this lucky.

Using a Scripting Functoid

The last item that we need to move from the source data to the output data is the name. The target has a FullName node; the source has UserFirstName and UserLastName nodes. At first, this looks like a simple concatenation like you did earlier. But we're adding a wrinkle. We want the FullName node to contain a job description followed by the values from the UserLastName and UserFirstName nodes. Your output should be in the format <job description><last name>, <first name>.

We want the FullName value to contain either Customer or Supplier as the job description. The job description value must be derived from the value in the UserCode node, which can be either 001 or 002. The value 001 signifies that the address is for a customer while 002 signifies that the address is for a supplier. And last, you must not output the comma if the UserFirstName node has no data. We can do all this using only the Scripting functoid as follows:

1. Drag the Scripting Functoid to the grid.

2. Drag the UserCode to the Scripting functoid as the first input.

3. Drag the UserLastName to the Scripting functoid as the second input.

4. Drag the UserFirstName to the Scripting functoid as the third input.

The result should look like Figure 1-31.

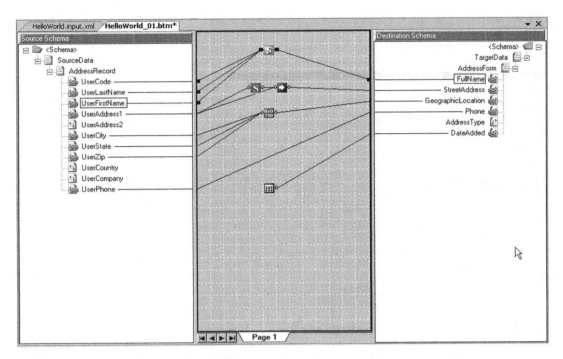

Figure 1-31. *Using the Scripting functoid*

Now, right-click the Scripting functoid, and select Configure Functoid Script to bring up the Configure Functoid Script window shown in Figure 1-32.

Note You can also reach the Configure Functoid Script window by left-clicking the Scripting functoid, going to the Properties window, and clicking the ellipsis next to Configure Functoid Script. Having several paths to choose from is typical of the development environment; it's a feature that allows you to devise a methodology that best fits you.

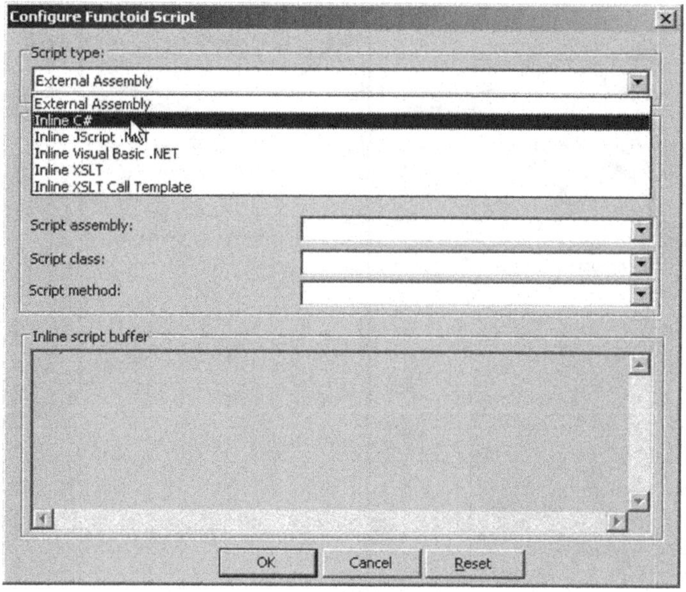

Figure 1-32. *The Configure Functoid Script window*

Go to the "Script type" drop-down box, and select Inline C#. The "Inline script buffer" box
will display a sample script, as shown in Figure 1-33.

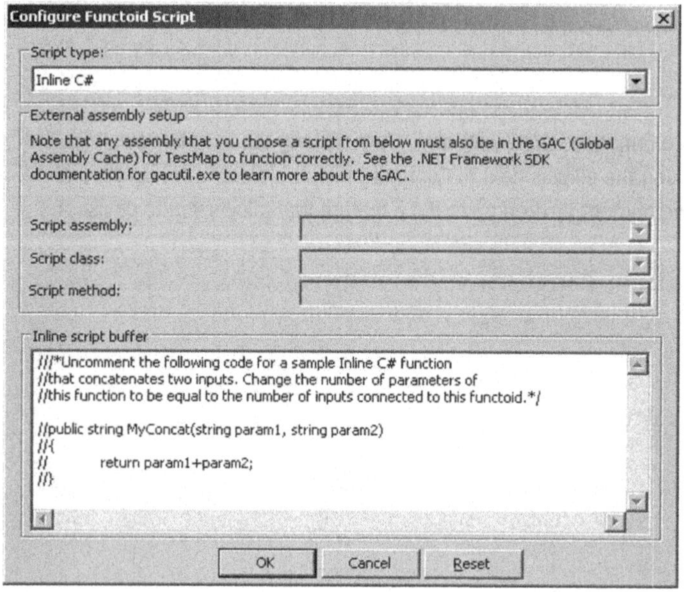

Figure 1-33. *The Configure Functoid Script window with sample code*

You can enter the script by typing it directly in the "Inline script buffer" box, but we don't recommend that you do. The window cannot be resized, making it difficult to keep track of more than ten or so lines. We create simple scripts in a text-editing window and then copy the script into the functoid window. The script used in this map is shown in Listing 1-2.

■**Tip** If the script has complex logic or is just long, you may want to create and test the script in a development studio project. In this example, the project would be a C# project.

Listing 1-2. *C# Code to Paste into the Configure Functoid Script Window*

```
public string HelloWorld(string inCode, string inLastName, string inFirstName)
{
string retval = "MISC: ";
if (inCode == "001")
    retval = "CUSTOMER: ";
else if (inCode == "002")
    retval = "SUPPLIER: ";
retval = retval + inLastName;
if (inFirstName != "")
    retval = retval + ", " + inFirstName;
return retval;
}
```

The variable `retval` is populated in three steps. First, the code puts `"CUSTOMER: "` or `"SUPPLIER: "` into the variable depending on the value in the input variable `inCode`, or it uses `"MISC: "` if there is no value in the input. The second step appends the value from the input variable `inLastName` to that data. Finally, if the input variable `inFirstName` contains a value, then a comma, a space, and the value from `inFirstName` are appended. The Scripting functoid returns the value in `retval` as output to the map. Figure 1-34 contains the output from the completed map.

```
┌─────────────────────────────────────────────────────────────────┐
│ C:\...\HelloWorld_05_output.xml │ HelloWorld_05.btm │             │
├─────────────────────────────────────────────────────────────────┤
│ URL:  C:\Documents and Settings\Administrator\Local Settings\Temp\_MapData\HelloWorld_05_output.xml │
│                                                                   │
│   - <TargetData>                                                  │
│     - <AddressForm>                                               │
│         <FullName>CUSTOMER: Wainwright, John</FullName>           │
│         <StreetAddress>7008 Robbie Drive</StreetAddress>          │
│         <GeographicLocation>Raleigh NC</GeographicLocation>       │
│         <Phone>555-612-2222</Phone>                               │
│         <DateAdded>2009-01-10</DateAdded>                         │
│       </AddressForm>                                              │
│     - <AddressForm>                                               │
│         <FullName>SUPPLIER: Dawson, Jim</FullName>                │
│         <StreetAddress>230 Shadow Smoke Lane</StreetAddress>      │
│         <GeographicLocation>Siler City NC</GeographicLocation>    │
│         <Phone>555-444-3331</Phone>                               │
│         <DateAdded>2009-01-10</DateAdded>                         │
│       </AddressForm>                                              │
│     - <AddressForm>                                               │
│         <FullName>MISC: Accounts Payable</FullName>               │
│         <StreetAddress>7008 RedWing Drive</StreetAddress>         │
│         <GeographicLocation>Apex NC</GeographicLocation>          │
│         <Phone>555-876-1234</Phone>                               │
│         <DateAdded>2009-01-10</DateAdded>                         │
│       </AddressForm>                                              │
│   </TargetData>                                                   │
└─────────────────────────────────────────────────────────────────┘
```

Figure 1-34. *Output from map with Scripting functoid*

Now you have completed your first map. See how easy it is?

Summary

One thing that we learn again and again as we explore the world of BizTalk mapping is that there is *never* only a single way to solve a mapping problem. Quite often, deciding which way is best can be difficult. The map you created in this chapter would look very different if we had chosen other ways for you to implement the steps. When you encounter a mapping issue, use your imagination and look at different approaches to finding a solution. Give John and Jim the same mapping specification and two things can be guaranteed: First, both maps will produce the same output. Second, the maps will not look the same.

This chapter introduced you to the methods and tools that are used to create a map in BizTalk. For many of you, this may have been your first look at Visual Studio and at BizTalk. You cannot create maps in BizTalk without understanding the fundamentals of these environments. This book focuses on mapping and does not discuss those topics in detail, thus you should add books on your version of BizTalk and your version of Visual Studio to your reference library.

In this chapter, we covered the basic steps required to create a map in BizTalk. However, what you saw in the map editor when you completed the work was a graphical depiction of a map, not the map. The map is an XSLT file that is generated when you validate the map. In Chapter 2, we will examine the XSLT that is generated from the work you did in this chapter.

CHAPTER 2

■■■

How BizTalk Maps Work

Most people start out with the BizTalk Map Editor just like we did: Jump right into the tool by opening up a map and dragging links from source to destination. Then, as mapping challenges are encountered, begin to experiment with icons and scripts. Become frustrated as some experiments work as expected and some do the opposite of what is expected. If you had these same early experiences at mapping, you also know there is a mystery as to why some techniques work and others don't.

Over time, we learned that, to figure out which mapping techniques work and which don't, we needed to understand BizTalk map functionality beyond knowing how to drag and drop links and what each functoid did. We needed to understand which code was generated when we created links between objects, when we added functoids to the grid, and when we inserted scripts.

As we progressed as mappers, we began to see the value of digging deeper and examining the XSL code that was being constructed by our actions. Not long after we began digging, we realized that we should have begun poking and prying a bit earlier. Doing so would have saved us a lot of frustration. We hope this chapter will do the same for you by helping you to avoid some of those same frustrations.

Understanding How BizTalk Maps Work

If you have experience with other mapping tools, the first thing that you notice with BizTalk is that the BizTalk mapping engine works in a different way than most other tools. Traditional mapping tools, particularly those that are designed specifically for Electronic Data Interchange (EDI) transactions, follow the same generic model:

1. The source is parsed from beginning of file to end of file.

2. Data is extracted from the source in the order that it is encountered.

3. Mapping rules are constructed as the source is parsed.

4. Data is pushed to an output file structure based on the structure and content of the source.

The better traditional engines are two-pass, meaning that they parse the source twice. The first time they extract and store all of the source data in a manner that makes any data accessible at any time in the rest of the process. The second time they go through the source to build the rules of the map. Most of the traditional engines that are not two-pass provide means, such as variables, in which the mapper may store data for later processing.

BizTalk maps work in exactly the opposite fashion. The mapping rules for a BizTalk map are built not from the source but from the target:

1. The BizTalk mapping engine traverses the target from beginning to end.

2. Mapping rules are constructed and executed as links are encountered on the output side.

3. Data is extracted from the source when a link is encountered in the target.

4. Data is pulled into the file structure based on the structure of the output schema.

These are very high-level models of traditional and BizTalk mapping engines but suffice to show that the basic flow of the map differs between them. This basic difference is the source of much frustration for mappers who are transitioning from other engines to BizTalk.

Fortunately, one great thing about BizTalk mapping is that the code that forms the map is easily accessible and relatively easy to understand. This chapter reviews in detail the HelloWorld map from the previous chapter. We will pry the lid off that map and examine the code that is generated when the map is compiled. Let's begin by reviewing that map, shown in Figure 2-1.

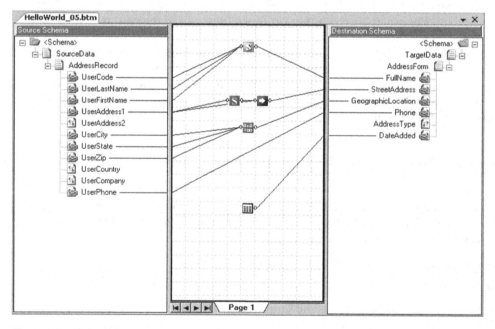

Figure 2-1. *The HelloWorld map*

Constructing Map Rules

When you look at the five mapping links in Figure 2-1, you might intuitively assume that the map created from these links first reads the source file and pulls out the needed data, then executes the functoids, and finally places the data into the target. That would be exactly backward from what actually happens.

Remember that BizTalk maps are constructed specifically to write XML output. The map graphically displayed is actually an XSLT (Extensible Stylesheet Language Transformation) style sheet built to write output into the specific format defined by the output schema. The rules in the XSL style sheet are processed in the sequence required to create the output nodes. When the map is compiled those rules are translated into XPATH queries and use XSLT functions to transform the data. They also are built and processed in the order that they are encountered in the schema definition of the target.

You can easily generate the .xsl file containing the map code at any point in the development of your map and look to see how the map rules are being generated. Doing so can help you spot potential problems in your map that may not be apparent in the map editor graphics. If you are not familiar with the XPATH query statement, you may find the code verbose and somewhat confusing—even more so if you are generating code based on an X12 schema. We will examine the code underlying the HelloWorld map in this chapter, and you will find that untangling the XPATH query is not as hard as it first appears.

Generating the Underlying Map

You can generate the underlying code by executing the Validate Map function, found by right-clicking the map name in the Solution Explorer, as shown in Figure 2-2.

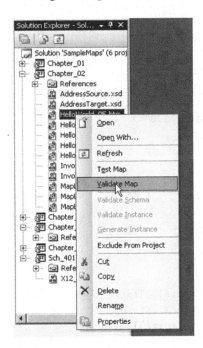

Figure 2-2. *The Validate Map option*

When the generation of the underlying code is complete the Output window displays the pathname to the resulting XSL file, as shown in Figure 2-3.

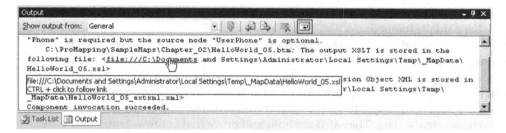

Figure 2-3. *The Output window display of the path to the XSL file*

You may Ctrl-click the pathname to open the XSL file and view the code. Listing 2-1 shows the map code for our final version of the HelloWorld map from the last chapter.

■ Note Comments have been included in the code to help everyone understand what the code does. Comments are not generated in the XSL code when you compile the maps.

Listing 2-1. *XSL Code for HelloWorld Map*

```
<?xml version="1.0" encoding="UTF-16"?>
<xsl:stylesheet xmlns:xsl="http://www.w3.org/1999/XSL/Transform"
  xmlns:msxsl="urn:schemas-microsoft-com:xslt"
  xmlns:var="http://schemas.microsoft.com/BizTalk/2003/var"
  exclude-result-prefixes ="msxsl var userCSharp" version ="1.0"
  xmlns:userCSharp="http://schemas.microsoft.com/BizTalk/2003/userCSharp">
<xsl:output omit-xml-declaration="yes" method="xml" version="1.0"/>
<xsl:template match="/">
  <xsl:apply-templates select="/SourceData"/>
</xsl:template>
<xsl:template match="/SourceData">
// The code begins here.
  <TargetData>
// Begin a loop, one output record for each AddressRecord in the source
    <xsl:for-each select="AddressRecord">
// Create and populate local variables v2, v4, v5
      <xsl:variable name="var:v2" select=
        "userCSharp:LogicalIsString(string(UserAddress1/text()))"/>
      <xsl:variable name="var:v4" select="userCSharp:StringConcat(string
        (UserCity/text()) ,&quot; &quot; , string(UserState/text()) ,
        &quot; &quot; , string(UserZip/text()))"/>
      <xsl:variable name="var:v5"select=
        "userCSharp:DateCurrentDate()"/>
// Begin creation of the target AddressForm node
    <AddressForm>
// Create and populate local variable v1 and output it to the FullName node
```

```
            <xsl:variable name="var:v1" select=
              "userCSharp:HelloWorld(string(UserCode/text()) ,
              string(UserLastName/text()) ,
              string(UserFirstName/text())))"/>
            <FullName><xsl:value-of select="$var:v1"/></FullName>
// Check to see if v2 (from source UserAddress1 node) had a value
            <xsl:if test="string($var:v2)='true'">
//  If so, output v3 to the StreetAddress node
               <xsl:variable name="var:v3" select="UserAddress1/text()"/>
                 <StreetAddress>
                    <xsl:value-of select="$var:v3"/>
                  </StreetAddress>
            </xsl:if>
//  Output the GeographicLocation node, filling it with v4
            <GeographicLocation>
               <xsl:value-of select="$var:v4"/>
            </GeographicLocation>
//  Check to see if the source node UserPhone had data, and if so,
//  output the Phone node
            <xsl:if test="UserPhone">
               <Phone><xsl:value-of select="UserPhone/text()"/></Phone>
            </xsl:if>
//  Output the DateAdded node, filling it with v5
            <DateAdded><xsl:value-of select="$var:v5"/></DateAdded>
          </AddressForm>
          </xsl:for-each>
      </TargetData>
</xsl:template>//  Identify the script type as C#<msxsl:script language="C#"
          implements-prefix="userCSharp">
<![CDATA[
//Script from the String Concatenate functoid
public string StringConcat(string param0, string param1, string param2,
          string param3, string param4)
{
return param0 + param1 + param2 + param3 + param4;
}
//  Script from the Date functoid
public string DateCurrentDate()
{
DateTime dt = DateTime.Now;
return dt.ToString("yyyy-MM-dd", System.Globalization.CultureInfo.InvariantCulture);
}
//  Script from the Logical String functoid
public bool LogicalIsString(string val)
{
return (val != null && val !="");
}
```

```
// Custom HelloWorld Script
public string HelloWorld(string inCode, string inLastName, string inFirstName)
{
//  Initialize the return value
string retval = "MISC: ";
//  If the source UserCode node contains "001", change the return value
if (inCode == "001")
  retval = "CUSTOMER: ";
//  If the source UserCode node contains "001", change the return value
  else if (inCode == "002")
    retval = "SUPPLIER: ";
//  Append the contents from source node UserLastName to the return value
retval = retval + inLastName;
//  Check to see if the source node UserFirstName contains data
//  If it does, append a comma, space, and the data to the return value
if (inFirstName != "")
retval = retval + ", " + inFirstName;
  return retval;
}
]]></msxsl:script>
</xsl:stylesheet>
```

Now, let's dig into the map to help you understand it.

Examining the Hidden Constructs in Maps

Before we tackle the visible aspects of the map as they appear in the code, let's examine some unexpected constructs that we find in the code. These are created when BizTalk helps out a little by inferring some algorithms in the code on its own.

Compiler-Generated Links

Because we have links in our map that connect source elements in a repeating group to target elements in a repeating group, BizTalk assumes that we want to loop through the data in the source. The result of that assumption is that the first unexpected rule we encounter in the code is a for-each loop that tells the map to create one instance of the target node AddressForm for each instance of the source node AddressRecord (see Listing 2-2).

Listing 2-2. *Compiler-Inferred For-Each Loop*

```
<TargetData>
<xsl:for-each select="AddressRecord">
:
:
</xsl:for-each>
</TargetData>
```

This code examines the source document and processes the code found within the TargetData node once for each occurrence of the source AddressRecord node. Thus if there are seven AddressRecord nodes, the code executes seven times and creates seven instances of the TargetData node. Notice that this looping rule is created even though we have not used a Looping functoid in the map.

Since these rules may alter the behavior of your map, you should become familiar with how and when the compiler generates them. You can view the links that represent these compiler-generated rules in your map editor, but you must manually activate them in the display. To see them, go to the main menu, and select View ➤ Error List as shown in Figure 2-4.

Figure 2-4. *Opening the Error List window*

This opens the error window with which you will become very familiar once you begin testing maps. Select the Warnings tab, as shown in Figure 2-5.

		Description	File	Line	Column	Project
⊗	1	File Copy of HelloWorld_05.btm has duplicate values for namespace and type name properties.	Copy of HelloWorld_05.l			
⊗	2	File HelloWorld_05.btm has duplicate values for namespace and type name properties.	HelloWorld_05.btm			
⚠	3	The destination node "Phone" is required but the source node "UserPhone" is optional.	HelloWorld_05.btm			
⚠	4	Double-click here to show/hide compiler links.	HelloWorld_05.btm			

Error List — 2 Errors — 2 Warnings — 0 Messages

Figure 2-5. *Error List Warnings tab*

You will see the line "Double-click here to show/hide compiler links." When you double-click, additional links will appear on your map. Look at Figure 2-6.

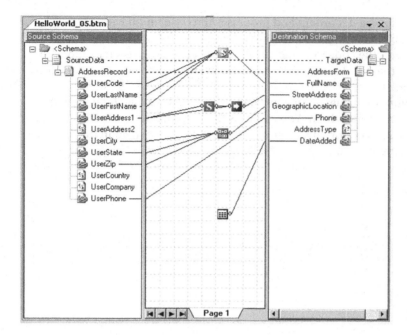

Figure 2-6. *Compiler-generated links*

See the two dotted lines that have appeared? These represent the links that have been generated by the compiler based on the links that we created.

■**Note** You can find out more details about hidden compiler links in Chapter 11. We won't address their use and impact further here except to note that hidden links can sometimes cause your map to behave in unexpected ways. If this occurs, always check out the compiler-generated links to make sure the compiler hasn't misinterpreted your intentions.

Compiler-Generated Variables

When you examine the code in Listing 2-1 you find many unexpected variables. The compiler creates and uses internal variables for its own use, most often to contain the output of functoids. Any time a logical operation produces output that must be consumed by another operation or placed into the target model, the compiler creates an internal variable in which the value can be stored temporarily. The code for the HelloWorld map creates five internal variables right away. See Listing 2-3.

Listing 2-3. *Internal Variables*

```
//  Create and populate local variables v2, v4, v5
<xsl:variable name="var:v2" select=
    "userCSharp:LogicalIsString(string(UserAddress1/text()))"/>
```

```
<xsl:variable name="var:v4" select="userCSharp:StringConcat(string(UserCity/text()),
     &quot; &quot; , string(UserState/text()) ,
     &quot; &quot; , string(UserZip/text()))"/>
<xsl:variable name="var:v5"select=        "userCSharp:DateCurrentDate()"/>
// Begin creation of the target AddressForm node
<AddressForm>
// Create and populate local variable v1 and output it to the FullName node
  <xsl:variable name="var:v1" select=
       "userCSharp:HelloWorld(string(UserCode/text()) ,
       string(UserLastName/text()) ,
       string(UserFirstName/text()))"/>
  <FullName><xsl:value-of select="$var:v1"/></FullName>
// Check to see if v2 (from source UserAddress1 node) had a value
  <xsl:if test="string($var:v2)='true'">
// If so, output v3 to the StreetAddress node
     <xsl:variable name="var:v3" select="UserAddress1/text()"/>
     <StreetAddress>
       <xsl:value-of select="$var:v3"/>
     </StreetAddress>
  </xsl:if>
```

At first glance it appears that the variables are not created in order but are created in the sequence v2, v4, v5, v1, and v3. On closer inspection, though, you see that the sequence is driven by the output. Stop and think about how the map is created. The first thing that happens is that the mapper sees the need for a for-each loop as we saw in Listing 2-2. The next thing the compiler sees is the need to create a FullName node, then a StreetAddress node, a GeographicLocation node, and finally a DateAdded node. There is no need for an internal variable for the Phone node since that is a direct link with no interim operation. Now compare the order in which the compiler sees these nodes with the variable numbers:

- v1: FullName
- v2 *and* v3: StreetAddress
- v4: GeographicLocation
- v5: DateAdded

See that, although the order these variables appear in the code is not sequential, the actual order in which they were created is sequential according to the output file format.

Why use internal variables like this? Practically speaking, using local variables is the easiest way of referring to the output of interim operations on the data. Think of a piece of data as an object. If you move the source object directly to the output object, you can do so without modifying the source object. But if you are changing the object between the source and destination, you need some place to put the changed value. You don't want to modify the actual source object, and you may want to use the new value more than once in the map. These internal variables are the best means for the compiler to do this. Also, a simple variable name is much easier to repeat in the code than it would be to have to put the fully qualified name each time the value is needed, as with var:v4 as opposed to userCSharp:StringConcat(string(UserCity/text().

BizTalk uses compiler-generated variables liberally, but untangling them is less confusing than untangling the code without them. Tracing the flow of data through these variables is another good way to determine what the map is actually doing when your output isn't quite what you expect.

Compiler-Generated Scripts

Another of the hidden features of the code we generated for the HelloWorld map is the C# scripting for the functoids. You might expect to see the script that was manually added to the map in a Scripting functoid appear in the code, but the appearance of these additional scripts might be a surprise.

In addition to the script `public string HelloWorld` that we wrote to create the `FullName` value, you also see these scripts:

- `public string StringConcat`
- `public string DateCurrentDate`
- `public bool LogicalIsString`

Each of these scripts represents a C# function that was created as the result of placing a functoid on the grid. These scripts, along with any custom scripts that you add using scripting functoids, are found in the CDATA section at the end of the map.

Caution The detailed scripts may not appear in the code for some functoids.

Note that even if you put multiple instances of a functoid on the mapping grid (same script in several Scripting functoids), BizTalk will only create one instance of the script's code in the map. We will limit the discussion of custom scripts here to this simple example of how the scripts are included in the CDATA section, and present an extended discussion of various script types and their use in maps in Chapter 3.

Computer-generated links, computer-generated variables, and computer-generated scripts are three features of mapping that are not obvious when you look at the map in the map editor. Now, let's move on to some of the mapping constructs that would be obvious.

Digging into the HelloWorld Map Rules

When we speak of *rules*, we refer to actions defined in the map that affect the movement of data from the source to the target. The simplest rule in a map is the basic rule created by dragging the link from a source element node to a target element node.

Drag-and-Drop Link Rule

In our HelloWorld map, the simplest rule in this map is created by the link between the UserPhone node and the target Phone node. The underlying code is as straightforward as the line on the mapping grid. Look at Listing 2-4.

Listing 2-4. *The Drag-and-Drop Rule from the HelloWorld Map*

```
<xsl:if test="UserPhone">
   <Phone><xsl:value-of select="UserPhone/text()"/></Phone>
</xsl:if>
```

This simple rule is slightly different than you might have suspected. That is because both the source and the target nodes are optional. Although the mapping grid graphically indicates an unconditional link between the source node UserPhone and the target node Phone, the code generated by the compiler reveals a test to be conducted to see if the source node is present in the source file. Only if the source node is present is the value placed into the output node. If we make the source element mandatory rather than optional, the generated code is simplified to that presented in Listing 2-5.

Listing 2-5. *Simplified Drag-and-Drop Rule*

```
...
<Phone><xsl:value-of select="UserPhone/text()"/></Phone>
...
```

Caution Changing the target node to mandatory while leaving the source node optional will not change the rule from the original rule shown in Listing 2-4. However, in that case, the compiler will issue a warning to indicate that while the target node is mandatory the source node is optional.

Also note that the source value as the rule refers to it is UserPhone/text(), so technically, this addresses not the source node UserPhone but the text within that node. This rule then actually states that the value to be placed in the target node Phone is the text that is found in the source node UserPhone. Throughout this book, we show code as it is generated by the compiler but refer to the data object by the node name only.

Caution There is a difference between UserPhone/text() and UserPhone in practice. The Logical Existence functoid, for example, tests for the presence of the node, not the presence of the text. The Logical String functoid tests for the presence of the text. Thus the node <UserPhone></UserPhone> will cause the If Exists functoid to return true while the Is String functoid returns false. Such cases as this will be pointed out throughout this material.

We will see the Logical String functoid mentioned in the preceding Caution in our next rule from our map.

Using the Logical String Functoid Rule to Qualify a Data Extract

The Logical functoid group generally performs by testing an input variable for some condition and then returning a literal value of true or false based on the result of that test. Our Hello-World map uses the Logical String functoid to build such a rule for use in creating the value to be output in the StreetAddress target node.

The code generated for this rule contains three separate operations. First, evaluate the UserAddress1/text() node to see if there is data present in the node. Second, if the evaluation is true, put the data from Address1 into the internal variable v3. Third, put the value contained in v3 into the target node StreetAddress. Listing 2-6 shows the code excerpt from the map that pertains to this rule.

Listing 2-6. *XSL Code for the StreetAddress Rule*

```
1  <xsl:variable name="var:v2" select=
      "userCSharp:LogicalIsString(string(UserAddress1/text()))"/>
2  <xsl:if test="string($var:v2)='true'">
3       <xsl:variable name="var:v3" select="UserAddress1/text()"/>
4       <StreetAddress>
5             <xsl:value-of select="$var:v3"/>
6       </StreetAddress>
7  </xsl:if>
```

■**Note** Code excerpts such as the one in Listing 2-6 and other listings in this book are composite extracts. This means that the lines of code may not occupy the same relative positions in the full map file as in the listing. In Listing 2-6, for example, we have pulled line 1 from early in the XSL and placed it with lines 2–7 to facilitate the discussion. Line 1 actually occurs much earlier in the XSL than lines 2–6.

Let's use the line numbers seen in the listing to examine what the code does. Line 1 calls the C# library routine LogicalIsString(string (UserAddress1/text())) and places the return value from that routine into the variable v2. The exposed code for this library routine, as seen in the CDATA section, is in Listing 2-7.

Line 2 evaluates variable v2, populated in line 1, to see if the value is true. If so, the code between lines 2 and 7 is executed. If not, lines 2 through 7 are not executed.

When the value is true, line 3 obtains the value from UserAddress1 and places it into variable v3. Lines 4 and 6 define the target node StreetAddress, and line 5 places the value from variable v3 into that node.

Listing 2-7. *C# Code for the LogicalIsString Function Exposed*

```
public bool LogicalIsString(string val)
{
return (val != null && val !="");
}
```

The result of the code in this discussion is to output the `StreetAddress` node and data contents only if the `Address1` node in the source contains data.

Note The code for most of these functoid scripts is relatively simple and is placed in the CDATA section of the map in exactly the same fashion as your C# (or other types) of scripting. We frequently encounter resistance to using scripts in maps, mainly because anecdotal "evidence" has given mappers the impression that scripting causes performance degradations. Even with extensive use of scripting, we have never found this to be true, and we encourage the use of scripts as an important tool in the mapper's arsenal.

Manipulating Strings Using a Concatenate Functoid Rule

One of your most frequent activities in mapping will be manipulating string data. In our Hello-World map, you see two separate examples of string manipulation. The first is a simple string concatenation action where we concatenate three city, state, and ZIP strings into a single string. Here in Listing 2-8 is the XSL code for this concatenation.

Listing 2-8. *Code for Concatenating City, State, and ZIP*

```
1  <xsl:variable name="var:v4"
       select="userCSharp:StringConcat(string(UserCity/text()) ,
       &quot; &quot; , string(UserState/text()) ,
       &quot; &quot; , string(UserZip/text())))"/>
2  <GeographicLocation>
3     <xsl:value-of select="$var:v4"/>
4  </GeographicLocation>
```

Line 1 appears strange on first inspection. The second and fourth variables passed to the function look like this: " ". This is because both the single and double quotation marks are reserved characters in XML files and have to be escaped when used. " " translates to ' ' (single quotation mark, space, single quotation mark).

Line 1 also contains a call to a library routine, triggered by the addition of the String Concatenate functoid. The C# for that routine is shown in Listing 2-9.

Listing 2-9. *C# Code for the StringConcat Function Exposed*

```
public string StringConcat(string param0, string param1, string param2,
     string param3, string param4)
{
return param0 + param1 + param2 + param3 + param4;
}
```

Now, let's walk through the rule. Line 1 creates the variable v4 to hold the results of the `StringConcat` function. That result is created from the five inputs to the functoid: the contents of the source `UserCity`, `UserState`, and `UserZip` nodes and two space characters to separate the other values.

Lines 2 and 4 create the output node `GeographicLocation`; line 3 populates that node with the contents of variable v4. Note that we assumed that the source data would be present since we have placed no provisions to handle any situation where any or all of the three source nodes lacks data.

As you see, the underlying code for this rule is not complex. By spending time familiarizing yourself with how the BizTalk mapper constructs code, as we are doing here, and by learning the basics of XSLT, you can make this code even more efficient. XSLT has a `concat()` function, thus you could use a Scripting functoid containing the XSLT shown in Listing 2-10 to achieve the same results.

Listing 2-10. *Inline XSLT to Concatenate City, State, and ZIP*

```
<GeographicLocation>
    <xsl:value-of select="concat(./UserCity, ' ', ./UserState), ' ', ./UserZip"/>
</GeographicLocation>
```

The second example of string manipulation in this map is covered next when we look at the custom script in our HelloWorld map.

Manipulating Scripts with a Custom Script Rule

As we discuss this rule from our HelloWorld map, we will touch on the subject of custom scripting in maps. Custom scripting is covered in detail in the next chapter, so here, we will limit the discussion to the information necessary to understand the rule.

In the preceding examples, you saw how C# scripts are invoked from the XSLT code generated by the map when a functoid is added to the map. Now, you will see what happens when a Scripting functoid is added to the map and filled with a script.

■**Caution** Adding a Scripting functoid and links to/from it to a map without inserting a script into it will cause a map validation error.

When you place a Scripting functoid in the map and put your script into it, your script is built into the map XSL exactly as are scripts from the standard functoids. In the HelloWorld map, our Scripting functoid contains code that generates the contents of the output node `FullName`. This is done by collecting values from three source nodes and creating a single output value based on business rules. Listing 2-11 contains the custom script.

Listing 2-11. *Custom Script from HelloWorld Map*

```
public string HelloWorld(string inCode, string inLastName, string inFirstName)
{
    string retval = "MISC: ";
    if (inCode == "001")
        retval = "CUSTOMER: ";
    else if (inCode == "002")
        retval = "SUPPLIER: ";
```

```
    retval = retval + inLastName;
    if (inFirstName != "")
        retval = retval + ", " + inFirstName;
    return retval;
}
```

The source values for this script come from the UserCode, LastName, and FirstName nodes. The script creates the variable retval and fills it with the value MISC, which will be the default output value.

The input value inCode (the source value from UserCode) is then tested to determine which of two actions might be taken. If the value is "001" the script puts the value "CUSTOMER: " into the retval variable (replacing the value MISC). If the value is 002, the script replaces MISC with the value "SUPPLIER: ". Next, the input value from LastName is appended to the value in the retval variable. Finally, if the FirstName variable contains data, that data is appended to the retval variable along with a comma (,). We do not test for the presence of data in the UserCode or LastName nodes, because we know both those nodes are mandatory.

The content of the output value, retval, from the script is placed in the target node FullName.

Employing the Current Date Rule

The next rule from the HelloWorld map that we will discuss obtains the current date from the system. As you might expect by now, this rule is done in two parts. First, a variable is created to hold the system date returned from the C# function DateCurrentDate(). The content of the variable is then assigned to the output node. The two lines of code, extracted from different locations in the XSL, are displayed in Listing 2-12.

Listing 2-12. *Code for Obtaining the Current Date*

```
<xsl:variable name="var:v5"select="userCSharp:DateCurrentDate()"/>
<DateAdded><xsl:value-of select="$var:v5"/></DateAdded>
```

The exposed code for the C# function, userCSharp:DateCurrentDate(), is shown in Listing 2-13.

Listing 2-13. *C# Code for the DateCurrentDate Function Exposed*

```
public string DateCurrentDate()
{
DateTime dt = DateTime.Now;
Return dt.ToString("yyyy-MM-dd", System.Globalization.CultureInfo.InvariantCulture);
}
```

The date is returned in the format CCYY/MM/DD. If you are passing this date to an output node that requires a different format, you have to reformat it yourself. Chapter 8 contains several examples of reformatting date and time fields as well as other aspects of handling dates and times.

Now that we have covered the rules in our HelloWorld map, let's discuss some other important concepts in understanding how BizTalk maps work.

Looking Deeper into Understanding Maps

The order in which links are attached has a great impact on the output of a map. That this is so is not readily apparent, nor is the impact easily predictable.

Sequencing Links

Sometimes, we get calls asking for help in resolving a mapping problem where the caller has carefully examined the map as it is depicted in the map editor, even to the point of opening functoids and validating that the values inside are correct. But the cause of the problem is still not apparent.

Quite often, we find that the cause is the order in which links are attached to their target. The target could be a functoid or a node in the output schema. The simple fact is that the order in which you attach links to an object can directly impact how the underlying code is generated.

Perhaps the simplest example of this occurs with the Value Mapping functoid. Look at the example depicted in Figure 2-7.

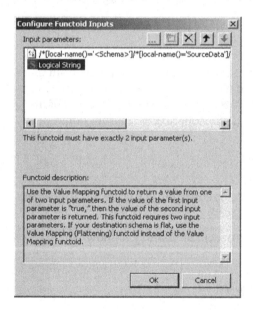

Figure 2-7. *Incorrect order of inputs to the Value Mapping functoid*

The Value Mapping functoid expects either `true` or `false` as the first input, as would be provided from a Logical String functoid or one of the other Logical Group functoids. If the first input is `true`, the second input becomes the output of the Value Mapping functoid. If the first input is not `true`, the Value Mapping functoid does not output anything. Notice that we say "if the first input is not `true`" as the second test rather than saying "if the first input is `false`". This is because the Value Mapping functoid interprets any value other than `true` as the equivalent of `false`.

Because of this, when you attach the links backward, the first input and second input are reversed. The `true`/`false` value becomes the return value, and the return value becomes the `true`/`false` value that is evaluated by the Value Mapping functoid. In the HelloWorld map, we use the Value Mapping functoid in combination with the Logical String functoid to control the output to the StreetAddress node. Whether or not a value is output in that case depends on the output of the Logical String functoid.

If we reverse the inputs, as shown in Figure 2-7, the value from the source node UserAddress1 becomes the first input to the Value Mapping functoid (the value which is tested for true/false). Since the likelihood that UserAddress1 contains the value true is slight, the result of this mix-up is that the Value Mapping functoid never passes data to the output.

Some link reversals will not stop the process but will change the value of the data. The order in which you attach links to a String Concatenate functoid, for example, determines the order of the output string.

Considering the Impact of the Order of Source Links on Output

Now, let's look at an example where the sequence in which source links are attached to a node affects the order of output. In the map shown in Figure 2-8, we intend to create two separate output nodes, one for a ShipToAddress and one for a BillToAddress.

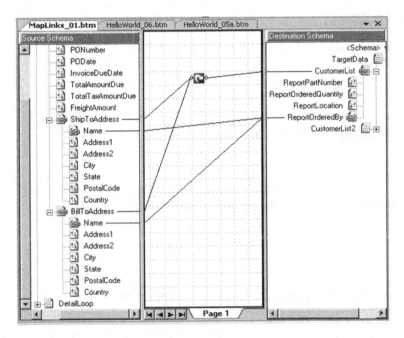

Figure 2-8. *Creating two output nodes*

We connect the Name field from each source input node to the target ReportOrderedBy node. To force two and only two output CustomerList nodes, we add the Looping functoid. Though it's not apparent from looking at the map, the order in which the source Name nodes will be written to the ReportOrderedBy node is determined by the sequence in which the two address nodes are connected to the Looping functoid. The input parameter window in Figure 2-9 shows that we've connected the link line from the ShipToAddress node first and from the BillToAddress node second.

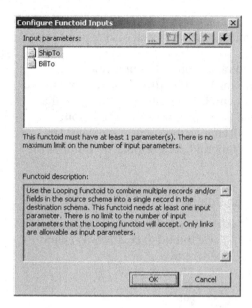

Figure 2-9. *Inputs to the Looping functoid*

Tip Right-click a link in the mapping grid, and type a name in the Label field of the Properties window. This will replace the path name with the Label when you open an input window.

This map outputs two `CustomerList` nodes, with the name of the shipping company in the first and the name of the accounting company in the second, as shown in Listing 2-14.

Listing 2-14. *Output of a Map with the ShipToAddress Link First*

```
<TargetData>
    <CustomerList>
        <ReportOrderedBy>Good Company Receiving</ReportOrderedBy>
    </CustomerList>
    <CustomerList>
        <ReportOrderedBy>Good Company Accounting</ReportOrderedBy>
    </CustomerList>
</TargetData>
```

Listing 2-15 shows the code that is generated for this map. You can see that one for-each loop is generated for each of the source address nodes, with the `ShipToAddress` being generated first.

Listing 2-15. *Code Generated by Map with ShipToAddress Link First*

```
<TargetData>
// Start FOR-EACH loop to generate one CustomerList node for each source
// ShipToAddress node
  <xsl:for-each select="InvoiceHeader/ShipToAddress">
// Output Customer List node
    <CustomerList>
// Check to see if the source node Name has data, and if so, output that data in the
// ReportOrderedBy node
        <xsl:if test="Name">
        <ReportOrderedBy>
          <xsl:value-of select="Name/text()" />
        </ReportOrderedBy>
      </xsl:if>
    </CustomerList>
  </xsl:for-each>
// Finished with the first loop, now start the FOR-EACH loop to output a
// CustomerList node for each BillTo address using the same logic
  <xsl:for-each select="InvoiceHeader/BillToAddress">
    <CustomerList>
      <xsl:if test="Name">
        <ReportOrderedBy>
          <xsl:value-of select="Name/text()" />
        </ReportOrderedBy>
      </xsl:if>
    </CustomerList>
  </xsl:for-each>
</TargetData>
```

Change the order of the links to the Looping functoid so that the link for the
BillToAddress node is first and the sequence in which the two for-each loops in the code
are created is reversed. Now, when the map is run, the accounting company record will be
output first, and the shipping company will be output second.

Considering the Impact of the Order of Target Links on Output

What about changing the order of the link connections to the target nodes? Changing the order
of the link sequence to the target can also alter the sequence of the output. Unfortunately,
when you connect multiple links to an output node, there is no place where you can look to
see the order of the links, as you could in the last example. The only way you can check in this
case is to inspect the code.

Our example here writes each output node using simple inline XSLT scripts. The map for
this example is shown in Figure 2-10.

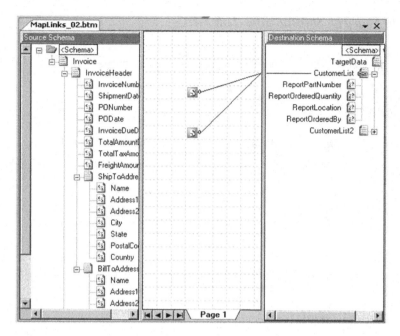

Figure 2-10. *A map for illustrating effect of reordering output links*

The top Scripting functoid contains an inline XSLT script that outputs a CustomerList node and a child ReportOrderedBy node filled with data from the source ShipToAddress node. The bottom Scripting functoid contains an inline XSLT script that outputs a different CustomerList node and ReportOrderedBy node, this time filled with data from the source BillToAddress node. The top Scripting functoid is the first connection to the CustomerList node, which means we expect the ShipToAddress information to be output first. That this is correct is obvious when we look at the code generated for the map, shown in Listing 2-16.

Listing 2-16. *Code Generated for Illustrating the Effect of Reordering an Output Links Map*

```
<TargetData>
//  Just output one instance of the CustomerList node with the ShipToAddress/Name
//  data in the ReportOrderedBy node.
    <CustomerList>
        <ReportOrderedBy>
            <xsl:value-of select="//ShipToAddress/Name"/>
        </ReportOrderedBy>
    </CustomerList>
//  Now output one instance of the CustomerList node with the BillToAddress/Name
//  data in the ReportOrderedBy node.
    <CustomerList>
        <ReportOrderedBy>
            <xsl:value-of select="//BillToAddress/Name"/>
        </ReportOrderedBy>
    </CustomerList>
</TargetData>
```

Reversing the order of the two links by connecting the BillToAddress link first and then connecting the ShipToAddress link will cause the two clauses to be reversed in the code, thus outputting the BillToAddress link first.

The Exception Makes the Rule: Processing Links Out of Order

Earlier in this chapter, we stated that the mapping engine processes rules by traversing the target model top to bottom. Also, we implied in early discussion that within a node, links are always processed in the order of connection. This would properly mean links to parent nodes are processed before links the child nodes of that parent. After all, the parent node must be output before the child nodes.

Well, there is a very important exception to the sequencing rule, and it is of most interest when you are using scripts, especially scripts that increment a counter. We can illustrate this by adding two scripts to the map from Figure 2-8, as shown in Figure 2-11.

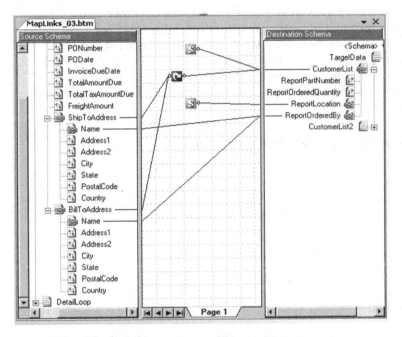

Figure 2-11. *A map that's an exception to the rule*

We've taken the original invoice map used to illustrate node sequencing, and we've added two scripts to the grid: The first is to define and increment a counter and the second to retrieve the incremented counter value and apply it to the ReportLocation output node.

The code in the scripts, shown in Listing 2-17, is very simple. The code in the top Scripting functoid contains a declaration of a counter variable and a statement to increment that counter. The code in the second Scripting functoid retrieves and outputs the current value of the counter.

Listing 2-17. *Scripts for Exception to the Rule Map*

```
//     First Script
int outputCounter = 0;
public void IncrementCounter()
{
    outputCounter += 1;
}

//     Second Script
public string ReturnCounter()
{
    return outputCounter.ToString();
}
```

Based on the order of connection, we would expect the first script to initialize the counter and increment the value when the mapping engine reaches the CustomerList node. We would then expect the second script to output the value 1, which would be the current value of the counter, when the mapping engine reaches the child node ReportLocation. On the second pass through the CustomerList node, we would expect the first script to increment the counter to 2 and the second script to output the value 2. Listing 2-18 contains the actual output of this map.

Listing 2-18. *Output of the Map Showing the Exception to the Rule*

```
<TargetData>
    <CustomerList>
        <ReportLocation>0</ReportLocation>
        <ReportOrderedBy>Good Company Receiving</ReportOrderedBy>
    </CustomerList>
    <CustomerList>
        <ReportLocation>1</ReportLocation>
        <ReportOrderedBy>Good Company Accounting</ReportOrderedBy>
    </CustomerList>
</TargetData>
```

As you can see, the output is not what we expected. The sequence in which the links are processed is to first create the CustomerList node, then to create the child nodes and execute the links attached to them, and finally to execute the link attached to the CustomerLink node. Let's look at part of the XSL generated for this map, shown in Listing 2-19.

Listing 2-19. *Code Generated for Exception to the Rule Map*

```
// A FOR-EACH loop was generated to control all output
<xsl:for-each select="InvoiceHeader/ShipToAddress">
// Everything goes into the CustomerList nodes
<CustomerList>
// Get the ReturnCounter value by calling the ReturnCounter script
    <xsl:variable name="var:v1" select="userCSharp:ReturnCounter()"/>
```

```
//  Output the counter value to the ReportLocation node
        <ReportLocation>
            <xsl:value-of select="$var:v1"/>
        </ReportLocation>
//  Check to see if the source node Name has data, and if so, output the data
//  to the ReportOrderedBy node.
        <xsl:if test="Name">
            <ReportOrderedBy>
                <xsl:value-of select="Name/text()"/>
            </ReportOrderedBy>
        </xsl:if>
//  Increment the counter by calling the IncrementCounter script
        <xsl:variable name="var:v2" select="userCSharp:IncrementCounter()"/>
        <xsl:value-of select="$var:v2"/>
    </CustomerList>
</xsl:for-each>
```

This code fragment contains the for-each loop for the ShipTo company processing. As you see, the first operation executed is to fill variable v1 with the current contents of the counter, using the userCSharp:ReturnCounter() that is in the second Scripting functoid, the one attached to the child ReportLocation node. Variable v1 is then output to the ReportLocation node.

Next, the map executes the code for the ReportOrderedBy node, the second child of CustomerList with a link attached. Only now, after both the links to both child nodes have been executed, is the link to the parent node CustomerList executed. Thus, at the point that the counter is first output, the value has never been incremented so the output value is 0. When the CustomerList node has been output once, the counter is incremented once, and the value output is 1.

■ **Note** This problem using the counter to illustrate that the links to child nodes are executed before links to the parent node was constructed to make the point. There are many ways to solve the problem, some of which you will see later in this book.

The Exception to the Exception: Executing Parent Node Links First

Our last example clearly indicated that links to child nodes are executed before links to the parent node of those child nodes. Well, that's not always true either. Sometimes, we want to block the output of a node unless a certain condition is met. Here's our starting map, in Figure 2-12.

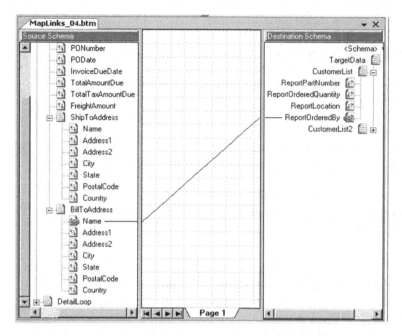

Figure 2-12. *A map illustrating the exception to the exception*

We only want one instance of CustomerList to be output, containing data from the source ShipToAddress/Name node. The output of this map is shown in Listing 2-20.

Listing 2-20. *The Map Illustrating the Exception to the Exception*

```
<TargetData>
  <CustomerList>
    <ReportOrderedBy>Good Shipping Company</ReportOrderedBy>
  </CustomerList>
</TargetData>
```

But what if we only want to output the CustomerList node when the ShipToAddress/Name node contains the value ACME? We add an Equal functoid to the map, as shown in Figure 2-13, and connect its output to the CustomerList node.

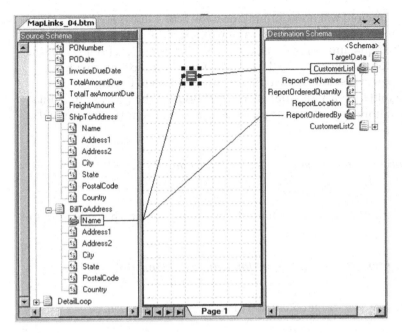

Figure 2-13. *The map illustrating the exception to the exception with the Equal functoid*

The Equal functoid compares the parameters shown in Figure 2-14.

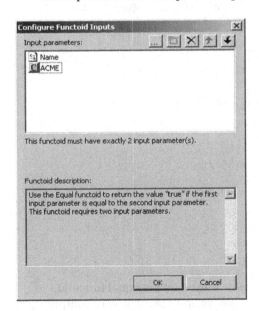

Figure 2-14. *Parameters for the Equal functoid of the map illustrating the exception to the exception*

As you know, the Equal functoid will now output true if the Name value is ACME and false if it is not. Since our Name value is Good Shipping Company, we expect the output to be false. We connect the output of the Equal functoid to the target node CustomerList, hoping that the value false will block the output of the node. By the rules you saw in the example with the counter, though, we might expect the node to be built and the children to be output before the link from the Equal functoid is activated. After all, the exception to the rule was that links to child nodes are executed before the links to the parent of those children. The output of this map is shown in Listing 2-21.

Listing 2-21. *Output of Exception-to-the-Exception Map with the Equal Functoid*

```
<TargetData />
```

As you can see, the CustomerList node was blocked from being output. The code from this map is in Listing 2-22.

Listing 2-22. *Code for the Exception-to-the-Exception Map with Equal Functoid*

```
<TargetData>
//  A FOR-EACH loop to create one target CustomerList node for each source
//  ShipToAddress node
  <xsl:for-each select="InvoiceHeader/ShipToAddress">
//  Check to see if the source node Name contains the string "ACME" and put the
//  result in v1.
    <xsl:variable name="var:v1" select="userCSharp:LogicalEq(string(Name/text()) ,
          "ACME")" />
//  Test the result
    <xsl:if test="$var:v1">
//  If the result is true then output the CustomerList node
        <CustomerList>
//  Check to see if the source node Name has data, and if so, output
//  the target node ReportOrderedBy
          <xsl:if test="Name">
              <ReportOrderedBy>
                  <xsl:value-of select="Name/text()" />
              </ReportOrderedBy>
          </xsl:if>
        </CustomerList>
    </xsl:if>
  </xsl:for-each>
</TargetData>
```

The first action taken by the map is to obtain the value output by the Equal functoid, which in this case compares the values Good Shipping Company and ACME. The value output from the Equal functoid is placed into variable v1. The next operation is an if statement that tests variable v1 to see if it contains true. If it does, the code within the if statement is executed. If not, none of that code is executed. The code in question is the creation of the target CustomerList node.

You see that, in this example, the link to the parent node was executed before the link to the child node. This is the exact opposite of the mapping example shown in Figure 2-11: "for every action, there are one or more different reactions."

Summary

Our goal in this chapter was to introduce you to the code that underlies the maps you see in the map editor and to illustrate how important understanding that code can be to successful mapping. Being an XSLT expert is not a requirement for being a good BizTalk mapper, but having no less than an apprentice's understanding of XSLT is mandatory if you want to be an expert BizTalk mapper.

As we discussed the XSL code, you saw several C# scripts that were also produced when the map was compiled. You saw the code for the custom script that we added to the map in a Scripting functoid. There is no way around the fact that, if you work with mapping in BizTalk, you can't avoid using custom scripts. Like with XSLT, you do not have to be an expert, but you must have a basic understanding of at least one scripting language. For that reason, we will delve into the how, when, why, and which language questions next in Chapter 3.

CHAPTER 3

■ ■ ■

Using Scripting in Maps

You saw in our first two chapters that we've already introduced custom scripting in maps. There is a good reason we did so. Even a very simple map like our HelloWorld map is easier to create by using custom scripts. We'll go so far as to state that complex maps cannot be completed without them. This chapter introduces some basic concepts and techniques of using custom scripts in maps.

Choosing Between Scripts and Functoids

When you should use a script rather than a functoid chain is not always driven by the complexity of the rule. Sometimes, the choice is a matter of preference. Many people do the entire map in XSLT, with the only function of the companion map created in the BizTalk editor being to invoke the XSLT map. Others resist putting any scripts in their maps, even to the point of using a series of maps to complete a transformation that could be accomplished in one map.

Although we generally use functoids unless the functoid chain becomes too complex to unravel easily, there are good reasons to resort to scripting even when a couple of functoids will do the trick easily. One perfect example is the need to reformat the date from an unpunctuated format of YYYYMMDD to a punctuated format of YYYY/MM/DD. This, as well as the reverse rule where you need to remove the punctuation, is a very common rule in EDI mapping.

You can easily implement this rule with standard functoids. As you can see in Figure 3-1, only four functoids are needed. Three string extraction functoids break the date into century and year, month, and day. A String Concatenate functoid then builds the new string.

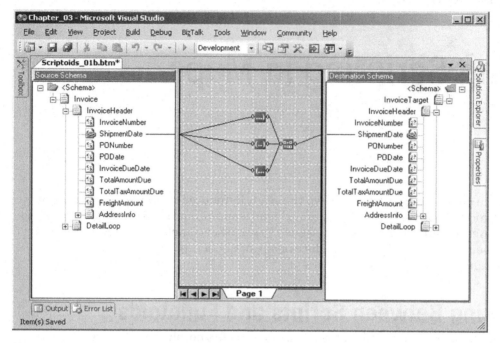

Figure 3-1. *A functoid chain to reformat a date*

This functoid chain takes only a few minutes to build. However, many maps have multiple instances of source dates that must be reformatted. Look at the InvoiceHeader record in Figure 3-1. There are three source nodes with dates in that one record, which means you would have to replicate this functoid chain three times in the first record—that's 12 functoids in total. This case presents an opportunity to use a custom script to reduce the amount of work needed to accomplish a rule.

Listing 3-1. *Script to Reformat a Date*

```
public string Format8Date(string inDate)
{
    if (inDate != "")
        return inDate.Substring(0,4) + "/" + inDate.Substring(4,2) + "/"
                + inDate.Substring(6,2);
    else
        return "";
}
```

The script in Listing 3-1 replaces the four functoids used in Figure 3-1. We keep a library of such scripts, so adding them to a map is a simple matter of copying the code and pasting it into a Scripting functoid. Once this has been done in a map, invoking the same code in another instance is accomplished by copying the functoid call Format8Date(string inDate) {} into a new Scripting functoid. Using this method to reformat the dates in the InvoiceHeader requires only four functoids instead of twelve, three of which would hold exactly the same line of code.

> **Tip** We said "library of such scripts" when discussing Listing 3-1. In this case, we are not talking about a `.dll` library. Each time we write a script, we save a copy of the code in a text or XML file. When we want to reuse a script later in a different map, all we need to do is open the correct file, copy the script, and paste it into the new Scripting functoid.

This example leads us to a question that we are often asked: When should scripting be used instead of functoids? Our answer is, "It depends."

Our Guidelines for Scripts vs. Functoids

Four primary factors have lots of traction with us when we decide whether or not to use a functoid or to use a script:

- *Maintainability*: You should always consider the likelihood that someone else will maintain your maps. The more complex the logic in your map, the more difficulty others will have understanding what you did, and the harder it will be for them to modify the map. Elegant maps are impressive when you deliver them but not so impressive when you are called back in six months to modify them and even you can't figure out what you did.

- *Readability*: Make the map easy to understand. Once you move beyond simple functoid chains, untangling the logic of a complex functoid chain is time consuming. By the same token, the simple concatenation of several strings requires only one functoid; using a script only complicates that action.

- *Level of effort*: Choose the method that reduces the development time. Don't spend hours wrestling with a complex functoid chain that keeps falling apart each time you touch it. Write a script. Don't write a script that would take more time to create and test than would be needed to accomplish with a few functoids.

- *Reusability*: Until the time comes that you can copy a chain of functoids from one spot in your map and paste the copy somewhere else, consider using a script when a function must be repeated several times in the map.

Using the Rule of Six

We sometimes refer to our simple method of deciding between scripts and functoids as our Rule of Six. Simply stated, this rule says, "If you need more than six functoids to accomplish a rule, you should consider using a script. If you need six or less functoids, you should not use a script."

Obviously, the date formatting example we just presented violates this rule. Reusability overrode the rule in that case, thus the rule is really just a basis for quick decisions on when to use a script. We don't want to spend an inordinate amount of time on every rule trying to decide what to do, so we operate on the basis that if more than six functoids are needed for a rule, a script is probably the easier and simpler method to use.

■**Caution** The Rule of Six is a guideline for new mappers, not a fixed rule. We violate it all the time and so will you once you find your comfort level with BizTalk mapping. The more experience you have, the more you will rely on the four guidelines and the less you will rely on this rule.

Let's take our HelloWorld map and modify the rule that creates and outputs the string to the FullName node. In the original form, this rule used the script shown in Listing 3-2 to concatenate the last and first name, separate them with a comma, and prefix the name with a literal string based on the UserCode.

Listing 3-2. *Original Script to Form and Output the FullName*

```
public string HelloWorld(string inCode, string inLastName, string inFirstName)
{
string retval = "MISC: ";
if (inCode == "001")
    retval = "CUSTOMER: ";
else if (inCode == "002")
    retval = "SUPPLIER: ";
retval = retval + inLastName;
if (inFirstName != "")
    retval = retval + ", " + inFirstName;
return retval;
}
```

This script resided in one Scripting functoid. Now let's replace the script with functoids that perform the same logic, as shown in Figure 13-2.

You can see the 11 functoids that are needed to accomplish the same function as the simple script in Listing 3-2. Worse, the functoid chain in Figure 13-2 is not complete, as it does not test to see if the UserFirstName node is empty. That must be done in order to suppress the inserted comma when there is no data in UserFirstName.

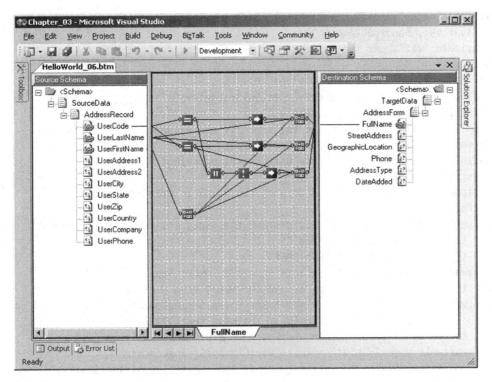

Figure 3-2. *Too many functoids*

In order to include the UserFirstName test, the value in UserFirstName must be captured and tested in a separate functoid chain, stored in a global variable, and then pulled into this chain through a scripting functoid. That would add at least two more functoids to the procedure, for a total of 13. If you validate this map, you will see that the underlying code for just this one logical rule is actually larger than the entire map we created earlier. The code for this map is shown in Listing 3-3. The code generated by the map with the script is shown in Listing 3-5. As you see, this simple map creates code that is difficult to follow.

Listing 3-3. *Code Generated for the Too-Many-Functoids Map*

```
<xsl:template match="/SourceData">
 <TargetData>
// Begin an output loop to output one AddressFormRecord for each AddressRecord
   <xsl:for-each select="AddressRecord">
// Create variable "v1", set the value to "'true" if the UserCode is "001",
// false if not
    <xsl:variable name="var:v1" select="userCSharp:LogicalEq
         (&quot;001&quot; , string(UserCode/text()))"/>
// Create variable "v5" and put the UserCode as the value
    <xsl:variable name="var:v5" select="string(UserCode/text())"/>
// Create variable "v6", set the value to "true" if "v5" (UserCode) is "002",
// false if not
```

```
      <xsl:variable name="var:v6" select="userCSharp:LogicalEq
            ($var:v5 , &quot;002&quot;)"/>
// Create variable "v12", set the value to "true" if either "v1" or "v6" is true.
// This checks
// to see if the UserCode is either "001" or "002"
      <xsl:variable name="var:v12" select="userCSharp:LogicalOr
            (string($var:v1) , string($var:v6))"/>
// Create variable "v13", set the value to "true" if the value of "v12" is false,
// and vice versa.  This controls which functoid path fires.
      <xsl:variable name="var:v13" select="userCSharp:LogicalNot
            (string($var:v12))"/>
//  Begin outputting the AddressForm node when the value in UserCode is "001"
    <AddressForm>
//  Is the UserCode value "001"?  If so, perform the lines inside the IF statement
     <xsl:if test="string($var:v1)='true'">
//  Set "v2" to contain the string "CUSTOMER"
        <xsl:variable name="var:v2" select="&quot;CUSTOMER: &quot;"/>
//  Set "v3" to contain a comma, a space, and the value from UserFirstName.
        <xsl:variable name="var:v3" select="userCSharp:StringConcat
              (&quot;, &quot; , string(UserFirstName/text()))"/>
//  Set "v4" to contain the value from UserLastName plus the value from "v3"
        <xsl:variable name="var:v4" select="userCSharp:StringConcat
              (string($var:v2) , string(UserLastName/text()) , string($var:v3))"/>
//  Output the value from "v4" into the Fullname Node
         <FullName><xsl:value-of select="$var:v4"/></FullName>
     </xsl:if>
//  Begin outputting the AddressForm node when the value in UserCode is "002"

     <xsl:if test="string($var:v6)='true'">
//  Set "v7" to contain the string "SUPPLIER"
        <xsl:variable name="var:v7" select="&quot;SUPPLIER: &quot;"/>
//  Set "v8" to contain the value from UserFirstName
        <xsl:variable name="var:v8" select="string(UserFirstName/text())"/>
//  Set "v9" to contain comma, space, then the value from "v8" (UserFirstName)
        <xsl:variable name="var:v9" select="userCSharp:StringConcat
                (&quot;, &quot; , $var:v8)"/>
//  Set "v10" to contain the value from UserLastName
        <xsl:variable name="var:v10" select="string(UserLastName/text())"/>
//  Set "v11" to contain "v7", "v10", and "v9" ("SUPPLIER" + UserLastName +
//  comma, space, UserFirstName)
        <xsl:variable name="var:v11" select="userCSharp:StringConcat
                (string($var:v7) , $var:v10 , string($var:v9))"/>
```

```
           <FullName><xsl:value-of select="$var:v11"/></FullName>
        </xsl:if>
//  Test "v13" to see if the UserCode was neither "001" nor "002"
        <xsl:if test="string($var:v13)='true'">
//  Set "v14" to contain "MISC"
           <xsl:variable name="var:v14" select="&quot;MISC: &quot;"/>
//  Set "v15" to contain the value from UserFirstName
           <xsl:variable name="var:v15" select="string(UserFirstName/text())"/>
//  Set "v16" to contain a comma, space and the value from "v14" (UserFirstName)
           <xsl:variable name="var:v16" select="userCSharp:StringConcat
                 (&quot;, &quot; , $var:v15)"/>
//  Set "v17" to contain the value from UserLastName
           <xsl:variable name="var:v17" select="string(UserLastName/text())"/>
//  Set "v18" to contain the values from "v14", "v17", and "v18"
//  ( "MISC" + UserLastName + comma, space, UserFirstname)
           <xsl:variable name="var:v18" select="userCSharp:StringConcat
                 (string($var:v14) , $var:v17 , string($var:v16))"/>
//  Output the value of "v18" into the FullName node
           <FullName><xsl:value-of select="$var:v18"/></FullName>
        </xsl:if>
      </AddressForm>
    </xsl:for-each>
   </TargetData>
</xsl:template>
```

This map reflected only three conditionals, represented by the Equal functoids, in the chain. Needing five or more conditionals is not unusual in EDI mapping. Imagine how complex the functoid chain would be in such cases. This map is a good example of when to apply our Rule of Six.

Selecting from Available Scripting Languages

Since maps are created in the .NET environment, you may choose from a wide range of scripting languages. To see your choices, first drag a Scripting functoid onto the grid, right-click the functoid, and select Configure Functoid Script. The Configure Functoid Script window shown in Figure 3-3 opens.

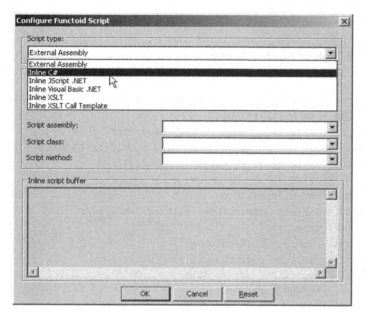

Figure 3-3. *Configure Functoid Script window*

When the window comes up, you'll see that the first drop-down window, "Script type", presents six choices for the scripting language:

- External Assembly
- Inline C#
- Inline JScript .NET
- Inline Visual Basic .NET
- Inline XSLT
- Inline XSLT Call Template

Let's build a date conversion script for each of these. We'll first look at the three more traditional programming languages (C#, JScript, and Visual Basic). Next, we'll examine the two XSLT methods, and finally, we'll create the external assembly example.

C#

Our C# script is a single function that accepts a date as input and returns a converted date. The script also checks to make sure that the input is not an empty string. Begin by selecting Inline C# in the Configure Functoid Script window to get the screen shown in Figure 3-4.

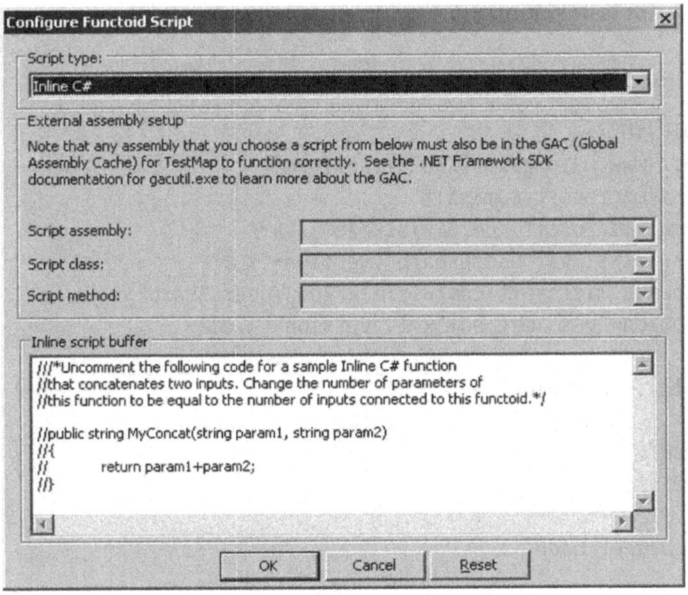

Figure 3-4. *Inline C# input window*

You see that BizTalk provides sample C#, commented out, in the "Inline script buffer" window. Delete all seven lines, as typing your code into the buffer is easier than working with the sample. You should always put in a comment that describes the purpose of the script. In C# comments begin with a double slash (//), as shown in the sample text. Finally, type your code directly into the buffer.

■**Tip** You do not have to type your code into the buffer. You can type and edit it in any text editor, such as Notepad, and then copy and paste it into the buffer. The Visual Studio IDE can be used to create and test scripts as well.

We put the script in Listing 3-4 into the buffer for our C# example.

Listing 3-4. *DateFormat Script in C#*

```
public string Format8Date(string inDate)
{
    if (inDate != "")
        return inDate.Substring(0,4) + "/" + inDate.Substring(4,2) + "/"
                + inDate.Substring(6,2);
    else
        return "";
}
```

The code generated with this script is in Listing 3-5.

Listing 3-5. *Code Generated with Format8Date Script*

```
<?xml version="1.0" encoding="UTF-16"?>
<xsl:stylesheet xmlns:xsl="http://www.w3.org/1999/XSL/Transform"
        xmlns:msxsl="urn:schemas-microsoft-com:xslt"
        xmlns:var="http://schemas.microsoft.com/BizTalk/2003/var"
        exclude-result-prefixes="msxsl var userCSharp" version="1.0"
    xmlns:userCSharp="http://schemas.microsoft.com/BizTalk/2003/userCSharp">
    <xsl:output omit-xml-declaration="yes" method="xml" version="1.0"/>
    <xsl:template match="/">
        <xsl:apply-templates select="/Invoice"/>
    </xsl:template>
    <xsl:template match="/Invoice">
//  Begin outputting the InvoiceTarget node.
        <InvoiceTarget>
//  Begin outputting the InvoiceHeader node
            <InvoiceHeader>
//  set the contents of variable "v1" to the value returned by the C#
//  function "Format8Date"
//  Pass the function the value from the source node InvoiceHeader/PODate
            <xsl:variable name="var:v1" select=
                    "userCSharp:Format8Date(string(InvoiceHeader/PODate/text()))"/>
//  Begin outputting the PODate node
            <PODate>
//  Output the value from "v1" (the reformatted date"
                <xsl:value-of select="$var:v1"/>
            </PODate>
            </InvoiceHeader>
            </InvoiceTarget>
    </xsl:template>
//  Specify the script language used in the map
<msxsl:script language="CSharp" implements-prefix="userCSharp">
//  Begin the CDATA section of the map, where all the C# scripts reside
<![CDATA[
//  Here is the script that is contained in the Scripting functoid.  It is the same
//  script as we typed into the buffer (see Listing 3-4)
public string Format8Date(string inDate)
{
  if (inDate != "")
    return inDate.Substring(0,4) + "/" + inDate.Substring(4,2) +
            "/" + inDate.Substring(6,2);
  else
    return "";
}
```

```
]
]></msxsl:script>
</xsl:stylesheet>
```

A CDATA section has been created in the map to hold the Format8Date script.

Caution When you first create a script, remember to give it a new name. We named the script in Listing 3-5 Format8Date. As noted earlier, all scripts with the same name are treated as one by the compiler.
Subsequent occurrences of the same function do not get created in the CDATA section of the map. Thus
if you create two different scripts but name both the same, when the map is generated the code from the
second instance will not appear in the compiled map. It will still appear in the functoid, however, thereby
misleading you when you try to debug the map. This is true of all scripts, not just C# scripts.

Suppose we want to pass the date through to another output node, but this time, we don't
want to reformat it. We add a second script to our map so that we have the scripts from Listing
3-4 and Listing 3-6 in our map.

Listing 3-6. *Second Format8Date Script*

```
public string Format8Date(string inDate)
{
string returnvalue = indate;
return indate
}
```

The second script has the same name but contains different code. Now look at Listing 3-7,
which is generated when we validate the map containing these two scripts.

Listing 3-7. *Code Generated for Map with Two Format8Date Scripts*

```
<?xml version="1.0" encoding="UTF-16" ?>
<xsl:stylesheet xmlns:xsl="http://www.w3.org/1999/XSL/Transform"
    xmlns:msxsl="urn:schemas-microsoft-com:xslt"
    xmlns:var="http://schemas.microsoft.com/BizTalk/2003/var"
    exclude-result-prefixes="msxsl var userCSharp" version="1.0"
    xmlns:userCSharp="http://schemas.microsoft.com/BizTalk/2003/userCSharp">
<xsl:output omit-xml-declaration="yes" method="xml" version="1.0" />
<xsl:template match="/">
<xsl:apply-templates select="/Invoice" />
</xsl:template>
<xsl:template match="/Invoice">
//  Begin outputting the InvoiceTarget node
<InvoiceTarget>
//  Begin outptting the InvoiceHeader node
```

```
    <InvoiceHeader>
//  Set variable "v1" to contain the value returned
//  from the C# functoid "Format8Date"
//  Pass the the value from InvoiceHeader/InvoiceNumber to the function
    <xsl:variable name="var:v1" select="userCSharp:Format8Date
          (string(InvoiceHeader/InvoiceNumber/text()))" />
Begin outputting the InvoiceNumber node
    <InvoiceNumber>
//  Output the value from "v1" into the InvoiceNumber node
      <xsl:value-of select="$var:v1" />
    </InvoiceNumber>
//  Set variable "v2" to contain the value returned
//  from the C# functiod "Format8Date"
    <xsl:variable name="var:v2" select="userCSharp:Format8Date
          (string(InvoiceHeader/PONumber/text()))" />
Begin outputting the PONumber node
    <PONumber>
//  Output the value from "v3" into the PONumber node.
      <xsl:value-of select="$var:v2" />
    </PONumber>
  </InvoiceHeader>
  </InvoiceTarget>
</xsl:template>
//  Specify the script language used in the map
<msxsl:script language="CSharp implements-prefix="userCSharp">
//  Begin the CDATA section of the map, where all the C# scripts reside
<![CDATA[
//  Here is the script that is contained in the Scripting functoid.  It is the same
//  script as we typed into the buffer (see Listing 3-4).
public string Format8Date(string inDate)
{
if (inDate != "")
return inDate.Substring(0,4) + "/" + inDate.Substring(4,2) +
  "/" + inDate.Substring(6,2);
else
return "";
}
]]>
</msxsl:script>
</xsl:stylesheet>
```

Notice that only the code for the first version of the Format8Data script, the one from Listing 3-4, appears in the CDATA section. The code from the second script, the one shown in Listing 3-6, was not compiled. If we had two Scripting functoids in a map, one with the script from Listing 3-4 and one with the script from Listing 3-6, both would call the script in the CDATA section. When the map was executed, the output of the second Scripting functoid would not be what we expected.

■**Caution** When calculating byte positions in a string in scripts or for String functoid parameters, make sure you recognize which notation should be used. In C#, for example, character positions are zero based. In String functoids, character positions are one based. Thus the character "C" in the string ABCD is in position two in C#, and three in a String functoid.

VB.NET

Next, we replace the C# code selection with Inline Visual Basic .NET. When we select this type in the drop-down, we again get sample code in the buffer. Remove the sample code. The Visual Basic (VB) script is shown in Listing 3-8.

Listing 3-8. *DateFormat Script in VB.NET*

```
Public Function Convert8Date(ByVal inDate As String) As String
    If inDate = "" Then
        Return ""
    Else
        Return inDate.Substring(0, 4) & "/" & inDate.Substring(4, 2)
                & "/" & inDate.Substring(6, 2)
    End If
End Function
```

You can see that there are noticeable differences in the syntax of VB as compared to C# even when the logic is the same. The difference in the way the underlying code is created is minor, however, as you can see in Listing 3-9.

Listing 3-9. *DateFormat Script in Visual Basic .NET*

```
<?xml version="1.0" encoding="UTF-16"?>
<xsl:stylesheet xmlns:xsl="http://www.w3.org/1999/XSL/Transform"
        xmlns:msxsl="urn:schemas-microsoft-com:xslt"
        xmlns:var="http://schemas.microsoft.com/BizTalk/2003/var"
                exclude-result-prefixes="msxsl var userVB" version="1.0"
        xmlns:userVB="http://schemas.microsoft.com/BizTalk/2003/userVB">
  <xsl:output omit-xml-declaration="yes" method="xml" version="1.0" />
  <xsl:template match="/">
    <xsl:apply-templates select="/Invoice" />
  </xsl:template>
  <xsl:template match="/Invoice">
// Begin outputting the InvoiceTarget node
  <InvoiceTarget>
// Begin outputting the InvoiceHeader node
      <InvoiceHeader>
// Set variable "v1" to the value returned by the VB function "Convert8Date"
// Pass the value from InvoiceHeader/ShipmentDate to the function
        <xsl:variable name="var:v1" select=
```

```
                "userVB:Convert8Date(string(InvoiceHeader/ShipmentDate/text())))" />
//  Begin outputting the ShipmentDate node
        <ShipmentDate>
//  Output the value from "v1" into the ShipmentDate node
          <xsl:value-of select="$var:v1" />
        </ShipmentDate>
      </InvoiceHeader>
    </InvoiceTarget>
  </xsl:template>
//  Specify the script language used in the map
  <msxsl:script language="VB" implements-prefix="userVB">
//  Begin the CDATA section of the map, where all the VB scripts reside
<![CDATA[
Public Function Convert8Date(ByVal inDate As String) As String
    if inDate = "" then
        Return ""
    else
        Return inDate.Substring(0, 4) & "/" & inDate.Substring(4, 2)
            & "/" & inDate.Substring(6, 2)
    End if
End Function
]]></msxsl:script>
</xsl:stylesheet>
```

We changed the script name and used different nodes in the schemas, so those values are different in this map, but those changes have nothing to do with the fact that we switched to VB in this map. The changes in the code due to the switch are shown in bold in Listing 3-9.

JScript .NET

As you might expect, we can create a format date script using JScript, as shown in Listing 3-10.

Listing 3-10. *DateFormat Script in Inline JScript .NET*

```
function JScriptFormatDate(inDate)
{
    var retval = "";
    if (inDate == "")
        retval = "";
    else
      retval = inDate.substr(0,4) + "/" + inDate.substr(4,2) + "/"
            + inDate.substr(6,2);
    return retval;
}
```

The underlying XSL map, depicted in Listing 3-11, differs very little from the C# and VB maps you just saw.

Listing 3-11. *Code for DateFormat Script in Inline Jscript .NET*

```
<?xml version="1.0" encoding="UTF-16"?>
<xsl:stylesheet xmlns:xsl="http://www.w3.org/1999/XSL/Transform"
    xmlns:msxsl="urn:schemas-microsoft-com:xslt"
    xmlns:var="http://schemas.microsoft.com/BizTalk/2003/var"
        exclude-result-prefixes="msxsl var userJScript" version="1.0"
    xmlns:userJScript="http://schemas.microsoft.com/BizTalk/2003/userJScript">
    <xsl:output omit-xml-declaration="yes" method="xml" version="1.0"/>
    <xsl:template match="/">
      <xsl:apply-templates select="/Invoice"/>
    </xsl:template>
    <xsl:template match="/Invoice">
//  Begin outputting the InvoiceTarget node
        <InvoiceTarget>
//  Begin outputting the InvoiceHeader node
          <InvoiceHeader>
//  Set variable "v1" to the value returned from the Jscript "JScriptFormatDate"
//  Pass the value from InvoiceHeader/ShipmentDate to the script as input
            <xsl:variable name="var:v1" select="userJScript:JScriptFormatDate
                (string(InvoiceHeader/ShipmentDate/text()))"/>
//  Begin outputting the ShipmentDate node
            <ShipmentDate>
//  Output the value from "v1" into the ShipmentDate node
              <xsl:value-of select="$var:v1"/>
            </ShipmentDate>
          </InvoiceHeader>
        </InvoiceTarget>
    </xsl:template>
//  Specify the script language used in the map
    <msxsl:script language="JScript" implements-prefix="userJScript"><!
//  Begin the CDATA section of the map, where all the JScript scripts reside
  [CDATA[
function JScriptFormatDate(inDate)
{
    var retval = "";
    if (inDate == "")
        retval = "";
    else
      retval = inDate.substr(0,4) + "/" + inDate.substr(4,2) + "/" +
          inDate.substr(6,2);
    return retval;
}
]]>
</msxsl:script>
</xsl:stylesheet>
```

XSLT Call Template

An XSLT call template builds one or more output nodes from scratch. In this example, we accept a date as the input parameter. We could have used an XPATH query instead of the input parameter.

Note The two XSLT scripting methods differ in whether or not an input parameter can be used. Inline XSLT, which we discuss after this XSLT call template discussion, accepts input via XPATH queries but does not accept input parameters. XSLT call templates accept input via both methods. The XPATH query you will see in the inline XSLT discussion is the same type as would be used in the XSLT call template.

Listing 3-12. *DateFormat Script in XSLT Call Template*

```
<xsl:template name="BuildShipmentDate">
    <xsl:param name="inDate"/>
    <ShipmentDate>
        <xsl:if test="$inDate != '' ">
            <xsl:value-of select="concat(substring($inDate,1,4), '/',
                    substring($inDate,5,2), '/',
                    substring($inDate,7,2))"/>
        </xsl:if>
    </ShipmentDate>
</xsl:template>
```

Notice that the language of the call template, shown in Listing 3-12, is similar to code that is generated when a map compiled.

Note Simple XPATH queries are especially useful when creating outbound EDI segments like the REF or DTM segments, because you can collect data from source nodes that are not in the current context node of your source data and use this data to create repeating instances of a single output node. We'll show examples of this in Part 4 of this book.

Using Inline XSLT

Inline XSLT scripts are different from those created with the other scripting languages, because they do not use input parameters. Look at Listing 3-13.

Listing 3-13. *DateFormat Script in Inline XSLT*

```
<xsl:variable name="inDate" select="//ShipmentDate" />
<xsl:if test="$inDate != '' ">
    <ShipmentDate>
```

```
        <xsl:value-of select="concat(substring($inDate,1,4), '/',
                substring($inDate,5,2), '/',
                substring($inDate,7,2))" />
      </ShipmentDate>
</xsl:if>
```

We use an XPATH query statement to retrieve the date, loading it directly into the variable inDate. The query gets the date from the source node //ShipmentDate. Since there is only one instance of ShipmentDate in the source, we are able to use an abbreviated pathname to that node.

Note Does is matter whether or not to use the variable inDate? Not really. But our good practice rule says that if you will use the input data in more than one place, you should use a variable. Your XSLT will then construct and use variables in the same way that a BizTalk map constructs and uses internal variables. (We are a bit more creative in naming variables than BizTalk, though!)

Like the XSLT call template, inline XSLT code is almost identical to that created when C#, JScript, and VB scripts are compiled. The inline XSLT code is in Listing 3-14.

Listing 3-14. *DateFormat Script in Inline XSLT*

```
<xsl:stylesheet xmlns:xsl="http://www.w3.org/1999/XSL/Transform"
    xmlns:msxsl="urn:schemas-microsoft-com:xslt"
    xmlns:var="http://schemas.microsoft.com/BizTalk/2003/var"
    exclude-result-prefixes="msxsl var" version="1.0">
  <xsl:output omit-xml-declaration="yes" method="xml" version="1.0"/>
  <xsl:template match="/">
    <xsl:apply-templates select="/Invoice"/>
  </xsl:template>
  <xsl:template match="/Invoice">
    <InvoiceTarget>
      <InvoiceHeader>
        <xsl:variable name="inDate" select="./ShipmentDate"/>
        <xsl:if test="$inDate != '' ">
          <ShipmentDate>
            <xsl:value-of select="concat(substring($inDate,1,4), '/',
                substring($inDate,5,2), '/',
                substring($inDate,7,2))"/>
          </ShipmentDate>
        </xsl:if>
      </InvoiceHeader>
    </InvoiceTarget>
  </xsl:template>
</xsl:stylesheet>
```

Caution Here are two notes to keep in mind when working with XSLT call templates and inline XSLT. First, when input parameters are used in an XSLT call template, the input values arrive through links from the source nodes to the Scripting functoid. If the source data is in a loop, the value input to the Scripting functoid depends on how many times the loop has been accessed before the script is executed. Second, when you need a system variable such as System Date as input, you may have to use a call template and not inline XSLT. Releases of BizTalk that do not use Version 2.0 or higher of XSLT do not have access to XSLT functions that can access system variables.

Using External Assemblies

Although listed with the other script types in the drop-down in the Configure Functoid Window of the Scripting functoid, external assemblies are not a different type of script. The External Assemblies selection provides a method for you to call .NET assemblies from a Scripting functoid. The five scripting languages we have just reviewed all can be used to create such a .NET assembly.

One reason to put your script in a .NET assembly stored in the global assembly cache (GAC) is that you can call the same routine from multiple Scripting functoids in multiple maps. This means that you can change the way all those maps work by modifying and replacing the assembly in the GAC.

Another reason is that assemblies allow you access to functions that are not available from scripts written directly in the Scripting buffer, such as SQL functions that reside in the System. Data assembly.

Caution Since there may be multiple instances of a map running at the same time, the code used in an assembly called from a Scripting functoid must be thread safe.

The date conversion process we used for the other scripting examples can be used as an external assembly as well. Since we are creating a library routine, we want to expand the functionality and make the script more universal in usage.

Creating an external assembly to perform the date conversions is more complex than simply putting a script in a Scripting functoid. Since you develop code for external assemblies in the Development Studio, you must create a class library project as shown in Figure 3-5.

Open the development studio, and select File ➤ New ➤ Project. When the project window opens, select the project type Visual C# and the template type Class Library. Name your project (we've named ours SSPS_Commonfunctions).

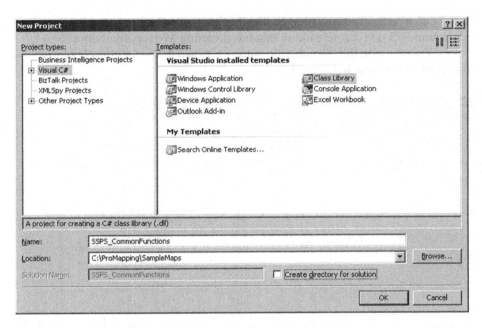

Figure 3-5. *Creating a Class Library project*

■ **Note** Which language you use in your external assembly is a matter of your choice. We use C# because we feel that C# is the most commonly used language with BizTalk and because we are most familiar with it.

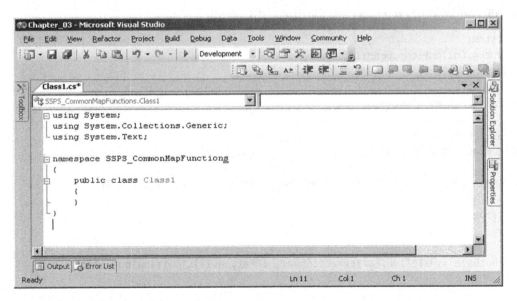

Figure 3-6. *The default window for the new C# library routine*

When you click OK, a code window will open like the one shown in Figure 3-6. Change the default module name (class1.cs) to a name that has meaning. We renamed ours SSPS_ CommonMapFunctions. Do the same thing for the file name as shown in the Solution Explorer. Now the window looks like the one in Figure 3-7.

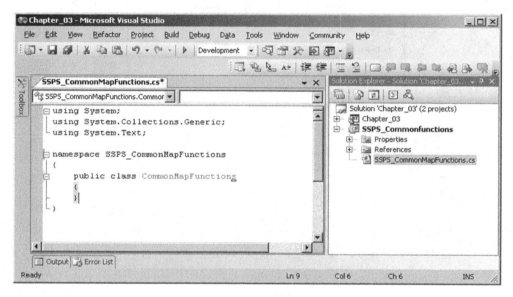

Figure 3-7. *Window for the new C# library routine with the new names*

Next add the method that will format dates. The code is shown in Listing 3-15. Notice that this script allows you to specify the format of the input date and the format for the output date.

Listing 3-15. *Format Date Function Code for External Assembly*

```
using System;
using System.Collections.Generic;
using System.Text;

namespace SSPS_CommonFunctions
{
  [Serializable]
  public class CommonMapFunctions
  {
    public string FormatDateTime(string inVar, string inFmt, string outFmt)
    {
      string outDate = "";
      try
      {
        outDate = DateTime.ParseExact(inVar, inFmt, null).ToString(outFmt);
      }
      catch
      {
```

```
        outDate = "INVALID";
    }
    return outDate;
  }
 }
}
```

■**Note** We will not discuss the .NET aspects of this code in detail, as that is beyond the scope of this material. If you are not familiar with .NET programming, we recommend you obtain a manual on the .NET language of your choice.

Before the class library function can be called from your map, you must deploy the .dll to the GAC. Begin by compiling the assembly with a strong-named key. Right-click the project, and select Properties to open the Properties window. Then, click the Signing tab to get the window displayed in Figure 3-8. Make sure the "Sign the assembly" check box is checked, and use the drop-down under "Choose a strong name key file" to select the key file.

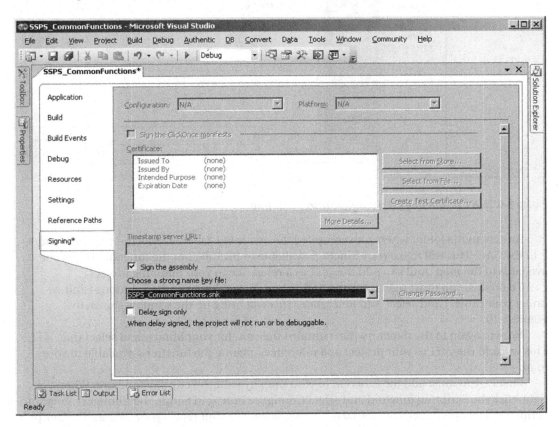

Figure 3-8. *Adding a strong-named key*

Next, you install the .dll into the GAC. Go to your Start menu, and select Settings ➤ Administrative Tools ➤ Microsoft .NET Framework 2.0 Configuration, or the equivalent for the version of .NET Framework that you have installed. The window that will open will differ depending on several things, including the preferences that have been set for the tool. The screen shot in Figure 3-9 shows the default view using version 2.0, after selecting Add an Assembly.

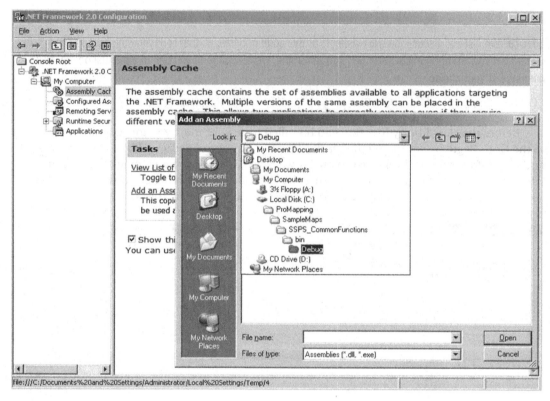

Figure 3-9. *.NET Framework 2.0 configuration window*

Browse to the folder where you compiled the assembly. Double-click the .dll file to add it to the GAC. This will make your function available to BizTalk, but the function will not be available to the map until you add the .dll as a reference to your mapping project.

To do this, you must right-click the References folder shown in the Solutions window under your project and select Add Reference. This will bring up the window shown in Figure 3-10.

Browse again to the directory that contains the .dll for your library, and select that .dll. This will add the .dll to your project as a reference, making the functions available to your map.

Finally, you must add the function to your map by using a Scripting functoid. When you right-click the Scripting functoid and select Configure Functoid Script, the Configure Functoid Script window opens. Select External Assembly as your "Script type", your .dll as the "Script assembly", your script class, and the name of your function. You will then have a window similar to the one in Figure 3-11.

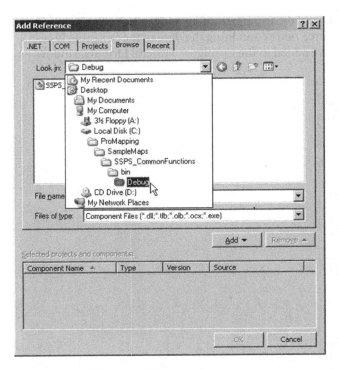

Figure 3-10. *Adding the .dll as a reference to your map project*

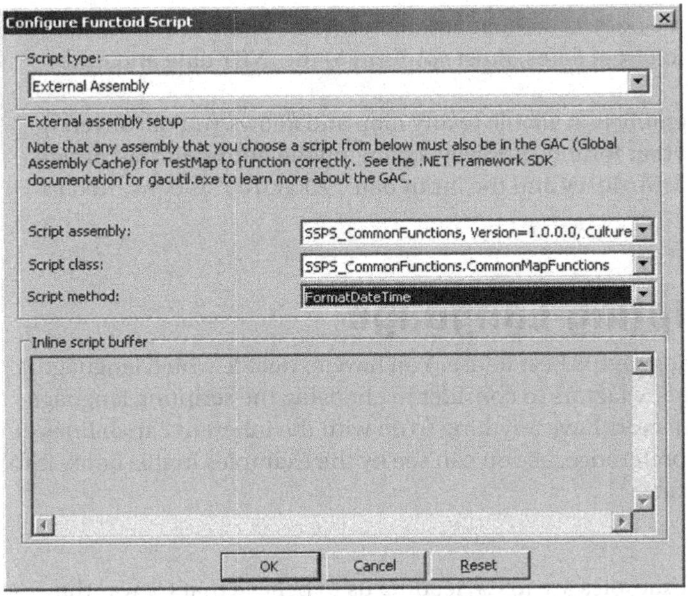

Figure 3-11. *Configuring the Scripting functoid for an external assembly*

The final step that you must do is to add the input parameters to the Scripting functoid. The first parameter is a link from the source node containing the date to the Scripting functoid. The second and third parameters are added in the Configure Functoid Inputs window, as shown in Figure 3-12.

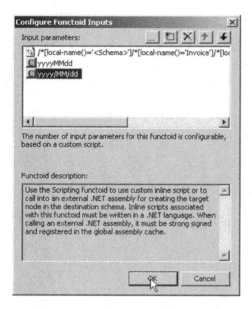

Figure 3-12. *Configuring the inputs*

Notice that the link to the source node is the first parameter. The second and third parameters, the formats for the source and target dates, must conform to the .NET date and time syntax requirements.

This quickly built external assembly is available to any map and allows you to convert a valid date from one format to any other format simply by changing the output format parameter. Change the output format to MM/dd/yy and the input date "20080704" is converted to 04/07/08. It's as easy as that.

Choosing Your Scripting Language

We can't tell you which scripting language is best to use. You have to decide which language is best for your situation. There are many factors to consider in choosing the scripting language for your maps. Only a few of those factors have anything to do with the inherent capabilities of one language versus another. Our preference, as you can see by the examples in this book, is to use C# and XSLT. We chose C# because

- We are familiar with C#.

- Most of the Microsoft SDK examples are in C#, leading us to believe that C# was the language of choice for BizTalk development.

We chose XSLT because we found that some of the more difficult mapping problems that needed scripting were easier to solve with XSLT than with C#. We were not familiar with XSLT prior to working with BizTalk maps, so we had to learn how to use it. Let's examine some of the factors that may help you decide which language, or languages, you should use.

- *Familiarity with the language*: If you are already familiar with one of the scripting languages, you should use that language for your scripts. You shouldn't learn a new language unless one of the other factors discussed here indicates that you should.

- *Company standards*: Many organizations have a standard development language. We have clients that insist that entire BizTalk maps be written is XSLT, not just the scripts. You must use the scripting language that is dictated by the standards for the organization.

- *Complex data extracts*: Your best bet when doing complex queries against the source data is to use inline XSLT or an XSLT call template. This allows you to take advantage of the powerful capabilities of XPATH queries, which are very helpful when you need to extract data from a variety of different source nodes to create common output records.

- *Loop controls*: The BizTalk mapper does not provide a method to control looping other than the Looping functoid, which is insufficient in many cases. This is because the iterations of a loop are determined by the instances of data in the source node. Also, multiloop to single loop iterations are not supported. Sometimes, you need to force a greater or smaller number of loops than would be produced by the default mechanisms. XSLT scripting provides the means to control looping in such instances.

- *Complex logic*: As discussed earlier, complex functoid chains should be replaced with scripts. Complex logic is more difficult to implement in XSLT, particularly when variables must be manipulated. C#, VB, or JScript are better choices when complex logic is needed.

- *Database lookups*: Custom database access should be done in an external assembly. You can use any language for this purpose. The one you should use will be driven by external factors, such as the type of database.

- *External cross-reference files*: In some cases, particularly with EDI mapping, you may need to access external data that resides in flat files. C# and VB are the best choices for this.

As a simple illustration of how flexible the mapping tool is with respect to language choice, let's look at an example of how the FullName script from our original HelloWorld example can be coded just as easily with an XSLT call template. The C# script was shown in Listing 3-2. Here is the equivalent XSLT call template in Listing 3-16.

Listing 3-16. *FullName Script in XSLT*

```
<xsl:template name="PutFullName">
    <xsl:param name="UserCode"/>
    <xsl:param name="UserLast"/>
    <xsl:param name="UserFirst"/>
    <xsl:variable name="NewFirst">
        <xsl:if test="$UserFirst != '' "><xsl:value-of
```

```
                select="concat(', ', $UserFirst)"/></xsl:if>
    </xsl:variable>
    <xsl:variable name="UserType">
        <xsl:choose>
            <xsl:when test="$UserCode = '001' ">CUSTOMER: </xsl:when>
            <xsl:when test="$UserCode = '002' ">SUPPLIER: </xsl:when>
            <xsl:otherwise>MISC: </xsl:otherwise>
        </xsl:choose>
    </xsl:variable>
    <FullName>
        <xsl:value-of select="concat($UserType, $UserLast, NewFirst)"/>
    </FullName>
</xsl:template>
```

The resulting code is a bit more verbose, but it is also more readable. Notice that we were able to easily build in the test to put the comma into the FullName only if the FirstName was actually present. That test was also easy to do in C#, but there was no easy way to do it using only functoids.

Combining Types of Scripting

You can also access one type of script from another type. As you've seen from some of our simple coding examples, the XSL map code generated as you place functoids on the grid calls C# routines. There is no reason why you can't do the same thing in your scripted solutions.

For example, sometimes an XPATH query is the best choice for 90 percent of your needs but doesn't have the horsepower to do everything you need. On the other hand, C# can do the other 10 percent but is not the best choice for the other 90 percent. Combining the two languages is a perfect solution.

Let's look at an example where we call a C# script from an inline XSLT script. We take the map that used a C# script to convert a date, and we add an inline script to populate the output node LineNumber. Because the XSLT script doesn't connect to the source, we've also added a looping functoid to insure that the target map knows it is supposed to iterate through all instances of LineItem in the source. The map is shown in Figure 3-13.

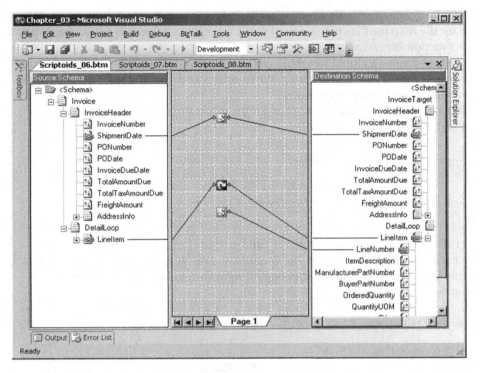

Figure 3-13. *A map with scripts calling scripts*

The top Scripting functoid in the map holds the script that converts the date. Now, we add a second function, a line counter, to that functoid. We inserted the new script following and outside the scope of the existing script, as shown in Listing 3-17. This enables the compiler to compile the new function and place it in the CDATA section of the map without making it a part of the script executed when the functoid is accessed to reformat the date.

Listing 3-17. *Date Conversion Scripting Functoid with Counter Function*

```
public string Format8Date(string inDate)
{
  if (inDate != "")
    return inDate.Substring(0,4) + "/" + inDate.Substring(4,2) + "/"
          + inDate.Substring(6,2);
  else
    return "";
}

int LineCount = 0;
public string ReturnCounter()
{
    LineCount += 1;
    return LineCount.ToString();
}
```

Since the mapping engine compiles only the first script in the functoid by default, the XSL code generated for the map for the conversion of the ShipmentDate value will not contain any reference to the function ReturnCounter().

The new functoid creates a global variable LineCount and initializes it to 0. This makes the variable available to code anywhere in the map. When referenced, the function increments the variable and returns the new value to the caller.

Next, we add a new Scripting functoid to output the LineNumber. This functoid contains the inline XSLT script shown in Listing 3-18.

Listing 3-18. *Script to Output the Line Number*

```
<LineNumber>
   <xsl:value-of select="userCSharp:ReturnCounter()" />
</LineNumber>
```

This script calls the function ReturnCounter() and outputs the value returned from that function. Since each call increments the global variable, the result is that the output from this Scripting functoid is an incrementing number beginning with 1. Listing 3-19 is the map code created for this map.

Listing 3-19. *Code for a Map with a C# Script Called by the Inline XSLT Script*

```
<?xml version="1.0" encoding="UTF-16"?>
<xsl:stylesheet xmlns:xsl="http://www.w3.org/1999/XSL/Transform"
            xmlns:msxsl="urn:schemas-microsoft-com:xslt"
            xmlns:var="http://schemas.microsoft.com/BizTalk/2003/var"
            exclude-result-prefixes="msxsl var userCSharp" version="1.0"
            xmlns:userCSharp="http://schemas.microsoft.com/BizTalk/2003/userCSharp">
    <xsl:output omit-xml-declaration="yes" method="xml" version="1.0"/>
    <xsl:template match="/">
        <xsl:apply-templates select="/Invoice"/>
    </xsl:template>
    <xsl:template match="/Invoice">
//  Begin outputting the InvoiceTarget node
        <InvoiceTarget>
//  Begin outputting the InvoiceHeader node
            <InvoiceHeader>
//  Set "v1" to value returned from C# Format8Date script
//  Pass value from InvoiceHeader/ShipmentDetail node to script
                <xsl:variable name="var:v1"
                    select="userCSharp:Format8Date(string
                    (InvoiceHeader/ShipmentDate/text()))"/>
//  Begin outputting the ShipmentDate node
                <ShipmentDate>
//  Output the value from "v1" into the Shipment Date node
                    <xsl:value-of select="$var:v1"/>
                </ShipmentDate>
```

```
                    </InvoiceHeader>
//  Begin outputting the DetailLoop node
                <DetailLoop>
//  Output one loop for each source DetailLoop/LineItem node
                    <xsl:for-each select="DetailLoop/LineItem">
//  Begin outputting the LineItem node
                        <LineItem>
//  Begin outputting the LineNumber node.  The next three lines are inline XSLT
//  contained in a Scripting functoid.  The inline XSLT calls the C#
//  functoid "ReturnCounter"
                            <LineNumber>
//  Output the value returned from the C# function "ReturnCounter"
//  into the LineNumber node
                                <xsl:value-of select="userCSharp:ReturnCounter()"/>
                            </LineNumber>
                        </LineItem>
                    </xsl:for-each>
                </DetailLoop>
            </InvoiceTarget>
        </xsl:template>
//  Specify the script language used in the map
        <msxsl:script language="C#" implements-prefix="userCSharp">
//  Begin the CDATA section of the map, where all the C# scripts reside
<![CDATA
[
//  Here is the C# script that formats a date
public string Format8Date(string inDate)
{
  if (inDate != "")
    return inDate.Substring(0,4) + "/" + inDate.Substring(4,2) + "/"
                + inDate.Substring(6,2);
  else
    return "";
}
Here is the global variable "LineCount"
int LineCount = 0;
Here is the C# script that increments and returns the "LineCount" counter
public string ReturnCounter()
{
    LineCount += 1;
    return LineCount.ToString();
}
]]></msxsl:script>
</xsl:stylesheet>
```

There are many other ways, better ways, that the preceding example could have been implemented. We used this method just to illustrate how two languages could be used together to solve a problem.

■**Tip** Chapter 17, which discusses the HL loop found in X12 EDI, contains a great example of how to blend together two types of scripting.

Examples of When You Should Use a Script

Earlier we discussed general rules of when to use scripting. Now, let's look at some specific situations that we have encountered where we found scripting to be the better solution.

- *Compound if-else*: A single if-else condition is something like "if the code equals '1' then the return value equals 'a'; otherwise the return value equals 'b'." Implementing this with functoids is pretty easy. When the equation involves multiple if-else conditions, however, using functoids to replicate the equation becomes difficult if not impossible.

- *Modifying text strings*: There are functoids that can be used to pad strings and/or replace characters in strings. These are fine for simple padding and replacing, but in most cases, using a library script that you have developed is quicker and easier than adding multiple functoids to the map and entering their parameters.

- *Rounding and formatting output numbers*: The Rounding functoid has one practical limitation in that it suppresses trailing zeros. When this is a problem, using a string format script is much easier.

- *Multiple value substitution*: When you must evaluate several source values and replace the one received with a different value, you should turn to a case-function type script.

This is a short list of examples where scripting may be the better choice method. We end this chapter with an example map that demonstrates how much you can rely on Scripting functoids. We again use the HelloWorld map as our basis. The map is in Figure 3-14.

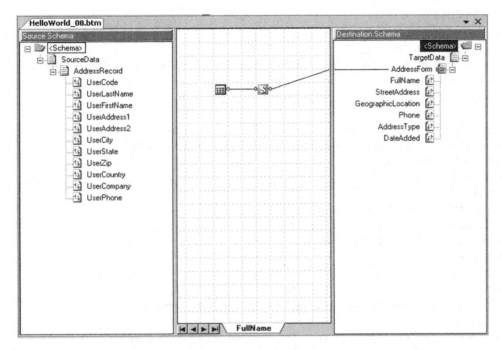

Figure 3-14. *XSLT map*

This map uses an XSLT call template to build the output file. The only direct input into the script is the output of the Date functoid. XPATH statements in the script extract the other input from the source file. The code generated for this map, which builds the entire AddressForm node, is in Listing 3-20.

Listing 3-20. *Code Generated for XSLT Map*

```
<xsl:template name="PutAddressRec">
  <xsl:param name="SysDate"/>
// Begin a loop for each source AddressRecord node
  <xsl:for-each select="//AddressRecord">
// Put the value from the source UserCode node into the variable "UserCode"
    <xsl:variable name="UserCode" select="./UserCode"/>
// Put the value from the source UserLastName node into the variable "UserLast"
    <xsl:variable name="UserLast" select="./UserLastName"/>
// Put the value from the source UserFirstName node into the variable "UserFirst"
    <xsl:variable name="UserFirst" select="./UserFirstName"/>
// Create the empty variable "NewFirst" for the revised first name
    <xsl:variable name="NewFirst">
// Only do the first name work if there is a value in the variable "UserFirst"
      <xsl:if test="$UserFirst != '' ">
// Add a comma and a space to the beginning of the "UserFirst" variable
        <xsl:value-of select="concat(', ', $UserFirst)"/>
      </xsl:if>
```

```
      </xsl:variable>
//    Create the variable "UserType"
      <xsl:variable name="UserType">
//    Fill the variable "UserType" based on the contents of the variable "UserCode"
//    If the value of "UserCode" is neither "001" nor "002", put the string "MISC"
//    into "UserType"
        <xsl:choose>
          <xsl:when test="$UserCode = '001' ">CUSTOMER: </xsl:when>
          <xsl:when test="$UserCode = '002' ">SUPPLIER: </xsl:when>
          <xsl:otherwise>MISC: </xsl:otherwise>
        </xsl:choose>
      </xsl:variable>
// Begin outputting the AddressForm node
    <AddressForm>
//    Begin outputting the FullName node
        <FullName>
//    Join the values of the variables "UserType", "UserLast", and "NewFirst
//    and put the result into the FullName node
          <xsl:value-of select="concat($UserType, $UserLast, $NewFirst)"/>
        </FullName>
//    If the source node UserAddress1 contains a value, output that value
//    into the StreetAddress node        <xsl:if test="./UserAddress1 != '' ">
          <StreetAddress><xsl:value-of select="./UserAddress1"/></StreetAddress>
        </xsl:if>
//    Output the GeographicLocation node using the value obtained by joining the
//    "UserCity", "UserState", and "UserZip" variables separated by spaces
        <GeographicLocation>
          <xsl:value-of select="concat(UserCity, ' ', UserState, ' ', UserZip)"/>
        </GeographicLocation>
//    Output the Phone node using the value from the source UserPhone node
        <Phone><xsl:value-of select="UserPhone"/></Phone>
//    Output the system date into the DateAdded node
        <DateAdded><xsl:value-of select="$SysDate"/></DateAdded>
      </AddressForm>
    </xsl:for-each>
</xsl:template>
```

■**Caution** When building a target node with an XSLT script, that target node and all of its children *must* be created by that script.

Summary

In this chapter, we presented a high-level overview of when and how to use scripting in Biz-Talk maps. We can't dictate, or even recommend, specifics in this area, because the factors that influence these choices are outside our control. You must decide when and where to use scripts and which language or languages you will use based on your own skills and on the requirements of the organization for which you do mapping.

As you saw, becoming familiar with XSLT is almost a prerequisite to becoming adept at BizTalk mapping—not only because you need the ability to read the code generated by the map but also because there are some constructs that are very difficult, if not impossible, to create without using XSLT.

Before we begin to get into the basic techniques for creating maps, we've got one more topic to cover, so in the next chapter, we will take a detailed look at how to test BizTalk maps. In many ways, we consider developing good testing techniques to be the key to becoming a good BizTalk mapper. Learning how to test the maps will raise your comfort level with all aspects of BizTalk mapping.

CHAPTER 4

■■■

Testing BizTalk Maps

The first three chapters covered the basics, explaining how BizTalk maps work, walking you through how they are created, and showing you how to enhance them with scripts. We touched on testing maps in those chapters as we examined the code and output files. Now, in this chapter, we expand the discussion of map testing methods.

The BizTalk Map Editor has no debugger or trace feature. Data goes in one side of a map, and the new data either comes out the other side or it doesn't. If it does come out, it may not be correct. Even small changes to a working map can cause the map to fail to produce output or to output incorrect data.

The alternative to testing in the map editor is deploying the map to a BizTalk application and creating and configuring the artifacts—ports, parties, pipelines, and so on—necessary to process a file through the map. We call testing in this manner end-to-end testing and won't spend time on it in this chapter because you must be thoroughly familiar with configuring BizTalk artifacts such as parties, ports, and pipelines to do this type of testing. End-to-end testing is not the preferred method of testing a map during its development.

Caution There are differences in behavior in the two types of testing. When you have a decimal point in a number or trailing zeros after a decimal point, for example, the map may fail in the map editor but not fail in end-to-end testing. Why? Because you configure some features, such as allow trailing zeros, in the party. End-to-end testing accesses the party configuration, whereas the map editor does not. This is one of the reasons most of your testing in the editor will be done with output validation disabled.

Incremental Testing

We recommend incremental testing of BizTalk maps. Incremental testing is where you test your map immediately after adding or changing a rule. You may test a map as you develop it tens or hundreds of times, but by testing so often, you will find that bugs are easier to locate and fix. A modification in one area of the map can cause a bug to appear in a seemingly unrelated area; you want to find such a bug immediately rather than hours or days later.

Let's look at an example of what we mean. Figure 4-1 presents our map.

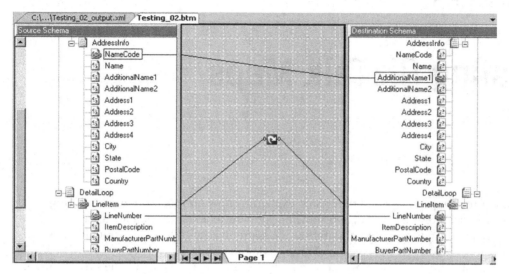

Figure 4-1. *Our working map*

This map produces the output seen in Listing 4-1. This output is correct. There are two addresses in the source data and four line items in the source data. We have two AddressInfo nodes and four LineItem nodes in the output.

Listing 4-1. *Output from Our Working Map*

```
<InvoiceTarget>
  <InvoiceHeader>
// There are two AddressInfo loops, one for BT and one for SF
    <AddressInfo>
        <AdditionalName1>BT</AdditionalName1>
    </AddressInfo>
    <AddressInfo>
        <AdditionalName1>ST</AdditionalName1>
    </AddressInfo>
  </InvoiceHeader>
  <DetailLoop>
//  There are four LineItem loops, one for each line item
    <LineItem>
        <LineNumber>1</LineNumber>
    </LineItem>
    <LineItem>
        <LineNumber>2</LineNumber>
    </LineItem>
    <LineItem>
        <LineNumber>3</LineNumber>
    </LineItem>
    <LineItem>
        <LineNumber>4</LineNumber>
```

```
        </LineItem>
      </DetailLoop>
</InvoiceTarget>
```

Now, let's make a minor modification to the map, performing these three actions:

1. We link the source ItemDescription node to the target node Name.

2. We remove the link from the source node NameCode to the target node AdditionalName1.

3. We realize the last step was a mistake and reattach the line between NameCode and AdditionalName1.

Now the map looks like Figure 4-2. We can continue mapping, or we can run an incremental test to make sure things are still working.

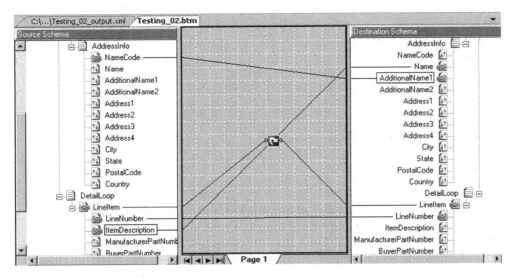

Figure 4-2. *Our updated map*

Let's run the incremental test. Listing 4-2 shows the output from the test.

Listing 4-2. *Output of Our Updated Map*

```
<InvoiceTarget>
  <InvoiceHeader>
//  Now there are four AddressInfo loops instead of two, and only the BT is output
//  The ST has been lost
    <AddressInfo>
      <Name>LITTLE WIDGET</Name>
      <AdditionalName1>BT</AdditionalName1>
    </AddressInfo>
    <AddressInfo>
      <Name>BIG WIDGET</Name>
      <AdditionalName1>BT</AdditionalName1>
    </AddressInfo>
```

```
  <AddressInfo>
    <Name>BROKEN WIDGET</Name>
    <AdditionalName1>BT</AdditionalName1>
  </AddressInfo>
  <AddressInfo>
    <Name>FREE WIDGET</Name>
    <AdditionalName1>BT</AdditionalName1>
  </AddressInfo>
  </InvoiceHeader>
  <DetailLoop>
//  The LineItem loop is still correct.
    <LineItem>
      <LineNumber>1</LineNumber>
    </LineItem>
    <LineItem>
      <LineNumber>2</LineNumber>
    </LineItem>
    <LineItem>
      <LineNumber>3</LineNumber>
    </LineItem>
    <LineItem>
      <LineNumber>4</LineNumber>
    </LineItem>
  </DetailLoop>
</InvoiceTarget>
```

The two changes to our working map, adding one link and disconnecting and reconnecting a second link, have broken parts of our map that were working. We can immediately work to solve this problem, because we know that one of the two changes is the cause. We can remove those changes and set the map back to the way it was. Then, we can make the changes one at a time to find out what happened.

However, imagine that we did not perform the incremental test and instead continued to add links to the map, perhaps even completing the map. When we finally ran a test and discovered this problem, would we know where to begin looking for the cause?

Addressing Architecture Considerations

How you structure your BizTalk applications, solutions, projects, and so forth has a major impact on testing, an impact that may reverberate up through your QA and production environments. We offer here some recommendations that are based on the way we set up our testing environments. Note that we are addressing the organization as it relates to the maps and schemas used by the maps. We do not address the organization of artifacts such as pipelines, orchestrations, and so forth, none of which affect testing of the maps.

Organizing Your BizTalk Applications

When we set up our BizTalk applications to which we will deploy our maps, we create separate applications for trading partners and for common artifacts as shown in Figure 4-3.

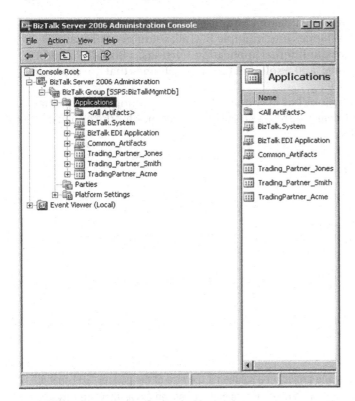

Figure 4-3. *BizTalk applications*

The two default applications in our group are the BizTalk.System application and the Biz-Talk.EDI.Application. We added four applications. One is called Common_Artifacts, while the others are named for the trading partners with whom we exchange messages. These could just as easily be named for different applications or even departments within our organization.

The Common_Artifacts application is where we place all of our schemas. Normally, schemas are used by more than one map, especially when there is more than one trading partner. By placing the schemas in the common application, we can keep them all in one place and reference them by application. One key thing to remember is that everything in the common application may be referenced by multiple other applications, thus a modification in that area may have a wider impact than you think.

The three trading partner applications each contain artifacts, including maps, that are unique to the particular customer. We know that modifying anything in a customer application should not cause problems with another customer. We can even remove and replace an entire customer application without fear that we may accidentally delete an object needed elsewhere.

Organizing Your BizTalk Solutions

We like to continue separation of function and customer in the way we organize our BizTalk solutions. The BizTalk application layout shown in Figure 4-3 comes close to the way our solutions structure looks.

The exception is that there may be more than one solution in the Common_Artifacts application, because we separate our schemas into multiple BizTalk solutions. For example, in this case, we have a BizTalk solution for our internal application schemas, a BizTalk solution for each customer-unique set of schemas, and a solution for those schemas that are common to all trading partners.

Each of the trading partner applications has only one solution, containing the maps that are specific to that trading partner. Listing 4-3 shows one way the schemas for the applications shown in Figure 4-3 might be organized.

Listing 4-3. *BizTalk Solution Organization*

```
Common_Artifacts Application
    EDI_Schemas_Solution
    Internal_Application_Schemas_Solution
Trading_Partner_Jones Application
    Jones_Maps Solution
Trading_Partner_Smith Solution
    Smith_Maps Solution
Trading_Partner_Acme Solution
    Acme_Maps Solution
```

■**Tip** You may be forced to have more than one project in a solution if the size of the project .dll that is formed when you build your solution is too large. This often occurs with EDI schemas, as they are very large. You may also decide to have separate solutions for pipelines and orchestrations.

Organizing Your BizTalk Projects

We prefer to place each artifact in its own BizTalk project: one project per map, one schema per map, and so forth. Let's extend the organization shown in Listing 4-3 to that shown in Listing 4-4.

Listing 4-4. *BizTalk Solution and Project Organization*

```
Common_Artifacts Application
    EDI_Schemas_Solution
        X12_4010_850_Schema Project
        X12_4010_810_Schema Project
    Internal_Application_Schemas_Solution
        My_internal_PO_Schema Project
        My_internal_IN_Schema Project
```

```
Trading_Partner_Jones Application
    Jones_Maps Solution
        Jones_PO_to_850_Map Project
        Jones_810_to_PO_Map Project
Trading_Partner_Smith Solution
    Smith_Maps Solution
        Smith_PO_to_850_Map Project
        Smith_810_to_PO_Map Project
Trading_Partner_Acme Solution
    Acme_Maps Solution
        Acme_PO_to_850_Map Project
        Acme_810_to_PO_Map Project
```

The purpose of this organization is to allow the manipulation of artifacts as independent entities. When you deploy a project from this structure, only that project and its unique referenced projects need be deployed. Since the referenced projects contain only schemas, deploying a map that uses the same schema as a previously deployed map does not deploy a second copy of that schema.

Separating Schemas and Maps

You cannot deploy the same schema twice. If you do, any artifact that uses that schema will throw an error, because BizTalk will not be able to decide which schema is the correct one. Separating schemas from the maps is a simple method of avoiding this problem.

Tip Changing the file name of a schema does not make a new schema. You could modify schema namespaces or root node names, or you could assign version numbers to the schemas—all these methods enable BizTalk to differentiate among schemas. Our problem with these methods is that they shift the responsibility for tracking which schema goes with which map to us, forcing us to remember whether version 1 goes with map A or map B, for example. We prefer our solution architecture, which minimizes this by ensuring that the schema file name matches the schema name in the Solution Explorer, which in turn matches the schema name in any map using the schema.

Look at Listing 4-5, which shows a solution setup that we often encounter at client sites.

Listing 4-5. *Common Architecture*

```
Our Solution
    Our Project
        Jones_PO_to_850_Map
        Jones_810_to_PO_Map
        Smith_PO_to_850_Map
        Smith_810_to_PO_Map
        X12_4010_850_Schema
```

```
X12_4010_810_Schema
My_internal_PO_Schema
My_internal_IN_Schema
```

Notice that any change to any artifact forces us to undeploy and redeploy the entire solution. Unfortunately, this solution architecture often ends up in production, meaning that a simple change to one artifact affects the movement of the entire solution up the deployment channel. Separating your schemas from your maps prevents this situation from occurring.

Test Data

Map development and map testing are intertwined, especially since you should begin incremental testing as soon as you add your first rule to your map. Of course, in order to test, you must have data. Ideally, you have production data from your trading partner and from your applications that can be used but often that is not possible. But what if you have no test data?

Generating Test Data from a Schema

Sadly, this is often the case. You do have a source schema, though, and you can generate data using that. Right-click your source schema in the Solution Explorer window, and select Properties to get the window shown in Figure 4-4.

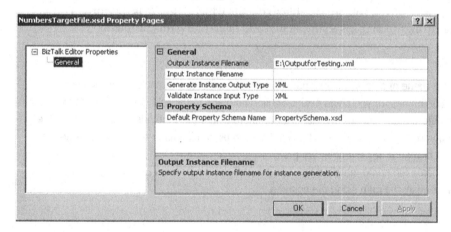

Figure 4-4. *Setting schema properties to create an instance*

Specify an output location and file name in Output Instance Filename. Make sure the Generate Instance Output Type is set to XML. Close the window. Then, right-click your schema name, and select Generate Instance. The engine will then create the file you specified in Output Instance Filename, including multiple nodes for looping nodes. Listing 4-6 shows an excerpt from such a file.

Listing 4-6. *Except from a Generated Instance*

```
<LineItem>
  <LineNumber>LineNumber_0</LineNumber>
  <PartNumber>PartNumber_0</PartNumber>
  <PartDescription>PartDescription_0</PartDescription>
  <UnitQuantity>UnitQuantity_0</UnitQuantity>
  <UnitPrice>UnitPrice_0</UnitPrice>
  <UnitDiscountPercentage>UnitDiscountPercentage_0</UnitDiscountPercentage>
  <UnitDiscountAmount>UnitDiscountAmount_0</UnitDiscountAmount>
  <ExtendedPrice>ExtendedPrice_0</ExtendedPrice>
  <NetUnitPrice>NetUnitPrice_0</NetUnitPrice>
  <TotalUnitPrice>TotalUnitPrice_0</TotalUnitPrice>
</LineItem>
```

Notice that the engine has filled every node with a string. You must replace this information with meaningful test information by hand, paying particular attention to dates, numbers, and code fields, since your map will fail if those fields are in the wrong format or have values that are illegal. We use values that have positional meaning. See Listing 4-7.

Listing 4-7. *Excerpt with Replace Values*

```
<LineItem>
  <LineNumber>1</LineNumber>
  <PartNumber>1111</PartNumber>
  <PartDescription>FirstPartLoop</PartDescription>
  <UnitQuantity>1</UnitQuantity>
  <UnitPrice>1</UnitPrice>
  <UnitDiscountPercentage>1</UnitDiscountPercentage>
  <UnitDiscountAmount>1</UnitDiscountAmount>
  <ExtendedPrice>1</ExtendedPrice>
  <NetUnitPrice>1</NetUnitPrice>
  <TotalUnitPrice>1</TotalUnitPrice>
  </LineItem>
<LineItem2>
```

The second `LineItem` loop would have twos in the data. This mechanism allows us to look at the output generated by the map and verify that output without having to look back at the source data. Knowing where part number 1111 was in the source is automatic, compared to trying to remember in which instance of the source loop BN3764-AA72 appeared.

Generating Test Data from a Flat File

You can test your map using an original flat file without transforming it into XML if you desire. Figure 4-5 shows you the map properties window. Put the name of your data file in Testing Input Instance, and set Testing Input to Native.

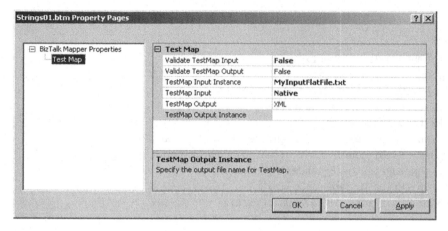

Figure 4-5. *Map properties for testing with native data*

You can convert your flat file to XML using your schema. Open your schema properties window, as shown in Figure 4-6.

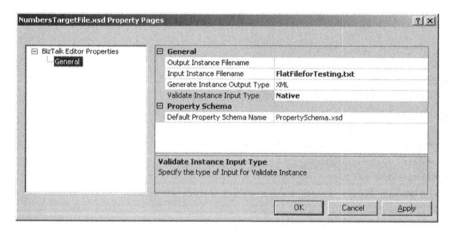

Figure 4-6. *Configuring your schemas properties to validate a flat file*

Put your flat file information into Input Instance Filename, and set Validate Instance Input Type to Native. Now, go back to your schema, right-click, and select Validate Instance. The engine will output your data file in XML format, ready for use in map testing.

Caution Always examine the output file from Validate Instance carefully. We have found cases where the output was not complete even though the validation process did not indicate there was an error in processing. Remember to press CTRL and click the link to the output file in the Output window to open the file.

Generating Test Data from an EDI File

You can generate an XML test file from your EDI data as well by using the Validate Instance option in your schema properties. There is one exception, and that is the screen shown in Figure 4-7.

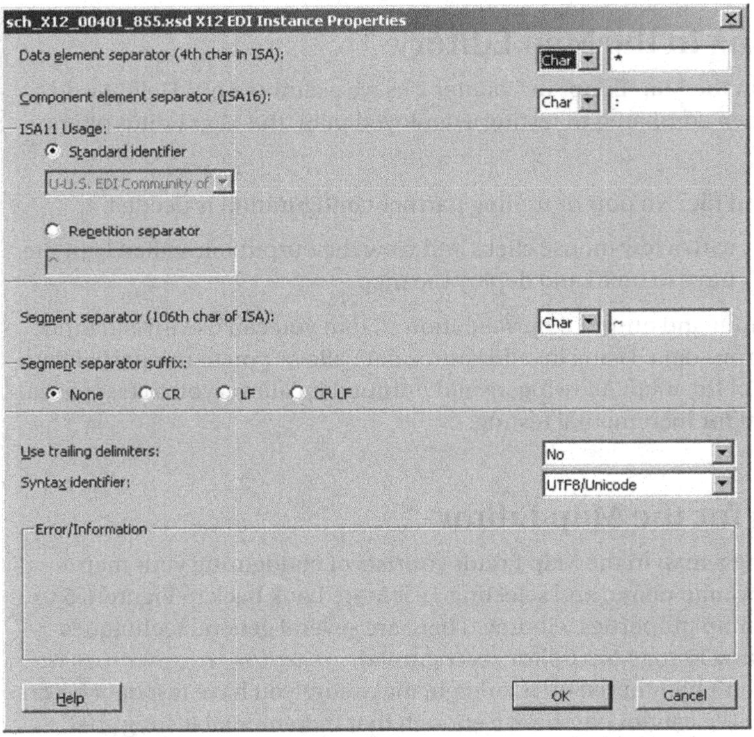

Figure 4-7. *X12 parsing parameters screen*

This screen appears after you select Validate Instance in your schema. An EDI file (in this case an X12 file) contains information needed to parse the file, such as the data element separator, the segment terminator, and so forth. This information is discussed in detail in the Chapter 13, the first chapter in the EDI section of this book.

Testing in the Map Editor

We believe so strongly that map building and map testing are synonymous that we repeat the incremental testing concept in this paragraph. The process of testing maps begins in the Map Editor as soon you create your first rule in the map and continues throughout the creation of the map. Map testing begins, then, in the Map Editor. Add a rule to the map; test the rule. Determine success by examining the output file to see if the structure and format are correct. Repeat.

The Map Editor is not a friendly place to do testing. There is neither a debugger nor an automated way to step through the map rule by rule. Testing becomes a process of analysis and detection, where you make a small change to your map, test it, and then analyze the output file to see what changed there. You have to find other methods to pry under the covers of your maps to see what is happening.

Advantages to Testing in the Map Editor

We touched on map testing in the Map Editor in Chapter 2 as we examined our HelloWorld map and ran a quick test. When compared to testing a deployed map, the Map Editor offers several advantages:

- You need only an input file. No port or trading partner configuration is needed.

- You can execute a test with a few mouse clicks and view the output immediately in the Map Editor. You don't have to build and deploy the map.

- You can deactivate input and output data validation so that you can use invalid input data or get invalid output data. Using invalid source data allows you to use partial data to focus on a portion of the map. Allowing invalid output data allows you to test partial maps. Both are critical for incremental testing.

Testing Techniques for the Map Editor

As you've already seen, testing a map in the Map Editor consists of configuring your map properties, right-clicking your map name, and selecting Test Map. Look back to Figure 4-5 to refresh your memory on the map properties window. There are several general techniques that you can use to make testing in the Map Editor even simpler.

First, just in case we haven't hammered on it enough, make sure you have test data before you begin creating your map. We cannot emphasize enough that incremental testing goes hand in hand with map development, and you cannot do incremental testing without test data.

Second, limit the size of your test data. Remember that you need to be able to quickly evaluate the output of your map to determine whether or not the map is working. Large data files are great for stress testing the end-to-end process, but when you want to see if your loop counter is working, you don't want to have to count 257 loops to find out. We usually use three iterations of each loop at this level of testing.

Third, modify your test data to simulate different conditions. If data arrived from the source in perfect form all the time, mapping would be much easier. But that doesn't happen. Analyze production data and the business process supported by your map to determine where anomalies may occur, and alter your test data accordingly to see how your map will respond.

Trapping Interim Results from Functoids

Sometimes, the data that appears in your output is incorrect, but you cannot pin down where the problem occurs, particularly when the data is passing through a long functoid chain or through a complex script. Let's look at a way to debug such a problem. Figure 4-8 shows a simple map to illustrate the point.

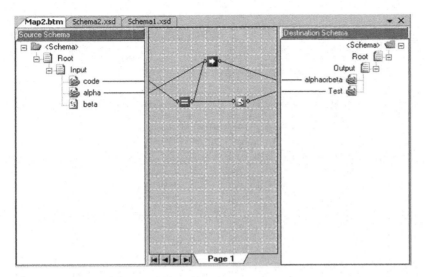

Figure 4-8. *Capturing interim results*

The scripting functoid in Figure 4-8 is there to solve a problem. The functoid chain of Equal and Value Mapping is not functioning correctly. We suspect that the Equal functoid is returning the incorrect value. We add the scripting functoid, with the script shown in Listing 4-8, to check that value. The map produces the output in Listing 4-9.

Listing 4-8. *Script to Check the Equal Functoid Output*

```
public string test(string x)
{
return x;
}
```

Listing 4-9. *Output of Capturing Interim Results Map*

```
<nsO:Root xmlns:nsO="http://Chapter_03.Schema2">
  <Output>
    <alphaorbeta>alpha</alphaorbeta>
    <Test>true</Test>
  </Output>
</nsO:Root>
```

The output tells us that the Equal functoid is returning the correct value. We examine the Value Mapping functoid and find that we had the inputs reversed. This is a very simple example of the technique. Imagine the value of this technique in resolving problems with the functoid chain in Figure 4-9.

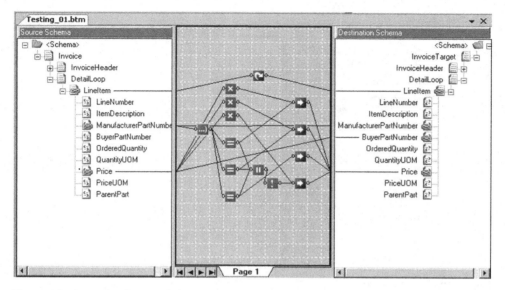

Figure 4-9. *Complex functoid chain*

Not only could you use the script to test the output from the logical functoids, you can also check the output of the String Left functoid and/or the Multiplication functoids by adding a link from the one to be tested to an output node; LineNumber would be a good choice in this case. Then, when you test the map, the output of the selected functoid would appear in the LineNumber node.

■**Caution** You should set Validate Testmap Output to False to use this method of testing, as shown in Figure 4-5.

Trapping Interim Results from Scripts

The same technique can be used to test scripts. Let's use the script in Listing 4-10 to illustrate how this is done.

Listing 4-10. *Trapping Interim Results from a C# Script*

```
public string BuildName()
{
string name;
  name = lastname;
  if (firstname != "")
    name = lastname + ", " + firstname;
  return name;
}
```

This script uses two global variables, lastname and firstname, that are found elsewhere in the map. The script either outputs the lastname or outputs lastname, firstname if there is data in the firstname variable. If you are testing the map and not getting the correct output from this script, you need to confirm that the input to the script is what you expect. You could do that quickly by inserting an early return line in the code as shown in Listing 4-11.

Listing 4-11. *Early Return Line to Check Input*

```
public string BuildName()
{
string name;
//  Insert early return to check value of firstname at this point in map
return firstname;
  name = lastname;
  if (firstname != "")
    name = lastname + ", " + firstname;
  return name;
}
```

The line inserted allows us to return just the contents of the variable firstname at the point the variable is accessed by the script. We may know that we loaded the variable with the correct value earlier, but perhaps something has modified that value between that time and the time this script runs.

Listing 4-12 shows how to check multiple inputs.

Listing 4-12. *Early Return Line to Check Multiple Inputs*

```
public static string Strings()
{
  string value = a + b;
  value = value + c;
//Insert line to check input value
return "a=" + a + "b=" + b + "c=" + c;
  return value;
}
```

If this script returns the string ajkxjkjlm, you can validate that this is the correct output by using the interim return line shown. The output using that line is a=ajk b=xjk c=jlm. Now, you can validate ajkxjkjlm as valid output.

Note You should create and test your scripts in the proper type of project (e.g., an empty C# project for C# scripting) in the IDE. The IDE provides syntax checking for your code and watch windows that allow you to observe line-to-line changes to variables. However, just because your script works in the IDE does not mean it will work in your map. You must test the script in your map as well.

You can use a variant of the early return technique with XLST scripts to check interim results from inside the script. Listing 4-13 contains an XSLT template and the output from the map.

Listing 4-13. *XSLT Script and Correct Output*

```
Script
<xsl:template name="InvoiceHeader">
 <xsl:param name="code" />
 <xsl:param name="invoicenum" />
 <xsl:param name="ponum" />
 <xsl:if test="$code != '' ">
    <xsl:element name="InvoiceHeader">
      <xsl:element name="InvoiceNumber">
       <xsl:value-of select="$invoicenum"/>
      </xsl:element>
      <xsl:element name="PONumber">
        <xsl:value-of select="$ponum"/>
      </xsl:element>
    </xsl:element>
  </xsl:if>
</xsl:template>
```

```
Output
<InvoiceTarget>
  <InvoiceHeader>
    <InvoiceNumber>IN12345</InvoiceNumber>
    <PONumber>PO67890</PONumber>
  </InvoiceHeader>
</InvoiceTarget>
```

The script only outputs the InvoiceNumber and PONumber nodes if the input parameter code contains the value AA. In Listing 4-13, the value was correct, so the two nodes were output. If the nodes had not been output, we could test to see what was in the parameter code. Look at Listing 4-14, which contains an adjusted script and output.

Listing 4-14. *XSLT Script to Check Value of code*

```
Script
<xsl:template name="InvoiceHeader">
 <xsl:param name="code" />
 <xsl:param name="invoicenum" />
 <xsl:param name="ponum" />
// Inserted line before IF statement to check value of "code"
 <xsl:if test="$code = 'AA' ">
<xsl:element name="InputCode"><xsl:value-of select="$code"/></xsl:element>
    <xsl:element name="InvoiceHeader">
      <xsl:element name="InvoiceNumber">
```

```
        <xsl:value-of select="$invoicenum"/>
      </xsl:element>
      <xsl:element name="PONumber">
          <xsl:value-of select="$ponum"/>
      </xsl:element>
    </xsl:element>
  </xsl:if>
</xsl:template>

Output
<InvoiceTarget>
  <InputCode>AB</InputCode>
</InvoiceTarget>
```

This example shows that if we were running the map and getting no output from the script we could insert a line to output a fake node with the code parameter. Now, we see that the code value was AB, which means the script is functioning correctly. The true value of the ability is not to check the input parameters but to check interim variables in a complex script.

Testing Output Structures

Often, the problem with a map is not the contents of the output but the structure of the output file. Problems of too many loops, not enough loops, or no loops in the output data can be very difficult to unravel, particularly once your map is producing reams of data. Here, in Figure 4-10 is the beginning of a map.

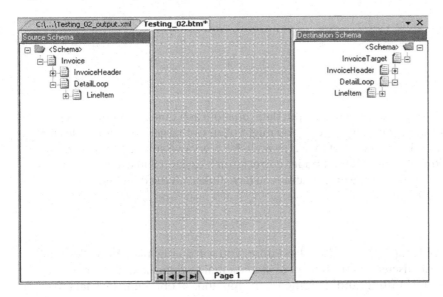

Figure 4-10. *A new map*

Let's look at the source and target LineItem nodes. We have a data file that is 82 lines of data, and we manually count four LineItem nodes in that file. We can easily see what the looping should produce by adding a Looping functoid to the map as shown in Figure 4-11.

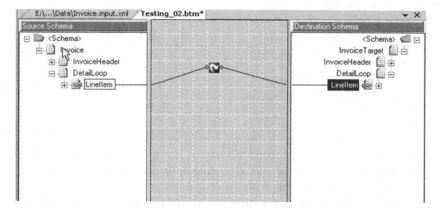

Figure 4-11. *Using the Looping functoid to determine looping structure*

Now, we test the map using our 82-line data file and get the output shown in Listing 4-15.

Listing 4-15. *Output Using a Looping Functoid to Determine Looping Structure*

```
<InvoiceTarget>
  <DetailLoop>
    <LineItem />
    <LineItem />
    <LineItem />
    <LineItem />
  </DetailLoop>
</InvoiceTarget>
```

There are four LineItem nodes in the output data, one for each LineItem node in the source data. The output is what we expected. You might need two target LineItem nodes for each source LineItem node or one target LineItem node for every two source LineItem nodes. You will find getting the number of target nodes correct much easier if you use this approach than you will if you try to control the output after you have linked all the data items.

Summary

This chapter introduced map testing in the Map Editor. You will do the majority of your mapping in this tool. We also discussed the concept of incremental testing, looked at architectural considerations to facilitate testing, and examined some methods of obtaining test data. We closed the chapter with some specific testing techniques. All of these factors work together to help you untangle problems in your maps.

We stress incremental testing, because that approach helps you minimize the mistakes that you carry deep into a map. You see mistakes as soon as you make them, and you have only a few changes to unravel to find the cause. Waiting until a large portion of the map, or the entire map, is completed to begin testing is a recipe for disaster.

Next, we begin looking at some basic mapping techniques. We will start in the next chapter with a look at how conditional logic works in BizTalk maps before moving on to numbers, strings, dates, times, and so forth. The next few chapters provide a detailed look at some of the basic techniques that appear in most maps.

PART 2

Step-by-Step Mapping

CHAPTER 5

■ ■ ■

Mapping Conditionals

Data mapping often involves decisions. One data element gets mapped to the target only under certain conditions. Another gets mapped every time, but the target changes depending on some variable. These if/else constructs are frequent requirements in mapping. This chapter discusses many of the conditional mapping situations that are encountered in mapping in BizTalk.

These situations use fairly simple source and target schemas that reflect a common problem encountered in mapping: needing to rearrange address information. Look at Figure 5-1. Notice that the target schema we use contains two separate but identical address record nodes, AddressRecord and AddressRecord2. This format allows us to show two methods of achieving the same result in one map.

We've included scripts as a method even in cases where we would not elect to use them, because they are always a viable alternative to functoids. As a general rule, however, we don't use scripts where functoid chains are simple. Recall our general Rule of Six: use a script when the number of functoids required exceeds six functoids. When the functoid chain becomes too complex, maintenance of the map becomes complex as well.

From this chapter on, we introduce functoids from the toolbox into our example maps. You should review the functoids in the toolbox so that you are familiar with their appearance, and basic functions, to more easily follow the discussion.

Tip The functoids from the Logical Functoids group in the toolbox are the most valuable for conditional operations. In this chapter, we lean heavily on the Logical String, Equal, Logical NOT, and a couple of others from that group. You can interchange many of these functoids to produce different logic. The Logical Numeric functoid could replace the Logical String functoid if you wanted to test for a number instead of a string, for example. The Logical AND functoid could replace the Logical OR functoid to produce a different logic gate. For the most part, the basic methodology used in the map would not change; only the output would change.

Checking If Data Exists

Many simple conditions are expressed easily with Logical functoids. In Figure 5-1, the objective is to move a UserLastName value to the target only when data exists in the source.

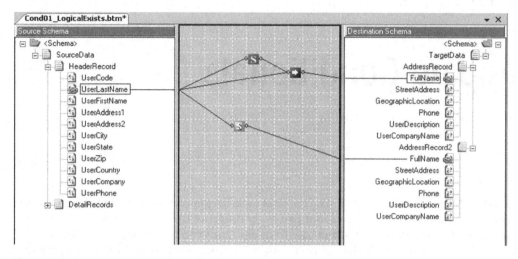

Figure 5-1. *Create output nodes only when data exists.*

The Logical String functoid in Figure 5-1 returns a true/false value based on whether or not there is data in the UserLastName node. This value is passed as the first input into the Value Mapping functoid. If the value is true, the Value Mapping functoid outputs the value received from its second input, the UserLastName node, to the target node FullName. If the value is false, the Value Mapping functoid outputs no data.

Caution We often see maps that use the Logical Existence functoid instead of the Logical String functoid. The Logical String interrogates the source node, in this case UserLastName, for the presence of text data. This is distinctly different than the function of the Existence functoid, which interrogates the XML document for the presence of the UserLastName node, not for the data in the node. Since XML files often have empty nodes, the Logical Existence functoid will return true if the node is present even when the node contains no data. This can result in data being output when it should not be output.

The Scripting functoid in Figure 5-1 contains a C# script, shown in Listing 5-1, that accomplishes the same action as the Value Mapping functoid.

Listing 5-1. *If-Exists C# Script*

```
public string CheckUserName(string inName)
{
if (inName != "")
  return inName;
else
  return "";
}
```

This simple script returns the value from the UserLastName node if there is a value; otherwise, it returns a null string. This is a case where using a script makes no sense, as the action performed by the script duplicates the action of one functoid.

Blocking Output When Data Doesn't Exist

In many situations, you want to create an output node only if a certain condition is met in the source. Our previous example has a flaw in that the target node, FullName, is created by the C# script even when there is no data in the source. This is because the script returns a value whether or not there is any data in the source node. Even a null string is treated as a value by the mapping engine and triggers creation of an empty FullName node. The node AddressRecord2 as created by the map in Figure 5-1 is in Listing 5-2.

Listing 5-2. *AddressRecord2 Output by Figure 5-1 Map*

```
<AddressRecord2>
  <FullName/>
</AddressRecord2>
```

Whether or not the empty FullName node is a problem depends on the syntax of the output schema. If the FullName node is mandatory, the map fails.

■Tip Always consider the downstream receiver of the file that is sent by BizTalk as well as considering the requirements of the map and schemas. In this case, the FullName node could be optional, meaning that the presence of the empty node is not a problem, and the map would not fail. However, if the message was sent from BizTalk with an empty node, a failure might occur in the receiving application due to the presence of the empty node.

We add a Logical String functoid to test the output of the Scripting functoid and to block the creation of the FullName node in AddressRecord2 if no data is output, as shown in Figure 5-2.

Look at the AddressRecord2/FullName node in Figure 5-2. There are two links to that node, one from a Logical String functoid and one from a Scripting functoid. The mapping engine evaluates the link to the Logical String functoid before it evaluates the link to the Scripting functoid. If the output of the Logical String functoid is true, the engine then evaluates the link to the Scripting functoid and builds the FullName node. If the output of the Logical String functoid is false, the engine stops processing the FullName node and does not build it. Let's look at the full output of the map in Figure 5-2. See Listing 5-3.

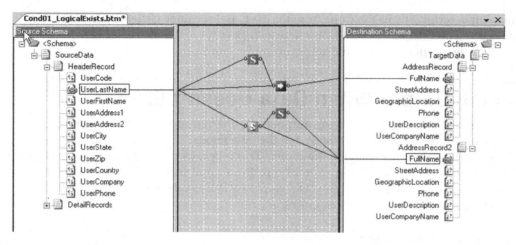

Figure 5-2. *Blocking output of an empty FullName node*

Listing 5-3. *Output of Figure 5-2 Map*

```
<ns0:TargetData xmlns:ns0="http://IfElse.TargetFile">
<AddressRecord />
<AddressRecord2 />
</ns0:TargetData>
```

Now, the AddressRecord2 node does not contain an empty FullName node. However, there are two empty nodes in the output, AddressRecord and AddressRecord2. We can block these nodes by moving the output links of the Logical String functoids as shown in Figure 5-3.

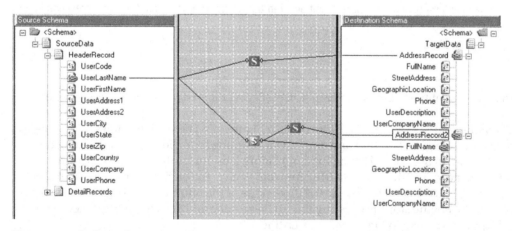

Figure 5-3. *Blocking the output of empty records*

We made three changes, two of which were moving the Logical String output links to the AddressRecord and AddressRecord2 nodes. The third was to remove the Value Mapping functoid. Since we are blocking the entire record if there is no value in the UserLastName node, there is no reason to block the FullName field using the Value Mapping functoid. As you know, the engine evaluates a conditional link placed on a record before it evaluates the child nodes of the record. If the conditional link returns false, the engine skips the children of that record and moves to the next record. Since we block both records in this map, the output is one line: `<nsO:TargetData xmlns:nsO="http://IfElse.TargetFile" />`. The two address records are suppressed.

Let's also take a look at an example of an inline XSLT script as a solution for this case, to illustrate a different methodology that we can use to block the output. The map looks the same as the only thing we do is replace the C# script with an inline XSLT script inside the Scripting functoid.

■**Note** We are using examples of inline XSLT scripts here, because the XSLT grammar and syntax are very different from the grammar and syntax of C#, VB, and JScript (whose grammar and syntaxes are similar). These examples of XSLT provide a brief and very high-level introduction to some of the more commonly used conditional XSLT statements, whether as inline code or in call templates. For a more detailed treatment of XSLT, we highly recommend *Beginning XSLT 2.0: From Novice to Professional* by Jeni Tennison (Apress, 2005).

Listing 5-4. *If-Exists XSLT Script to Check If Data Exists*

```
<xsl:variable name="inName"  select="//HeaderRecord/UserLastName"/>
<xsl:if test="$inName != '' ">
    <AddressRecord2>
        <FullName><xsl:value-of select="$inName"/></FullName>
    </AddressRecord2>
</xsl:if>
```

The Scripting functoid containing the code fragment shown in Listing 5-4 should be linked to the AddressRecord2 node on the target schema. This script blocks output of both the AddressRecord2 node and the FullName node. To block only the FullName node, delete from the script the AddressRecord2 start and end tags, and move the link to the FullName node.

■**Note** We could consider blocking the creation of empty record and element nodes in all the maps in this chapter, since there may or may not be data output. We did so in this first example to show how it is done. We will not block nodes from here on, because we want to keep the maps uncluttered.

Checking If a Specific Condition Exists

Our previous example depended on the presence of source data in the UserLastName node to determine if we should create a FullName node. Now, let's look at an example where two source nodes are involved. One contains the data we want to output to the target; the other contains a key that controls whether or not we output data. Look at the source schema in

Figure 5-4. We will use the value from the UserCode node to determine whether or not we should output the data contained in the UserLastName node to the target. In this example, the source UserCode name may contain many values, but we only want to output the target FullName nodes when the value is BY.

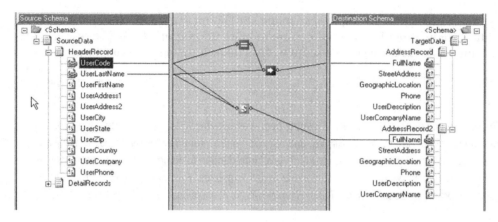

Figure 5-4. *Checking to see if a specific condition exists*

Replace the Logical String functoid with an Equal functoid, and enter the value BY into the Equal functoid as the second parameter. Now, the Equal functoid will compare the value received from the UserCode node to the value BY, returning true only when the two values match. The Value Mapping functoid outputs the value from the UserLastName node only when the output of the Equal functoid is true.

■**Caution** Remember that the underlying code for functoids is C#. This means any variable, such as BY in this example, is case sensitive.

The Scripting functoid has been modified also, as shown in Listing 5-5. It now accepts two inputs, the values from the UserCode and the UserLastName nodes. The C# script evaluates the value from UserCode to see if the value is equal to BY. The script returns the value from UserLastName if the answer is true and returns a null string if the answer is false. Listing 5-6 contains two outputs of the map, the first when the UserCode value is not BY and the second when the UserCode value is BY.

Listing 5-5. *Script That Checks If a Specific Condition Exists*

```
public string CheckUserCode(string inCode, string inName)
{
if (inCode == "BY")
return inName;
else
return "";
}
```

Listing 5-6. *Outputs of the Map That Checks If a Specific Condition Exists*

```
<ns0:TargetData xmlns:ns0="http://IfElse.TargetFile">
  <AddressRecord />
  <AddressRecord2>
      <FullName />
  </AddressRecord2>
</ns0:TargetData>

<ns0:TargetData xmlns:ns0="http://IfElse.TargetFile">
  <AddressRecord>
    <FullName>WAINWRIGHT</FullName>
  </AddressRecord>
  <AddressRecord2>
    <FullName>WAINWRIGHT</FullName>
  </AddressRecord2>
</ns0:TargetData>
```

We can accomplish the exact same functionality with the XSLT script in Listing 5-7.

Listing 5-7. *XSLT Script for Checking If a Specific Condition Exists*

```
<xsl:if test="//HeaderRecord/UserCode = 'BY' ">
  <FullName>
    <xsl:value-of select="//HeaderRecord/UserLastName"/>
  </FullName>
</xsl:if>
```

An alternate and slightly more compact method of performing the same conditional test could be written using an XSLT predicate expression, as shown in Listing 5-8.

Listing 5-8. *XSLT Predicate Expression Script for Checking If a Specific Condition Exists*

```
<FullName>
  <xsl:value-of select="//HeaderRecord[UserCode = 'BY']/UserLastName"/>
</FullName>
```

Checking If a Specific Condition Does Not Exist

What about the opposite situation? What if you want to output FullName only when the UserCode node does not contain a specific value? Let's modify the map to output the FullName node only when the UserCode value is not equal to SH. We accomplish this by replacing the Equal functoid with a Not Equal functoid and changing the parameter in the Not Equal functoid from BY to SH. The map is in Figure 5-5.

Tip You don't have to delete the Equal functoid. Just drag the Not Equal functoid onto the grid until your pointer is on the Equal functoid, and release the mouse button. The Not Equal functoid will replace the Equal functoid, retaining the links and the input values.

Once you replace the Equal functoid, the map will look like Figure 5-5.

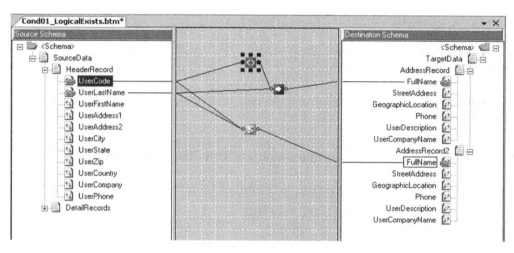

Figure 5-5. *A map to check if a specific condition does not exist*

The script undergoes an even smaller change, as shown in Listing 5-9.

Listing 5-9. *Script for the Map That Checks If a Specific Condition Does Not Exist*

```
public string CheckUserCode(string inCode, string inName)
{
if (inCode != "SH")
  return inName;
else
  return "";
}
```

Notice that the only change was to modify == (equals) to != (not equals). Using the same source data (where the UserCode node contains BY) as the previous map, this map will produce the same outputs as in Listing 5-6. This time, the first output is produced when the UserCode value is equal to SH; the second output is produced when the UserCode value is not equal to SH.

Again, the XSLT alternate is much the same. You need to change the = in the predicate expression to !=, and you'll accomplish the same thing here. See Listing 5-10.

Listing 5-10. *XSLT Predicate Expression Script for Checking If a Specific Condition Does Not Exist*

```
<FullName>
  <xsl:value-of select="//HeaderRecord[UserCode != 'BY']/UserLastName"/>
</FullName>
```

■**Caution** Be careful when you move back and forth between scripting languages. The C# symbol for equivalence is the double equals sign, but in XSLT, the single equals sign serves as both an equivalence and an assignment operator.

An If/Else Condition

Sometimes, the problem is not to block output when a condition is false, but to output an alternate value. Now, if the UserCode node contains the value SH, you want to output the value from the UserLastName node. Otherwise, you want to output the string NO SHIPPER NAME. The map is in Figure 5-6.

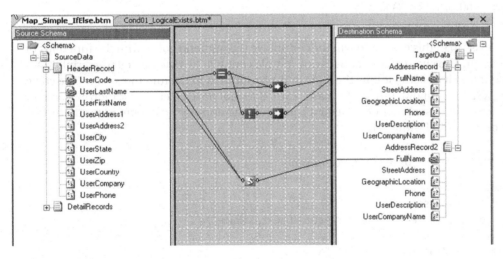

Figure 5-6. *An if/else condition map*

We add two more functoids to our map, a second Value Mapping functoid and a Logical NOT functoid. The Equal functoid checks to see if the UserCode node contains the value SH and returns either true or false as appropriate.

The first Value Mapping functoid passes the value from UserLastName to the FullName node if the value received from the Logical Equal functoid is true. If that value is false, this Value Mapping functoid outputs no data.

The second Value Mapping functoid does not receive the output of the Equal functoid. That output goes to the Logical NOT functoid. The Logical NOT functoid inverts the received value. If the output of the Equal functoid is true, the Logical NOT functoid outputs false. If the Equal functoid returns false, the Logical NOT functoid returns true. The second Value Mapping functoid operates off the output of the Logical NOT functoid. If the output is true the Value Mapping functoid passes the string "NO SHIPPER NAME" to the FullName node. If the value is false, the second Value Mapping functoid does not produce any output.

The net result of this functoid chain is that if the value of the UserCode node is SH, the value from the UserLastName node will be output in the FullName node. Otherwise, the string "NO SHIPPER NAME" will be output in the FullName node.

Although the functoid chain in this map consists of only four functoids, the script in the Scripting functoid is even simpler. Look at Listing 5-11.

Listing 5-11. *Script for If/Else Condition Map*

```
public string CheckUserCode(string inCode, string inName)
{
  if (inCode == "SH")
    return inName;
  else
    return "NO SHIPPER NAME";
}
```

It's a toss-up in this case as to whether or not we recommend going with the functoids or with the script. The chain of functoids is not complex enough to justify using the script, but some might find it easier to follow the logic in the script than in the functoid chain. The corresponding XSLT is a bit different in this case. XSLT does not have an else condition so you have to make use of an if statement for the first condition and another if statement for the alternate condition, as in Listing 5-12.

Listing 5-12. *XSLT Script for the If/Else Condition*

```
<FullName>
  <xsl:if test="//UserCode = 'BY' ">
    <xsl:value-of select="//HeaderRecord/UserLastName"/>
  </xsl:if>
  <xsl:if test="//UserCode != 'BY' ">
    <xsl:value-of select=" 'NO SHIPPER NAME"/>
  </xsl:if>
</FullName>
```

The double if statement method is a bit awkward. Fortunately, using the XSLT equivalent of a case statement is an easier way to deal with if/else conditions, as illustrated in Listing 5-13.

Listing 5-13. *XSLT Script for If/Else Condition Using an XSLT case-Type Statement*

```
<FullName>
  <xsl:choose>
    <xsl:when test="//HeaderRecord/UserCode = 'BY' ">
```

```
        <xsl:value-of select="//HeaderRecord/UserLastName"/>
    </xsl:when>
    <xsl:otherwise>NO SHIPPER NAME</xsl:otherwise>
  </xsl:choose>
</FullName>
```

Caution In this script, we took advantage of the fact that in this schema there is only one UserCode node. This allowed us to use a shorthand notation in the XPATH statement for the test, the //. Using // returns the first instance of UserCode that is found in the document. When there is more than one instance of a node, the XPATH statement must be explicit.

Using the Logical OR for a Single Return Value

So far, we have looked at situations where a single condition drives output. Now, we examine a situation where data must be mapped when a source value meets any one of several conditions. This construct outputs a value when the UserCode node contains any of several values and outputs a default value if none are present. We are looking for the values SH, ST, and BY in order to pass the contents of UserLastName to the FullName node. If neither of those values is present, we will pass the string Unknown Address Type to the FullName node. The map is shown in Figure 5-7.

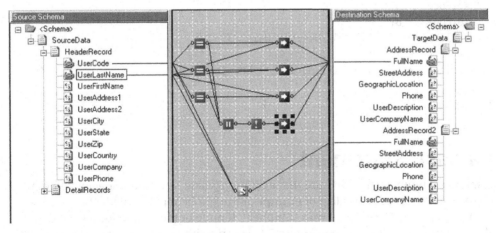

Figure 5-7. *Using the Logical OR functoid for a single return value*

The functoid chain builds a logical gate that is interpreted as saying, "If UserCode equals SH, ST, or BY, output UserLastName to FullName, else output the string "Unknown Address Type to FullName". There are seven functoids in this cascading flow, about the maximum number we would want to use in one chain. Adding more conditionals to the evaluation would cause the mapping grid to become crowded with functoids and make the flow hard to interpret. The script contained in the Scripting functoid that might replace the functoid chain is shown in Listing 5-14.

Listing 5-14. *Script for Using the Logical OR Functoid for a Single Return Value*

```
public string CheckUserCode(string inCode, string inName)
{
  if (inCode == "SH" || inCode == "ST" || inCode == "BY")
    return inName;
  else
    return "Unknown Address Type";
}
```

Again, the logic appears to be much simpler to understand in the script as opposed to in the functoid chain. Notice that you would have to see the second parameter for all three Equal functoids in order to identify the codes that you want; whereas those are readily apparent in the script. Still, we consider this functoid chain to be on the borderline as to whether or not we would recommend using the script. As you might expect, the equivalent XSLT statement in Listing 5-15 is not all that different.

Listing 5-15. *XSLT Script for Using Logical OR for a Single Return Value*

```
<FullName>
  <xsl:choose>
    <xsl:when test="//UserCode = 'SH'
      or //UserCode = 'ST'
      or //UserCode = 'BY'">
            <xsl:value-of select="//UserLastName"/>
    </xsl:when>
    <xsl:otherwise>Unknown Address Type</xsl:otherwise>
  </xsl:choose>
</FullName>
```

Using a case Statement

A more complex conditional would require that a different value be output for each different value received from the UserCode node. For example, BY might be replaced with "Buyer", SE replaced with "Seller", and SH replaced with "Shipper". If none of these were found, a default value would be output. The map, seen in Figure 5-8, is eerily similar to the last map we viewed.

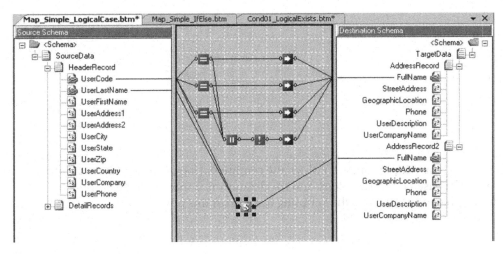

Figure 5-8. *Using a case statement*

Look closely, and you will see that three links from the UserCode node to the Value Mapping functoids have been removed. We put the desired output values, Buyer, Seller, and Shipper, in the Value Mapping functoids.

Each Equal and Value Mapping functoid pair works the same. The Equal functoid returns true if it finds a match, false if it does not find a match. The Value Mapping functoid paired with the Equal functoid outputs the desired value if the value of the Equal functoid is true. Nothing is output if the value is false.

The Logical OR/Logical NOT/Value Mapping functoid chain works the same as in the previous example. If none of the Logical Equal functoids return true, the Logical OR functoid returns false. The Logical NOT functoid converts the false to true, causing the paired Value Mapping functoid to output the default string.

This change in logic did not increase the number of functoids needed. Also, the logic flow still is not hard to figure out. Notice that you now have to open six functoids to determine what the desired UserCode values are and what the outputs of the Value Mapping functoids are. Now, look at the script in Listing 5-16. This script, which uses a case statement, replaces the functoids.

Listing 5-16. *Script for Using a case Statement*

```
public string CheckUserCode(string inCode, string inName)
{
string retval;
switch (inCode)
{
  case "SH":
    retval ="Shipper";
    break;
  case "ST":
    retval ="Ship To";
    break;
```

```
    case "BY":
      retval ="Buyer";
      break;
    default :
      retval ="Unknown Address Type";
      break;
  }
  return retval;
}
```

You can see all three input values on which the conditional logic is based, all three values that will be output based on those values, and the default value that might be output. We would definitely recommend using the Scripting functoid at this point.

Note There are some other functoids and constructs that are useful for conditional logic in a map. Most notable are the Value Mapping (Flattening) functoid and the Table Looping and Table Extractor pair of functoids. Both of these are more useful in situations where the source data is in a loop and are covered in the chapters on looping (Chapters 11 and 12) and EDI looping (Chapters 14 and 17) as appropriate.

The XSLT choose construct serves well for implementing a case-like structure. Listing 5-17 contains the same logic from the CheckUserCode script in Listing 5-16 presented as XSLT.

Listing 5-17. *XSLT Script for Using a case-like Statement*

```
<FullName>
  <xsl:choose>
    <xsl:when test="//UserCode = 'SH'">Shipper</xsl:when>
    <xsl:when test="//UserCode = 'ST'">Ship To</xsl:when>
    <xsl:when test="//UserCode = 'BY'">Buyer</xsl:when>
    <xsl:otherwise>Unknown Address Type</xsl:otherwise>
  </xsl:choose>
</FullName>
```

Summary

The simple conditional examples that we examine in this chapter could be solved in ways other than described here. As noted at the beginning of the chapter, many of the logical functoids are interchangeable in the sense that you can use different ones in the same location to alter the logic. We felt that repeating maps whose only change was the specific functoids used would not add any benefit. You can easily do the substitution yourself to learn the different effects.

Use the sample maps to try different ways of approaching same problems. Perhaps you can change the last map so that the UserLastName is output if any of the three UserCode values is present, else the UserFirstName is output. Everything you need to know is in this chapter.

This chapter began the basic mapping section of the book, where we examine how to address basic solutions for BizTalk mapping. Next, we examine methods for handling numbers and problems relating to numbers. Later, we will move on to strings, dates, and times, all simple constructs that introduce their own sets of problems into mapping.

CHAPTER 6

■ ■ ■

Dealing with Numbers

You might think handling numbers in the BizTalk mapper would be pretty straightforward. You would be almost right. The truth is that you may encounter many problems dealing with numbers. Although most will not be difficult to solve, some will be tricky, and others will sneak up on you. In this chapter, we provide some examples of techniques that are useful in working with numbers.

Many, perhaps most, of the instances where you will need to manipulate numbers in a map can be accomplished using standard functoids. Others, the more complex cases, may require you to use scripts. We use both methods in this chapter. Our examples are those you may encounter when working with common business information such as quantity, price, discount percentages, accumulated totals, and so forth. Since math is not our strong point, we will not discuss problems of a scientific mathematical nature.

Caution When you use scripts to handle numbers, remember that some languages are strongly typed. Strong typing means that you can't do implied conversions. For example, if the input into a C# function is an integer that must be converted into a real number with a specified number of decimal places, you must explicitly convert the integer to a double type. The same goes for returning variables. If your function is a string type and you are working with real numbers inside it, you must convert the number to a string before you return from the function.

Is This a Number?

This question might seem ridiculous at first glance. After all, an element of data is either a number or it is not a number, correct? The answer is, "Maybe." Suppose you have a source node that is of string type but that you expect to contain a number. Such a situation exists more often than you might suspect. Since you cannot be certain that the input value is a number, you must validate the data.

> **Note** How could someone build a schema that should contain a number in a node but define that node as a string? There are many cases where you will not control the schema definition. Sometimes, an ERP builds the schema; other times, a customer-written application has a custom designed schema. Combine these with data entry screens that do not validate the typed data, and there is no way to ensure that a node contains a number.

Fortunately, BizTalk provides the Logical Numeric functoid, which accepts one input variable. The functoid returns the value `true` if the input variable is a number and `false` if not. The Logical Numeric functoid in combination with the Value Mapping functoid provides a means for you to control your output based on whether or not the input value is a number. Figure 6-1 shows an example of this usage.

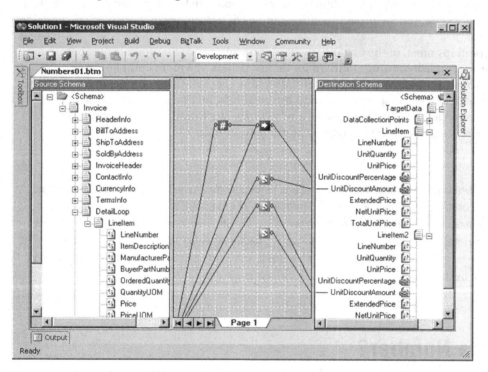

Figure 6-1. *Is the input value a number?*

We are working with the top two functoids, the Logical Numeric and Value Mapping functoids. The code generated for this example is shown in Listing 6-1.

Listing 6-1. *Code Generated for the Logical Numeric and Value Mapping Functoids Example*

```
<xsl:variable name="var:v1"
  select="userCSharp:LogicalIsNumeric(string(DiscountPercent/text()))"/>
  <LineItem>
```

```
<xsl:if test="string($var:v1)='true'">
   <xsl:variable name="var:v2" select="DiscountPercent/text()"/>
   <UnitDiscountPercentage>
      <xsl:value-of select="$var:v2"/>
   </UnitDiscountPercentage>
</xsl:if>
</LineItem>
```

Note that the target node UnitDiscountPercentage is only populated with the source value received from the source DiscountPercent node if the return value from the call to LogicalIsNumeric(string(DiscountPercent/text())) equals true. The C# code for that functoid is shown in Listing 6-2.

Listing 6-2. *C# Code for the Logical Numeric Functoid*

```
public bool IsNumeric(string val)
{
    if (val == null)
        return false;
    double d = 0;
    return Double.TryParse(val,
            System.Globalization.NumberStyles.AllowThousands |
            System.Globalization.NumberStyles.Float,
            System.Globalization.CultureInfo.InvariantCulture,
            out d);
}
```

Sometimes, the Logical Numeric and Value Mapping functoid pair is not the best choice for determining whether or not a value is numeric. For example, this question may be embedded inside a larger chain of logic. In such an instance, you may need to perform the test inside a script. Let's look at three examples where this might be the case.

Determining if a String Is a Number

Listing 6-3 is an example where you control the output based on whether or not the input value is numeric, but where the input value is a string type.

Listing 6-3. *Is That String a Number?*

```
public string NumberTest(string inNumber)
{
    double d = 0;
    if (Double.TryParse(inNumber, System.Globalization.NumberStyles.Float,
       System.Globalization.CultureInfo.InvariantCulture, out d))  d = d/2;
    return d.ToString();
}
```

The code in Listing 6-3 returns 0 if the input string does not consist entirely of numeric characters. If the input string does contain all numeric characters, the code returns the input value divided by 2. Notice that the string is converted to a double for the test and then converted back to a string before being output.

Using a Regular Expression to Check for a Number

Another scripting method we use to determine if an input value is numeric is to use a regular expression (regex). The expression checks all the characters in the string to make sure they are numeric. Listing 6-4 contains the code for this method.

Listing 6-4. *Checking for a Number Using a Regular Expression*

```
public  string RegExIsNumeric(string input)
{
  double outNum = 0;
  if(System.Text.RegularExpressions.Regex.IsMatch(input, "^\\d+$"))
    outNum = Convert.ToDouble(input);
  return outNum.ToString();
}
```

Tip Many functions can be performed with regular expressions, as you will see in later chapters. Sometimes, regular expressions can accomplish in short form things that would otherwise take large blocks of code. You should keep a reference on regular expressions handy.

Testing for a Numeric Value with the XSLT Number Function

Our final example of using a script to test for a numeric value, shown in Listing 6-5, uses the XSLT number() function in an XSLT call template. The same function is used in an inline XSLT script, and it converts the input string to a number. If the conversion fails, as will happen if the value is not numeric, the script returns the number 0. If the conversion succeeds, the script returns the input value.

Listing 6-5. *Checking for a Number with the XSLT number() Function*

```
<xsl:template name="BuildDiscPercent">
  <xsl:param name="inDisc"/>
    <xsl:variable name="DiscPct">
      <xsl:value-of select="number($inDisc)"/>
    </xsl:variable>
    <xsl:element name="UnitDiscountAmount">
      <xsl:choose>
        <xsl:when test="$DiscPct != 'NaN' ">
          <xsl:value-of select="$DiscPct"/>
```

```
      </xsl:when>
        <xsl:otherwise>0</xsl:otherwise>
      </xsl:choose>
    </xsl:element>
</xsl:template>
```

Using an inline XSLT script instead of a call template would mean retrieving the variable directly from the data rather than receiving it as a parameter, as shown in Listing 6-6.

Listing 6-6. *Checking with the XSLT number() Function Using Inline XSLT*

```
<xsl:variable name="inDisc"/>
  <xsl:value-of select="./DiscountPercent"/>
</xsl:variable>
<xsl:variable name="DiscPct">
  <xsl:value-of select="number($inDisc)"/>
</xsl:variable>
<xsl:element name="UnitDiscountAmount">
  <xsl:choose>
    <xsl:when test="$DiscPct != 'NaN' ">
      <xsl:value-of select="$DiscPct"/>
      </xsl:when>
        <xsl:otherwise>0</xsl:otherwise>
  </xsl:choose>
  </xsl:element>
```

These few examples can be modified to fit your needs when you need to determine whether or not a value pulled from a source node is numeric. Now, let's narrow that test even more.

Is This Number an Integer?

Sometimes, just knowing that the value is numeric is not sufficient. You may also need to know whether or not the value is an integer or decimal number. At first glance, you may think that the Integer functoid in the Mathematical Functoids group of the mapping toolbox would do this. That functoid, however, converts a decimal number to an integer by removing the decimal and all digits to the right of the decimal, and that result is not what you need. You might be surprised to learn that we use a functoid from the String Functoids group to determine whether a number is an integer.

The String Find functoid requires two inputs: the string value to be searched and the string for which to search. The String Find functoid returns the starting position of the search string if the search is successful or 0 if the search is not successful. In this example, we ask the String Find functoid to search the input string for a decimal (.). Look at the map in Figure 6-2.

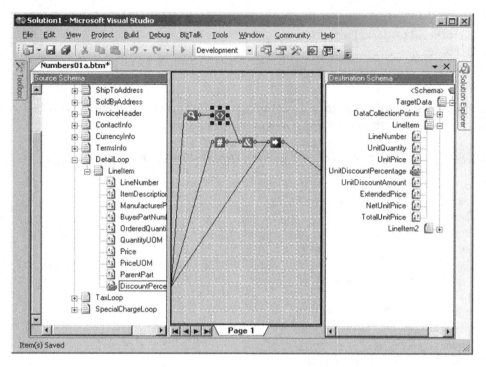

Figure 6-2. *Functoid map to output a value that is both numeric and decimal*

We want to output the UnitDiscountPercentage node only if the value from the source node DiscountPercent is a decimal number. A chain of five functoids is needed. Here, in Listing 6-7, is an excerpt from the code generated for this map.

Listing 6-7. *Code Excerpt for Map to Output a Value That is Both Numeric and Decimal*

```
<xsl:variable name="var:v1" select=
    "userCSharp:StringFind(string(DiscountPercent/text()) , ".")" />
<xsl:variable name="var:v2"
    select="userCSharp:LogicalNe(string($var:v1) , "0")" />
<xsl:variable name="var:v3" select="string(DiscountPercent/text())" />
<xsl:variable name="var:v4" select="userCSharp:LogicalIsNumeric($var:v3)" />
<xsl:variable name="var:v5"
    select="userCSharp:LogicalAnd(string($var:v2) , string($var:v4))" />
<LineItem>
  <xsl:if test="string($var:v5)='true'">
    <xsl:variable name="var:v6" select="DiscountPercent/text()" />
    <UnitDiscountPercentage>
      <xsl:value-of select="$var:v6" />
    </UnitDiscountPercentage>
</xsl:if>
```

The logic is straightforward. In one path, the source value is searched for the presence of a decimal and the result of that search is placed into the variable v1. The result will either be a positive number or a zero, with the zero indicating that the value did not contain a decimal. The value contained in v1 is then tested for zero by the Logical Not Equal functoid. This functoid returns true if the value is not zero and false if the value is zero.

In a different path, the Logical Numeric functoid tests the source value to determine whether or not the value is numeric. The functoid returns true if the value is a number, false if not.

The outputs of these two paths are both passed to the Logical AND functoid, which evaluates the pair of values. If both values equal true, the Logical AND function returns true. If either or both values are not equal to true, the function returns false.

The output value of the Logical AND function is then evaluated by the Value Mapping functoid. If the value is true, the source value is output to the target node. If the value is false, no value is output. Thus the net effect is just what we want, the target node UnitDiscountPercentage is only populated if the source value is a decimal number.

You can track this logic in both the map and in the script.

Rounding Numbers

The BizTalk mapper has limited capability in rounding numbers. The Round functoid rounds a number up or down to the precision specified in the input parameters. Let's extend the previous map by rounding the number before we put it into the target node, as depicted in Figure 6-3.

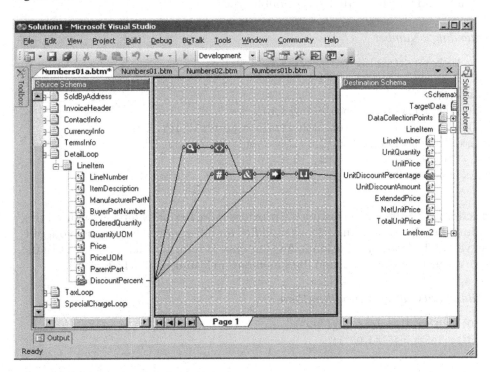

Figure 6-3. *Rounding a number*

The Rounding functoid in Figure 6-3 ensures that the decimal number passed to the target node UnitDiscountPercentage will be a decimal number with no more than two digits to the right of the decimal. The first input into the Rounding functoid is the source value; the second input is the number of decimal places to which the value should be rounded. The additional code generated for the map for the rounding is in Listing 6-8.

Listing 6-8. *Rounding Code*

```
<xsl:variable name="var:v7" s
    Select="userCSharp:MathRound(string($var:v6) , "2")" />
```

Of course, variable v7 becomes the output variable instead of v6, and the C# code for the rounding is added to the CDATA section. Otherwise, the code is the same as in Listing 6-7.

There is one limitation to using the Rounding functoid. If you specify two digits of precision, the functoid will round to that level only if the digits to the right of the decimal are greater than zero. The number 2.16 becomes 2.2, and the number 2.00 becomes 2, for example. This does not cover the situation where the requirement is to have trailing zeros, as when the number 2.16 becomes 2.20. Rounding with trailing zeros is not the same as padding, where trailing zeros are added when a number does not meet the minimum length requirements.

If you require the output number have a specific number of digits to the right of the decimal, then you will need a script such as the one shown in Listing 6-9. For the sake of brevity, we assume that the inPrice parameter will always be numeric. Also notice the inputs are accepted as strings and then converted to the double type.

Listing 6-9. *Extending a Number*

```
public string NumberTest(string inDisc, string inPrice)
{
  double disc = 0;
  double unitPrice = Convert.ToDouble(inPrice);
  if(Double.TryParse(inDisc, System.Globalization.NumberStyles.Float,
        System.Globalization.CultureInfo.InvariantCulture, out disc))
        disc = disc * unitPrice * .01;
  return disc.ToString("#0.00");
}
```

Using a script such as the one in Listing 6-9 provides more flexibility for you in formatting your output numbers. The script can easily be modified for different needs. Suppose your output should have two decimals of precision unless the value is zero, in which case you want the output to have no decimal. You could add the statements in Listing 6-10 to Listing 6-9.

Listing 6-10. *Additional Code for Formatting Zero*

```
If (disc == 0) return disc.ToString("#0");
else return disc.ToString("#0.00");
```

Summing Numbers

Sometimes, you must provide the sum of two or more source values as output to a target node. Often, this is merely a matter of adding two numbers together with the Addition functoid. That functoid works well for 2 to 100 parameters that are all available at the same time but does not work well when the source data is embedded in loops.

Using the Cumulative Sum Functoid to Sum Data

The Cumulative Sum functoid is found in the Cumulative Functoids group in the mapping Toolbox. The functoid accepts two inputs as shown in Figure 6-4. The first is the source of the values to be summed; the second, and optional, input is the scope.

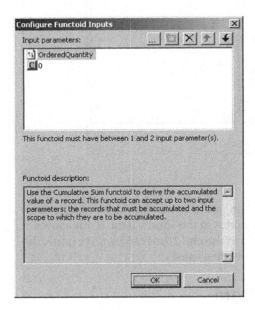

Figure 6-4. *Input parameters to the Cumulative Sum functoid*

The map is in Figure 6-5.

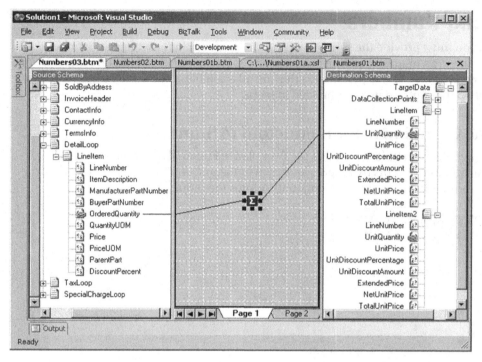

Figure 6-5. *Cumulative Sum map*

In this case, we've specified a scope of zero, which means that we want to obtain the sum of all `Invoice/DetailLoop/LineItem/OrderedQuantity` nodes in the source data. If our source data contained five `LineItem` records, each with a value in the child `OrderedQuantity` node, the target node `UnitQuantity` would contain the sum of those five values.

Using an Inline XSLT Script to Sum Data

The summing of data can also be accomplished with a simple inline XSLT script that makes use of the XSLT `sum()` function, as shown in Listing 6-11.

Listing 6-11. *Summing Data with an XSLT Script*

```
<xsl:element name="UnitQuantity">
  <xsl:value-of select="sum(//OrderedQuantity)"/>
</xsl:element>
```

You can exercise the same level of control over the scope here as you could with the Cumulative Sum functoid, in this case by modifying the XPATH statement in the `sum()` function. Use care, though, because the `Context` node issue discussed earlier comes into play in this case. For example, if the XPATH path `"(//OrderedQuantity)"` in Listing 6-11 is changed to `"(./OrderedQuantity)"`, then a zero will be output. That is because the `Context` node would be the `Invoice` node, and there is no `Invoice/OrderedQuantity` node in the source schema.

Summing Complex Data

At times, you need to sum data in an asymmetric fashion. When summing numbers from a repeating node, you may want to include only those numbers that meet some specific criteria. Figure 6-6 shows a map that sums the values from OrderedQuantity only when the value in ManufacturerPartNumber begins with "ABA".

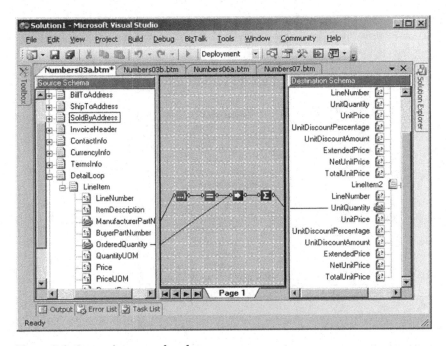

Figure 6-6. *Summing complex data*

We accomplish this using a functoid chain. The String Left functoid extracts the first 3 bytes from the values received from the ManufacturerPartNumber node and provides them to the Logical Equal functoid. The Logical Equal functoid tests to see if the first 3 bytes are equal to "ABA" and outputs true or false accordingly to the Value Mapping functoid. Only when the Logical Equal functoid outputs true does the Value Mapping functoid pass the value from the OrderedQuantity node to the Cumulative Sum functoid. The Cumulative Sum functoid continues to pull the values from the ManufacturerPartNumber and OrderedQuantity pairs until the data is exhausted. When that occurs, the final sum is output.

Counting Records

Many times, you need to count the number of occurrences of a source node and output the result. When processing an inbound invoice, for example, you might need to count and output the number of line items found in the source. Let's look at simple and complex examples of this.

Counting Records Simply

The easiest way to perform a count of source record instances is to use the Record Count functoid, which provides the number of occurrences of a specified source node. See Figure 6-7. The result output to the LineNumber node in this map is the total number of LineItem nodes found in the source file.

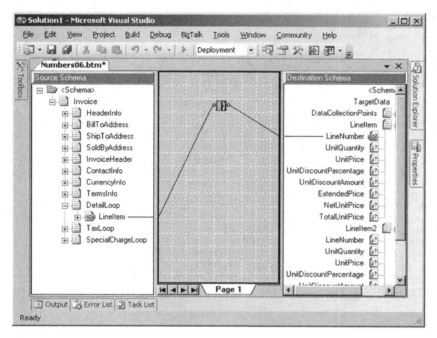

Figure 6-7. *Counting records simply*

You can also use an XSLT script for this count, with the XSLT count() function, as shown in Listing 6-12.

Listing 6-12. *A Simple Record Count Using XLST*

```
<xsl:element name="LineNumber">
    <xsl:value-of select="count(//LineItem)" />
</xsl:element>
```

The standard Record Count functoid and XSLT function are the best means to perform this count. Neither C# nor VBScript provides a good way to perform this count.

Counting Qualified Records Simply

A qualified count of source records is when you need to determine how many instances of the source record meet some criteria. When the criteria are simple, you may be able to perform the entire count with a functoid chain. The functoid chain in Figure 6-8 counts the number of source LineItem nodes that contain an OrderedQuantity node with a value greater than 15. The result is placed in the output node LineNumber.

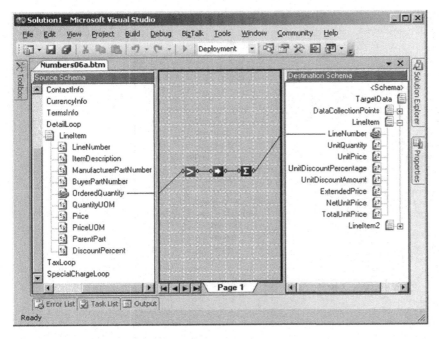

Figure 6-8. *Counting qualified records simply*

The second parameter in the Greater Than functoid is the number 15, which is the test criterion for our example. When the value received from the source node OrderedQuantity is greater than 15, the Greater Than functoid outputs the value true. The second parameter in the Value Mapping functoid is the value 1. When the input from the Greater Than functoid is true, the Value Mapping functoid sends 1 to the Cumulative Sum functoid. The Cumulative Sum functoid sends the sum of all the 1 values to the target node LineNumber. Thus if the source node OrderedQuantity contains the four values 9, 16, 12, and 23, the functoid chain will output the value 2 to the target LineNumber functoid.

Counting Complex Qualified Records

When the qualifying rules for counting get complex, you must turn to scripting to help solve the problem. How do you determine the number of target LineItem nodes you will create based on the contents of multiple source nodes? The map in Figure 6-9 provides an example of this problem and a solution.

The map in Figure 6-9 examines the source LineNumber, OrderedQuantity, and Price nodes to determine the number of target LineItem records that will be output. Note that we say "will be output" because the map as shown does not depict the code that would output a target LineItem node. Only that part of the map associated with the value to be output into the target LineNumber node is presented.

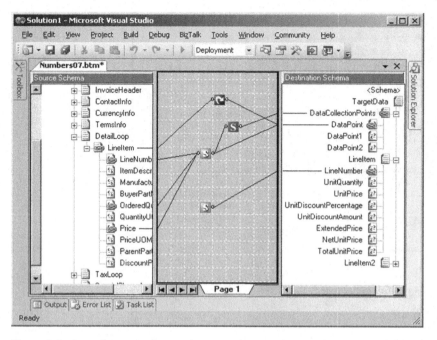

Figure 6-9. *Complex record counting*

The DataCollectionPoints node and its children exist for the express purpose of allow-ing the counting script to execute before processing of the actual target data records begins. The Looping functoid causes the DataPoint node to repeat until all the source data has been pulled through the Scripting Functoid. The Logical String functoid blocks output of the DataCollectionPoints node, since we never want that node to appear in the output file. Look at Listing 6-13, which is from the top Scripting functoid. For the sake of brevity, we do not check to see if any of the input parameters is null in the script as we should.

Listing 6-13. *Counting the Line Items*

```
int LineCounter = 0;
public string CountLines(string inLineNumber, int inQuantity, string inPrice)
{
double Price = Convert.ToDouble(inPrice);
if (inLineNumber != "" && inQuantity > 15 && Price > 25)  LineCounter += 1;
return "";
}
```

The first thing done is to create the global variable, LineCounter, which will be available for reference throughout the rest of the map. The script then evaluates the three inputs to see if the criteria for outputting a line item are met. The criteria are that the Quantity must be greater than 15, the Price must be greater than 25, and there must be a LineNumber. If either of those is not true, no line item will be output. If all three are true, a line item will be output, and the script increments the value of LineCounter. The script always returns a null string, "", which is passed to the Logical String functoid to control creation of the DataCollectionPoints node.

The lower scripting functoid outputs the final count to the target LineNumber node. The output value is pulled from the global variable, LineCounter, as you can see in Listing 6-14.

Listing 6-14. *Outputting the Counter*

```
public string PutLineCounter()
{
return LineCounter.ToString();
}
```

Converting Real Numbers to Integers (and Back Again)

Another common problem that you will see is the need to translate real numbers from a format with explicit decimals to an integer format with implied decimals, and the reverse. X12 standards-based documents use an implied decimal notation in many elements, thus this issue is particularly relevant when working with those schemas. Figure 6-10 depicts a map that uses the Multiplier functoid to do this.

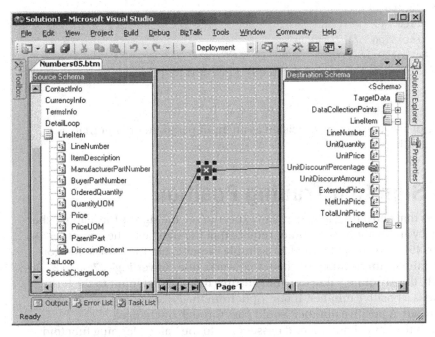

Figure 6-10. *Converting a real number to decimal*

The Multiplier functoid would have as the second input the power of ten needed to remove the decimal. For example, for an output with two implied decimals, you multiply by 100. For example, 12.55 multiplied by 100 becomes 1255.

Listing 6-15 contains a simple scripting example that can also be used for the same purpose. The script uses an input parameter to supply the precision, making the script reusable even though each use needs a different precision.

Listing 6-15. *Script for Converting Real Numbers to Decimals*

```
Public string RtoN(string inputString, int ipower)
{
double inboundNumber = Convert.ToDouble(inputString) * Math.Pow(10,ipower);
return inboundNumber.ToString("#0");
}
```

The Multiplier functoid and the script from Listing 6-14 can perform the opposite conversion as well. When we converted 12.55 to 1255, we multiplied with the value 100. We move the decimal in the opposite direction by multiplying 1255 by .01.

Although we find that manipulating numbers with scripts is easier with C#, you can accomplish the same objectives with XSLT. Listing 6-16 contains an XSLT script that does the same conversions.

Listing 6-16. *XSLT Script for Converting Numbers*

```
 <xsl:template name="ComputePrice">
<xsl:param name="inPrice" />
<xsl:param name="inPrecision" />
<xsl:element name="NetUnitPrice">
  <xsl:value-of select="format-number($inPrice * $inPrecision, '#0.00')" />
</xsl:element>
</xsl:template>
```

This example script also accepts the precision as an input parameter rather than as a hard-coded value, extending its usability.

Moving the Sign to a Trailing Position

Most numeric formats that allow for a negative sign expect to see the sign as the leading character, as in –455. Legacy applications sometimes require that the sign be in the low-order, or trailing position, as in 455–. This might seem like a simple exercise, but there are some gotchas. Figure 6-11 contains a simple functoid chain that works fine converting –27.50 to 27.50–.

In the upper path, the Absolute Value functoid ensures that the first input to the String Concatenate functoid is a positive number. If our input from the Price node is -27.50, the value 27.50 will be output. A positive number would pass through unchanged.

In the bottom path the Less Than functoid passes true to the Value Mapping functoid only if the number received from the Price node is negative. The second input value to the Value Mapping functoid is the negative sign (-). When true is received from the Less Than functoid, the Value Mapping functoid passes the negative sign as the second input to the String Concatenate functoid.

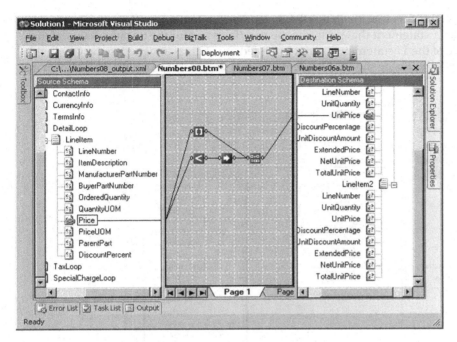

Figure 6-11. *Changing a leading sign to a trailing sign*

The String Concatenate functoid joins the two inputs, 27.50 and -, into the string 27.50-.
You would expect, if the source node Price contained the positive number 27.50, that no conversion would be made and the original value output. That is not what happens.

The problem with this functoid chain is that the output of positive numbers is blocked by
the Less Than functoid. Thus when you have two Price nodes, one with -27.50 and one with
40.50, your output will have only one UnitPrice node, the one containing the value 27.50-.
The XSLT code in Listing 6-17 shows us why this happens.

Listing 6-17. *Why Is the Positive Number Blocked?*

```
<xsl:for-each select="DetailLoop/LineItem">
<xsl:variable name="var:v1" select="userCSharp:MathAbs(string(Price/text()))"/>
<xsl:variable name="var:v2" select="string(Price/text())"/>
<xsl:variable name="var:v3" select="userCSharp:LogicalLt($var:v2 , '0')"/>
<LineItem>
  <xsl:if test="string($var:v3)='true'">
    <xsl:variable name="var:v4" select=" '-' "/>
    <xsl:variable name="var:v5" select="userCSharp:StringConcat(string($var:v1) ,
                             string($var:v4))"/>

    <UnitPrice>
      <xsl:value-of select="$var:v5"/>
    </UnitPrice>
  </xsl:if>
</LineItem>
</xsl:for-each>
```

As you can see, this functoid chain has the assignment statement for the output variable, v5, inside the if statement that performs the true/false test for the negative value. If the instructions inside of the if statement are not executed, no value is assigned to the v5 variable. We can correct this by splitting the if statement into two statements using the map shown in Figure 6-12.

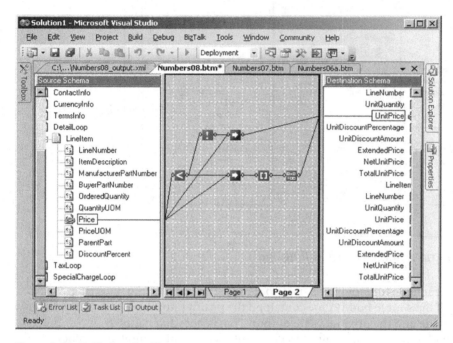

Figure 6-12. *Splitting the if statement*

Now, the Less Than functoid drives the output of both positive and negative numbers. Positive values are output by the top path; negative values are output by the lower path. Which path is followed is determined by the output of the Less Than functoid, which will pass true to one path and false to the other path.

The Logical NOT functoid in the top path flips the value received for that path, changing true to false and vice versa. This causes true to be passed when the output of the Less Than functoid is false, as it would be when the input was positive. The code shows the two paths clearly. Look at Listing 6-18.

Listing 6-18. *Code for Splitting the if Statement*

```
<xsl:for-each select="DetailLoop/LineItem">
<xsl:variable name="var:v6" select="string(Price/text())"/>
<xsl:variable name="var:v7" select="userCSharp:LogicalLt($var:v6 , '0')"/>
<xsl:variable name="var:v11" select="userCSharp:LogicalNot(string($var:v7))"/>
<LineItem2>
  <xsl:if test="string($var:v7)='true'">
```

```
<xsl:variable name="var:v8" select="Price/text()"/>
<xsl:variable name="var:v9" select="userCSharp:MathAbs(string($var:v8))"/>
<xsl:variable name="var:v10" select=
                   "userCSharp:StringConcat(string($var:v9) , '-')"/>
<UnitPrice>
  <xsl:value-of select="$var:v10"/>
</UnitPrice>
</xsl:if>
<xsl:if test="string($var:v11)='true'">
  <xsl:variable name="var:v12" select="Price/text()"/>
  <UnitPrice>
    <xsl:value-of select="$var:v12"/>
  </UnitPrice>
</xsl:if>
</LineItem2>
</xsl:for-each>
```

In this script, there are two assignment statements, each lying within a separate if statement. This is another one of the cases where implementation using a script might be easier regardless of the number of functoids. Look at the script in Listing 6-19.

Listing 6-19. *Script to Convert Leading Signs to Trailing Signs*

```
public static string TrailingSign(double inNumber)
{
double absNum = Math.Abs(inNumber);
if (inNumber < 0)
    return absNum.ToString() + "-";
else
    return inNumber.ToString();
}
```

The script is much simpler (is it not?) than struggling to get the functoid chain working correctly.

Converting a Number to or from Sign-Trailing Overpunch Format

Occasionally, you run across a requirement for a number to be translated to or from a legacy format that uses a sign-trailing overpunch character in the low-order digit of the number. In this format, the number usually contains a low-order alphanumeric character that represents both the numeric digit and the sign. For example, a +1 would be represented by the letter "A", while a –1 would be represented by the letter "J". For additional examples, see Table 6-1.

Table 6-1. *Sign-Trailing Overpunch Conversions*

Value	Character	Value	Character
+0	{	−0	}
+1	A	−1	J
+2	B	−2	K
+3	C	−3	L
+4	D	−4	M
+5	E	−5	N
+6	F	−6	O
+7	G	−7	P
+8	H	−8	Q
+9	I	−9	R

This type of conversion requires a script. One solution for converting to the sign-trailing overpunch format would be to isolate the low-order digit of the number and then do a value substitution. You could do an extended if-else construct, use a SWITCH statement, or use a substitution array. The latter is seen in the script in Listing 6-20; the if-else construction is shown in Listing 6-21.

Listing 6-20. *Converting to the Sign-Trailing Overpunch Format*

```
public static string AddTrailingSignOverpunch(string inputString)
{
double inboundNumber = Convert.ToDouble(inputString);
string inboundString = inboundNumber.ToString("#0");
string replacement = "0";
string[] CheckPos = new String[10] { "{", "A", "B", "C", "D", "E", "F",
                                          "G", "H", "I"};
string[] CheckNeg = new String[10] { "}", "J", "K", "L", "M", "N", "O",
                                          "P", "Q", "R"};
int lastDigit = Convert.ToInt16(inboundString.Substring(inboundString.Length - 1));

if(inboundNumber >= 0)
     replacement = CheckPos[lastDigit];
else
     replacement = CheckNeg[lastDigit];

inboundNumber = Math.Abs(inboundNumber);
inboundString = inboundNumber.ToString("#0");
return inboundString.Substring(0,inboundString.Length - 1) + replacement;
}
```

The script in Listing 6-21 converts from the sign-trailing overpunch format by replacing the nonnumeric digit in the input number. Don't forget to multiply the resulting number by −1, if required, to make it negative.

Listing 6-21. *Converting from Sign-Trailing Overpunch Format*

```
public string RemoveTrailingSignOverpunch(string inString)
{
Int64 outputNum = 0;
string lastDigit = inString.Substring(inString.Length - 1);

if (lastDigit == "{") outputNumber = Convert.ToInt64(inString.Replace("{", "0"));
  else if (lastDigit == "A") outputNum =
       Convert.ToInt64(inString.Replace("A", "1"));
  else if (lastDigit == "B") outputNum =
      Convert.ToInt64(inString.Replace("B", "2"));
  else if (lastDigit == "C") outputNum =
      Convert.ToInt64(inString.Replace("C", "3"));
  else if (lastDigit == "D") outputNum =
      Convert.ToInt64(inString.Replace("D", "4"));
  else if (lastDigit == "E") outputNum =
      Convert.ToInt64(inString.Replace("E", "5"));
  else if (lastDigit == "F") outputNum =
      Convert.ToInt64(inString.Replace("F", "6"));
   else if (lastDigit == "G") outputNum =
      Convert.ToInt64(inString.Replace("G", "7"));
  else if (lastDigit == "H") outputNum =
      Convert.ToInt64(inString.Replace("H", "8"));
  else if (lastDigit == "I") outputNum=
      Convert.ToInt64(inString.Replace("I", "9"));
  else if (lastDigit == "}") outputNum =
      Convert.ToInt64(inString.Replace("}", "0")) * -1;
  else if (lastDigit == "J") outputNum =
      Convert.ToInt64(inString.Replace("J", "1")) * -1;
  else if (lastDigit == "K") outputNum =
      Convert.ToInt64(inString.Replace("K", "2")) * -1;
  else if (lastDigit == "L") outputNum =
      Convert.ToInt64(inString.Replace("L", "3")) * -1;
  else if (lastDigit == "M") outputNum =
      Convert.ToInt64(inString.Replace("M", "4")) * -1;
  else if (lastDigit == "N") outputNum =
      Convert.ToInt64(inString.Replace("N", "5")) * -1;
  else if (lastDigit == "O") outputNum =
      Convert.ToInt64(inString.Replace("O", "6")) * -1;
  else if (lastDigit == "P") outputNum =
      Convert.ToInt64(inString.Replace("P", "7")) * -1;
  else if (lastDigit == "Q") outputNum =
      Convert.ToInt64(inString.Replace("Q", "8")) * -1;
  else if (lastDigit == "R") outputNum =
      Convert.ToInt64(inString.Replace("R", "9")) * -1;
return outputNum.ToString();
}
```

Summary

BizTalk provides 11 mathematical functoids that allow the basic manipulation of numbers. You can add, subtract, multiply, round, find the square root, and determine the absolute value. It would be nice if the mapping situations involving numbers were all simple enough to be solved with these functoids, but this chapter has shown that such is not the case; sometimes, we can't even be sure that a value is numeric without testing it. We also see that the definition of "number" varies from environment to environment, forcing us to develop techniques to reformat numbers. The examples in this chapter not only depict some of the problems that might be encountered but also illustrate that the business rules behind these problems are important.

Now, let's move to strings. Like numbers, strings are basic structures in BizTalk mapping. The two even overlap, since in many instances, a number is presented as a string of digits. In fact, from the map point of view, the schema may define a data node as a number, a date, a string, a time, and so on, but the map views the data as a string unless otherwise instructed. As we move through the next chapter, you will see ways to restructure strings, learn how to search and replace characters, and examine other basic methods for working with them.

■■■

CHAPTER 7

Manipulating Strings

Strings, like numbers, require manipulation in just about every BizTalk map. String Functoids available in BizTalk handle many string manipulation requirements, but we resort to scripts for the same reasons that we did when working with numbers. Scripts allow us to perform complex string operations that are beyond the capability of functoids; they enable us to replace complicated functoid chains with simpler code; and they are often more reusable than functoid chains.

String operations are prevalent in BizTalk mapping, so you will find many more string handling examples embedded in the more complex maps found throughout the remaining chapters. As with numbers, several functoids are provided to assist you in manipulating strings. These functoids each perform a very simple, easy-to-understand operation. The same is true of the examples that we discuss in this chapter. We present the basic methods of dealing with strings, methods that provide a foundation for the more complicated exercises that will come later.

Trimming Strings

One common string exercise is trimming data from the beginning or from the ending of a string. Data from fixed-length flat files is often padded to fill out the field, and this padding must be removed or added depending on the direction of flow. Although schemas provide default padding options, these are not practical to use in many cases. Both spaces and zeros are common padding characters.

Caution Leading and trailing white space is suppressed by many XML viewers. They don't remove it; they just don't display it. This is one good reason to examine your data in an editor that does not suppress white space. Unexpected errors and incorrect results from string manipulations are often due to white space that is not visible when you view the data in an XML viewer. We use XMLSpy by Altova (www.Altova.com/XMLSpy) and UltraEdit by IDM Computer Solutions, Inc. (http://www.ultraedit.com/products/ultraedit.html).

BizTalk provides two functoids for trimming strings, String Left Trim and String Right Trim, both of which are shown in Figure 7-1. These functoids trim leading and trailing spaces from the data. For example, the map in Figure 7-1 changes the string " abcd " into the string "abcd".

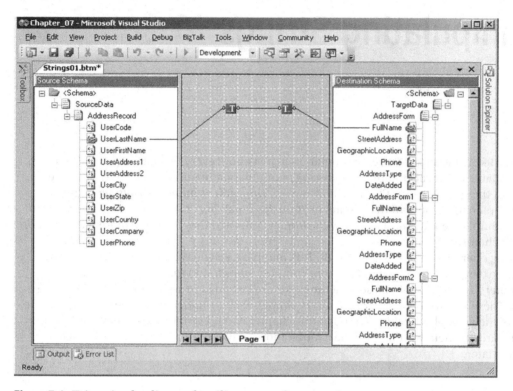

Figure 7-1. *Trimming leading and trailing spaces from a string*

These two functions call the C# functions `string.TrimStart` and `string.TrimEnd`. A third C# function is available that could replace both functoids with one Scripting functoid. The `String.Trim` function, shown in Listing 7-1, removes leading and trailing spaces.

Listing 7-1. *C# String Trim Function*

```
public string StripSpace(string inputString)
{
    return inputString.Trim();
}
```

The XSLT function `normalize-space()` is also easy to invoke. An example is shown in Listing 7-2.

Listing 7-2. *XSLT String Trim Function*

```
<xsl:template name="PutFullName">
  <xsl:param name="UserLast"/>
  <FullName><xsl:value-of select="normalize-space($UserLast)"/></FullName>
</xsl:template>
```

Caution The `normalize-space()` function not only trims leading and trailing spaces, but it also normalizes white space. That means that any instances of multiple spaces inside the string are reduced to a single space. For example, the string " ab   cd   " is reduced to "ab cd".

We don't expect the `UserLastName` field to have any extra spaces other than those in the leading and trailing positions in this map, so we can be comfortable using the XSLT function. We wouldn't want to use this function with a part number field, because such fields may have strings of more than one space inside the string.

This situation also illustrates one of the traps you encounter using the browser in the Dev Studio. We inserted six spaces in the `UserLastName` field of the `AddressRecord` node, making the input look like that in Listing 7-3. The `UserLastName` data is in bold.

Listing 7-3. *Source Data*

```
<SourceData>
  <AddressRecord>
    <UserCode>001</UserCode>
    <UserLastName>  Wain     wright   </UserLastName>
    <UserFirstName>John</UserFirstName>
    <UserAddress1>7008 Robbie Drive</UserAddress1>
    <UserAddress2/>
    <UserCity>Raleigh</UserCity>
    <UserState>NC</UserState>
    <UserZip/>
    <UserCountry>USA</UserCountry>
    <UserCompany>Second Star Professional Services, LLC.</UserCompany>
    <UserPhone>919-604-1812</UserPhone>
  </AddressRecord>
</SourceData>
```

The `UserLastName` field has both leading and trailing spaces and several spaces inside the name. We run this data through the functoid chain in Figure 7-1, the C# code in Listing 7-1, and the XSLT code in Listing 7-2. We expect the functoid chain and the C# script to strip the leading and trailing spaces but leave the internal spaces intact, so that " Wain   wright " becomes "Wain   wright". We expect the XSLT to trim the leading and trailing spaces and to reduce the number of internal spaces to one. Here in Listing 7-4 is the output of the XSLT script as shown in the browser window, with comments added.

Listing 7-4. *Output as Viewed in Browser Window*

```
<TargetData>
// Output from functoid chain
  <AddressForm>
    <FullName>Wain wright</FullName>
  </AddressForm>
 // Output from C# Script
```

```
<AddressForm1>
   <FullName>Wain wright</FullName>
</AddressForm1>
// Output from XSLT script
  <AddressForm2>
    <FullName>Wain wright</FullName>
  </AddressForm2>
</TargetData>
```

Looking at this output might lead us to believe that all three methods are removing internal spaces, not just the XSLT functoid. Now, open the file using a text or XML editor, and you see the output seen in Listing 7-5.

Listing 7-5. *Output as Viewed in a Text or XML Editor*

```
<TargetData>
// Output from functoid chain
  <AddressForm>
    <FullName>Wain      wright</FullName>
  </AddressForm>
// Output from C# Script
  <AddressForm1>
    <FullName>Wain      wright</FullName>
  </AddressForm1>
 // Output from XSLT script
  <AddressForm2>
    <FullName>Wain wright</FullName>
  </AddressForm2>
</TargetData>
```

Here, you can see that the three operations performed as expected. Neither the functoid chain nor the C# script changed the number of spaces in the center of the field. You must never assume that data is as it appears without validating it carefully. Now, let's move from trimming spaces to trimming other characters.

Trimming Nonblank Characters from a String

Sometimes, you must trim characters other than spaces from your data. You cannot use the String Left Trim and String Right Trim functoids for this purpose, because they only trim spaces. You must turn to scripts, such as the C# functions string.TrimStart and string.TrimEnd mentioned earlier. Fortunately, both these functions allow you to specify the character to be trimmed.

Perhaps the most common instance where you must trim characters other than spaces is when you must trim zeros. There are many cases where numbers in string form have leading and/or trailing zeros. Pallet ID fields, native to the shipping industry, and bar code label fields are two examples. Fixed length flat files often pad numbers with leading or trailing zeros. Listing 7-6 shows the string.TrimStart function that we use in a Scripting functoid to remove leading zeros.

Listing 7-6. *Trimming Leading Zeros*

```
public string StripZero(string inputString)
{
    return inputString.TrimStart(Convert.ToChar("0"))
}
```

Listing 7-7 shows the `string.TrimEnd` function we use to remove trailing zeros.

Listing 7-7. *Trimming Trailing Zeros*

```
public string StripSign(string inputString)
{
    return inputString.TrimEnd(Convert.ToChar("0"))
}
```

Padding a String

Another common string manipulation that requires a chain of string functoids is padding strings. This situation occurs when you have an input field that may be shorter than the desired output field and you want to make sure the input field is lengthened to meet the requirement. You must know the pad character and the length of the output field.

Our example consists of a product ID number that may vary in length, a pad character of zero, and a required output field length of 15 bytes. Our map is in Figure 7-2.

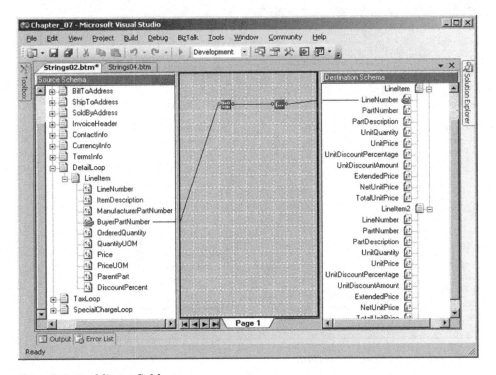

Figure 7-2. *Padding a field*

We use two string functoids in this example. The String Concatenate functoid appends 15 zeros to the start of the string received from the BuyerPathNumber node. The String Right functoid then captures the last 15 characters of the string output by the String Concatenate functoid. The source value BP12345 becomes 000000000000000BP12345 and then is cut to the target value of 00000000BP12345. Naturally, there is a simple C# function that serves the same purpose, as shown in Listing 7-8.

Listing 7-8. *C# Function to Pad a Field*

```
public static string PadNumber(string inNum, int padLen, string padChar)
{
  return inNum.ToString().PadLeft(padLen, Convert.ToChar(padChar));
}
```

We made all three parameters, pad length, pad character, and string, input variables to the function. Doing so allows us to use this script multiple times for different fields by allowing us to set all the variables in the Configure Functoid Inputs screen of the Scripting functoid.

Selecting Substrings from String Data

Substringing is just extracting a fixed number of bytes from a larger string, whether the extract is from the beginning, middle, or end of the string. The String Left, String Extract, and String Right functoids perform those extractions. Our map in Figure 7-3 uses the String Left functoid.

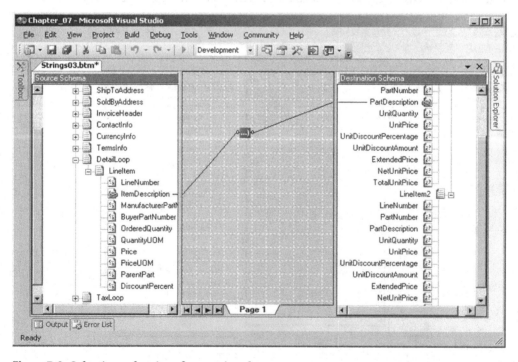

Figure 7-3. *Selecting substrings from string data*

We set the second input to the String Left functoid, the number of characters to be selected, to 8. If the source node `ItemDescription` contains the value `PN1295D1000STD`, the map will output value `PN1295D1` to the `PartDescription` node. We can also use the script in Listing 7-9 to achieve this.

Listing 7-9. *C# Code to Extract the Left Eight Characters from a String*

```
public string TruncateField(string inDesc)
{
if (inDesc.Length > 8)
  return inDesc.Substring(0,8);
else
  return inDesc;
}
```

Notice that we also add a check to make sure that the input string is at least as long as the string we want as output. Without the check, the script will throw an error if the input string is shorter than the target string. You can't select an eight-character string from a five-character string. Extracting the rightmost eight characters is slightly more difficult. Since our C# substring functoid requires the start position for the extraction, we must be able to determine where that position is. Listing 7-10 illustrates this.

Listing 7-10. *C# Code to Extract the Right Eight Characters from a String*

```
public string TruncateField(string inDesc)
{
// Get the length of the input string
Int strLen = inDesc.Length;
// Only do the extraction if the input string is longer than 8 bytes
if (strLen > 8)
// C# positions are zero-based, so we move the start position back seven, not eight
  return inDesc.Substring(strLen - 7,8);
else
  return inDesc;
}
```

Tip The zero-based position calculation shown in Listing 7-10 can be confusing. Let's look at an example. We have the string "abcdefghijklm". We normally think of the "e" as being the fifth character of the alphabet. That is because in one-based counting, "e" is character number five. When we use zero-based counting, however, we start counting with zero instead of one. Thus the letter "a" becomes the zero character, "b" the one character, and so on until "e", which is the fourth character. The length of our string is twelve in zero-based indexing, so to get the last eight characters, we must move the pointer back to character five (12 − 7 = 5) which is the character "f".

We find the start position for the extraction by determining the length of the whole string. Once we have that, we can set the extraction to begin at the length of the string minus eight. That will give us the last eight characters. Sometimes, we can't extract from the beginning or the end of a string. That's when we use the substring function seen in Listing 7-11.

Listing 7-11. *C# Code to Extract Eight Characters from Inside a String*

```
public string TruncateField(string inDesc)
{
Int strLen = inDesc.Length;
if (strLen > 8)
// Five is the zero-based start position; eight is the number of
// characters to extract.
  return inDesc.Substring(5,8);
else
  return inDesc;
}
```

Here, we need the eight-character string that begins with the fifth character in the string. Again, remember that C# scripts are zero-based, so the positions are counted as 012345..., so from the string "abcdefghijklmn", we are looking to extract the string "fghijklm".

We can also extract substrings using XSLT scripting. The example in Listing 7-12 extracts 40 characters starting from the first byte of the string. Notice that XSLT scripting is one-based, thus the positions are counted as 12345...

Listing 7-12. *XSLT Code to Extract First 40 Characters from a String*

```
<xsl:template name="TruncatePartDescription">
  <xsl:param name="inPart"/>
// One is the start position, forty is number of characters to extract
    <PartDescription>
      <xsl:value-of select="substring($inPart,1,40)"/>
    </PartDescription>
</xsl:template>
```

XSLT also offers left and right string selections, in the forms depicted in Listing 7-13.

Listing 7-13. *XSLT Code to Extract from the Beginning and End of a String*

```
<xsl:template name="SubstringLeftandRight">
// Select all of the string following the character '|'  (right string)
  <xsl:param name="inPart"/>
  <xsl:param name="inName"/>
  <PartDescription>
      <xsl:value-of select="substring-After($inPart,'|')"/>
  </PartDescription>
// Select all of the string before the string " WAINWRIGHT" (left string)
  <FirstName>
```

```
        <xsl:value-of select="substring-before($inName,'  WAINWRIGHT)"/>
    </FirstName>
</xsl:template>
```

The first section searches for the pipe character (|) and returns all of the string that follows that character. Thus the string "abc|def" becomes "def". The second section searches for the string " WAINWRIGHT" and returns all of the preceding string. Thus "JOHN WAINWRIGHT" becomes "JOHN".

Concatenating Strings

Concatenating strings is a frequent mapping requirement. You saw examples of concatenation in the HelloWorld map, where we joined the last and first names to create a full name. We also concatenated strings in Chapter 3. We will expand on those cases here, starting with the map in Figure 7-4.

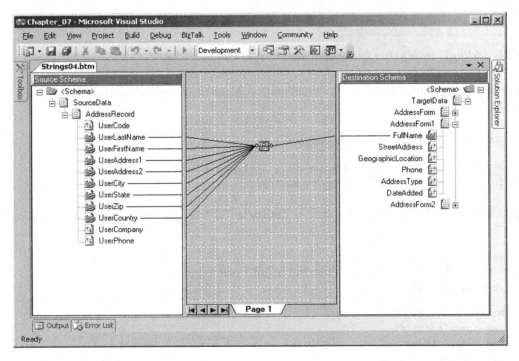

Figure 7-4. *Simple concatenation*

The String Concatenate functoid will serve for most of your simple concatenation requirements. It takes up to 100 inputs, including literals. Figure 7-5 shows the Configure Functoid Input window for this String Concatenate functoid. As you see, we have separated the address strings with commas.

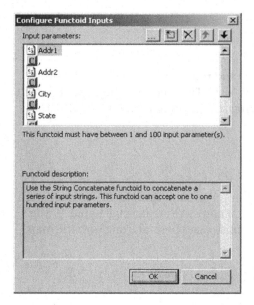

Figure 7-5. *Adding literals to the String Concatenate functoid*

The C# script version of this string concatenation is equally simple, as shown in Listing 7-14.

Listing 7-14. *C# Script for Concatenating Strings*

```
Public string ConcatAddress (string inAddr1, string inAddr2, string inCity,
string inState, string inZip, string inCountry)
{
  Return inAddr1 + ", "+ inAddr2 + ", " + inCity + ", "  + inState + inZip +
          " "+ inCountry;
}
```

Performing the same function with an inline XSLT call template is more verbose, but equally straightforward:

```
<xsl:template name="PutAddress">
<xsl:param name="Addr1"/>
<xsl:param name=" Addr2"/>
<xsl:param name="City"/>
<xsl:param name="State"/>
<xsl:param name="Zip"/>
<xsl:param name="Country"/>
<GeographicLocation>
  <xsl:value-of select="concat($Addr1,',' ,$Addr2,',',$City,',',$State,'',$Zip)"/>
</ GeographicLocation >
</xsl:template>
```

These concatenation examples expect all of the input data to be present. In each case, if an input element is missing, the output string may be incorrectly formatted. If no address data were in the input, for example, the output string could be ", , , ,". Unless you know the input fields are mandatory in the source data, you must provide for the possibility that data may be missing.

Searching String Data

Often, you need to determine if a character or a string exists within another string. One example would be the need to determine whether or not a part number begins with a certain prefix. The simplest method is to use the String Find functoid shown in the map in Figure 7-6.

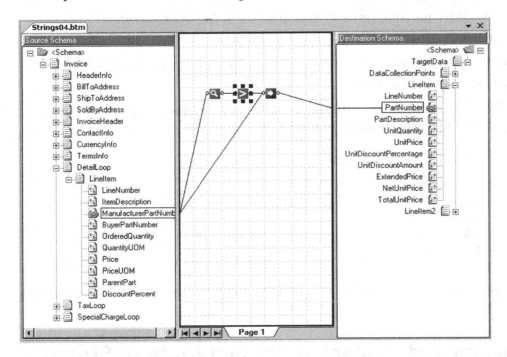

Figure 7-6. *Using the String Find functoid*

This map uses the String Find functoid to determine whether or not to output a value to the target PartNumber node. The functoid returns one of two values. If the search succeeds the functoid returns the starting position of the string for which you searched within the source string. If the target string is not found, the functoid returns a zero.

The map uses a Greater Than functoid to see if the String Search functoid was successful in finding the target string. The Value Mapping functoid uses the output of the Greater Than functoid, which is either true or false, to decide whether or not to output the source value to the target PartNumber node. Suppose we only want to output a PartNumber if the value from ManufacturerPartNumber begins with the string "ABA". The logic in the map would follow these steps:

1. Get the value from ManufacturerPartNumber.

2. Search for the string "ABA" in that value (using the String Find functoid).

3. Output a positive number if "ABA" is found; output zero if "ABA" is not found.

4. Test the output from the String Find functoid (using the Greater Than functoid).

5. Output true if the output is positive; output false if the output is zero.

6. Test the output from the Greater Than functoid (using the Value Mapping functoid).

7. If the value is true, output the ManufacturerPartNumber to the PartNumber node.

8. If the value is false, do nothing.

Listing 7-15 shows the C# script that performs the same string search and output logic, replacing all three functoids shown in the map.

Listing 7-15. *C# Code for Searching a String*

```
public string SearchPart (string inpart)
{
  if (inpart.IndexOf("ABA",0) != -1);
    return inpart;
  else return "";
}
```

The script uses the C# IndexOf function, which returns a –1 if the search string is not found and the position of the search string if it is found.

Removing and Replacing Characters from Strings

Often, you must remove characters from data, such as a dash embedded in a part number. As shown in Figure 7-7, this can be done with functoids but not as simply as you might expect.

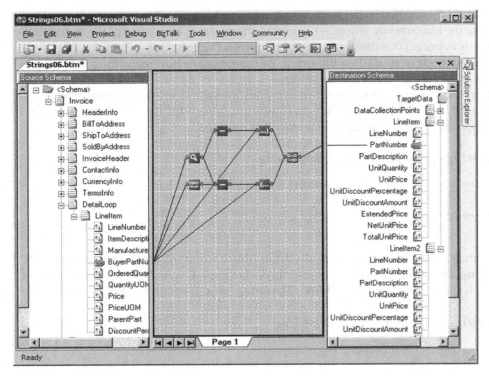

Figure 7-7. *Removing a dash*

The map accomplishes removal of the dash by capturing in one path the string before the dash, capturing in another path the string following the dash, and then joining the captured strings together. The string "ab-cd" becomes "ab" and "cd", which are joined to form "abcd". The process follows these steps:

1. Find the position of the dash in the string (using the String Find functoid).

2. Determine the length of the string (using the Size functoid).

3. Before capturing the string before the dash, subtract one from the value returned from the String Find functoid. If the string is "ab-cd", the value is reduced from 3 to 2.

4. Pass this value to the String Left functoid so that the first two characters from the string are captured. The string "ab-cd" becomes "ab".

5. Before capturing the string after the dash, subtract the value returned from the String Find functoid from the value returned from the Size functoid. If the string is "ab-cd", the size value would be 5, the position of the dash would be 3, and the final value would be 2.

6. Pass this final value to the String Right functoid so that the last two characters from the string are captured. The string "ab-cd" becomes "cd".

7. Pass both strings to the String Concatenate functoid in the correct order so that they are joined. The strings "ab" and "cd" become "abcd".

Using functoids to remove a single character works. What about when there are multiple occurrences of the character or, worse yet, multiple characters to be removed? We needed seven functoids to extract one dash, and we did not protect against cases where there is no data in the source node or no dash in the string. You can imagine how many functoids we would need to address either of these situations.

The C# and XSLT functions that remove or replace characters are not complex. The C# function uses the `string.Replace()` function, shown in Listing 7-16. The code will remove or replace all occurrences of the string to be removed or replaced.

Listing 7-16. *C# Code to Remove Dashes from a String*

```csharp
public  string ReplaceDash(string inputString)
{
    return inputString.Replace("-","");
}
```

The example in Listing 7-16 removes all dashes from a string by replacing each dash with an empty string. The string "ab-cd" becomes "abcd". Listing 7-17 shows the same functoid set up to replace the dash with the string "1234". The string "ab-cd" becomes "ab1234cd".

Listing 7-17. *C# Code to Replace Dashes in a String*

```csharp
public  string ReplaceDash(string inputString)
{
    return inputString.Replace("-","1234");
}
```

The corresponding function in XSLT uses the `translate()`function. Three parameters, the string to be searched, the character to be replaced, and the replacing character, are required. The script in Listing 7-18 searches for the dash and removes it by replacing it with nothing. Again, the string "ab-cd" becomes "abcd".

Listing 7-18. *XSLT Code to Replace Dashes in a String*

```xml
<xsl:template name="ReplaceDash">
  <xsl param name="inPart"/>
  // note that the quotes with in the parentheses are single quotes.
  // The '-' is the search object; the '' (two single quote marks with no data
 //between them) is the replacement object.
  <xsl:if test="translate($inPart, '-','' ) != '' ">
    <Part><xsl:value-of select="$inPart)"/></Part>
  </xsl:if>
</xsl:template>
```

The XSLT script does not behave in the same manner as the C# script. The `translate()` function allows sets of search and replacement characters. When more than one character is present in the search set, the function uses the character in the matching position in the replacement set as the replacement character. If the original string is "A1B2C3", the search characters are "ABC", and the replacement characters are "a2D", the result is "a122D3".

Using the RegEx Function to Remove Garbage from a String

We often need to sanitize free-form strings by removing characters that are illegal for use in the situation. We find that the RegEx function provides a simple method of doing this. The function requires three inputs, the string to be searched, the set of characters to be removed, and the replacement character, as shown in Listing 7-19.

Listing 7-19. *Testing the RegEx function*

```
public string TestRegex(string inString)
{
    return System.Text.RegularExpressions.Regex.Replace
                                (inString, "[*#$%<>^{|}@~]", "");
}
```

Notice that even though you can have many characters to be replaced, you may have only one replacement character. This function converts the string "a*#%<^~d" to the string "ad".

Summary

Our focus in this chapter is on basic methods of manipulating strings. The set of String functoids available in BizTalk are flexible and, when used in chains, can solve more difficult problems. Scripting extends your string manipulation capabilities even more by allowing you to address complex problems that are beyond the scope of the functoids. These complex problems are not discussed in this chapter but will be encountered as you work through the later chapters.

Next, we will continue looking at basic BizTalk mapping concepts by examining the manipulation of dates and times. Date and time fields appear in almost every document that you process, so understanding the basic concepts of working with them is another important mapping basic.

CHAPTER 8

■ ■ ■

Manipulating Dates and Times

Anyone from North America who has ever tried to keep track of European-style dates knows that dates can be confusing: Is 07/06 July 6 or June 7? EDI mappers know that EDI date formats often do not match date formats in XML schemas. We have to manipulate date, time, and date/time values in almost every map we do. You can be sure that at some point you will encounter the same.

Many times, the manipulation of a date/time type value is no more than modifying the format by rearranging the characters, for example, changing 103108 to 2008/10/31. These kinds of manipulations are no more than string manipulations. We covered string manipulations in Chapter 7, so we will focus on other type of date/time manipulations in this chapter and present only one example of handling a date as string here. The mapping toolbox contains several functoids that are specific to date and time usage.

BizTalk Date and Time Functoids

BizTalk provides four date and time functoids (see Figure 8-1). Three of these retrieve system date/time information; the fourth provides a means to add days to a date.

Figure 8-1. *Date/Time functoids in the Toolbox*

Use of the Date and Time, Date, and Time functoids is very straightforward. No inputs may be entered. The Date and Time functoid returns the system date/time format CCYY-MM-DDThh:mm:ss. The Date functoid returns the system date in the format YYYY-MM-DD.

The Time functoid returns the system time in the format HH:MM:SS. We use the Date and Time functoid for our example in Figure 8-2.

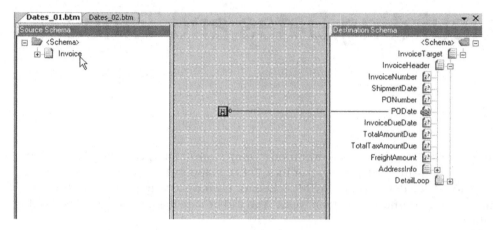

Figure 8-2. *The Date and Time functoid in action*

The underlying code for the functoid is exposed in the CDATA section of the map generated when you validate this map. As you've seen before, the XSLT code in the map calls a C# function. Here, the call is to the DateCurrentDateTime() function shown in Listing 8-1.

Listing 8-1. *DateCurrentDateTime Function*

```csharp
public string DateCurrentDateTime()
{
// retrieve system date and time
  DateTime dt = DateTime.Now;
// pull the date out of the datetime string and format
  string curdate = dt.ToString("yyyy-MM-dd",
                  System.Globalization.CultureInfo.InvariantCulture);
// pull the time out of the datetime string and format
  string curtime = dt.ToString("T",
                  System.Globalization.CultureInfo.InvariantCulture);
// concatenate the date and time together, separated by a "T"
  string retval = curdate + "T" + curtime;
  return retval;
}
```

The Date functoid and Time functoid perform in the same manner. The Date functoid calls the C# function DateCurrentDate(); the Time functoid calls the C# function DateCurrentTime(). All three C# functions call the same C# function, DateTime.Now, which returns a string in the format of MM/DD/YYYhh:mm:ss. The three functoids then perform string manipulations to pick out that part of the string that they require.

Tip If you want a different format, you can modify either of these functions to output the format you need. Just remember to rename the function before using it in a map. If you decide to use the DateTime.Now function, be aware that the format returned from this function depends on the default date/time format as it is set for your operating system. For example, if you set that property to display the time in a 12-hour format, the output from the DateTime.Now function will also have an AM/PM indicator.

Altering the Format of a Date

In our experience, the most common date and time manipulations encountered are adding, removing, or changing the punctuation characters. You've already seen a few examples of this in earlier chapters and know that the mechanisms for adding, removing, and replacing characters are similar. Rather than send you off to find one of those examples, let's look here at removing punctuation. Our map is in Figure 8-3.

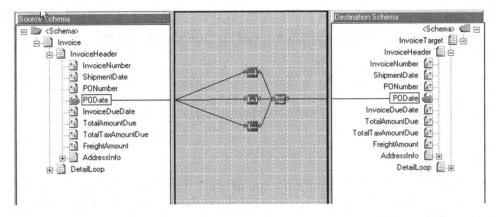

Figure 8-3. *Removing characters from a date*

This map appears identical to the map you saw in Figure 3-1 of the chapter on scripting where we changed a date from YYYYMMDD to a punctuated format of YYYY/MM/DD. But this map is different, changing YYYY?MM?DD to YYMMDD. The question mark in the first string is a wildcard character, indicating that any characters in those positions will be removed. Figure 8-4 shows why the two maps produce different results.

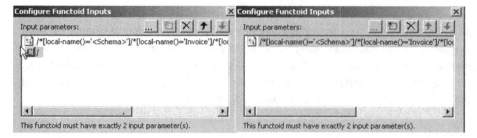

Figure 8-4. *Inputs to the String Concatenate functoids in Figures 3-1 and 8-3*

The left pane is a close-up of the input to the String Concatenate functoid in Figure 3-1. The right pane is a close-up of the input to the String Concatenate functoid in Figure 8-3. Now you see why the first map added a slash character (/) between the year, month, and day and why the second map removes any character that is in the same position.

Manipulating the format of a date or time field is simple using functoids, but doing so is even simpler using scripts. Listing 8-2 has the C# script that reformats CCCC?MM?DD to CCCCMMDD.

Listing 8-2. *C# Script to Remove Characters from Between the Year, Month, and Day*

```
public string FormatDate(string inDate)
{
if (inDate != "")
    return inDate.Substring(6,4) + inDate.Substring(0,2) + inDate.Substring(3,2);
else
    return "";
}
```

Since the Substring call will fail if there is not enough data, the script checks to make sure the date is in the data before reformatting it. Listing 8-3 shows that an inline XSLT script can also remove the punctuation from a date.

Listing 8-3. *Inline XSLT Script to Remove Characters from Between the Year, Month, and Day*

```
<xsl:variable name="inDate" select="//ShipmentDate" />
  <xsl:if test="$inDate != '' ">
    <ShipmentDate>
        <xsl:value-of select="concat
            (substring($inDate,7,4, substring($inDate,1,2),
            substring($inDate,4,2))" />
    </ShipmentDate>
</xsl:if>
```

When the order of the remaining characters in the output string is the same as in the input string after the punctuation character has been removed, the C# function in Listing 8-4 is useful.

Listing 8-4. *Using the C# Replace Function to Remove Characters from the Date*

```
public string RemoveFormatFromDate(string inDate)
{
  if (inDate != "")
      return inDate.Replace("/","");
  else
      return "";
}
```

And finally, of course, you can use the inline XSLT translate function, as shown in Listing 8-5.

Listing 8-5. *Using Inline XSLT Translate Function to Remove Characters from the Date*

```
<xsl:variable name="inDate" select="//ShipmentDate" />
  <xsl:if test="$inDate != '' ">
    <ShipmentDate>
      <xsl:value-of select="translate($inDate, '/', '' )" />
    </ShipmentDate>
</xsl:if>
```

Sometimes, you need to extract only part of a date or time. You can do this using the appropriate string extraction functoid or using the simple script shown in Listing 8-6.

Listing 8-6. *C# Script to Obtain Part of a Date or Time*

```
public string ReturnDatePart(string inDate, string inPart)
{
// Convert the input string date to a DateTime object
  DateTime inParse = Convert.ToDateTime(inDate);
// Extract the portion of the DateTime specified by the
// inPart input
  return inParse.ToString(inPart).ToUpper();
}
```

Notice that, in this script, we no longer treat the data as a string; instead, we use a DateTime object. The inPart parameter might be one of those listed in Listing 8-7.

Listing 8-7. *Input Parameters for Date and Time Format Extractions*

```
yy     Year without the century
yyyy   Year with the century
MM     Month of the Year
dd     Day of the Month
ddd    Short Day Name
hh     Hour
mm     minutes
ss     Seconds
zz     Time zone offset
```

Calculating a Due Date

Another common date manipulation in maps is calculating a new date based on an input date. One example is when your map receives an invoice date in the input and you must also output a due date for payment. Basic arithmetic using dates is performed with the fourth Biz-Talk Date/Time functoid from the toolbox, the AddDays functoid. This functoid requires two inputs: A valid date and the number of days (positive or negative) you wish to add to the date.

Our map in Figure 8-5 uses the Date functoid as the source for the date. The AddDate functoid adds 10 days to the date obtained from the Date functoid.

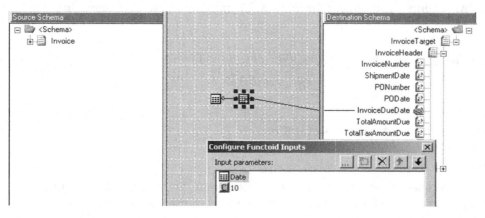

Figure 8-5. *Adding dates*

As shown in the Configure Functoid Inputs window, the AddDate functoid is set to add 10 days to the date received from the Date functoid. The AddDate functoid performs validation behind the scenes, checking to insure that the input date is a valid date and that the number of days is a valid number. If either of the inputs is invalid, it will return an empty string. The C# script called by the AddDate functoid is in Listing 8-8.

Listing 8-8. *C# Script Used by the AddDate Functoid*

```
public string DateAddDays(string date, string days)
{
  string retval = "";
  double db = 0;
  if (IsDate(date) && IsNumeric(days, ref db))
  {
    DateTime dt = DateTime.Parse(date);
    int d = (int) db;
    dt = dt.AddDays(d);
    retval = dt.ToString("yyyy-MM-dd",
            System.Globalization.CultureInfo.InvariantCulture);
  }
return retval;
}
```

Comparing Date Intervals

Occasionally, you must compare a date in your map to another date, perhaps to check a schedule. Doing this with functoids is not easy, so we turn to scripts right away. We use an example where we evaluate whether the date in the data is later than an effective date and report the results.

Our script, shown in Listing 8-9, accepts the two dates as input. The script converts both dates into the standard DateTime format (yyyy-mm-dd) for the computations. A call to the function DateTime.Compare() determines the difference between the dates, returning –1 if the first date is earlier, 0 if the dates are the same, or 1 if the first date is later.

If the two dates are not the same, we use a System.TimeSpan struct to calculate the difference in the number of days and then output a message describing the result.

Listing 8-9. *Comparing Dates*

```
public string CalcDaysOverdue(string inDueDate, string inTransDate)
{
    string message = "";
  int daysOverdue = 0;
// Check to see if either date is null, set message to show invalid dates if so
  if (inTransDate == "" || inDueDate == "")  message = "Invalid Date(s)";
// Convert both dates from string types to DateTime types.
// Use Convert.ToDateTime instead of DateTime.Parse just for
// illustration.
  DateTime dueDate = Convert.ToDateTime(inDueDate);
  DateTime transDate = Convert.ToDateTime(inTransDate);
// Determine the difference in the two dates
  int overdue = DateTime.Compare(transDate, dueDate);
// If the difference is not zero, convert the interval between them into a time span
// of format days.hours:minutes:seconds and extract the value for days
  if (overdue != 0)
  {
    System.TimeSpan diff1 = transDate.Subtract(dueDate);
    string diff2 = diff1.ToString();
   daysOverdue = Convert.ToInt16( diff2.Substring(0,diff2.IndexOf(".",0)));
  }
// format the number of days into a message string
  if (daysOverdue < 0)
  {
    daysOverdue = Math.Abs(daysOverdue);
    message = "Transaction is due in " + daysOverdue + " days";
  }
  else if (daysOverdue > 0)
    message = "Transaction is " + daysOverdue + " days overdue";
  else
    message = "Transaction is due today";
```

```
// return the message string
return message;
}
```

For the sake of brevity, the script assumes that the input dates are in a format compatible for conversion. Figure 8-6 displays both the map and a sample output.

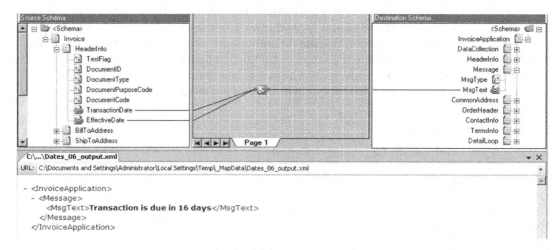

Figure 8-6. *Map and output for comparing dates*

Performing Time Zone Conversions

Another useful date manipulation is converting from one time zone to another. Our example here uses the format of yyyy-MM-dd hh:mm zz. zz is the time zone offset and states the difference in number of hours between the time given from UTC, or Coordinated Universal Time (also referred to as Greenwich Mean Time [GMT]) . Thus if the given date is in the Pacific Daylight time zone, the offset would be –7. If you were in the Eastern Daylight time zone, you would need to adjust that time by adding three hours. Note that this might also affect the date.

This example uses the CurrentTimeZone property of the DateTime object. We retrieve the current time zone offset from the system and then compute the difference between the given zone and the current zone. The difference is added to the given date to adjust that date to our local date. Listing 8-10 contains the script.

Listing 8-10. *Time Zone Conversion Script*

```
public string ConvertDateTime(string inDate)
{
// retrieve the local timezone offset  in format "zz:00:00"
   string systemZone = TimeZone.CurrentTimeZone.GetUtcOffset
                    (DateTime.Now).ToString();
```

```
// Strip of the first two characters to get the hours difference
   int localZone = Convert.ToInt16(systemZone.Substring(0,systemZone.IndexOf(":")));
// retrieve the time zone offset from the input string
   int inZone = Convert.ToInt16(inDate.Substring(20));
// determine the difference between time zones
   double zoneDiff = localZone - inZone;
// convert input date to standard date format by adding the offset hours
   DateTime dueDate = Convert.ToDateTime(inDate.Substring(0,18));
   return dueDate.AddHours(zoneDiff).ToString();
}
```

Figure 8-7 shows the map, the input date, and the map output. Notice that that the conversion rolled the date from August 31 to September 1, changing both the day and the month.

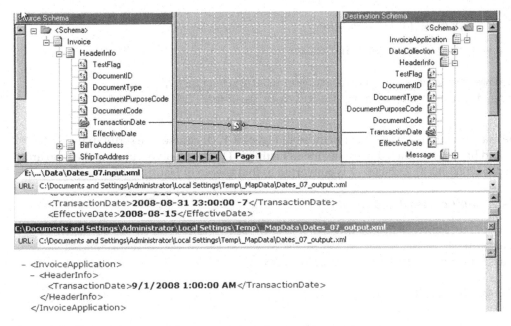

Figure 8-7. *Time zone conversion map, input date, and output*

Converting Gregorian Dates to Ordinal Dates

An ordinal date consists of a year and a day of the year, where the day of the year ranges between 1 and 366. ISO-8601 defines the format for the ordinal date as YYYY-DDD, but we see it often in the format YYYYDDD. Purchase order numbers, for example, sometimes use an ordinal-style date as part of the number, thus conversions to and from ordinal dates may be required in maps.

■**Caution** You may see ordinal dates referred to as Julian dates. This is incorrect. The ordinal date is just a different method of displaying the date and the year based on the Gregorian calendar. A Julian date is computed from a different starting date than the Gregorian calendar. There is an extensive set of methods associated with the Julian Calendar class in C# that can be used to manipulate true Julian dates. However, you should not use them because they are intended for use with only true Julian dates, not ordinal representations of Gregorian dates.

This type of conversion is easy using the built-in functions available in C#. To find the ordinal representation of a date, we need only to extract the DayOfYear property from the date and concatenate that value with the year. The code is in Listing 8-11.

Listing 8-11. *Script to Get the Ordinal Date*

```
public string GetOrdinalDate(string inDate)
{
    DateTime testDate = Convert.ToDateTime(inDate.Substring(0,10));
    return testDate.Year.ToString() + testDate.DayOfYear.ToString("000") ;
}
```

The map and input are identical to those in Figure 8-7. Of course, the script in the Scripting functoid has been replaced with the one in Listing 8-11. The result of running the map are that the date 2008-08-31 23:00:00 –7 is converted to that shown in Listing 8-12.

Listing 8-12. *Date Converted to Ordinal*

```
<InvoiceApplication>
  <HeaderInfo>
    <TransactionDate>2008244</TransactionDate>
  </HeaderInfo>
</InvoiceApplication>
```

Converting Ordinal Dates to Gregorian Dates

The requirement to convert a date from the ordinal format of YYYYDDD to the Gregorian format pops up every once in a while. Unfortunately, there is not a simple method of doing this, so you will have to write your own code. Keep in mind that you need to determine whether or not the year in question is a leap year. Any year that is equally divisible by four is a leap year.

■**Caution** If your calculations involve dates earlier than 1901 or later than 2099, you must take into account that century years are not leap years unless they are evenly divisible by 400. Since the year 2000 is likely to be the only one you in which you will be interested for some time, this more obscure part of the leap year determination can usually be overlooked.

Listing 8-13 presents a script that will convert an ordinal date into a standard date.

Listing 8-13. *Script to Convert Ordinal Date to Standard Date*

```
public string GetOrdinalToGreg(string inDate)
{
// Initialize the variables to the correct values, including extracting
//  the year and day from the input ordinal date
  int year = Convert.ToInt32(inDate.Substring(0,4));
  int day = Convert.ToInt32(inDate.Substring(4,3));
  int month = 0;
  int dayOfMonth = 0;
  int div = 4;
// create arrays month values for ordinal days in leap and non-leap years
  int[] LeapArray = new int[13] { 0,31,60,91,121,152,182,213,244,274,305,335,366};
  int[] DateArray = new int[13] { 0,31,59,90,120,151,181,212,243,273,304,334,365};
// if the year is evenly divisible by 4, copy the LeapArray to the DateArray since
// the DateArray is used through the rest of the script
  if ( (year % div ) == 0)
  {
    LeapArray.CopyTo( DateArray, 0 );
  }
// search the DateArray to find the month in which the dayOfYear falls by checking
// to see where the day variable is greater than the current array value
// and less than the next array value.  The counter "I" keeps
// place of the month.
  for (int i = 0;i < 13;i ++)
  {
    if (day > DateArray[i] && day <= DateArray[i + 1])
  {
//  The array is zero-based, so increment the value before assigning the month
  month = i+1;
//  Calculate the day of the month by subtracting the array value from the day value
  dayOfMonth = day - DateArray[i];
//  Leave the For loop once the target is found
  break;
}
}
// return the concatenate and formatted pieces of the date
return year.ToString("0000") + "/" + month.ToString("00") + "/" +
      dayOfMonth.ToString("00");
}
```

The script converts the date 2008048 to 2008/02/17.

Converting Dates and Times Using the ParseExact Method

All the scripts to this point in this chapter accept dates in the format that they are given, which causes them to sometimes have to convert the date from one format into another in order to work properly. We can overcome the need to do this explicit conversion by using the C# ParseExact() method. We just have to supply a second parameter defining the format of the input date. Here is the script in Listing 8-14.

Listing 8-14. *Using the ParseExact Method*

```
public string GetOrdinalDate(string inVar, string inFmt)
{
  string returnDate = "";
// Here we use a try-catch block to ensure that the input parameters are correct
  try
  {
// Use the ParseExact method to read the input date
    DateTime testDate = DateTime.ParseExact(inVar, inFmt, null);
// Convert the date into the format you want
    returnDate = testDate.Year.ToString() + testDate.DayOfYear.ToString("000") ;
}
//  If an error occurred in the try code this catch code will be executed
  catch
  {
    returnDate = "INVALID";
  }
  return returnDate;
}
```

Getting Dates and Times for an XSLT Script

If you use an extensive amount of XSLT scripting in your maps, you will need to do date manipulating within some scripts. Since we are limiting our discussion here to XSLT functions available in the basic version of XSL 1.0, many date functions from later versions are not available.

That doesn't mean that you can't take advantage of scripting to do date manipulations. The map shown in Figure 8-8 uses a combination of C# and XSLT to calculate an invoice due date by adding days to the current date.

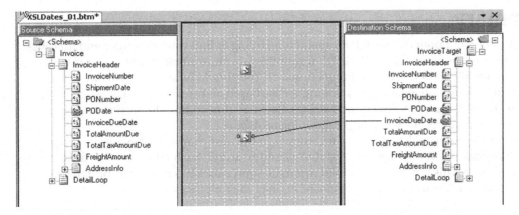

Figure 8-8. *Getting dates and times for an XSLT script*

There are two Scripting functoids in the map. The top one, which is not linked to anything, contains a C# script that does the date manipulation. The script retrieves the system date, adds the number of days specified by the XSLT script, and formats the result to yyyyMMdd. Listing 8-15 contains this script.

Listing 8-15. *C# Script Called by the XSLT Script*

```
public string ReturnDueDate(int inDays)
{
  DateTime currDate = DateTime.Now;
  return currDate.AddDays(inDays).ToString("yyyyMMdd");
}
```

The XSLT script receives the return value from the C# script, the newly calculated InvoiceDueDate. The XSLT script is in Listing 8-16.

Listing 8-16. *XSLT Script to Output the InvoiceDueDate*

```
<xsl:template name="CalculateDate">
  <xsl:param name="inDays"/>
  <InvoiceDueDate>
    <xsl:value-of select="userCSharp:ReturnDueDate($inDays)" />
  </InvoiceDueDate>
</xsl:template>
```

The XSLT script has one input parameter, the number of days to add to the system date. In this map, we put the value as a parameter in the Configure Functoid Inputs for the Scripting functoid that holds the XSLT script. We could have provided the value via a link from an input node as well.

Summary

As you've no doubt noticed, we did not spend time trying to find ways of using standard func-toids to do date manipulations. We feel that scripting is a more efficient way since the date handling capabilities of C# are rich in functionality. You should be able to solve most of your date and time handling issues by developing scripts based on the ones we show in this chapter. As with conditionals, numbers, and strings, date and time manipulation techniques are fundamental methods of solving larger mapping problems.

We continue this look at the basic techniques in the next chapter by looking at methods of collecting data from the source into global variables, arrays, hash tables, and so forth for use later in the map. This is especially helpful when the source data has numerous nested loops and the data in all the loops must be exposed at one time for processing.

CHAPTER 9

■ ■ ■

Collecting Data

We have looked at techniques for manipulating some basic objects such as dates, numbers, and strings by processing data pulled from the source. Now, let's look at how we get that data. This is the first of two chapters that discuss how to retrieve and organize data that is not readily available. This chapter focuses on retrieving data from the source file. The next chapter will focus on data that is not in the source file and must be retrieved from an external source such as a flat file or a database.

Collecting Nonlooping Data from the Source

Let's begin with an example of this type of issue. Our source file looks like Listing 9-1. Notice that the data consist of one nonlooping record, SourceRecord, and one looping record, SourceLoop. We have numbered the data so that you can tell to which source loop the data belongs. A1 is the first data item in the first SourceLoop node, for example.

Listing 9-1. *Source Data*

```
<ns0:Source xmlns:ns0="http://chapter9.Source1">
  <SourceRecord>
      <SourceRecordData>SourceRecordData</SourceRecordData>
  </SourceRecord>
  <SourceLoop>
      <SourceA>A1</SourceA>
      <SourceB>B1</SourceB>
      <SourceC>C1</SourceC>
    </SourceLoop>
  <SourceLoop>
      <SourceA>A2</SourceA>
      <SourceB>B2</SourceB>
      <SourceC>C2</SourceC>
  </SourceLoop>
  <SourceLoop>
      <SourceA>A3</SourceA>
      <SourceB>B3</SourceB>
      <SourceC>C3</SourceC>
  </SourceLoop>
</ns0:Source>
```

The first thing that we want to illustrate is that in BizTalk mapping data is available throughout the map. In other words, data is not consumed when used. Our map is shown in Figure 9-1.

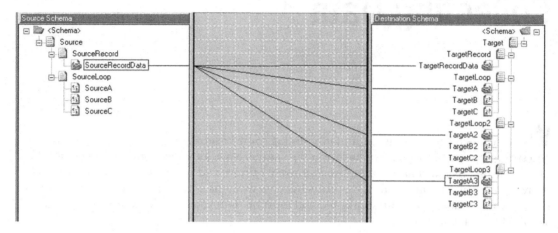

Figure 9-1. *Data is available throughout the map.*

Our source file contains one instance of SourceRecordData. There are four links to the target that request the data from that node. Listing 9-2 contains the output from this map, which illustrates that source data persists after use in the BizTalk mapping engine.

Listing 9-2. *Output of Data Is Available Throughout the Map*

```
<nsO:Target xmlns:nsO="http://chapter9.Target1">
  <TargetRecord>
      <TargetRecordData>SourceRecordData</TargetRecordData>
  </TargetRecord>
  <TargetLoop>
      <TargetA>SourceRecordData</TargetA>
  </TargetLoop>
  <TargetLoop2>
      <TargetA2>SourceRecordData</TargetA2>
  </TargetLoop2>
  <TargetLoop3>
      <TargetA3>SourceRecordData</TargetA3>
  </TargetLoop3>
</nsO:Target>
```

Although there is only one instance of SourceRecordData in the source data, each of the four target nodes receives the data.

Collecting Looping Data from the Source

Now, let's change to the map to look like the one shown in Figure 9-2 and see what happens.

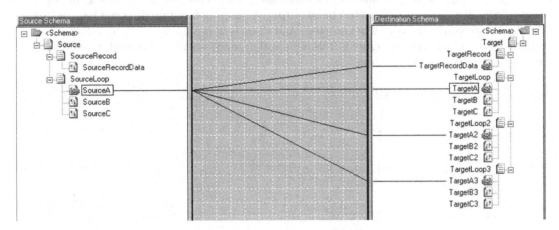

Figure 9-2. *Too much data*

Our desire in the Figure 9-2 map is to output the data from the SourceA node into four different target nodes. But when we run the map with validate output activated, the map fails. With validation deactivated, we get the output shown in Listing 9-3.

Listing 9-3. *Too Much Data Output*

```
<ns0:Target xmlns:ns0="http://chapter9.Target1">
// We get three target record nodes, one fore each SourceA node.
  <TargetRecord>
      <TargetRecordData>A1</TargetRecordData>
  </TargetRecord>
  <TargetRecord>
    <TargetRecordData>A2</TargetRecordData>
  </TargetRecord>
  <TargetRecord>
    <TargetRecordData>A3</TargetRecordData>
  </TargetRecord>
// We then get nine TargetLoop nodes, all with the same three values as this node.
  <TargetLoop>
    <TargetA>A1</TargetA>
  </TargetLoop>
  <TargetLoop>
    <TargetA>A2</TargetA>
  </TargetLoop>
  <TargetLoop>
    <TargetA>A3</TargetA>
  </TargetLoop>
// The output continues with three TargetLoop2 nodes and three TargetLoop3 nodes.
```

```
// We've clipped the nodes to shorten this listing.
</ns0:Target>
```

Since the mapping engine does not extract data based on the min/max values set on the target nodes, all of the source data has been output. A Looping functoid does not help in this case. And since you have no way of knowing what value is in the source node, conditional structures do not help either. Figure 9-3 shows another map, where we have added a child looping node to the source schema.

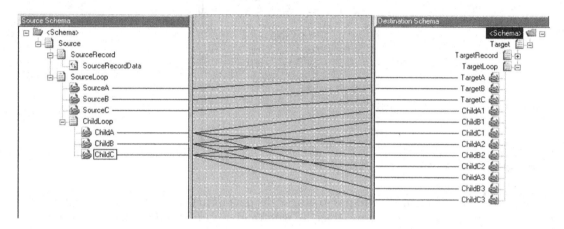

Figure 9-3. *A map with a child loop*

What we are trying to output in this map is a TargetLoop node for each instance of the SourceLoop node, with all the data from three ChildLoop nodes output in the same TargetLoop node as their parent. Such a result would produce three TargetLoop nodes. Here, in Listing 9-4, is the source data. Again, note that we've keyed the data so that you can tell from which node each piece is retrieved.

Listing 9-4. *Source Data for a Map with a Child Loop*

```
<ns0:Source xmlns:ns0="http://chapter9.Source1">
  <SourceRecord>
    <SourceRecordData>SourceRecordData</SourceRecordData>
  </SourceRecord>
  <SourceLoop>
    <SourceA>SourceA</SourceA>
    <SourceB>SourceB</SourceB>
    <SourceC>SourceC</SourceC>
    <ChildLoop>
      <ChildA>ChildA1</ChildA>
      <ChildB>ChildB1</ChildB>
      <ChildC>ChildC1</ChildC>
    </ChildLoop>
    <ChildLoop>
      <ChildA>ChildA2</ChildA>
```

```xml
      <ChildB>ChildB2</ChildB>
      <ChildC>ChildC2</ChildC>
    </ChildLoop>
    <ChildLoop>
      <ChildA>ChildA3</ChildA>
      <ChildB>ChildB3</ChildB>
      <ChildC>ChildC3</ChildC>
    </ChildLoop>
  </SourceLoop>
  <SourceLoop>
    <SourceA>SourceA2</SourceA>
    <SourceB>SourceB2</SourceB>
    <SourceC>SourceC2</SourceC>
    <ChildLoop>
      <ChildA>ChildA1-2</ChildA>
      <ChildB>ChildB1-2</ChildB>
      <ChildC>ChildC1-2</ChildC>
    </ChildLoop>
    <ChildLoop>
      <ChildA>ChildA2-2</ChildA>
      <ChildB>ChildB2-2</ChildB>
      <ChildC>ChildC2-2</ChildC>
    </ChildLoop>
    <ChildLoop>
      <ChildA>ChildA3-2</ChildA>
      <ChildB>ChildB3-2</ChildB>
      <ChildC>ChildC3-2</ChildC>
    </ChildLoop>
  </SourceLoop>
  <SourceLoop>
    <SourceA>SourceA3</SourceA>
    <SourceB>SourceB3</SourceB>
    <SourceC>SourceC3</SourceC>
    <ChildLoop>
      <ChildA>ChildA1-3</ChildA>
      <ChildB>ChildB1-3</ChildB>
      <ChildC>ChildC1-3</ChildC>
    </ChildLoop>
    <ChildLoop>
      <ChildA>ChildA2-3</ChildA>
      <ChildB>ChildB2-3</ChildB>
      <ChildC>ChildC2-3</ChildC>
    </ChildLoop>
    <ChildLoop>
      <ChildA>ChildA3-3</ChildA>
      <ChildB>ChildB3-3</ChildB>
      <ChildC>ChildC3-3</ChildC>
```

```
    </ChildLoop>
  </SourceLoop>
</ns0:Source>
```

When we run the map, we get the output shown in Listing 9-5, which looks nothing like we expected. Since the map is a multiple-loop–to–single-loop map, the compiler was unable to figure out the logic. Adding looping functoids does not help either.

Listing 9-5. *Output from the Map with the Child Loop*

```
<ns0:Target xmlns:ns0="http://chapter9.Target1">
  <TargetLoop>
//  The next six nodes are correct
    <TargetA>SourceA</TargetA>
    <TargetB>SourceB</TargetB>
    <TargetC>SourceC</TargetC>
    <ChildA1>ChildA1</ChildA1>
    <ChildB1>ChildB1</ChildB1>
    <ChildC1>ChildC1</ChildC1>
//  Oops.  This data has already been output.  It should be the values from
//  the second and third child loops, but it is two repetitions of the data from
//  the first child loop.
    <ChildA2>ChildA1</ChildA2>
    <ChildB2>ChildB1</ChildB2>
    <ChildC2>ChildC1</ChildC2>
    <ChildA3>ChildA1</ChildA3>
    <ChildB3>ChildB1</ChildB3>
    <ChildC3>ChildC1</ChildC3>
  </TargetLoop>
  <TargetLoop>
//  Oops again.  These three nodes should have the data from the second
//  SourceLoop but instead repeat the same data
    <TargetA>SourceA</TargetA>
    <TargetB>SourceB</TargetB>
    <TargetC>SourceC</TargetC>
//  And these three nodes should have been the third, fourth, and fifth nodes
    <ChildA1>ChildA2</ChildA1>
    <ChildB1>ChildB2</ChildB1>
    <ChildC1>ChildC2</ChildC1>
//  Now we're back to repeating the data
    <ChildA2>ChildLoopA2</ChildA2>
    <ChildB2>ChildLoopB2</ChildB2>
    <ChildC2>ChildLoopC2</ChildC2>
    <ChildA3>ChildLoopA2</ChildA3>
    <ChildB3>ChildLoopB2</ChildB3>
    <ChildC3>ChildLoopC2</ChildC3>
  </TargetLoop>
... and so on for seven more TargetLoop nodes, none of which are correct.
```

Again, the Looping functoid is of no value in solving this problem. The problem we face is removing only the data that we desire from the source for each TargetLoop node. The method we use most often is to collect the data that we need at the beginning of the map in one or more structures that allow us to pick and choose what pieces we output. We'll see the solution to this specific problem at the end of the chapter. Before that, let's look at the underpinnings that will allow us to solve the problem.

Modifying the Target Schema for Data Collection

When you need to collect data, you must perform the collection as near to the beginning of the map as possible. You can use any target node as your collection node as long as that node meets these criteria:

- The node must occur before the parent node of any node where you will output the data.

- The node must be a looping node if the source data is looping and you will not be using a Cumulative Concatenate functoid.

- The normal use of the node must remain unaffected by attachment of the link that collects the data.

Sometimes, you may not be able to find a node that you can use. In that case, you may modify the target schema to create the needed nodes. Look the target schema in Figure 9-4, where we have added three nodes for data collection, a parent and two children.

Figure 9-4. *A map with target schema data collection nodes*

The receiving application or trading partner should not receive the data collection nodes in the file that is output by the map. Therefore, these nodes must be optional so you can block them from being output. All three data collection nodes are unbounded optional nodes that can loop as many times as necessary.

Modifying the target schema using the unbounded nodes is our preferred method of choosing a node for collecting data, but sometimes, the schema cannot or should not be modified. In those cases, we choose an unused node when one is available and meets the criteria. Our least favorite choice is to piggyback data collection on a node that is also receiving output data.

Using Global Variables for Data Collection

Without global variables, we could not collect data for processing. Global variables provide a place for us to store the collected data until we are ready to use it. Once a global variable has been created, the content of that variable is available to the rest of the map. Listing 9-6 shows a script that creates some global variables and contains a functoid to get and increment a global counter.

Listing 9-6. *Declaring Global Variables and Returning a Counter*

```
// Declare the global Variables before the function
int line_counter = 0;
string default_description = "None";
string[] stores = new string[999];

public int GetLineCounter ()
{
    line_counter++;
    return line_counter;
}
```

Note Declaring a variable outside the brackets that contain the code for the function makes that variable global in scope and accessible by any scripts that are called afterward. The one exception to this is in XSLT, where the variable must be declared inside the scope of the script (making the variable local and not available outside the script).

In general, it doesn't matter where you place the declaration of the global variable. Remember that you may have many Scripting functoids in your map, and you don't want to have to search for the one with a particular global variable. You should decide how to manage your global variables early and use the same technique in every map.

Tip We put all global variables in the first Scripting functoid in the map. Sometimes, this is the first data collection Scripting functoid, and sometimes, the Scripting functoid is specifically for the global variables. This method means we always know where our global variables are, as well as making it easy for a different mapper who must modify the map.

Accumulating an Output Counter in a Script

When you need to capture and output the number of occurrences of a particular input record, you use the Record Count functoid. But what if you need the number of occurrences of the input record that contain a specific value or that have a particular child element or record?

You turn to a global variable counter, of course. But rather than use the one from Listing 9-7, we will create a new one, so we can show the full organization. We will have three scripts.

The first script is in Listing 9-7 and must be linked to an output node that occurs before both of the other scripts. Note that this script does nothing but create the global variable store_counter.

Listing 9-7. *Creating the Global Variable for a Store Counter*

```
int store_counter;
public void DeclareVariables ()
{}
```

The second script is in Listing 9-8. This script increments the global variable store_counter each time a string is received that has a length greater than zero. This script must complete all processing before the third script executes.

Listing 9-8. *Incrementing the Store Counter*

```
public void IncrementStoreCounter (string store)
{
// If the input parameter has a value increment the counter
if (store.Length > 0) store_counter++;
}
```

The final script, shown in Listing 9-9, outputs the final value of the global variable store_counter.

Listing 9-9. *Output Final Value of Store Counter*

```
public int OutputStoreCounter ()
{
return store_counter;
}
```

Notice that the first two scripts, both with void return types, do not have output. They will still trigger the creation of the output node to which they are attached, however. Figure 9-5 presents our map.

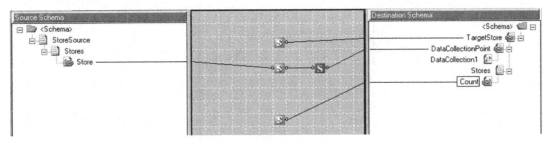

Figure 9-5. *The map for counting the number of stores*

The first script, which declares the global variable, is in the Scripting functoid attached to the root node `TargetPoint`. Since the script has no output and the root node is always output, we don't need to block anything. The second script, which tests for stores and increments the counter, is attached to the data collection record node. Even though the second script has no output, the data collection node would be created unless we block it. The Logical String functoid blocks the creation of that node. The third script, which outputs the number of stores, is attached to the output node into which we want that value placed. The source data and the output are shown in Listing 9-10.

Listing 9-10. *Source Data and Output of the Map for Counting the Number of Stores*

```
// Source data containing three Store nodes but only two stores
<ns0:StoreSource xmlns:ns0="http://chapter9.StoreSource">
  <Stores>
    <Store>Store</Store>
    <Store></Store>
    <Store>Store</Store>
  </Stores>
</ns0:StoreSource>

// Output of map
<ns0:TargetStore xmlns:ns0="http://chapter9.stores">
<Stores>
  <Count>2</Count>
</Stores>
</ns0:TargetStore>
```

Accumulating an Output Counter in an XSLT Script

Since you cannot declare global variables in an XSLT script, you are limited to local variables, which are only within the XSLT template. You can get around this problem by invoking a C# script from within the XSLT script. In the example shown in Listing 9-11, we use the same three C# scripts that you just saw. We modify the map by moving the output of the third script and by adding a fourth Scripting functoid. The map is shown in Figure 9-6.

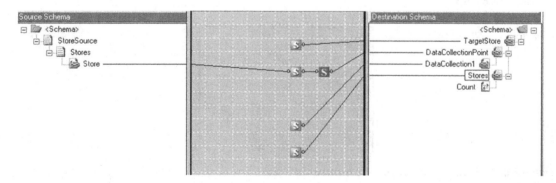

Figure 9-6. *A map using XSLT script to output accumulated data*

The Scripting functoid at the bottom contains the XSLT script from Listing 9-11 and will create the entire target Stores node. Notice that the Scripting functoid that holds the C# OutputStoreCounter script is now connected to the DataCollection1 node.

Listing 9-11. *XSLT Script to Output Accumulated Data*

```
// Create the target node Stores
<xsl:element name="ns0:Stores">
// Call the C# function OutputStoreCounter to retrieve the number of stores
  <xsl:variable name="TotalStores" select="userCSharp:OutputStoreCounter()"/>
// Create the child node Count
  <xsl:element name="Count">
// Output the number of stores
      <xsl:value-of select="$TotalStores"/>
  </xsl:element>
</xsl:element>
```

When the map in Figure 9-6 is run using the same input as shown in Listing 9-10, we get the same output as shown in Listing 9-10. Since both methods create exactly the same output, why would you want that added overhead of the XSLT script? Sometimes, when working with loops, you have to resort to XSLT to force the output of a node. You'll see examples of such cases in the four chapters that address looping.

Loading a Hard-Coded Reference List

Global variables provide the means to create lists of data that can be accessed throughout a map. Suppose you have many instances of a unit of measure in your source schema, and each value must be converted. "CA" would be converted to "CASE" for example. While a switch statement might suffice when only a few values were needed, a hash table is better when there are many values, because you can use the initial value as a key to look up the desired value.

Adding the hash table as a global variable is easy. We'll add it to our script from Listing 9-7 to get the script shown in Listing 9-12. We also choose to load the table using our DeclareVariables function.

Listing 9-12. *Adding the Global Variable for a Hash Table*

```
int store_counter;
System.Collections.Hashtable UOMTable = new System.Collections.Hashtable();

public void DeclareVariables ()
{
  UOMTable ["EA"] = "Per Each";
  UOMTable ["LB"] = "Pounds";
  UOMTable ["KG"] = "Kilograms";
}
```

The values are hard-coded. The value on the left (e.g., "EA") becomes the key while the value on the right (e.g., "Per Each") becomes the value to look up.

■**Caution** Hard-coded hash tables and arrays with global data should only be used for static lists with very little chance of modification. If a list is subject to modification, the hash table or array should be loaded from an external source when the map runs. We cover this type of loading in the next chapter.

Listing 9-13 contains the script that retrieves a value from the hash table. If the input parameter key is "LB", the script returns the value "Pounds".

Listing 9-13. *Script to Retrieve a Value from Hash Table*

```
public string ReturnUOM(string key)
{
//  Set default return value
  String retval = "Unknown";
//  Check to see if the key is found in the table
  if (UOMTable.ContainsKey(key))
//  If the key is there, retrieve the corresponding value
      retval = UOMTable[key].ToString();
  return retval;
}
```

Loading a Unique List from Input Data

One common situation where you need to collect data is when you must distill a list of values into a unique list. For example, your source data might contain many line items, each with the container number in which it is stored. Since many line items fit inside a container, any container numbers might occur several times. You might need to organize the output data by container number, thus you must create a method of controlling your output by container number. Listing 9-14 contains our script.

Listing 9-14. *Script to Load Container Numbers into a Hash Table*

```
System.Collections.Hashtable ContainerTable = new System.Collections.Hashtable();
public void LoadContainerTable(string item_number, string container_number)
{
// load the container number to the table
  ContainerTable[item_number] = container_number;
}
```

Now, we can traverse items each time we create a container output node and only output those items that belong to that container. The script to check to see if an item should be output in the current container is in Listing 9-15.

Listing 9-15. *Script to Check Line Item Container*

```
public string CheckContainer(string item_number, string container_number)
{
// Initialize return value to false
  string retval = "false";
// Get the container number for the item being processed
  string item_container = ContainerTable.Remove(item_number);
// If the item is in the container now being output, set the return value to true
  if (item_container == container_number) retval = "true";
  return retval;
}
```

Now, you can control your output using the hash table. Could you do the same thing using an array?

Arrays vs. Hash Tables

The examples to this point in this chapter show that a hash table is an effective method of providing a repository for data that has unique keys. In fact, a hash table may consist of keys that point to traditional arrays. The subject of hash tables and arrays is extensive and far too large for this book. We simplify it by saying that for our purposes, we determine which to use with three questions:

- Is there a unique key for each entry? If there is, the hash table scores a point. If there is no unique key, we must use the array.

- Are there multiple elements of data involved? Even when there is a unique key, the volume of data associated with each key may preclude use of a hash table. A social security number provides a unique key to an individual, but the amount of data available on the individual precludes using a hash table.

- What processing is required? If we need to sort the data once it is stored, an array is the better choice. If we need to maintain the order in which data is entered, we must use an array.

Using an Array to Control Data Selection for Output

Finally, let's look at the solution to the problem you saw at the beginning of this chapter. We build a map that uses an array to manipulate the source data in Listing 9-4. We divide the map into two pages so that we can see the layout better. Figure 9-7 shows the first page.

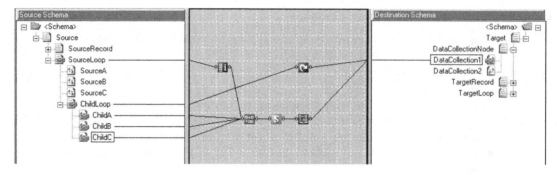

Figure 9-7. *Data collection page of an array map*

Every functoid on this page of the map is associated with collecting the data from the ChildLoop nodes for later output. Let's walk through the functionality step by step:

1. The Looping functoid causes the compiler to generate mapping code that causes the DataCollection1 node to loop once for each instance of the ChildLoop node.

2. The Cumulative Concatenate functoid (the right side of the Scripting functoid) is set to pull all the data that is present in source nodes ChildA, ChildB, and ChildC to the DataCollection1 node.

3. The Scripting functoid contains the code that will generate the array where we will store the data from the ChildLoop node.

4. The String Concatenate functoid (the left side of the Scripting functoid) performs two functions for us: it combines all the data into one string and formats the data.

5. The Iteration functoid (also on the left side of the map) provides a counter that tells us from which SourceLoop node we are receiving data. The counter returns 1 when the map begins to read the first ChildLoop node and continues to return 1 until all the ChildLoop nodes under that iteration of the SourceLoop node have been read. When the ChildLoop node is exited and then reentered, the Iteration functoid increments the counter.

■Note The map shown in Figure 9-7 does not block the output of the DataCollection node, because we want to see the data as it flows through the process. That is how we obtained the data in Listing 9-16.

Listing 9-16 shows what the data looks like when it leaves the String Concatenate functoid. There is one string for each of the nine ChildLoop nodes that are processed (three from each SourceLoop node).

Listing 9-16. *Data Strings As They Leave the String Concatenate Functoid*

```
1|ChildA1|ChildB1|ChildC1|
1|ChildA2|ChildB2|ChildC2|
1|ChildA3|ChildB3|ChildC3|
```

```
2|ChildA1-2|ChildB1-2|ChildC1-2|
2|ChildA2-2|ChildB2-2|ChildC2-2|
2|ChildA3-2|ChildB3-2|ChildC3-2|
3|ChildA1-3|ChildB1-3|ChildC1-3|
3|ChildA2-3|ChildB2-3|ChildC2-3|
3|ChildA3-3|ChildB3-3|ChildC3-3|
```

The data has been separated by pipe characters. Notice that the counter from the Iteration functoid is the first data item in each string and that the values of the counter indicate that there are three strings from each SourceLoop node. The string is terminated with a pipe as well. Figure 9-8 shows the inputs to the String Concatenate functoid.

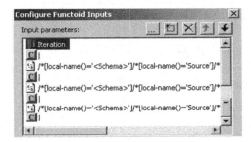

Figure 9-8. *Inputs to the String Concatenate functoid*

These strings of data pass one-by-one to the Scripting functoid, where the string is parsed and the data stored into an array. Listing 9-17 shows the script.

Listing 9-17. *Script that Parses the String and Puts Data into the Array*

```
// Define the array as a global variable for later access
string[,] childloopxref = new string[99,2];
// Initialize a row counter as a global so you can keep track
// of which row is to receive data
int row = 0;

public void CreateGlobals(string childloop)
{
// Define a length variable, a pipe position variable, and a
// storage variable for a string
  int len = 0;
  int pipe = 0;
  string sourceloop = "";

// Locate the offset into the input string of the first pipe
  pipe = childloop.IndexOf("|");
// Find the length of the input string
  len = childloop.Length - (pipe + 1);
```

```
// Get the first data item (the SourceNode counter)
   string source = childloop.Substring(0, pipe);
// Clip the characters just used including the pipe
   childloop = childloop.Substring(pipe + 1, len);

// Now loop once for each ChildLoop node in this SourceLoop node
   for (int i = 0; i < 3; i++)
   {
// Find the next position of the pipe
      pipe = childloop.IndexOf("|");
// Update the length of the string
      len = childloop.Length - (pipe+1);
//   Get the next ChildLoop node value from the string
      sourceloop = childloop.Substring(0, pipe);
// Put the current SourceLoop node counter value into the array
      childloopxref[row, 0] = source;
// Put the current ChildLoop node value into the second column of the array
      childloopxref[row, 1] = sourceloop;
// Clip the value and pipe just used
      childloop = childloop.Substring(pipe+1, len);
// Increment the array row counter
      row++;
   }
}
```

Figure 9-9 shows the first six rows of the array as populated by the script. The numbers of the parent SourceLoop nodes are in the 0 column, and the values from the ChildLoop nodes are in the 1 column. Once all data has been collected and placed into the array, we can begin outputting to the target.

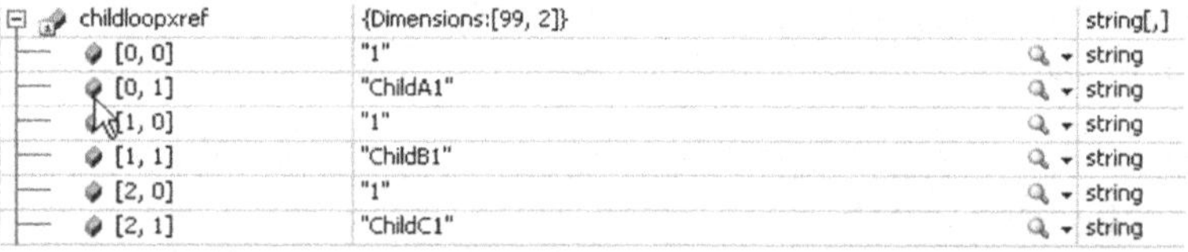

childloopxref	{Dimensions:[99, 2]}	string[,]
[0, 0]	"1"	string
[0, 1]	"ChildA1"	string
[1, 0]	"1"	string
[1, 1]	"ChildB1"	string
[2, 0]	"1"	string
[2, 1]	"ChildC1"	string

Figure 9-9. *Contents of the array*

The second page of the map, shown in Figure 9-10, is where we retrieve the data from the array and output it. Our goal is to output the correct ChildLoop data with each SourceLoop. We have four direct links on this page—three that output the data from SourceA, SourceB, and SourceC to the TargetA, TargetB, and TargetC nodes, respectively. The fourth outputs the data from the SourceRecordData node to the TargetRecordData node.

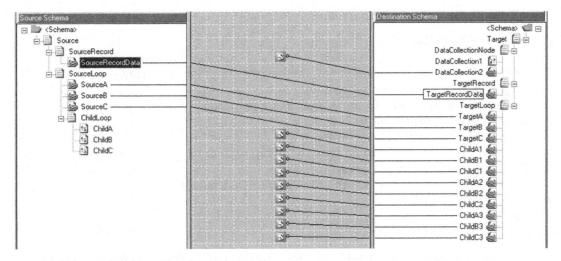

Figure 9-10. *The output page of the array map*

The Scripting functoids on the page contain the mechanisms by which we restructure the source data from multiple nodes to a single node. We are flattening the SourceLoop data. Notice that the first Scripting functoid is linked to a data collection node. The global variables we need to control the output have been placed there. The script is in Listing 9-18.

Listing 9-18. *Global Variables for Controlling Output*

```
// Create a variable to hold the number equating to the SourceLoop now being output
int outnode = 1;
// Create a variable to hold the current row number in the array for output
int outrow =0;

public void AnotherGlobals ()
{}
```

Tip You must have a function in the Scripting functoid even if the function does nothing and returns no value, as seen in Listing 9-18. Otherwise, you will get this error: XSL transform error: Unable to write output instance to the following <file:///C:\Documents and Settings\ Administrator\Local Settings\Temp_MapData\Map1_output.xml>. XSLT compile error at (10,37). See InnerException for details. 'userCSharp:()' is an invalid XPath expression. 'userCSharp:()' has an invalid qualified name.

The other nine Scripting functoids are each attached to one of the target nodes. Each outputs one value. The script for the first, connected to the target ChildA1 node, is in Listing 9-19.

Listing 9-19. *First Script in the Output Chain*

```
public string PutChildA1 ()
{
// Get the SourceLoop node number for the current row from the array
   string node = childloopxref[outrow, 0];
// Convert the node number to an integer for comparison
// to the current outnode value
   int nodenumber = Convert.ToInt16(node);
// If the SourceLoop node number from the array matches the current outnode
// return the value from the array
   if (nodenumber == outnode) return childloopxref[outrow,1];
// Else return nothing
   return "";
}
```

The next seven Scripting functoids, functoids two through eight, all contain the script in Listing 9-20, except for the function names, which are unique to each script.

Listing 9-20. *Script Used by Scripting Functoids Two Through Eight*

```
// The name changes to match the output node name
public string PutChildA2 ()
{
// Increment the row number so we point to the next row in  the array
   outrow++;
// Every thing else is the same as before
   string node= childloopxref[outrow, 0];
   int nodenumber = Convert.ToInt16(node);

   if (nodenumber== outnode) return childloopxref[outrow,1];
   return "";
}
```

Notice that the only difference between this script and the previous one, other than the function name, is that this one increments the row number. The ninth script is in Listing 9-21.

Listing 9-21. *Script Used by the Ninth Functoid*

```
// The name changes again to match the output node
public string PutChildC3 ()
{
// Increment the row pointer
   row++;
// Get the SourceLoop node number for the current row from the array
// and convert it to an integer
   string node= childloopxref[outrow, 0];
   int nodenumber = Convert.ToInt16(node);
// Initialize a return variable
```

```
  string retval = "";
// If the SourceLoop node number from the array matches the current outnode
//  put the array value into the return variable.
if (nodenumber== outnode) retval = childloopxref[outrow,1];
// Increment the current output node number for the next pass through the chain
  outnode++;
// Increment the current output row number for the next pass through the chain
  outrow++;
  return retval;
}
```

The main difficulty in managing the scripts in this map is that you must control the array pointers and keep track of where you are in the process in both collecting and outputting the data. Let's see the results of our map, shown in Listing 9-22.

Listing 9-22. *Output of the Array Map*

```
<ns0:Target xmlns:ns0="http://chapter9.Target1">
  <TargetRecord>
    <TargetRecordData>SourceRecordData</TargetRecordData>
  </TargetRecord>
  <TargetLoop>
    <TargetA>SourceA</TargetA>
    <TargetB>SourceB</TargetB>
    <TargetC>SourceC</TargetC>
    <ChildA1>ChildA1</ChildA1>
    <ChildB1>ChildB1</ChildB1>
    <ChildC1>ChildC1</ChildC1>
    <ChildA2>ChildA2</ChildA2>
    <ChildB2>ChildB2</ChildB2>
    <ChildC2>ChildC2</ChildC2>
    <ChildA3>ChildA3</ChildA3>
    <ChildB3>ChildB3</ChildB3>
    <ChildC3>ChildC3</ChildC3>
  </TargetLoop>
  <TargetLoop>
    <TargetA>SourceA2</TargetA>
    <TargetB>SourceB2</TargetB>
    <TargetC>SourceC2</TargetC>
    <ChildA1>ChildA1-2</ChildA1>
    <ChildB1>ChildB1-2</ChildB1>
    <ChildC1>ChildC1-2</ChildC1>
    <ChildA2>ChildA2-2</ChildA2>
    <ChildB2>ChildB2-2</ChildB2>
    <ChildC2>ChildC2-2</ChildC2>
    <ChildA3>ChildA3-2</ChildA3>
    <ChildB3>ChildB3-2</ChildB3>
    <ChildC3>ChildC3-2</ChildC3>
```

```
    </TargetLoop>
    <TargetLoop>
      <TargetA>SourceA3</TargetA>
      <TargetB>SourceB3</TargetB>
      <TargetC>SourceC3</TargetC>
      <ChildA1>ChildA1-3</ChildA1>
      <ChildB1>ChildB1-3</ChildB1>
      <ChildC1>ChildC1-3</ChildC1>
      <ChildA2>ChildA2-3</ChildA2>
      <ChildB2>ChildB2-3</ChildB2>
      <ChildC2>ChildC2-3</ChildC2>
      <ChildA3>ChildA3-3</ChildA3>
      <ChildB3>ChildB3-3</ChildB3>
      <ChildC3>ChildC3-3</ChildC3>
    </TargetLoop>
</ns0:Target>
```

We blocked output of the data collection nodes for this run. Notice that we have three `TargetLoop` nodes, each with data from the corresponding `SourceLoop` and `SourceLoop/ChildLoop` nodes.

Summary

In this chapter, we covered methods of collecting data from the source document and storing that data for later use in the map and illustrated how global variables are an invaluable tool for that process. We also presented some techniques for using hash tables and arrays to hold the source data for selective output.

The examples in this chapter are intentionally generic, and each one could be handled in multiple ways. In fact, each of us, the authors, may choose different methods to address the same issue. You will see many more examples of data collection and organization in subsequent chapters, particularly those that deal with EDI mapping.

Now that we have looked at how to handle data from the source file, we move in the next chapter to a similar but perhaps more imposing problem. What do you do if the data you need for your map is not available in your source file but has to be retrieved from some external location?

CHAPTER 10

■ ■ ■

Accessing External Data

In the previous chapters of Part 2, we discuss some of the basic techniques for handling data within a map. In all of the examples in those discussions, the data was available within the map, having arrived in the source data or having been entered as a constant, or literal, value. You can be certain that this will not always be the case.

At some point, you will find that you need data for a map that is not available in the source file and whose value is not known at run time, so it cannot be added as a constant. For example, we often encounter a problem with SAP transactions where a customer ID must be translated into an EDI sender ID or vice versa. The customer ID is in the SAP data file, but the EDI sender ID is not and must be picked up from an external source. Other business examples of the kind of translation that might require access to external data follow:

- Converting a delivery code into a specific carrier name and rate type

- Expanding a customer delivery address code into a complete address

- Transforming a customer part number into a manufacturer's part number

- Validating a code (such as a unit of measure) against a master list

The preferred solution to cases like the preceding one is to modify the application to add the needed data to the database. This way, the source file would contain the data in outbound transactions, and the application would do the lookup for translation in the inbound process. More often than not, of course, this solution is not practical. Costs, scheduling, complexity, lack of resources, and a number of other reasons may prevent you from modifying the database and/or application.

Another simple solution is hard-coding the needed data inside the map. Short lists of data can be coded into switch statements; longer lists can be loaded into global arrays or hash tables at the beginning of the map. These methods are effective when the amount of data is small and the values are static. If data values are volatile, the map must be modified, tested, and redeployed each time a value changes. Handling large volumes of data within the map may affect performance. This is when you must keep the data external to your map.

Getting to that data when you need it becomes the issue. In this chapter, we focus on two of several available methods of accessing external data: reading flat files and doing database table lookups. As we do this, we will also look at techniques for processing the retrieved data within a map. Although the information we cover is basic, the scripts in this chapter must be much more complex.

Using External Flat Files

One simple solution to retrieving lookup data is to use a flat file such as a comma-separated file derived by exporting data from a spread sheet. In such cases, nontechnical staff may be able to keep data in the file up to date. A flat file lookup mechanism requires only simple scripting, thus implementation is quick and easy. Also note that coordination with other groups such as database administration, security, and networking may not be required, further reducing the level of effort required. Finally, the flat file lookup method may be implemented as a temporary measure while more complex mechanisms are developed.

Retrieving a Single Value from a Flat File

We find that the most common requirement for this type of lookup is the need to retrieve one item from a list by key value. Many times, the list is very simple, looking like Figure 10-1.

Listing 10-1. *Example Flat File*

```
A344B2|88632
A20394|039485
A03249|78642
```

We would expect such a file to be much longer, of course. You could look up a value on either side of the pipe character in Listing 10-1, using A20394 to retrieve 039485 or using 039485 to retrieve A20394, for example. You only need one thing to perform such a lookup—a custom script to read the flat file and return the desired value. Look at Listing 10-2.

Listing 10-2. *Script to Look Up One Value*

```
public static string ShipToXref(string key)
{
// Hard-coded filename and other variables
  string xref = "C:\\FlatFile.txt";
  string line = "";
  string retval = "NOT FOUND";
  string match = "";
  int length = 0;
  bool found = false;
  int pipe = 0;

// Open the file for reading and create a line into which data is read
  FileStream filein = new FileStream(xref, FileMode.Open, FileAccess.Read);
  StreamReader readln = new StreamReader(filein);

// Continue reading until the end of file is reached
  while (readln.Peek() != -1)
  {
// Read a line from the file
    line = readln.ReadLine();
```

```
//  Find the position of the pipe character in the line
    pipe = line.IndexOf('|');
//  If no pipe is in the line (probable a comment line)
//  then go back to the start of the while loop
    if (pipe == -1) continue;
//  We are using the left side as our key, so substring the left value from the line
    match = line.Substring(0, pipe)
//  Check to see if the left value is our key
    found = match.Contains(key);
//  If we found our key, substring the right value and set it as the return value
    if (found)
       {
       length = line.Length;
       retval = line.Substring(pipe + 1, length - pipe -1);
//  We've found our value, so leave the while loop
       break;
       }
  }
//  Return either "NOT FOUND" or the value
  return retval;
}
```

Given A20394 as the search key, the script in Listing 10-2 returns the value 039485 from the list shown in Listing 10-2. The map is in Figure 10-1.

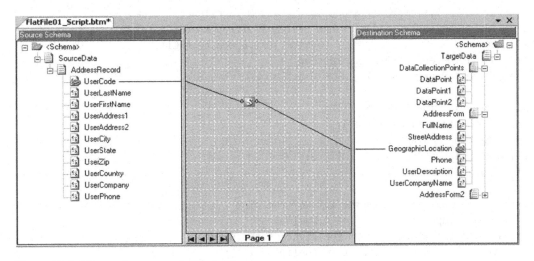

Figure 10-1. *Map using example file lookup*

Even if the list is simple many lookups may be required in each run of the map. When this is the case, using the method in Listing 10-2 is inefficient and a performance hog. We can solve those issues by loading the list into memory and keeping it there throughout the execution of the map. We need three things to do this:

- A global variable declaration that creates an array or a hash table into which we can store the contents of the file

- A custom script that reads the import file and loads the values into the global variable

- A custom script that retrieves values from the global variable and writes them to the correct nodes in the target

Listing 10-3 contains a script that creates a hash table as a global variable, reads data from a flat file, and loads the hash table.

Listing 10-3. *Script to Load Flat File Data into a Hash Table*

```
//  Create the hashtable that will hold the data
System.Collections.Hashtable XREFTable = new System.Collections.Hashtable();

public void LoadXREFTable()
{
  string inputLine;
  string keyval;
  string returnval;
  int delimPos = 0;
//  Hard-coded filename
  string tableLoc = "C:\\ProMapping\\SampleMaps\\Chapter_10\\Data\\ZipCodeXREF.txt";
//  Open the file and create a buffer into which data will be read
  System.IO.FileStream filein1 = new System.IO.FileStream(tableLoc,
               System.IO.FileMode.Open, System.IO.FileAccess.Read);
  System.IO.StreamReader reader1 = new System.IO.StreamReader(filein1,
                             System.Text.Encoding.ASCII);
//  Read until the end of file is reached
  while (reader1.Peek() != -1)
  {
//  Read the next line from the file
    inputLine = reader1.ReadLine();
//  Find the pipe character
    delimPos = inputLine.IndexOf("|", 0);
    if (delimPos > -1)
    {
//  Extract the key value from the left of the pipe
      keyval = inputLine.Substring(0, delimPos);
//  Extract the target value from the right of the pipe
      returnval = inputLine.Substring(delimPos + 1);
//  Insert the key value and return value into the next position in the hash table
      XREFTable[keyval] = returnval;
    }
  }
//  Close the file when the end of file is reached
  filein1.Close();
}
```

The script creates the hash table XREFTable as a global variable, opens the file, reads through each line in the file, and closes the file. As each line is read, the script adds an entry to the hash table. We did not include any error handling mechanisms for the sake of keeping the script simple. Whether or not you would need error handling depends on your confidence that the source file would exist and would have only valid data. Here are a couple of general points to note:

- The hash table is a global variable, because it is declared outside the LoadXREFTable function.

- The file locations in both these first scripts are hard-coded. Unless you have total control over the location of this script, you may want to make the file name and location input parameters to the Scripting functoid. Some alternate methods for getting the file name are discussed later in this chapter.

The input file used for this script is short, containing records with an ID code and a ZIP code, delimited with a pipe (|). Again, we would expect an actual file to be much longer.

Listing 10-4. *Flat File for Loading into Hash Table XREFTable*

```
0001|27607
0002|27344
```

The map uses a different script to output a value from the hash table. A sample such script, shown in Listing 10-5, receives the key from the source data as an input parameter. The script performs a hash table lookup to determine the target value and outputs the target value.

Listing 10-5. *Getting a Value from a Hash Table*

```
public string GetXREFValue(string inVal)
{
// Set a default value in case key is not found in hash table
  string retval = "Not Found";

// Get the value from the hash table based on the key.  If the key is found, put
// the value as the return value
  if ( XREFTable.ContainsKey(inVal))
      retval = XREFTable[inVal].ToString();
// Return either the value found in the hash table or the default value
 return retval;
}
```

Figure 10-2 presents a map that shows how this fits together. There are four functoids in the map:

- The top Scripting functoid contains the script (Listing 10-3) that reads the external file and fills the hash table. Scripting functoids that declare global variables and gather data should be linked to a node as close as possible to the top of the map, as shown here.

- The Logical String functoid blocks the output of the DataCollectionPoints node, since the top Scripting functoid has no output.

- The Looping functoid forces the output node AddressForm to loop once per iteration of the source node AddressRecord.

- The bottom Scripting functoid contains the script from Listing 10-5 that uses the key received from the source UserCode node to retrieve the correct value from the hash table and output it to the GeographicLocation node.

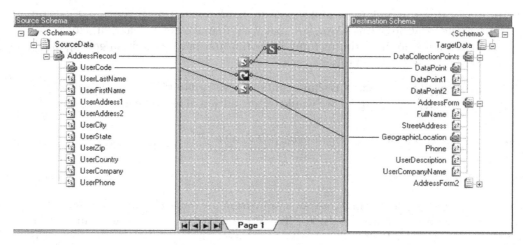

Figure 10-2. *A map for single value lookup*

Look at the output of the map in Listing 10-6. The input keys were 0001 and 0002 (there was no third key). If you look at Listing 10-4, you will see that the output values in Listing 10-6 are correct.

Listing 10-6. *Output of a Map for a Single Value Lookup*

```
<TargetData>
  <AddressForm>
    <GeographicLocation>27607</GeographicLocation>
  </AddressForm>
  <AddressForm>
    <GeographicLocation>27344</GeographicLocation>
  </AddressForm>
  <AddressForm>
    <GeographicLocation>Not Found</GeographicLocation>
  </AddressForm>
</TargetData>
```

Retrieving Multiple Values from a Flat File

Sometimes, your data file has many data fields, and you must retrieve multiple fields or a specific field from within the data. Listing 10-7 shows two records from our new flat file.

Listing 10-7. *Flat File Records for Retrieving Multiple Values*

```
0001|John|Wainwright|7008 Robbie Drive||Raleigh|NC|27607|USA
0002|Jim|Dawson|230 Shadowsmoke Lane||Siler City|NC|27344|USA
```

Notice that we still have data with keys, so we can continue using a hash table as the repository for the data we retrieve from the file. In fact, we will use the same script as before, the script in Listing 10-3, to load the data into the hash table. Again, this flat file has a key for each record. This time, the data will be stored in the table in the format in Listing 10-8.

Listing 10-8. *Data in the Hash Table*

```
Key              Data Value
0001        John|Wainwright|7008 Robbie Drive||Raleigh|NC|27607|USA
0002        Jim|Dawson|230 Shadowsmoke Lane||Siler City|NC|27344|USA
```

Since the hash table holds only two objects, the key and the value, we store the entire string as the value. This means that, when we retrieve a value from the hash table, we must break the string apart if we need to access specific fields such as the ZIP code. Our scenario requires us to do this as we must output different fields to different nodes in the map. Let's look at the map, which is in Figure 10-3.

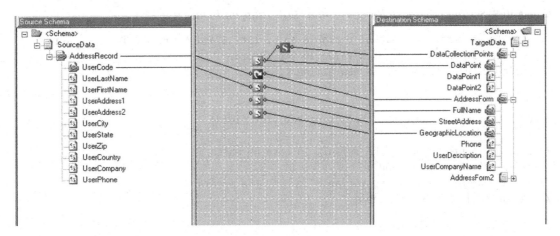

Figure 10-3. *A map for retrieving multiple values from a flat file*

This time we have six functoids in the map. Let's review what each does before we drill down to the scripts inside.

- The top Scripting functoid contains the script from Listing 10-3. That script, as you have already seen, reads the flat file and populates the hash table.

- The Logical String functoid serves the same purpose as before by blocking the output of the DataCollectionPoints node.

- The Looping Functoid forces the map to output one AddressForm node for each source AddressRecord node.

- The second Scripting functoid does several things. On each pass through the AddressForm loop, it extracts the appropriate record from the hash table, splits the fields of the record apart, and stores them into an array. It next extracts the full name from the array and outputs that value to the FullName node. The record that is extracted from the array is determined by the key, which is received from the UserCode node. A second input parameter, typed into the Configure Functoid Inputs pane of the Scripting functoid, identifies the field.

- The third Scripting functoid extracts the street address fields from the array and outputs the value to the StreetAddress node.

- The fourth Scripting functoid extracts the city, state, and ZIP fields from the array and outputs the value to the GeographicLocation node.

Let's examine the scripts in detail. We don't need to examine the script from the first Scripting functoid, since that is the same one we covered earlier. See Listing 10-3. That script read the flat file and placed the data into the hash table. Listing 10-4 shows the script from the second scripting functoid.

Listing 10-9. *Script to Extract a Record from a Hash Table and Place It in an Array*

```
// Create an array as a global variable so scripts 3 and 4 can use it.  The array
//  has 10 fields, one for each value in the record.
  public string[] AddressRec = new string [10];

//
  public string GetAddressString(string key, int field)
{
// Set the return value to the default in case no match is found
  string retval = "Not Found";
// Create a temporary string variable to hold the record
/  extracted from the hash table
  string addressString = "";

// initialize the array
  string initString = "|||||||||";
// fill the array with empty nodes in case there is no record for the key
  AddressRec = initString.Split(new char[1] { '|' });

// Check to see if the hash table contains the key
  if (XREFTable.ContainsKey(key))
```

```
  {
// The key was found, so pull the value from the hash table
// and put it into the variable
    addressString = XREFTable[key].ToString();
// Use the Split function to extract the fields from the string
// and place them into the array
    AddressRec = addressString.Split(new char[1] { '|' });
// Get the value from the specified field in the array and make it the return value
    retval = AddressRec[field];
  }
  return retval;
}
```

When the script in Listing 10-9 completes, a value is output to the FullName node. In the script, we only output one field, the last name, from the array. That's because the field parameter we put in the Scripting functoid is 1. Since arrays are zero-based, 1 points to the second field.

We could use this script in each Scripting functoid from here on, but doing so would cause the array to be rebuilt each time we extract data. Fortunately, we made the array a global variable, so we can use a shorter script to extract data from here on in the map.

Note We chose to output one value to each target node in this example. If you wanted to output "Last name, First name" as a value you could do so. However, that would require a field parameter to be interpreted as requesting that format and additional code to recognize that parameter, extract two fields from the array, and concatenate them into one value. We felt that the additional code to do this would make understanding the basic functionality of these scripts more difficult.

The third Scripting functoid outputs the street address, extracted from field two of the array that was created in the previous script. Obviously, this Scripting functoid must appear after the array has been created. The script, shown in Listing 10-10, extracts the desired field from the array and outputs the retrieved value to the StreetAddress node.

Listing 10-10. *Script to Extract a Value from the Previously Created Array*

```
// The input parameter field is typed into the Configure Functoid Inputs panel
// In this case the field parameter is set to "2".
public string GetAddressElement(string field)
{
// Initialize the return value in case the field has no data
  string retval = "Not Found";

// Extract the correct value from the array and store it in a temporary variable
  string addressString = AddressRec[field];
// Check to see if a value was retrieved from the array
```

```
    if (addressString != null)
// If a value was found, put it in the return variable, replacing the default value
        retval = addressString;
    return retval;
}
```

The script in Listing 10-10 used the global array built by the script in Listing 10-9. The fourth script, the one that outputs the geographic location, takes advantage of the script in Listing 10-10 by using the same function. See Listing 10-11.

Listing 10-11. *Script to Call the Function Used Earlier in the Map*

```
// Code is in previous Scripting functoid {TargetDate/AddressForm/StreetAddress}
public string GetAddressElement(string field)
{
}
```

As you can see, this script contains no operative code. Remember that when two or more Scripting functoids contain functions that have the same name, the code in the first one that is accessed becomes the default code for all of them. Thus the script in Listing 10-11 invokes the code contained in the script in Listing 10-10. Since the input parameter to the script in Listing 10-11 is 4, this time, a different field is returned.

Tip When you use a call to a previous script, as we did in Listing 10-11, always put a comment in the code that specifies the target node to which the original script is connected. That way, you can easily find and examine the code that is invoked. Otherwise, you have to click Scripting functoid after Scripting functoid trying to find the one that has the code.

When we test the map in Figure 10-3, we get the output shown in Listing 10-12.

Listing 10-12. *Output from the Map for Retrieving Multiple Values from a Flat File*

```
<TargetData>
  <AddressForm>
    <FullName>Wainwright</FullName>
    <StreetAddress>7008 Robbie Drive</StreetAddress>
    <GeographicLocation>Raleigh</GeographicLocation>
  </AddressForm>
  <AddressForm>
    <FullName>Dawson</FullName>
    <StreetAddress>230 Shadowsmoke Lane</StreetAddress>
    <GeographicLocation>Siler City</GeographicLocation>
  </AddressForm>
  <AddressForm>
    <FullName>Not Found</FullName>
    <StreetAddress>Not Found</StreetAddress>
```

```
      <GeographicLocation>Not Found</GeographicLocation>
    </AddressForm>
</TargetData>
```

Retrieving Values from a Flat File Using an Array

Sometimes, you aren't lucky enough to have a key in your flat file. Listing 10-13 shows our flat file with more records and with the key removed from each record.

Listing 10-13. *Revised Flat File with No Keys*

```
John|Wainwright|7008 Robbie Drive||Raleigh|NC|27607|USA
Jane|Smith|230 Shadowsmoke Lane||Montreal|QC|CAN
Jim|Dawson|230 Shadowsmoke Lane||Siler City|NC|27344|USA
```

As you see, none of the fields in these records are assured to have unique values, thus neither field can be used as a key. Listing 10-14 contains a script that reads the file and loads the data into an array.

Listing 10-14. *Script to Load an Unkeyed Flat File into an Array*

```
// Create global array.  Size must be greater than the possible number of records.
   string[,] AddressRec = new string [10,10];
// Create record counter for output scripts in later functoids
int outputrecord = 0;

public bool BuildAddressArray(string dummy)
{
// Hardcoded filename - could be input as a parameter
   string flatfile = "E:\\Solutions\\10_Using External Data\\10_Using External
         Data\\MapSamples_Chapter_10\\Chapter_10\\Data\\
         AddressXREF_noIndex.txt";
   string line = "";
   string field = "";
   string pipe = "|";
   int record = 0;
   int pipepos = 0;
   int length = 0;
// Open the file and create a stream reader
   System.IO.FileStream filein = new System.IO.FileStream(flatfile,
         System.IO.FileMode.Open, System.IO.FileAccess.Read);
   System.IO.StreamReader readln = new System.IO.StreamReader(filein);
// Loop through each record in the file until the end
   while (readln.Peek() != -1)
   {
// Read the next line from the file
      line = readln.ReadLine();
// Protect against blank lines at the end of the file,
```

```
//  exit while loop if line is blank
    if (line.Length < 1) break;
//  Loop through for statement once for each field in the record
//  (zero-based counter)
//  The variable i is the current field in the array
    for (int i = 0; i < 8; i++ )
    {
//  Find the first pipe in the line
        pipepos = line.IndexOf(pipe);
//  Substring the first field
        field = line.Substring(0, pipepos);
//  Put the field in the array
        AddressRec[record,i] = field;
//  Compute the length of the line minus the field just completed plus the pipe
        length = line.Length-pipepos-1;
//  Remove the field just processed by clipping that field plus the pipe
        line = line.Substring(pipepos+1, length);
    }
//  Move to the next row in the array
  record++;
}
//  Close the file
filein.Close();
//  Output boolean false to block output of DataCollectionPoints node
return false;
}
```

Notice that this time we use a Boolean return value to block output of the DataCollectionPoints node. When the script finishes, we have three records in our array, each with eight columns, as shown Table 10-1.

Table 10-1. *Contents of the Array Created by the Script in Listing 10-13*

0	1	2	3	4	5	6	7
0	John	Wainwright	7008 Robbie Drive	Raleigh	NC	27607	USA
1	Jane	Smith	230 Shadowsmoke Lane	Montreal	QC		CAN
2	Jim	Dawson	230 Shadowsmoke Lane	Siler City	NC	27344	USA

Figure 10-4 shows the map in which we use this script. The script is in the top Scripting functoid. The Logical String functoid blocks the output of the DataCollectionPoints node.

The Looping functoid forces one AddressForm node to be created for each AddressRecord node. None of our output comes from the source data, but there are three AddressRecord nodes in the source, and they drive the creation of three AddressForm nodes.

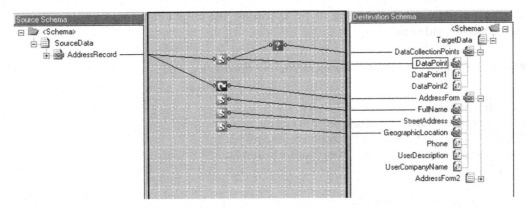

Figure 10-4. *A map using data from an array as output*

The bottom three Scripting functoids each output one field from the array. Listing 10-15 shows the three scripts that are in these Scripting functoids. Remember that the row indicator variable, outputrecord, is initialized as a global variable in the first script (Listing 10-14). On the first pass through the AddressForm node, outputrecord is 0. The last script increments outputrecord so that in the next pass the value is 1, and so forth.

Listing 10-15. *Scripts to Extract Data from the Array*

```
// Script to output to the FullName node
public string GetName()
  {
//  outputrecord is the number of the current row in the array; "1" is the field
//  in  the array where the name is stored
  return AddressRec[outputrecord,1];
  }

// Script to output to the StreetAddress node
public string GetAddress()
  {
//  outputrecord is the number of the current row in the array; "2" is the field
//  in the array where the address is stored
  return AddressRec[outputrecord,2];
  }

// Script to output to the GeographicLocation node
public string GetCity()
  {
//  outputrecord is the number of the current row in the array; "4" is the field
//  in the array where the city is stored
  return AddressRec[outputrecord++,4];
  }
```

The output of the map is in Listing 10-16. As you see, the output data corresponds to the data in the flat file and in the array.

Listing 10-16. *Output of the Map Extracting Data from the Array*

```
<TargetData>
  <AddressForm>
    <FullName>Wainwright</FullName>
    <StreetAddress>7008 Robbie Drive</StreetAddress>
    <GeographicLocation>Raleigh</GeographicLocation>
  </AddressForm>
  <AddressForm>
    <FullName>Smith</FullName>
    <StreetAddress>230 Shadowsmoke Lane</StreetAddress>
    <GeographicLocation>Montreal</GeographicLocation>
  </AddressForm>
  <AddressForm>
    <FullName>Dawson</FullName>
    <StreetAddress>230 Shadowsmoke Lane</StreetAddress>
    <GeographicLocation>Siler City</GeographicLocation>
  </AddressForm>
</TargetData>
```

Using the BizTalk Database Functoids with External Data

Sometimes, your data may be stored in a SQL server database rather than in a file. BizTalk includes several database functoids that provide access to information in a database table. Our next example uses three of those functoids to illustrate how to retrieve data from such a database table. We look at the Database Lookup, Error Return, and Value Extractor functoids.

■**Note** Of the ten database functoids available, we cover only three. The BizTalk help files contain a functoid reference (`Microsoft BizTalk Server 2006 R2 Help/Technical Reference/Developers Reference/Functoid Reference`). Space limitations preclude us from covering all the functoids in this book.

The Database Lookup functoid is used to extract information from a database and store it as a Microsoft ActiveX Data Object (ADO) record set. Four input parameters, in this order, are required:

1. Lookup value

2. Database connection string

3. Table name

4. Column name

We use the Error Return database functoid as a debugging tool to capture and return information about errors, such as database connection failures, that occur during run time. The only input parameter is a link from the Database Lookup functoid.

The Value Extractor functoid extracts the appropriate value from a record set returned by the Database Lookup functoid. Two inputs are required, in the following order:

1. Link to the Database Lookup functoid

2. Column name

Retrieving a Single Value Using Database Functoids

The Database Lookup Functoid is used when you need one value from a single row in a database table. We replace our flat file from the previous examples in this chapter with a custom table, custAddress, that resides in our ProMapping database. The table has eight columns, as shown in Figure 10-5.

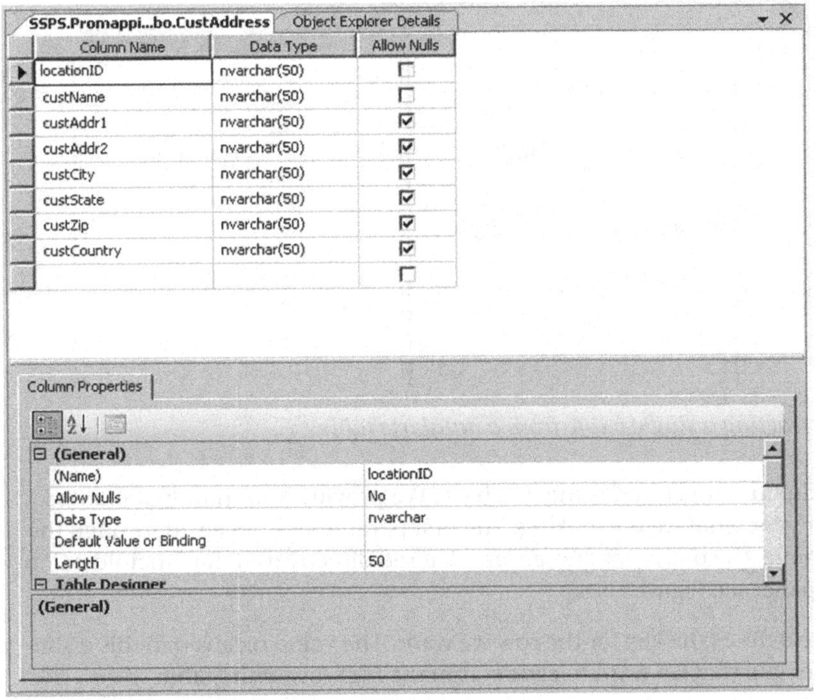

Column Name	Data Type	Allow Nulls
locationID	nvarchar(50)	☐
custName	nvarchar(50)	☐
custAddr1	nvarchar(50)	☑
custAddr2	nvarchar(50)	☑
custCity	nvarchar(50)	☑
custState	nvarchar(50)	☑
custZip	nvarchar(50)	☑
custCountry	nvarchar(50)	☑
		☐

Column Properties

(General)	
(Name)	locationID
Allow Nulls	No
Data Type	nvarchar
Default Value or Binding	
Length	50

Table Designer

(General)

Figure 10-5. *Column definitions of the custAddress table*

Figure 10-6 depicts the open data with the data visible. There are two rows populated with data and a third row that is empty.

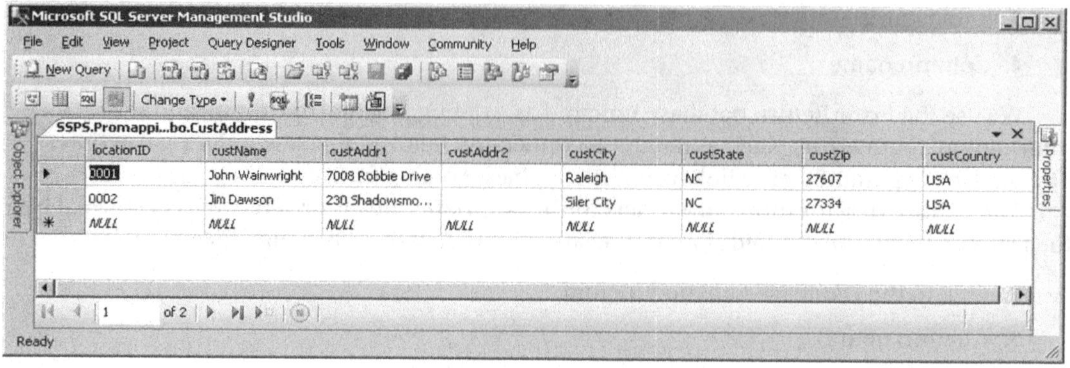

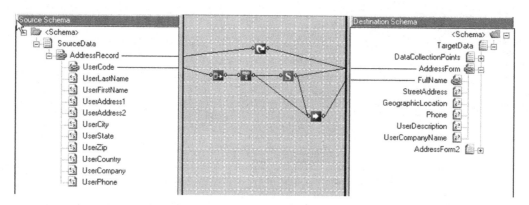

Figure 10-6. *View of the data in the custAddress table*

The map for this example is in Figure 10-7. The Looping functoid again forces the creation of one AddressForm node for each source AddressRecord node. The Logical String and Value Mapping functoids block the output of the FullName node if no value is returned from the database. These you've seen before in other maps. The Database Lookup functoid and the Value Extractor functoids are new.

Figure 10-7. *A map for extracting a single value from a database table*

The Database Lookup functoid queries the database. We provide four input parameters to that functoid to specify for what we are looking. The first parameter is received through the link from the UserCode node; the other parameters are entered directly into the functoid's Configure Functoid Inputs pane; see Figure 10-8:

- The lookup value defines the key for the row we want. The value received in this example is 0001, so the data that we want to extract is in the first row of the table.

- The connection string is Data Source=SSPS;Initial Catalog=ProMapping;Trusted_Connection=Yes;Provider=SQLOLEDB;.

- The table name is CustAddress.

- The column name, which tells us which column to use as the key, is locationID.

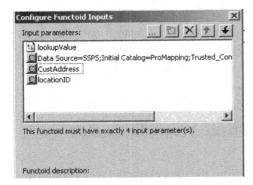

Figure 10-8. *Input parameters for the Database Lookup functoid*

The second database functoid is the Value Extractor, which has two inputs; see Figure 10-9. The first input is a link to the Database Lookup functoid. The second input is the column name containing the value we want.

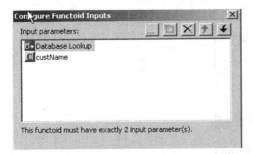

Figure 10-9. *Input parameters for the Value Extractor Functoid*

When these two database functoids execute, the Database Lookup functoid goes to the table and returns the requested row. The Value Extractor functoid then extracts the desired value from the returned row. If you look back at Figure 10-6, you will see that the value in the custName column of row one is John Wainwright.

Our source file for this map has two AddressRecord nodes, so we will produce two AddressForm nodes, forcing two queries to the database functoids. The output of the map is in Listing 10-17.

Listing 10-.17 Output of a Map for Extracting a Single Value from a Database Table

```
<TargetData>
  <AddressForm>
    <FullName>John Wainwright</FullName>
  </AddressForm>
  <AddressForm>
    <FullName>Jim Dawson</FullName>
  </AddressForm>
</TargetData>
```

■**Caution** The Value Extractor functoid returns a value only from the specified column. If more than one record is retrieved by the Database Lookup functoid, the Value Extractor functoid returns the value from the first record in the record set.

Retrieving Multiple Values Using Multiple Value Extractor Functoids

The same process can be used to return multiple fields from the data extracted by a Database Lookup functoid. See Figure 10-10.

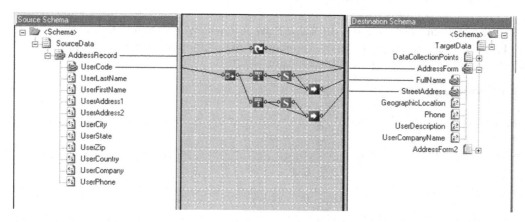

Figure 10-10. *A map using multiple Value Extractor functoids*

All we have done in this map is to add a second Value Extractor functoid along with an additional Logical String/Value Mapping pair of functoids. The column name input to the second Value Extractor functoid is custAddr1, which means that the StreetAddress node will also contain data when the map is executed.

■**Caution** Using the database functoids works well for outputting a few fields. However, each Value Extractor functoid causes the Database Lookup functoid to reconnect to the database. Outputting large numbers of fields might cause a performance issue. When this occurs, you should use an external assembly that is called from your map. Writing and deploying external assemblies is beyond the scope of this chapter.

Locating External Files with Path Names and Connect Strings

When you need to access external data, whether from a flat file or a database, you must provide the functoids and/or scripts with specific information on where to locate the data, the file name for the flat file and the connection string for database lookups, for example. In our examples, we have hard-coded the information in either the script or the functoid.

Hard-coding this information is a quick way to set up testing during development and for proof-of-concept models, but you should not hard-code the information for use in a production environment. Two major reasons are first, security and second, change control.

Security is an issue because usernames, passwords, and other secure information are often required in these strings. When you put this information as clear text in files or scripts, you are exposing your system.

Change control is another reason. Server names change, often as you move from development to QA to testing. File locations change. Database tables change names. You do not want to have to track down every instance of a server name, user, or password when one changes and then modify every place you find.

Fortunately, there are several places where you can store this kind of information securely and retrieve it only when needed. You also need to make a change in only one location when a change is necessary. We will cover three places.

Using the Machine Name

One simple solution to storing nonsecure information, especially when you have multiple environments, is to hard-code the string for each environment in a script. You can execute the script and store the value in a global variable for use throughout your map. Listing 10-18 shows an example.

Listing 10-18. *Using the Machine Name to Determine a Parameter*

```
// Make the string a global variable that can be used throughout the map
string fileLoc = "";

public string GetMachineName()
{
// If the map is on SSPS01, use this path
  if (machineName == "SSPS01")
     fileLoc = "c:\inputfile\mappingBook\Xref.txt;
// If the map is on SSPS02, use this path
  else if (machineName == "SSPS02")
     fileLoc = "d:\xreffiles\MapBookCustXref.txt;
return "";
}
```

This system works well in a very stable environment when there is no secure information involved. Of course, the script must be in every map that needs to access a flat file, so changing machines means recoding in every map.

Using System Environment Variables

A much better option is to use a system environment variable, or EVAR. This method eliminates hard-coding the values in your maps and scripts and is secure. You must be an administrator on a machine in order to implement this method on that machine. This means that you may need IT assistance to promulgate the implementation up through production. Let's see how to use an EVAR.

Open the Control Panel on your system, and double-click the System icon. Select the Advanced tab to get the view shown in Figure 10-11.

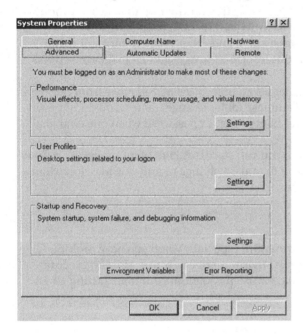

Figure 10-11. *System Properties Advanced Tab*

Next, click the Environment Variables button to get the Environment Variables dialog shown in Figure 10-12.

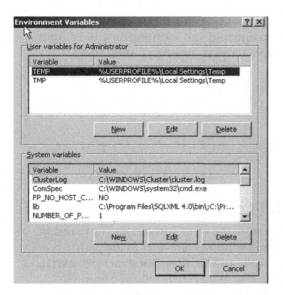

Figure 10-12. *Environment Variables dialog*

We are interested in the system variables displayed in the bottom pane. Click the New button at the bottom below the "System variables" pane to get the New System Variable pop-up window depicted in Figure 10-13.

Figure 10-13. *New System Variable editing window*

Type the name of your variable (make it a useful name) and the value for the variable. As you see, we named our variable MapBookConnectString and put the database connection string we used earlier as the value. Click OK three times to exit all three windows. Now, restart the machine.

Caution A major drawback to using environmental variables is the requirement to restart the server to register the variable with the system. Make sure your production machines can be restarted when you deploy the maps that use an environmental variable.

You use a simple custom script in a Scripting functoid to retrieve this variable for use in your map. When used with the Database Lookup functoid, the Scripting functoid output would be the second input to that functoid. A sample script is shown in Listing 10-19.

Listing 10-19. *Script to Retrieve an Environmental Variable*

```
public string ReturnConnectString()
{
  return System.Environment.GetEnvironmentVariable("MapBookConnectString");
}
```

Using the Machine Configuration File

Using the machine configuration file allows you to store the value without having to restart your machine. You can find this file under the default windows directory in the path `Microsoft.NET\Framework\<version>\CONFIG`. The file is an XML file named `machine.config`.

The machine configuration file has the root tag `<configuration>` followed immediately by the child node `<configSections>`. This node must always be the first child node. The `<configSections>` node should contain a child node that defines `appsettings`. That node would begin with `<section name="appSettings"` and continue with the definition of `appsettings`. If this node exists you can add your information to the file.

Insert a new node, `<appSettings>`, following the end tag of the `<configSections>` node. If an `<appSettings>` node already exists in the file, add your key node to the existing node. The result should look like Listing 10-20.

Listing 10-20. *Adding a Key to the <appSettings> Node*

```
<appSettings>
  <add key="MapBookConnectString" value="Data Source=SSPSI;Initial
                    Catalog=MappingBook;Trusted_Connection=Yes;" />
</appSettings>
```

Of course, if the `<appSettings>` node already existed, there would be other `<add key>` nodes. Once you modify the machine configuration file, you can access your key value from a Scripting functoid. An example of the code is in Listing 10-21.

Listing 10-21. *Script to Retrieve a Key Value from the Machine Configuration File*

```
public string GetConfigString(string custLoc)
{
  string connectString =
          System.Configuration.ConfigurationSettings.AppSettings.Get
                            ("MapBookConnectString");
return connectString;
}
```

> **Caution** This solution is deceptively easy to implement. However, you are making changes to a system file and if you make a mistake you might *really make a mistake*. Backup the `machine.config` file before you make changes!

Using an Application Configuration File

The `BTSNTSvc.exe.config` file, found in `Program Files\Microsoft BizTalk` is similar to the `machine.config` file but is specific to the BizTalk application. This file is safer to use.

In this file, the exact same `appSettings` node can be added, and it can be accessed by the same script noted previously. In fact, when the code executes, it will first check the machine configuration settings, and if the script is not found there, it will examine the application configuration file. The `appSettings` node should be inserted after the run time node.

> **Note** If you are testing your maps in Dev Studio, the BizTalk application configuration file will not be accessed. Instead, the application configuration file for Visual Studio, `devenv.exe.config`, is accessed. This configuration file is found in the `C:\Program Files\Microsoft Visual Studio 8\Common7\IDE` folder and looks similar to the `BTSNTSvc.exe.config` file.

BizTalk Cross-Reference Tables

The BizTalk cross-reference tables are built into the BizTalkMgmt database. As we have not yet chosen to use the tables, we shall not cover them except for a few notes. There are custom functoids available that access these tables, so custom scripts are not needed. An import wizard is available to assist you in populating the tables, and the tables can be deployed from environment to environment. The main drawback to using these tables and the custom functoids is that documentation on their use is inadequate.

Fortunately, there is reference material that provides a good view of the tables and good working examples of how to use them. We recommend you look at *BizTalk 2006 Recipes: A Problem-Solution Approach* by Mark Beckner, Ben Goeltz, Brandon Gross, Brennan O'Reilly, Stephen Roger, Mark Smith, and Alexander West (Apress, 2006); specifically, see Chapter 2, Recipes 2-9 through 2-13.

Summary

This chapter has provided a look at some ways of accessing data that does not arrive in the source file. The need for access to external data appears frequently in implementations, and the method chosen to provide that access is often driven by the client's desire to adhere to an existing process external to BizTalk.

Next, we move to one of the most problematic areas of BizTalk mapping—looping. The subject of looping is so critical that we dedicate four chapters to it. Next, Chapter 11 covers basic looping; then Chapter 12 goes into more difficult looping. Finally, in the EDI section, Chapter 14 addresses general EDI looping, and Chapter 17 discusses the dreaded HL loop.

PART 3

■■■

Looping

CHAPTER 11

■ ■ ■ ■

Using Basic Looping Controls

The most common and most challenging problems encountered with any mapping engine often involve looping. This chapter describes how the BizTalk mapping engine handles looping and presents a variety of techniques that may be used to solve basic looping problems. We will not discuss these techniques from a performance point of view, as each situation is different and may behave differently depending on the structure of the transactions and amount of data processed. If performance might be an issue, you should bench test different techniques with your data to determine if there is a significant performance difference in your situation.

Understanding Loops

A loop is repeated instance of a record. Listing 11-1 contains a loop of four DETAIL nodes.

Listing 11-1. *Loop of Four DETAIL Nodes*

```
<DETAIL>data</DETAIL>
<DETAIL>data</DETAIL>
<DETAIL>data</DETAIL>
<DETAIL>data</DETAIL>
```

Loops may also have child loops, called nested loops. In Listing 11-2 the first DETAIL node contains a nested SUBDETAIL loop.

Listing 11-2. *Nested SUBDETAIL Loops*

```
<DETAIL>data</DETAIL>
   <SUBDETAIL>data</SUBDETAIL>
   <SUBDETAIL>data</SUBDETAIL>
   <SUBDETAIL>data</SUBDETAIL>
<DETAIL>data</DETAIL>
<DETAIL>data</DETAIL>
<DETAIL>data</DETAIL>
```

■ **Note** BizTalk 2006 R2 and BizTalk 2009 schemas for EDI data always have loop header nodes that identify the start of each instance of a loop, with the name usually including the word "Loop". This means you can easily look at the data and determine where the loops are. BizTalk 2002 and 2004 schemas and non-BizTalk schemas, such as Covast schemas, may not use loop header nodes, forcing you to analyze the data and/or the document specification carefully to determine where the loops occur.

When the source and target loop structures are the same, mapping is normally not complicated by their presence. When the loop structures differ, mapping is often more difficult. Listing 11-3 shows matching source and target schemas. The node names differ between the two, but the data structure is the same since DETAIL data is LINE data and SUBDETAIL data is SUBLLINE data.

Listing 11-3. *Matching Looping Structures*

Source
```
<DETAIL>data</DETAIL>
  <SUBDETAIL>data</SUBDETAIL>
  <SUBDETAIL>data</SUBDETAIL>
  <SUBDETAIL>data</SUBDETAIL>
<DETAIL>data</DETAIL>
<DETAIL>data</DETAIL>
<DETAIL>data</DETAIL>
```

Target
```
<LINE>data</LINE>
  <SUBLINE>data</SUBLINE>
  <SUBLINE>data</SUBLINE>
  <SUBLINE>data</SUBLINE>
<LINE>data</LINE>
<LINE>data</LINE>
<LINE>data</LINE>
```

Listing 11-4 contains source and target structures that do not match. In the target schema the SUBLINE is no longer nested under the LINE loop.

Listing 11-4. *Looping Structures That Do Not Match*

Source
```
<DETAIL>data</DETAIL>
  <SUBDETAIL>data</SUBDETAIL>
  <SUBDETAIL>data</SUBDETAIL>
  <SUBDETAIL>data</SUBDETAIL>
<DETAIL>data</DETAIL>
<DETAIL>data</DETAIL>
<DETAIL>data</DETAIL>
```

Target
```
<LINE>data</LINE>
<LINE>data</LINE>
<LINE>data</LINE>
<LINE>data</LINE>
<SUBLINE>data</SUBLINE>
<SUBLINE>data</SUBLINE>
<SUBLINE>data</SUBLINE>
```

■Caution When the looping structure in the source does not match the structure in the target, you may need to override the compiler-generated looping. This is particularly true when you must map data from two or more looping nodes in the source to data within a single target node. In most cases, use of the Looping functoid will be sufficient. In other cases, you may need to use programming logic.

Understanding BizTalk Mapping Engine's Basic Looping Concepts

Understanding how to handle complex looping problems with BizTalk 2006 R2 begins with understanding the basic looping constructs that are built into the mapping engine. You must base your foundations on these concepts:

- The BizTalk mapping engine infers looping based on the source schema structure and generates XSLT code based on that inference.

- The Looping functoid overrides the inferred mapping in simple situations, causing the mapping engine to generate XSLT code based on the Looping functoid rather than on the schema structure.

- Complex looping situations, such as the one we just discussed, may cause the mapping engine to produce conflicting logic, no matter whether inferred mapping, the Looping functoid, or a combination of the two are used.

The BizTalk mapping engine infers looping. Let's first look at a simple map with no looping and then look at the same map with looping. We'll use the map in Figure 11-1 for the first example.

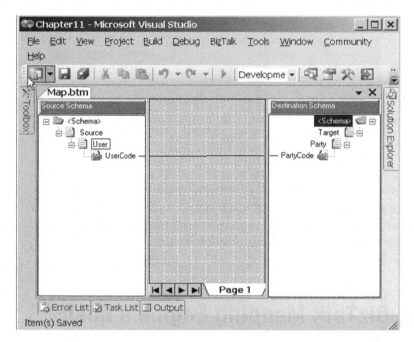

Figure 11-1. *A basic map*

In this basic map the source node UserCode minimum and maximum occurrences property is set to 1:1, which means it must occur once and only once, thus it is not a looping node. The source element PartyCode also is 1:1. The source node UserCode links to the target node PartyCode. Since both nodes should only occur once, we expect the map to create only one target PartyCode node. When you compile this map, the XSLT shown in Listing 11-5 is generated.

Listing 11-5. *Basic Map XSLT*

```
<ns0:Target>
  <Party>
    <PartyCode>
      <xsl:value-of select="User/UserCode/text()" />
    </PartyCode>
  </Party>
</ns0:Target>
```

Notice that there is no code in the XSLT that indicates that more than one instance of data is expected on either side of the map. Now, let's change the source schema so that the source node User has a minimum and maximum repetition of 1:100, making it a looping node. It now repeats one time to 100 times. We replace the source schema in the map with this modified schema and recompile the map. Now, look at the new XSLT shown in Listing 11-6.

Listing 11-6. *Inferred Loop XSLT*

```
<ns0:Target>
  <xsl:for-each select="User">
    <Party>
      <PartyCode>
        <xsl:value-of select="UserCode/text()" />
      </PartyCode>
    </Party>
  </xsl:for-each>
</ns0:Target>
```

Notice the difference? The XSLT for the Party node generation is now inside a for-each loop. The mapping engine inferred that since the source node User has a maximum iteration count greater than one, a loop is required to move the data from the source UserCode to the target PartyCode. Would a Looping functoid have any effect on the map? Figure 11-2 shows the map with the Looping functoid added.

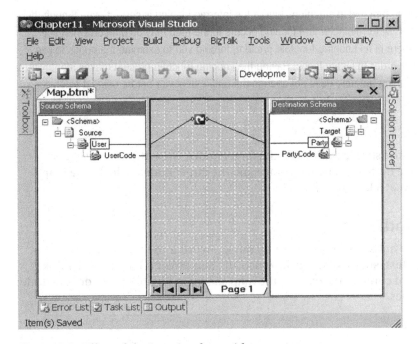

Figure 11-2. *Effect of the Looping functoid*

And here, in Listing 11-7, is the code generated by the map with the Looping functoid.

Listing 11-7. *Looping Functoid Code*

```
<ns0:Target>
  <xsl:for-each select="User">
    <Party>
      <PartyCode>
        <xsl:value-of select="UserCode/text()" />
      </PartyCode>
    </Party>
  </xsl:for-each>
</ns0:Target>
```

As you see, this code is identical to the code from the previous map, which did not have the Looping functoid. Thus we deduce that anytime the inferred looping is correct, there is no need to add a Looping functoid.

Tip We often use the Looping functoid in situations where the inferred looping is correct even though the Looping functoid has no impact. Determining where looping occurs in the map may be difficult when you examine the mapping grid if there is no Looping functoid present, forcing you to examine the nodes to see which ones are one-to-many in order to locate loops. Having the Looping functoid present makes identifying a loop easy. Make sure the Looping functoid does not change the map's behavior before using it solely for this purpose.

Finally, take note that the source nodes, not the target nodes, drive the generation of inferred loops. If the source node is a single instance and the target node is a loop, the mapping engine will not infer that a loop exists.

Adding Context Nodes

Suppose we wanted to go a house located at 101 Elm Street. In order to find that address, we need some additional context, such as the city in which 101 Elm Street is located. A BizTalk map needs the same kind of context. We will use the map shown in Figure 11-3 to demonstrate the concept of context nodes.

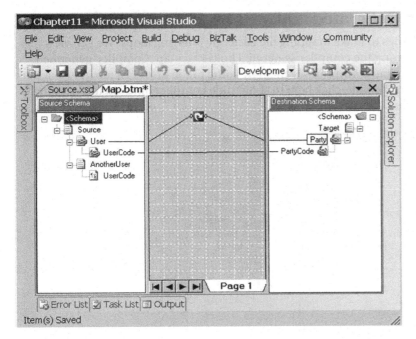

Figure 11-3. *Context nodes*

The code generated by this map is the same as our last map, shown in Listing 11-7. Look at that code, and you will see the selection statement that extracts the data from the source is `<xsl:value-of select="UserCode/text()" />`.

Notice that in this map, shown in Figure 11-3, there are two `UserCode` nodes in the source. In all the previous examples, the source had only one `UserCode` node. In this last map, to which of the two `UserCode` nodes is the selection statement referring? The answer is obvious to us in this simple map because of the one visible link, but it would not be as clear in a more complex map. How does the mapping compiler determine which node to use? We need to understand how the mapping engine determines which `UserCode` node should be used.

When the compiler builds the XSLT for a map it creates a context node for each loop by determining the parent source node for the loop. When the loop is inferred, the context node is the source node that causes the compiler to infer that a loop exists. When the loop is generated by a Looping functoid, the context node is the source node to which the Looping functoid is linked.

The context node in the examples to this point is the source `User` node. Any links from children of that node generate a relative XPATH statement to extract data. Thus our extract statement, `<xsl:value-of select="UserCode/text()" />`, assumes that the source node will be the `UserCode` node that is a child of the source `User` node.

Understanding the concept of the context node is important for you, because when looping is not working in a map, the cause is often that the compiler sees several possible context nodes and chooses the wrong one. When this happens, the XSLT select statement may retrieve data from the wrong source node or may fail to retrieve any data. Of course, loss of context causes the map to produce incorrect output. When our maps output incorrect data, our first step is to examine the XSLT code produced by the compiler to determine what context nodes were established by the compiler.

Adding Compiler-Generated Links

You just saw that BizTalk tries to make mapping life easier by inferring loops. We can view these inferred loops by viewing the compiler-generated links in a map. Compiler-generated links are not displayed by default. You can see them by going to the Error List tab in Visual Studio, finding the description "Double-click here to show/hide compiler links" in the Warning tab, and double-clicking that line. See Figure 11-4.

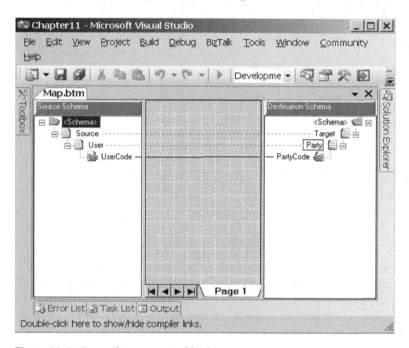

Figure 11-4. *Compiler-generated links*

The compiler-generated links are the red dotted lines. The compiler sees the link between the source UserCode and the target PartyCode and infers that there must be a relationship between the parents of those nodes. Thus we see an inferred link between the User and Party nodes and another inferred link between the Source and Target nodes.

Ideally, we'd be able to look at the grid and tell which compiler-generated links are inferred loops, but we cannot. Figure 11-4 appears the same whether the source User node is a looping node or is a single instance node.

The value of these compiler-generated links is that they tell you when you have unexpected links between the source and target nodes and tell you when you do not have an expected link between the two. Let's look at another example. In Figure 11-5, the source node User is a loop, and the target node Party is a loop, but the target node Party2 is not a loop.

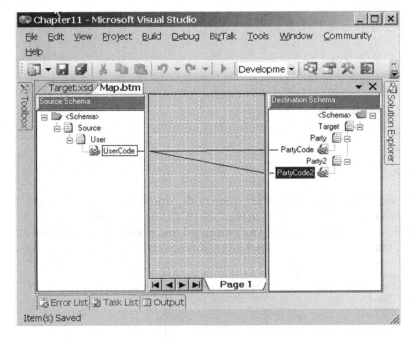

Figure 11-5. *More compiler-generated links*

Let's test the map using the data in Listing 11-8. Notice the source data has three itera-tions of the User loop, each with one instance of UserCode data.

Listing 11-8. *Source Data for the Map Testing More Compiler-Generated Links*

```
<ns0:Source xmlns:ns0="http://Chapter11.Source">
  <User>
    <UserCode>UserCode_1</UserCode>
  </User>
  <User>
    <UserCode>UserCode_2</UserCode>
  </User>
  <User>
    <UserCode>UserCode_3</UserCode>
  </User>
</ns0:Source>
```

The output of this test, shown in Listing 11-9, is different than we expect.

Listing 11-9. *Output of the Map of More Compiler-Generated Links*

```
<ns0:Target xmlns:ns0="http://Chapter11.Target">
  <Party>
    <PartyCode>UserCode_1</PartyCode>
  </Party>
  <Party>
```

```
        <PartyCode>UserCode_2</PartyCode>
    </Party>
    <Party>
        <PartyCode>UserCode_3</PartyCode>
    </Party>
    <Party2>
        <PartyCode2>UserCode_1</PartyCode2>
        <PartyCode2>UserCode_2</PartyCode2>
        <PartyCode2>UserCode_3</PartyCode2>
    </Party2>
</ns0:Target>
```

We expect to see three iterations of the target PartyCode node, since it is a looping node. But notice that our output contains three iterations of the PartyCode2 node as well, even though the PartyCode2 node is not a looping node. The minimum and maximum occurrences for PartyCode2 are set to 1:1. Maybe the compiler-generated links can tell us why this happened.

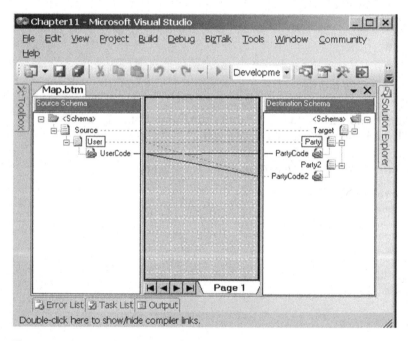

Figure 11-6. *Compiler-generated looping links*

We see that the compiler inferred a link between the source User node and the target PartyCode2 node as well as the expected links between the User and Party nodes and between the Source and Target nodes. The inferred link between the User node and the PartyCode2 node is created by our incorrectly mapping the two nodes directly to one another when we know that the data is mismatched.

Since looping output is driven by the source data, the map produces loops in both target records. This output would fail validation, of course (unless validation is turned off). We've seen many instances where someone creates a "working" map with validation turned off and then the map fails in quality assurance testing done with validation on.

The full value of the compiler-generated links is not apparent in this simple map, but the value becomes apparent when debugging a complex map that is spread over many pages. Often, we see incorrect output but cannot locate the problem by looking at the grid pages of the map. But viewing the compiler-generated links and following them back to the source nodes often helps us uncover an unexpected relationship between source and target.

The compiler-generated links in Figure 11-6 show that if the source User node is a looping node, we need to provide some type of control to prevent the PartyCode2 node from looping in the output.

Limiting the Output of a Loop

The problem we just encountered is that we have a loop on the source side and need to generate output records for only select iterations of that input loop. The map that we will use to illustrate how we solve this problem is in Figure 11-7.

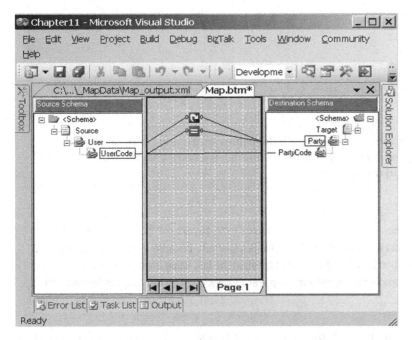

Figure 11-7. *Limiting the output of a loop*

Our source, the User node, has minimum and maximum occurrences of 1:unbounded, which means that the User node may occur many times. Regardless of whether or not our output Party node is a looping node, we only want to output one instance of it.

One stipulation about the input data is that a value of each UserCode node must be unique. This is because we want to find the UserCode node that contains the value BT and output only that value. Since we want just one output node, the value BT must appear only once in the source data.

Limiting the output in this example is very easy. As you see, we added one Equal functoid to the map. The two inputs to that functoid are the value from the source UserCode node and the constant value BT. The Equal functoid compares each value received from the source to BT. The output of the Equal functoid is either true or false, depending on the value received from the source data.

The output of the Equal functoid passes to the target Party node. The mapping engine evaluates the output of the Equal functoid before executing the link attached to the child node of Party, the PartyCode node. When the output is true, the link to the child PartyCode node is executed, and the value from the source UserCode node is stored in the target. When the value is false, the link to the child PartyCode node is ignored. Let's test the map in Figure 11-7 using the data in Listing 11-10.

Listing 11-10. *Source Data for the Map Limiting the Output of a Loop*

```
<ns0:Source xmlns:ns0="http://Chapter11.Source">
  <User>
    <UserCode>AB</UserCode>
  </User>
  <User>
    <UserCode>BT</UserCode>
  </User>
  <User>
    <UserCode>CD</UserCode>
  </User>
</ns0:Source>
```

We have three loops in the source data with the values AB, BT, and CD in the source UserCode node. Since the desired value, BT is in the middle, we know that the map can't just take the first or last value and output it.

Tip When testing the extraction of data from within a source loop, always put the desired value in a location other than the first or last instance of the loop. This is important, because in some cases, the map may only evaluate the first iteration of the loop or may only retain the last value encountered. If you put the desired value in the first or last instance, the map may appear to work properly but may not be doing so.

When we run our test data through the map we get the results in Listing 11-11. The value BT has been returned in the single iteration of the output node, which is exactly what we wanted to see.

Listing 11-11. *Output of the Map Limiting the Output of a Loop*

```
<ns0:Target xmlns:ns0="http://Chapter11.Target">
  <Party>
    <PartyCode>BT</PartyCode>
  </Party>
</ns0:Target>
```

The Equal functoid output successfully blocked the creation of the Party node when the source data was not equal to BT. Let's look at a more complex problem of this nature. We will use the new source and target schemas shown in Figure 11-8 for this example.

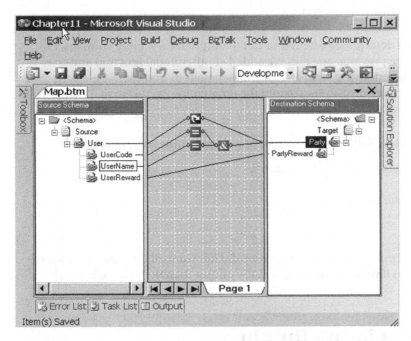

Figure 11-8. *Limiting the output of a loop using multiple criteria*

Again, the source User record is a looping record from which you must produce one PartyReward node. This output must occur when the source UserCode node contains BT and the UserName node contains SSPS. This time, the source data might contain more than one UserCode node with the value BT. It might also contain more than one UserName node with the value SSPS. The stipulation is that there will be only one User node whose child nodes both meet the criteria. We'll use the input data from Listing 11-12.

Listing 11-12. *Source Data for Limiting the Output of the Loop Shown in Figure 11-8*

```
<ns0:Source xmlns:ns0="http://Chapter11.Source">
  <User>
    <UserCode>AB</UserCode>
    <UserName>SSPS</UserName>
    <UserReward>DIRT</UserReward>
  </User>
  <User>
    <UserCode>BT</UserCode>
    <UserName>SSPS</UserName>
    <UserReward>HOUSE</UserReward>
  </User>
  <User>
```

```
      <UserCode>BT</UserCode>
      <UserName>NOTSSPS</UserName>
      <UserReward>FORK</UserReward>
    </User>
</ns0:Source>
```

The decision logic that determines whether or not to output data is more complex, but this map operates just as the previous one did. We added another Equal functoid and one Logical AND functoid. The underlying logic is "if UserCode equals BT and UserName equals SSPS, put the value from the source node UserReward into the target node PartyReward." Listing 11-13 shows the output of this map.

Listing 11-13. *Output of the Map Limiting the Output of a Loop As Shown in Figure 11-8*

```
<ns0:Target xmlns:ns0="http://Chapter11.Target">
  <Party>
    <PartyReward>HOUSE</PartyReward>
  </Party>
</ns0:Target>
```

We had to limit the output of this map because we did not want all the data in the source to be output. What happens if we need more data in the output than there are loops in the source?

Forcing Looping in the Output

You just saw how there may be times that there are more iterations of a source loop than we need for our output. Now, you will see that there are occasions where the reverse is true. This case is one where the source data does not loop, but the output data does. We have a single occurrence input node that will not cause the compiler to infer a loop. The input node has three child data nodes. The output structure is a single looping node with one child data node. Each child data node in the source must force one instance of the output loop. The input for the map is in Listing 11-14.

Listing 11-14. *Input for Forcing a Loop*

```
<Dates>
  <LoadDate>LoadDate</LoadDate>
  <ShipDate>ShipDate</ShipDate>
  <DeliveryDate>DeliveryDate</DeliveryDate>
</Dates>
```

You see that there are three dates in a single record. The map is in Figure 11-9.

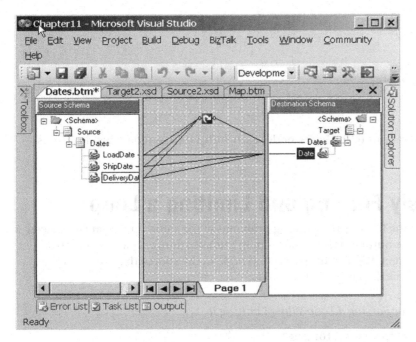

Figure 11-9. *Forcing a loop*

By connecting each of the source data elements to the Looping functoid, we tell the compiler to output one instance of the target Dates node for each child node in the source: LoadDate, ShipDate, and DeliveryDate. Without the Looping functoid, the map would output the data in Listing 11-15.

Listing 11-15. *Output for Forcing a Loop when a Looping Functoid Is Not Used*

```
<ns0:Target xmlns:ns0="http://_Chapter11.Target">
  <Dates>
    <Date>LoadDate</Date>
    <Date>ShipDate</Date>
    <Date>DeliveryDate</Date>
  </Dates>
</ns0:Target>
```

This output is not correct, as it has three child Date nodes in one instance of the Dates node. Since the child Dates node is 1:1, this output would fail validation if the map were executed with validation of output activated. Add the Looping functoid, as we did in Figure 11-9, and the output changes to that in Listing 11-16.

Listing 11-16. *Output for Forcing a Loop When a Looping Functoid Is Used*

```
<ns0:Target xmlns:ns0="http://_Chapter11.Target">
  <Dates>
    <Date>LoadDate</Date>
  </Dates>
```

```
<Dates>
  <Date>ShipDate</Date>
</Dates>
<Dates>
  <Date>DeliveryDate</Date>
</Dates>
</ns0:Target>
```

Now, we get three iterations of the Dates node, each with a different date inside. This is what we wanted to see.

Simultaneously Forcing and Limiting a Loop

Sometimes, we face both the forcing and limiting problems at the same time, that is, we need to force a loop and limit the output of the same loop. In this situation, we have one loop in both the source and the target. We also have a second node in the source that we will use to force the looping. The source data is in Listing 11-17.

Listing 11-17. *Source Data for Forcing a Loop While Limiting It*

```
<ns0:Source xmlns:ns0="http://Test.forcing2">
  <Dates>
    <EffectiveDate>EffectiveDate</EffectiveDate>
    <EndingDate>EndingDate</EndingDate>
  </Dates>
  <Users>
    <UserCode>AA</UserCode>
    <Name>ANDY</Name>
    <Company>ACME</Company>
  </Users>
  <Users>
    <UserCode>BT</UserCode>
    <Name>BEN</Name>
    <Company>BISCUIT</Company>
  </Users>
  <Users>
    <UserCode>CC</UserCode>
    <Name>CHARLIE</Name>
    <Company>CRISCO</Company>
  </Users>
</ns0:Source>
```

Our goal is to output exactly two loops, one containing the name BEN and the other containing the company BISCUIT. We must solve two problems. First, the source data has more loops than we need, so the computer-generated looping must be overridden to limit the number of output loops to exactly two: one for the Name, the other for the Company. Second, the data for both output loops must come from the one instance of the input loop, the one where the value in the UserCode node is BT. The map in Figure 1-10 uses the two techniques you saw earlier, modified to meet the new source format.

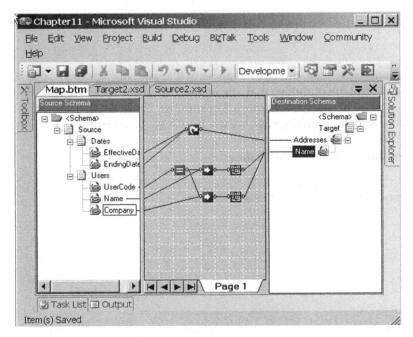

Figure 11-10. *Forcing and limiting loops*

Since we want to produce exactly two output iterations of the Addresses loop, we must search through the source structure to find two source nodes that each occur only once. We are fortunate in this case that the Dates node is a single-occurrence node with two child nodes. The two child nodes can drive two iterations of the Addresses node through the Looping functoid.

A different technique limits the output from the Users loop to only that iteration where the UserCode value is BT. We run each UserCode value through an Equal functoid to test for the value BT and then run the output from that functoid through the Value Mapping functoids. The Value Mapping functoids pass data through only when the Equal functoid output is true, so they will pass data only when the UserCode value is BT.

A new twist is that we use Cumulative Concatenate functoids to pull all the data from the Users loop through the Equal and the Value Mapping functoids. We did remember to set the scope for the Cumulative Concatenate functoids properly. We are almost there, but when we run the map, we get a validation error. Let's examine the output in Listing 11-18 to see what is wrong.

Listing 11-18. *Invalid Output from Forcing and Limiting Loops*

```
<nsO:Target xmlns:nsO="http://Test.forcingtarget">
  <Addresses>
    <Name>BEN</Name>
    <Name>BISCUIT</Name>
```

```
  </Addresses>
  <Addresses>
    <Name>BEN</Name>
    <Name>BISCUIT</Name>
  </Addresses>
</ns0:Target>
```

Oops. Name is a single-occurrence node, but two instances of it appear in each Addresses loop. We must find a way to control the output so that one instance appears in each loop. One neat way to control output in cases like this is to create a flag and then check the flag to determine which value to output in each loop. In this case, we use the C# script in Listing 11-19.

Listing 11-19. *Script to Control Output of the Name Node*

```csharp
bool FirstPass =true;
public string BuildFullName(string inName, string inCompany)
{
  if (FirstPass)
  {
    FirstPass = false;
    return inName;
  }
  else
    return inCompany;
}
```

The global variable FirstPass indicates which iteration, the first or the second, of the Addresses loop is being executed. When the first Addresses loop is output, the script returns the input value from the parameter inName. When the second Addresses loop is output, the script returns the value from inCompany. The updated map is shown in Figure 11-11.

This version of the map outputs the data in Listing 11-20. We have successfully forced two loops and extracted specific data to put into those loops.

Listing 11-20. *Invalid Output from Forcing and Limiting Loops*

```xml
<ns0:TargetData xmlns:ns0="http://Test.forcingtarget">
  <Addresses>
    <Name>BEN</Name>
  </Addresses>
  <Addresses>
    <Name>BISCUIT</Name>
  </Addresses>
</ns0:TargetData>
```

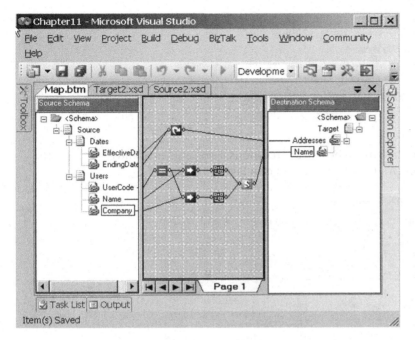

Figure 11-11. *Toggling a flag to control output*

Many-to-One Looping

Mapping becomes much more complex when multiple loops are involved. We refer to these
situations as many-to-one, one-to-many, and many-to-many looping. Let's take a look at a
many-to-one example where we want to generate one output loop from different input loops,
a common problem when mapping application data. The source data is in Listing 11-21.

Listing 11-21. *Source Data for Many-to-One Looping*

```
<ns0:ClientLists xmlns:ns0="http://Test.TwoClients">
  <FemaleClients>
    <FemaleName>AMY ANDREWS</FemaleName>
  </FemaleClients>
  <FemaleClients>
    <FemaleName>BETTY BOOP</FemaleName>
  </FemaleClients>
  <FemaleClients>
    <FemaleName>CINDY COOPER</FemaleName>
  </FemaleClients>
  <FemaleClients>
    <FemaleName>DARLEEN DARK</FemaleName>
  </FemaleClients>
  <MaleClients>
    <MaleName>ARTHUR ARCHER</MaleName>
```

```
    </MaleClients>
    <MaleClients>
      <MaleName>BOB BROWN</MaleName>
    </MaleClients>
    <MaleClients>
      <MaleName>CHARLES CROWN</MaleName>
    </MaleClients>
</ns0:ClientLists>
```

We want to move the data from the two source loops, FemaleClients and MaleClients, into the single output loop, AllClients. The map is in Figure 11-12.

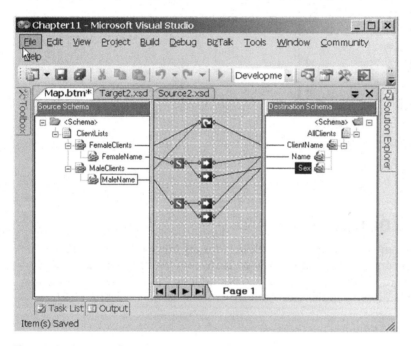

Figure 11-12. *Many loops to one loop*

Both source nodes are linked to the Looping functoid, which is, in turn, linked to the target node. One instance of either source node forces one instance of the target node. Thus if there were three FemaleClient nodes and two MaleClient nodes the map would produce five ClientName nodes.

The Logical String functoids test for the presence of data in the source nodes. When the FemaleClient node drives the loop the Logical String functoids return true for FemaleName and false for MaleName. The reverse is true when the MaleClient node drives the output. The map produces the output in Listing 11-22.

Listing 11-22. *Output from Many Loops to One Loop*

```
<ns0:AllClients xmlns:ns0="http://Test.AllClients">
  <ClientName>
    <Name>AMY ANDREWS</Name>
    <Sex>F</Sex>
  </ClientName>
  <ClientName>
    <Name>BETTY BOOP</Name>
    <Sex>F</Sex>
  </ClientName>
  <ClientName>
    <Name>CINDY COOPER</Name>
    <Sex>F</Sex>
  </ClientName>
  <ClientName>
    <Name>DARLEEN DARK</Name>
    <Sex>F</Sex>
  </ClientName>
  <ClientName>
    <Name>ARTHUR ARCHER</Name>
    <Sex>M</Sex>
  </ClientName>
  <ClientName>
    <Name>BOB BROWN</Name>
    <Sex>M</Sex>
  </ClientName>
  <ClientName>
    <Name>CHARLES CROWN</Name>
    <Sex>M</Sex>
  </ClientName>
</ns0:AllClients>
```

The output has the female clients and the male clients both in one loop, the `ClientName` loop, which is what we wanted.

One-to-Many Looping

Moving data from one loop into many loops, the reverse of the previous example, is our next case. We use the output of the previous map as the source data for this example. When we created that data, we added a `Sex` node to the data. The usefulness of this node becomes apparent in this example, as we must have a way to separate the source data into female and male clients. We use the map shown in Figure 11-13.

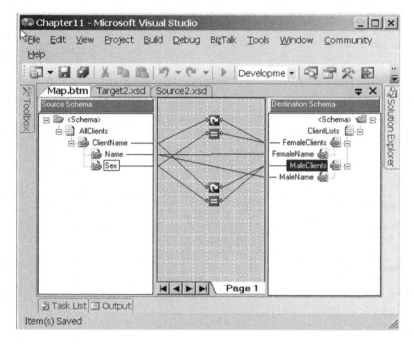

Figure 11-13. *One-to-many looping*

Notice there are two Looping functoids, both linked to the source ClientName. One Looping functoid drives the FemaleClients target loop; the other drives the target MaleClients loop. This generates the two output loops we need. Unfortunately, since the source loop has seven iterations, seven iterations of each target loop will be created without some control. We limit the number of target loops by using Logical Equal functoids to control output of the target nodes based on the sex of the client. The input for this map is in Listing 11-22; the output of this map is in Listing 11-21. As you can see, the maps in Figures 11-12 and 11-13 are complementary.

One-to-Nested Looping

The difficulty in handling loops becomes still more complex when nested loops are involved. A nested loop occurs when one loop is a child of another loop. First, let's examine one-to-nested looping. The source data contains nine clients, four parents and five children in no particular order, in a single loop. The target data should be in two loops, one for the parents and a second for the children. Each child loop must be nested under its parent loop, and children must be sorted by parents. The source data is in Listing 11-23.

Listing 11-23. *Source Data for One-to-Nested Looping*

```
<nsO:ClientsByName xmlns:nsO="http://Test.AllClients">
  <Name>
    <Name>ARTHUR ANDREWS</Name>
    <ParentChildFlag>P</ParentChildFlag>
```

```
    <ParentName />
  </Name>
  <Name>
    <Name>BONNIE BLUE</Name>
    <ParentChildFlag>P</ParentChildFlag>
    <ParentName />
  </Name>
  <Name>
    <Name>CINDY LOU</Name>
    <ParentChildFlag>P</ParentChildFlag>
    <ParentName />
  </Name>
  <Name>
    <Name>DIANE DOODY</Name>
    <ParentChildFlag>C</ParentChildFlag>
    <ParentName>DOUG DOODY</ParentName>
  </Name>
  <Name>
    <Name>BETTY BLUE</Name>
    <ParentChildFlag>C</ParentChildFlag>
    <ParentName>BONNIE BLUE</ParentName>
  </Name>
  <Name>
    <Name>ANDY ANDREWS</Name>
    <ParentChildFlag>C</ParentChildFlag>
    <ParentName>ARTHUR ANDREWS</ParentName>
  </Name>
  <Name>
    <Name>CHARLIE LOU</Name>
    <ParentChildFlag>C</ParentChildFlag>
    <ParentName>CINDY LOU</ParentName>
  </Name>
  <Name>
    <Name>DANDY DOODY</Name>
    <ParentChildFlag>C</ParentChildFlag>
    <ParentName>DOUG DOODY</ParentName>
  </Name>
  <Name>
    <Name>DOUG DOODY</Name>
    <ParentChildFlag>P</ParentChildFlag>
    <ParentName />
  </Name>
</ns0:ClientsByName>
```

The names are in no particular order, thus you cannot expect to extract the data based on position in the source. The map we use is in Figure 11-13.

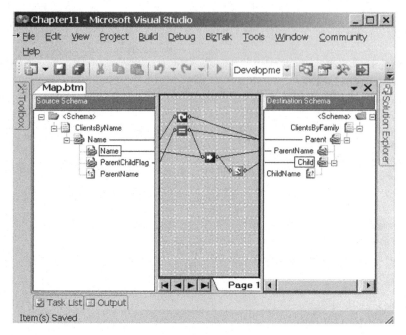

Figure 11-14. *One-to-nested looping*

The Looping functoid forces the map to generate one instance of the target Parent node for each instance of the source Name node. Since we have nine Name nodes in the source we will force nine Parent nodes to be output.

We also only want a Parent node created when the ParentChildFlag value is P. We put a P in the Equals functoid to block output of the Parent node unless the ParentChildFlag value is also P. Since we have four Name nodes whose ParentChildFlag value is P, we should only get four Parent nodes output.

The Equals functoid also controls the output of the ParentName node and the Child loop. The ParentName node is output when the value of the ParentChildFlag value is P.

The inline XSLT function in the Scripting functoid, also controlled by the Equals functoid, does not fire unless the ParentChildFlag value is P as well. The XSLT script, shown in Listing 11-24, creates and outputs the data to the Child node.

Listing 11-24. *XSLT Script Used in One-to-Nested Looping*

```
<xsl:template name="BuildChildRecords">
  <xsl:param name="inParent"/>
<-- Begin a for-each loop to search for children of this parent -->
<-- When one is found, output a Child loop with the data -->
  <xsl:for-each select="//Name[ ParentName = $inParent and
                        ParentChildFlag = 'C' ]">
    <xsl:element name="Child">
      <xsl:element name="ChildName">
        <xsl:value-of select="./Name"/>
      </xsl:element>
```

```
    </xsl:element>
  </xsl:for-each>
</xsl:template>
```

The XSLT uses the Name value received from the Value Mapping functoid to build a relative path for the XSLT selection statement. The selection statement then loops through the source data and extracts all the child nodes whose ParentName value is equal to the input Name value. Each time a match is found, the XSLT builds an output Child node. The output is in Listing 11-25.

Listing 11-25. *Output of the One-to-Nested Loop*

```
<ns0:ClientsByFamilyxmlns:ns0="http://Test.AllClients">
  <Parent>
    <ParentName>ARTHURANDREWS</ParentName>
    <Child>
      <ChildName>ANDYANDREWS</ChildName>
    </Child>
  </Parent>
  <Parent>
    <ParentName>BONNIEBLUE</ParentName>
    <Child>
      <ChildName>BETTYBLUE</ChildName>
    </Child>
  </Parent>
  <Parent>
    <ParentName>CINDYLOU</ParentName>
    <Child>
      <ChildName>CHARLIELOU</ChildName>
    </Child>
  </Parent>
  <Parent>
    <ParentName>DOUGDOODY</ParentName>
    <Child>
      <ChildName>DIANEDOODY</ChildName>
    </Child>
    <Child>
      <ChildName>DANDYDOODY</ChildName>
    </Child>
  </Parent>
</ns0:ClientsByFamily>
```

The data has been rearranged to contain four Parent loops, each with the correct Child loops.

Nested-to-One Looping

Now, we examine the opposite issue, nested-to-one looping. This time, the nested loops are in the source, and the data must be extracted from them and output into a single loop. The source data is in Listing 11-26.

Listing 11-26 .Source Data for Nested-to-One Looping

```
<ns0:ClientsByFamilyxmlns:ns0="http://Test.AllClients">
  <Parent>
    <ParentName>ARTHURANDREWS</ParentName>
    <Child>
      <ChildName>ANDYANDREWS</ChildName>
    </Child>
  </Parent>
  <Parent>
    <ParentName>BONNIEBLUE</ParentName>
    <Child>
      <ChildName>BETTYBLUE</ChildName>
    </Child>
  </Parent>
  <Parent>
    <ParentName>CINDYLOU</ParentName>
    <Child>
      <ChildName>CHARLIELOU</ChildName>
    </Child>
  </Parent>
  <Parent>
    <ParentName>DOUGDOODY</ParentName>
    <Child>
      <ChildName>DIANEDOODY</ChildName>
    </Child>
    <Child>
      <ChildName>DANDYDOODY</ChildName>
    </Child>
  </Parent>
</ns0:ClientsByFamily>
```

Four Parent loops, each with one or more nested Child loops must be flattened into a single Name loop, as shown in the map in Figure 11-15.

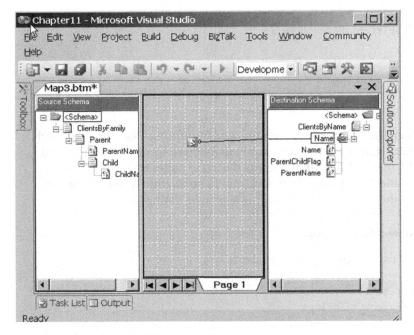

Figure 11-15. *Parent/Child loop to ClientByName loop map*

Nested-to-one looping is difficult to achieve with standard BizTalk functoids and links. We find inline XSLT templates are a better option. Our map in Figure 11-15 contains but one functoid, a Scripting functoid, in which we place our XSLT for this map.

Listing 11-27. *XSLT for Nested-to-One Looping*

```
<xsl:template name="BuildClientRecords">
<-- Begin a for each loop that searches for source Parent nodes -->
<-- When one is found, build the output nodes using data selected -->
<-- using XPATH select statements -->
  <xsl:for-each select="//Parent">
    <xsl:variable name="ParentName" select="./ParentName"/>
    <xsl:element name="Name">
      <xsl:element name="Name">
        <xsl:value-of select="$ParentName"/>
      </xsl:element>
      <xsl:element name="ParentChildFlag">P</xsl:element>
      <xsl:element name="ParentName"/>
    </xsl:element>
    <xsl:for-each select="./Child">
      <xsl:element name="Name">
        <xsl:element name="Name">
          <xsl:value-of select="./ChildName"/>
        </xsl:element>
        <xsl:element name="ParentChildFlag">C</xsl:element>
```

```
        <xsl:element name="ParentName">
          <xsl:value-of select="$ParentName"/>
        </xsl:element>
      </xsl:element>
    </xsl:for-each>
  </xsl:for-each>
</xsl:template>
```

The XSLT loops through the source nodes, creating and outputting a Name node for each source node found. The XSLT expects to find a Parent loop followed by one or more nested Child loops. Thus the XSLT for-each loop that outputs the Child nodes is nested within the for-each loop that outputs the Parent loops. Our code makes no attempt to sort the output; it just outputs the nodes in the order they are found, as shown in Listing 11-28.

Listing 11-28. *Output for Nested-to-One Looping*

```
<ns0:ClientsByName xmlns:ns0="http://Test.AllClients">
  <Name>
    <Name>ARTHUR ANDREWS</Name>
    <ParentChildFlag>P</ParentChildFlag>
    <ParentName />
  </Name>
  <Name>
    <Name>ANDY ANDREWS</Name>
    <ParentChildFlag>C</ParentChildFlag>
    <ParentName>ARTHUR ANDREWS</ParentName>
  </Name>
  <Name>
    <Name>BONNI EBLUE</Name>
    <ParentChildFlag>P</ParentChildFlag>
    <ParentName />
  </Name>
  <Name>
    <Name>BETTY BLUE</Name>
    <ParentChildFlag>C</ParentChildFlag>
    <ParentName>BONNI EBLUE</ParentName>
  </Name>
  <Name>
    <Name>CINDY LOU</Name>
    <ParentChildFlag>P</ParentChildFlag>
    <ParentName />
  </Name>
  <Name>
    <Name>CHARLIE LOU</Name>
    <ParentChildFlag>C</ParentChildFlag>
    <ParentName>CINDY LOU</ParentName>
  </Name>
  <Name>
```

```
    <Name>DOUG DOODY</Name>
    <ParentChildFlag>P</ParentChildFlag>
    <ParentName />
  </Name>
  <Name>
    <Name>DIANE DOODY</Name>
    <ParentChildFlag>C</ParentChildFlag>
    <ParentName>DOUG DOODY</ParentName>
  </Name>
  <Name>
    <Name>DANDY DOODY</Name>
    <ParentChildFlag>C</ParentChildFlag>
    <ParentName>DOUG DOODY</ParentName>
  </Name>
</ns0:ClientsByName>
```

Summary

This chapter presented some of the basic methods that we use to solve looping problems. There are many different approaches that may be used in each instance. Since the maps in this chapter use relatively simple schemas and business rules, only basic methods such as forcing loops and limiting loops are presented. Even the scripts are very basic. These methods are the building blocks for learning how to deal with looping in BizTalk maps.

We will come back to the subject of looping in the next chapter, examining two specific looping problems in great detail: one-to-many loops and many-to-one loops where there are nested loops involved. Then, in Part 4, "Mapping EDI Transactions," we will concentrate on looping in two more chapters: one extends the basic looping discussion to maps using EDI schemas, and the other discusses the X12 HL loop that has generated more requests for help from other mappers than any other mapping construct.

As you encounter more complicated schemas and more complex business rules, you will find that resolving looping presents more and more hurdles, so understanding these chapters is a key to becoming proficient with BizTalk mapping.

CHAPTER 12

■ ■ ■

Handling Advanced Looping

The previous chapter introduced some of the basic concepts of handling looping in maps. Now, we move on to examine how we might approach more difficult issues encountered when mapping loops. We don't spend much time in this chapter offering functoid solutions, because as you saw in Chapter 11, solving complex looping problems with functoids is very hard to do. We cover two mapping examples in the chapter, each one showing some specific approaches for solving problems associated with looping.

Many-to-One Looping with a Source Child Loop

You saw an example of many-to-one looping in the previous chapter. Here is another, more complex example: We have three source loops, two siblings and one child. The pallet loop is followed by the carton loop. The carton loop contains the package loop. You can see the structure in the source data shown in Listing 12-1.

Listing 12-1. *Source Data for Many-to-one Looping*

```
<ns0:Source xmlns:ns0="http://Chapter_12___Jim.ManyLoops">
 //  Two iterations of the first looping node, PalletLoop
 <PalletLoop>
     <PalletNumber>Pallet 1</PalletNumber>
 </PalletLoop>
 <PalletLoop>
     <PalletNumber>Pallet 2</PalletNumber>
 </PalletLoop>
//  Two iterations of the second looping node, CartonLoop
  <CartonLoop>
     <CartonNumber>Carton 1</CartonNumber>
//  Two iterations of the third, and child, node, PackageLoop
     <PackageLoop>
        <PackageNumber>Package 1a</PackageNumber>
     </PackageLoop>
     <PackageLoop>
        <PackageNumber>Package1b</PackageNumber>
     </PackageLoop>
  </CartonLoop>
```

```
<CartonLoop>
    <CartonNumber>Carton 2</CartonNumber>
// Two iterations of the third, and child, node, PackageLoop
    <PackageLoop>
        <PackageNumber>Package 2a</PackageNumber>
    </PackageLoop>
    <PackageLoop>
        <PackageNumber>Package 2b</PackageNumber>
    </PackageLoop>
</CartonLoop>
</ns0:Source>
```

We use incremental testing to see how well the compiler handles the looping, starting with the map in Figure 12-1.

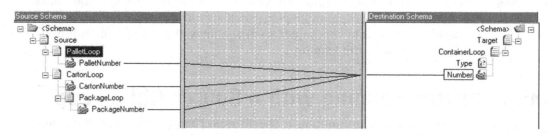

Figure 12-1. *The map for our first incremental test*

We simply attach the three data nodes to one output node and run the map. The output produced is in Listing 12-2.

Listing 12-2. *Output from the Map for Our First Incremental Test*

```
<ns0:Target xmlns:ns0="http://Chapter_12___Jim.OneLoop">
  <ContainerLoop>
    <Number>Pallet 1</Number>
    <Number>Carton 1</Number>
    <Number>Package 1a</Number>
  </ContainerLoop>
  <ContainerLoop>
    <Number>Pallet 2</Number>
    <Number>Carton 1</Number>
    <Number>Package 1a</Number>
  </ContainerLoop>
</ns0:Target>
```

Since we want one ContainerLoop output for each PalletLoop, CartonLoop, and PackageLoop node, we see right away that the source data cannot drive the output structure. The compiler has put an instance of each source loop in the two ContainerLoop nodes. The map also did not output the second PackageLoop in each CartonLoop. Perhaps using a Looping functoid can help, as shown in Figure 12-2. The Looping functoid is directing the compiler to generate a map that will output one ContainerLoop for each of the source loops.

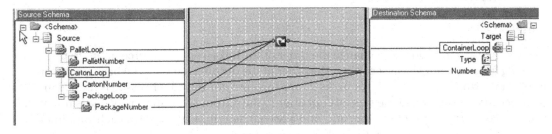

Figure 12-2. *A map for our second incremental test*

When we run the map in Figure 12-2, we get the output shown in Listing 12-3. The map did output one ContainerLoop node for each source loop node, eight in total. Unfortunately, carton and package information were output in the same loops and carton information was repeated.

Listing 12-3. *Output from the Map of Our Second Incremental Test*

```
<nsO:Target xmlns:nsO="http://Chapter_12___Jim.OneLoop">
  <ContainerLoop>
    <Number>Pallet 1</Number>
  </ContainerLoop>
  <ContainerLoop>
    <Number>Pallet 2</Number>
  </ContainerLoop>
  <ContainerLoop>
    <Number>Carton 1</Number>
    <Number>Package 1a</Number>
  </ContainerLoop>
  <ContainerLoop>
    <Number>Carton 1</Number>
    <Number>Package1b</Number>
  </ContainerLoop>
  <ContainerLoop>
    <Number>Carton 2</Number>
    <Number>Package 2a</Number>
  </ContainerLoop>
  <ContainerLoop>
    <Number>Carton 2</Number>
    <Number>Package 2b</Number>
  </ContainerLoop>
  <ContainerLoop>
    <Number>Carton 1</Number>
    <Number>Package 1a</Number>
  </ContainerLoop>
```

```
<ContainerLoop>
  <Number>Carton 2</Number>
  <Number>Package 2a</Number>
</ContainerLoop>
</ns0:Target>
```

We play around some and change the order of the links from the source nodes to the Looping functoid, but all we see is that the order of the output changes. The basic problems of duplicate carton numbers and two items in one loop are not solved. The issue is more complex, because we must add the type of container to the output loop, and that value is not in the source. We must control the output and find a way to determine the type of each container. Here, in Figure 12-3, is the map that solves the problems.

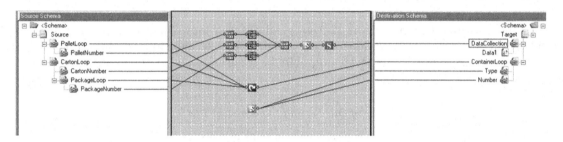

Figure 12-3. *A map solving our one-to-many looping problems*

We know that the Looping functoid used in the second test produced the correct number of `ContainerLoop` nodes, so we can continue to use it for that purpose. We take control of the data away from the compiler using a combination of functoids and scripts. The addition of a `DataCollection` node to the target schema allows us to gather the data before we hit the actual output nodes.

We gather data from each of the source looping nodes separately through the three String Concatenate/Cumulative Concatenate functoids. We then join the three strings of data in the fourth String Concatenate functoid. The Cumulative Concatenate functoids are set to pull all the data from the source nodes. Here's what the top pair of String Concatenate/Cumulative Concatenate functoids does to the data received from the `PalletNumber` node.

1. The data `Pallet 1` arrives at the String Concatenate functoid.

2. The string `P,` is prepended to the value `Pallet 1`.

3. The pipe character (`|`) is appended to the value `P,Pallet 1`.

4. The string `P,Pallet 1|` is passed to the Cumulative Concatenate functoid.

5. The Cumulative Concatenate functoid asks the String Concatenate functoid for more data.

6. The data `Pallet 2` arrives at the String Concatenate functoid.

7. The string `P,` is prepended to the value `Pallet 2`.

8. The pipe character (`|`) is appended to the value `P,Pallet 2`.

9. The string `P,Pallet 2|` is passed to the Cumulative Concatenate functoid.

10. The Cumulative Concatenate functoid appends the string P,Pallet 2| to the string P,Pallet 1|.

11. The Cumulative Concatenate functoid asks the String Concatenate functoid for more data. There is none, so the Cumulative Concatenate functoid passes the string P,Pallet 1|P,Pallet 2| to the fourth String Concatenate functoid.

The two other String Concatenate/Cumulative Concatenate pairs perform the same steps for the CartonLoop data and the PackageLoop data. The result is that three strings are passed to the fourth String Concatenate functoid. These strings are in Listing 12-4.

Listing 12-4. *Strings Passed to the Fourth String Concatenate Functoid*

```
P,Pallet 1|P,Pallet 2|
C,Carton 1|C,Carton 2|
K,Package 1a|K,Package1b|K,Package 2a|K,Package 2b|
```

We chose the character "K" for the package string, since "P" was used by the pallet string. The fourth String Concatenate functoid combines these strings into the string shown in Listing 12-5.

Listing 12-5. *String Output by the Fourth String Concatenate Functoid*

```
"P,Pallet 1|P,Pallet 2|C,Carton 1|C,Carton 2|K,Package 1a|K,Package1b|K,Package
2a|K,Package 2b|"
```

This string is passed to the Scripting functoid, where a script stores the entire string in a global variable. The script is in Listing 12-6.

Listing 12-6. *Script to Put the String in a Global Variable*

```
// Global variable to hold the string
string contents = "";

public string BuildGlobals (string input)
{
// put the input string into the global variable
contents = input;
// Return a null string so that the Logical String functoid will block
// output of the DataCollection node
return "";
}
```

The Logical String functoid blocks the output of the DataCollection node so that the preceding process is invisible to the output file. Now, you see the really neat trick. Notice that the bottom Scripting functoid outputs the Type and Number nodes—*both nodes*. How does one Scripting functoid output two different values to two different nodes? Let's look at the script that is inside that functoid. It is in Listing 12-7.

Listing 12-7. *Script to Output Two Values to Two Nodes*

```
public string OutputContents ()
{
//  Find the position of the comma in the string
//  held in the global variable contents,
//  then find the position of the pipe in the string and the length of the string,
//  and finally initialize a variable to hold the return value from this script
  int comma =  contents.IndexOf(",");
  int pipe =   contents.IndexOf("|");
  int length = contents.Length;
  string retval = "";

//  If there is no pipe we've have no string in contents so exit
  if (pipe == -1) return "no data";

//  Check to see if the comma is the second character in the string (zero-based
//  counting).  If it is, we know that we are doing the type, not the number.
//  Set the return value to the character in the first position of the string.  This
//   will be either a 'P', a 'C', or a 'K'.  Trim the first two characters
//  off the string in contents
  if (comma == 1)
  {
  retval =   contents.Substring(0,1);
  contents = contents.Substring(2,length-2);
  }

//  If the comma was not the second character, we must be doing the Number,
//  not the Type, so set the return value to the substring from before the first
//  pipe character and then trim the substring just used plus the first pipe
//  from the string in contents
  else
  {
  retval =   contents.Substring(0,pipe);
  contents = contents.Substring(pipe+1,length-pipe-1);
  }

//  Return either the Type or the Number, whichever was picked off this pass
return retval;
}
```

Here, in Listing 12-8, is what happens to our string that is in the global variable contents as the script runs. Notice that each pass removes the leftmost field, either the type or value.

Listing 12-8. *Our String in the contents Variable*

```
"P,Pallet 1|P,Pallet 2|C,Carton 1|C,Carton 2|K,Package 1a|K,Package1b|K,Package
    2a|K,Package 2b|"
"Pallet 1|P,Pallet 2|C,Carton 1|C,Carton 2|K,Package 1a|K,Package1b|K,Package
```

```
        2a|K,Package 2b|"
"P,Pallet 2|C,Carton 1|C,Carton 2|K,Package 1a|K,Package1b|K,Package
        2a|K,Package 2b|"
"Pallet 2|C,Carton 1|C,Carton 2|K,Package 1a|K,Package1b|K,Package 2a|
        K,Package 2b|"
"C,Carton 1|C,Carton 2|K,Package 1a|K,Package1b|K,Package 2a|K,Package 2b|"
"Carton 1|C,Carton 2|K,Package 1a|K,Package1b|K,Package 2a|K,Package 2b|"
"C,Carton 2|K,Package 1a|K,Package1b|K,Package 2a|K,Package 2b|"
"Carton 2|K,Package 1a|K,Package1b|K,Package 2a|K,Package 2b|"
"K,Package 1a|K,Package1b|K,Package 2a|K,Package 2b|"
"Package 1a|K,Package1b|K,Package 2a|K,Package 2b|"
"K,Package1b|K,Package 2a|K,Package 2b|"
"Package1b|K,Package 2a|K,Package 2b|"
"K,Package 2a|K,Package 2b|"
"Package 2a|K,Package 2b|"
"K,Package 2b|"
"Package 2b|"
""
```

Listing 12-9 is the output of the map.

Listing 12-9. *Output of the Solution Map*

```xml
<ns0:Target xmlns:ns0="http://Chapter_12___Jim.OneLoop">
    <ContainerLoop>
      <Type>P</Type>
      <Number>Pallet 1</Number>
    </ContainerLoop>
    <ContainerLoop>
      <Type>P</Type>
      <Number>Pallet 2</Number>
    </ContainerLoop>
    <ContainerLoop>
      <Type>C</Type>
      <Number>Carton 1</Number>
    </ContainerLoop>
    <ContainerLoop>
      <Type>C</Type>
      <Number>Carton 2</Number>
    </ContainerLoop>
    <ContainerLoop>
      <Type>K</Type>
      <Number>Package 1a</Number>
    </ContainerLoop>
    <ContainerLoop>
      <Type>K</Type>
      <Number>Package1b</Number>
    </ContainerLoop>
```

```
<ContainerLoop>
  <Type>K</Type>
  <Number>Package 2a</Number>
</ContainerLoop>
<ContainerLoop>
  <Type>K</Type>
  <Number>Package 2b</Number>
</ContainerLoop>
</ns0:Target>
```

In this instance, we did not care in which order the data was output. If we did care, we would need to use an array or hash table to keep track of the order. For that, we would use the techniques for collecting data presented in Chapter 9.

We used the technique of creating a single string both to hold the source values and to place the values into a discernable order. Then, we added a new technique that allowed us to use one Scripting functoid to output to two different nodes.

Next, we will look at our technique for handling a situation where we go from one source loop to two loops, a parent and child, on the target side. This example is further complicated by the need to reorder the data.

One-to-Many Looping with a Child Target Loop

Chapter 11 contained examples of one-to-many looping that included forcing the correct number of output loops and limiting the number of output loops using the Looping functoid and one or more Logical functoids. Combining those techniques with data collection can make creating a one-to-many map less difficult.

When the data from the single source loop must be separated into two target loops and the data determines whether or not one of those loops should be created, the problem becomes much more significant. Let's look at the source and target schemas in Figure 12-4.

Figure 12-4. *Source and target schemas for our one-to-many example*

We will retrieve data from the source DetailLoop node and put the data into both the target ItemInfo nodes and the children of those nodes, the SubItemInfo nodes. The movement of data is subject to these rules:

1. A new ItemInfo loop must be generated for each unique source part number found in the PartNumber nodes.

2. A new SubItemInfo node must be generated for each subpart number found in the Sub-PartNumber nodes.

3. Each SubItemInfo loop must be output inside the ItemInfo loop that contains the parent part number for that subpart number.

For example, look at the source data excerpt in Listing 12-10, which is the DetailLoop portion of the input. There are six LineItem nodes. Two are part number nodes, because they have no value in the SubPartNumber node. Four are subpart numbers, because they have a value in the SubPartNumber node. For this example, the order of the nodes is important as well. The part numbers must appear before their respective subpart numbers, which must be grouped behind their part number.

Listing 12-10. *Sample Source LineItem Loop Data*

```
<DetailLoop xmlns="">
  <LineItem>
    <PartNumber>ABX-9302</PartNumber>
    <SubPartNumber/>
  </LineItem>
  <LineItem>
    <PartNumber>ABX-9302</PartNumber>
    <SubPartNumber>9302-1977</SubPartNumber>
  </LineItem>
  <LineItem>
    <PartNumber>ABX-9302</PartNumber>
    <SubPartNumber>9302-1978</SubPartNumber>
  </LineItem>
  <LineItem>
    <PartNumber>ABA-1307</PartNumber>
    <SubPartNumber/>
  </LineItem>
  <LineItem>
    <PartNumber>ABA-1307</PartNumber>
    <SubPartNumber>1307-1982</SubPartNumber>
  </LineItem>
  <LineItem>
    <PartNumber>ABA-1307</PartNumber>
    <SubPartNumber>1307-1983</SubPartNumber>
  </LineItem>
</DetailLoop>
```

As usual, our first problem is how to produce a sufficient number of both output loops to hold the data. We try a couple of methods, shown in Figure 12-5. The top map generates twelve ItemInfo nodes but generates no SubItemInfo nodes. We must have both. The bottom map produces only six ItemInfo nodes, again enough total nodes but without the necessary SubItemInfo nodes.

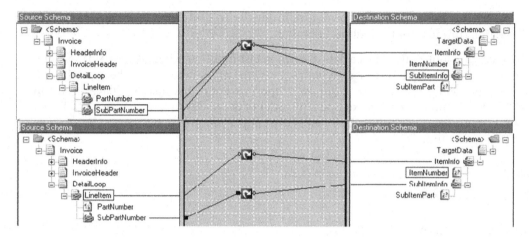

Figure 12-5. *A failed attempt to produce enough output nodes*

We have one more trick up our sleeve. We can try to use the nodes in the header to produce the looping we need. Figure 12-6 shows this map. We get 24 nodes, 12 ItemInfo nodes and 12 SubItemInfo nodes, more than enough to produce the output nodes we need.

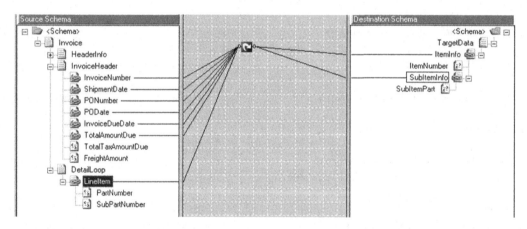

Figure 12-6. *Using the header nodes to produce looping*

Unfortunately, the nodes are paired; each ItemInfo node has one child SubItemInfo node, as shown in Listing 12-11. The listing contains an excerpt from the full output and shows 4 of the 12 nodes. Notice how each ItemInfo node contains a child SubItemInfo node. Despite there being enough loops to drive our output, this method will not allow us to drive more SubItemInfo loops than ItemInfo loops.

Listing 12-11. *Output of Using the Header Nodes to Produce Looping*

```
<ItemInfo>
  <SubItemInfo />
</ItemInfo>
```

```
<ItemInfo>
  <SubItemInfo />
</ItemInfo>
<ItemInfo>
```

Thank heavens for incremental testing. Otherwise, we might have assumed that we could produce the looping structure and thus gone right ahead and started mapping the data. A lot of time and effort could have been wasted. Of course, we could continue to search for ways to force the looping, and we might even discover one that would work in this case. However, doing so is not worth the time and effort involved. Remember that once we have the loops, we still would have to figure out a way to control their output. In any event, we would most likely end up using XSLT to output the child loop. Look at the map in Figure 12-7, where we take a different approach.

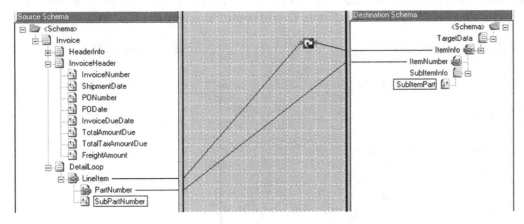

Figure 12-7. *A different approach to handling the looping*

Here, we decide to give up trying to force both `ItemInfo` and `SubItemInfo` loops. Instead, we plan to force only the `ItemInfo` loop and to output the `SubItemInfo` loop using an XSLT template. A quick test of the Looping functoid gives us six `ItemInfo` loops, and we only need two. We also get the `PartNumber` in each loop. That's good. The output from this map is in Listing 12-12.

Listing 12-12. *Output from Our Map Trying a Different Approach*

```
<ns0:TargetData xmlns:ns0="http://IfElse.TargetFile">
  <ItemInfo>
    <ItemNumber>ABX 9302</ItemNumber>
  </ItemInfo>
  <ItemInfo>
    <ItemNumber>ABX 9302</ItemNumber>
  </ItemInfo>
  <ItemInfo>
    <ItemNumber>ABX 9302</ItemNumber>
  </ItemInfo>
  <ItemInfo>
```

```
   <ItemNumber>ABA 1307</ItemNumber>
  </ItemInfo>
  <ItemInfo>
   <ItemNumber>ABA 1307</ItemNumber>
  </ItemInfo>
  <ItemInfo>
   <ItemNumber>ABA 1307</ItemNumber>
  </ItemInfo>
</ns0:TargetData>
```

Now, we have one problem. We must block the output of the second, third, fifth, and sixth ItemInfo nodes. Those are where we want to produce the four SubItemInfo nodes. We know from examining the source data in Listing 12-10 that we only want the ItemInfo node to be output when there is no SubPartNumber in the source LineItem loop. Logically then, we should be able to use the construct shown in Figure 12-8 to control this loop.

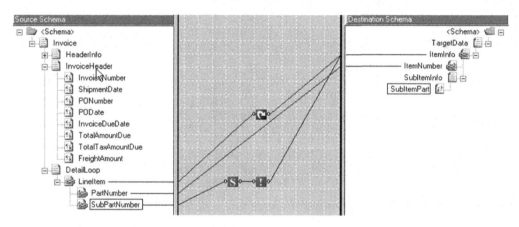

Figure 12-8. *Controlling the ItemInfo loop*

We run the map in Figure 12-8 and receive the output shown in Listing 12-13. Voilà! Just what we wanted, two ItemInfo loops each with the correct ItemNumber. Now, we can focus on producing the SubItemInfo node.

Listing 12-13. *Output of Controlling the ItemInfo Loop Map*

```
<ns0:TargetData xmlns:ns0="http://IfElse.TargetFile">
<ItemInfo>
    <ItemNumber>ABX-9302</ItemNumber>
  </ItemInfo>
<ItemInfo>
    <ItemNumber>ABA-1307</ItemNumber>
  </ItemInfo>
</ns0:TargetData>
```

Unfortunately, this is where our map falters. Neither functoids, nor XSLT templates, nor simple inline XSLT produce the correct output of the SubItemInfo loop. We have not yet eliminated the fundamental problem that we saw in the beginning of this example: we can't control the looping at the SubItemInfo level. At this point, we have spent several hours trying different approaches, only a few of which we have shown.

We know that we can use data collection techniques, such as an array, to organize the data and use a combination of C# scripting and XSLT to retrieve the data from the array and create the output file. The complexity of the problem means more complicated code than we would like to use, and we would continue on this approach only if our client placed restraints on us in regards to doing maps completely in XSLT. Here, in Figure 12-9, is our map that we use to solve this mapping problem.

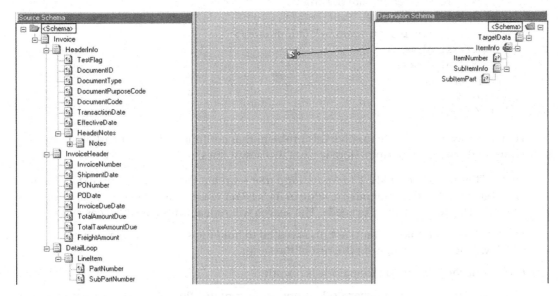

Figure 12-9. *Our XSLT map solution to this looping problem*

We use an inline XSLT script to parse the input file, organize the data, and generate and populate the output loops. The code is shown in Listing 12-14.

Listing 12-14. *Inline XSLT Script*

```
<!-- Select all Item records that have no sub-item part number -->
1  <xsl:for-each select="//DetailLoop/LineItem[ SubPartNumber = '' ]">
2     <xsl:variable name="CurrentPartID">
3        <xsl:value-of select="PartNumber"/>
4     </xsl:variable>
<!-- Write out an ItemInfo Loop node and an ItemNumber node-->
5     <xsl:element name="ItemInfo">
6        <xsl:element name="ItemNumber">
7           <xsl:value-of select="$CurrentPartID"/>
8        </xsl:element>

<!-- For the current ParentPartID, select Item nodes where the
 PartNumber is equal to the current part, and the
```

```
      SubPartNumber is not empty -->
9        <xsl:for-each select="//DetailLoop/LineItem[ PartNumber = $CurrentPartID
                              and SubPartNumber != '' ]">
10          <xsl:variable name="ChildPart">
11            <xsl:value-of select="SubPartNumber"/>
12          </xsl:variable>

      <!-- Write out a SubItemInfo loop and a SubItemPart for
      the current ChildPart -->
13          <xsl:element name="SubItemInfo">
14            <xsl:element name="SubItemPart">
15              <xsl:value-of select="$ChildPart"/>
16            </xsl:element>
17          </xsl:element>
18        </xsl:for-each>
19      </xsl:element>
20 </xsl:for-each>
```

That's twenty lines of code to solve this problem that confounded all our earlier attempts to use functoids and basic scripts. Here is what this script does:

Line 1: This line begins a XSLT for-each loop that searches through the source data for a LineItem loop that does not have a value in its SubPartNumber node. Lines 2–20 are executed each time the search succeeds. The search will repeat until it is unsuccessful.

Lines 2–4: The variable CurrentPartID is created to hold the source PartNumber value, which will be used throughout the rest of the script.

Line 5: The target ItemInfo loop node is output.

Lines 6–8: The target ItemNumber node is output; it contains the value from the variable CurrentPartID. This node is a child of the current ItemInfo loop.

Line 9: This line begins a XSLT for-each loop that searches through the source data for a LineItem loop that contains a SubPartNumber node, whose PartNumber node contains the same value as the CurrentPartID variable. In essence, this search looks for a child of the current ItemInfo loop. Lines 10–18 are executed each time the search succeeds. The search will repeat until it is not successful.

Lines 10–12: The variable ChildPart is created to hold the source SubPartNumber value.

Line 13: The target SubItemInfo node is output as a child of the current ItemInfo node.

Lines 14–16: The target SubItemPart node is output, and it contains the value from the variable ChildPart. This node is a child of the current SubItemInfo loop.

Line 17: This line outputs the end tag for the current SubItemInfo loop.

Line 18: This line ends the current search begun in line 9, returning the flow to line 9.

Line 19: This line outputs the end tag for the current ItemInfo loop.

Line 20: This line ends the current search begun in line 1, returning the flow to line 1.

This inline XSLT solution is so simple you may wonder why you'd bother with any other approaches to mapping. After all, you could write the entire map in XSLT. Here are some thoughts on that:

- The first, and foremost, reason is maintenance of the maps. The use of the XSLT solution in this map has increased the skill set required for modifying or maintaining the map to programmer—not just any programmer but one who has a working knowledge of XSLT.

- The fact is that the problem faced in this map was a simple problem from an XSLT standpoint. There are many problems where using a combination of functoids, C# scripts, and/or XSLT templates is easier than writing a complex, full-map XSLT script.

- Some clients do not want any scripts used in their maps and must be pushed to allow C# or Visual Basic scripts to solve the very complex issues that functoids cannot handle. Such clients will not allow XSLT.

Summary

The bottom line when tackling difficult looping problems is that you must review your mapping approach alternatives before you begin mapping. As you gain experience, you will recognize certain looping situations and will automatically reject approaches that you know will either not work or will be costly in time and effort.

Our exploration of the two looping problems in this chapter did not just present "here is the problem, and here is the solution" examples. In both cases, we took you through some of the exercises behind the search for the best solution. The incremental testing that quickly eliminated some of the approaches is perhaps the most valuable. Of course, analyzing the problem and defining possible courses of action for trial is also important.

This is the last chapter that focuses on general mapping techniques. The next five chapters deal strictly with the types of mapping problems that you will encounter when you must map to or from EDI schemas. These chapters focus on ANSI X12 and EDIFACT schemas. The next chapter does not discuss mapping but instead provides a broad overview of the EDI standards.

P A R T 4

■ ■ ■

EDI Mapping with BizTalk

CHAPTER 13

▪▪▪

Introducing Electronic Data Interchange (EDI)

Many BizTalk implementations are done purely to enable the exchange of EDI transactions with trading partners. Although EDI includes exchanging XML and flat files such as comma-separated variable files, when we speak of EDI in the context of this book, we refer to standardized formats such as those defined by ANSI X12 or EDIFACT. Many BizTalk experts know little or nothing about EDI and have difficulty understanding some of the business rules that affect mapping. This chapter provides a brief introduction to EDI and EDI transactions. If you are familiar with these subjects, you may skip this chapter.

EDI is the exchange of business documents in electronic format. This seems to be exactly what BizTalk was designed to accomplish—to pass electronic messages back and forth between applications and organizations. We might construe then that, strictly speaking, all messages passed to and from BizTalk are EDI messages. This is incorrect. EDI messages are those that adhere to specific formats and business rules for use as defined by EDI standards. Examples of EDI standards are ANSI X12, EDIFACT, SWIFT, TRADACOMS, and ODETTE. These standards and others like them define the formats, character sets, and data types that may be used in EDI business documents and forms.

The impact of these standards on BizTalk mapping is significant. Mapping EDI transactions is more complex than you might expect, even for those skilled in BizTalk mapping. Unlike recent message formats, which are often designed to work well with the design of the BizTalk mapping engine, EDI formats date as far back as the 1980s. The formats of these transactions often tax the capabilities of even mapping engines specifically designed for EDI.

If you find yourself faced with the structural complexities of an EDI document and/or if you have no understanding of the business rules embedded in the document, you may find your BizTalk mapping experience to be of little help. Untangling the complexities of an Advanced Ship Notice (ASN) with its single loop may frustrate you, especially since that single loop contains an inferred hierarchy that must be unraveled. We share that frustration as well, since we consider the ASN to be one of the most complicated of all transactions. We have even devoted a chapter, Chapter 17, in this book to it. Overall, EDI transactions present mapping challenges for several reasons:

- *Scope of the transactions*: Back-office, or application-to-application, transactions tend to be limited in scope. EDI transactions are wide in scope. For example, you would design the schema of an inventory update transaction sent from your warehouse inventory system to your purchasing system to hold only the data you want to exchange. The folks who design EDI transactions, on the other hand, attempt to encompass the superset of all information that might be used by anyone at anytime in their inventory update transaction. An EDI inventory update transaction contains hundreds of data items even though 90 percent of users use the same 10 percent of that data. The schemas for EDI transactions contain the full set of data.

- *Complex formats*: EDI schemas tend to be more complex than application-to-application data-transfer schemas. This is somewhat due to the wide scope mentioned before but is due more to these transactions often being arranged to represent the structure of the business activities they represent. Unraveling and flattening multiple inbound nested loops and building multiple outbound nested loops from flattened input are common requirements.

- *Highly formalized structure, loosely defined usage*: Because of the complicated business information that they convey, EDI schemas have the highly formalized structure, grammar, and syntax of their EDI Standard to ensure that both the sender and receiver of a document have a common understanding of the contents. As usual, mandatory/optional, maximum length, repetitions, order, and so forth are specified in the schema. But an EDI schema also reflects the EDI standards in that there often are several options on where specific data may be placed. Company information, for example, may appear in many locations in the same EDI transaction, with each location having a different business definition. The schema defines how this information must be formatted wherever it appears, but it does not specify which location is correct for your purpose. Does the company information go in the header, the order level, the shipment level, the item level, or the summary? You must know the business rule to make the correct choice.

We present a brief overview of X12 and EDIFACT standards in this chapter for those readers who are new to EDI transaction mapping.

EDI Standards-Based Transactions

EDI documents are based on carefully defined, public standards that define the structures of the data elements, records (segments), and messages. There are two widely used standards for EDI:

- American National Standards Institute Committee for Exchange of Data (ANSI X12)

- United Nations Electronic Data Interchange for Administration Commerce and Trade (UN EDIFACT)

Maintained by public standards organizations, both X12 and EDIFACT define a wide variety of electronic message formats and publish updated standards each year. X12 is maintained by the Data Interchange Standards Association (DISA), based in Washington D.C. EDIFACT standards are maintained by the United Nations Centre for Trade Facilitation and Electronic

Business (UN/CEFACT) under the UN Economic Commission for Europe Committee of the United Nations, based in Switzerland.

The X12 standards definitions are most widely used in North America; the EDIFACT definitions are more commonly used in the rest of the world. You will often see both transaction standards used by the same party, thus you can expect that most EDI translation software will process transactions from both standards bodies.

Purists refer to X12 documents as transactions and EDIFACT documents as messages. Now that we've stated that for the record, we note that we aren't purists and use the two terms interchangeably in this discussion. Also, since our discussion in this chapter is a high-level view of these standards, we are certain to further offend EDI purists of many different stripes. Debates over the minutia of message content and meaning frequently become theological with some of the most vociferous discussions occurring at standards meetings. We will ignore minutia in the practical interest of brevity in this chapter.

Versions and Releases

Both X12 and EDIFACT release new versions of their standards each year. X12 updates its primary yearly release twice during the year; EDIFACT issues a trial version and a final version.

Note There is nothing wrong with using older versions of standards. Standards do not have an expiration date. The introduction of a new standard does not require modifications to your EDI operations. Today, we often find companies that are still using transactions from X12 versions 002 and 003, which have been in use for 15 or more years. Companies with a large EDI infrastructure often use a variety of releases to accommodate the needs of their trading partners. Unless a new release contains a new feature that is required by your business or a trading partner decides to upgrade its transactions, the release of a new version should not affect your existing operation.

Here are some general guidelines about how the standards change from release to release:

- Additional segments, groups of related segments, or loops may be added, thereby changing the relative position of existing segments. This is important to note for BizTalk mapping because schemas often use position information in the names of segments.

- Elements do not change. When an element must be modified, a new data element with the new properties is added to the dictionary.

- The internal composition of a segment may change. New elements are appended to the segment; very rarely are they inserted into the segment.

X12

Each issue of an X12 standard has a unique version, release, and subrelease number. That's by the book. For example, one release is 4010 (referred to as "forty ten") and the first subrelease for 4010 is 4011. In reality, subreleases are infrequent, thus most often the unique version and release number define all the transactions for a given year.

X12 transactions from different releases will be similar but will *not* be upward compatible. As new releases of the standards are published, new transactions are added, and existing transactions are modified. In some cases, the definitions of basic elements are changed. This was the case with version 4010, in which the date format changed from six to eight digits.

EDIFACT

EDIFACT standards are issued twice each year. The first release each year is a trial version lettered "A"; the second is the final version and is lettered "B". The last two digits of the year identify the year of release, thus versions issued in 1999 are referred to as 99A and 99B. As you see, the EDIFACT naming convention is easier to untangle. The guidelines on how the EDIFACT standards change from release to release are the same as those for X12 as previously discussed.

Using the Basic Building Blocks of EDI Messages

EDI transactions are built from segments. Segments can be arranged in groups or looping groups or can stand alone. Segments are built from elements. Elements may stand alone or have a relationship with other elements in a segment. The basic building block of an EDI transaction is the data element.

Before we begin discussing the elements, segments, and messages, let's look at samples of an X12 850 and an EDIFACT ORDERS transaction. Listing 13-1 shows the X12 purchase order.

Listing 13-1. *An ASCII X12 PO Sample*

```
ISA*00*          *00*          *01*SENDER        *01*RECEIVER      *
        080211*1720*U*00303*000011253*0*P*:
GS*IN*SENDER*RECEIVER*080211*172040*11039*X*003030
ST*810*11039
BIG*080206*SI179831*080124*10520***DI
N1*RI*THIS COMPANY*92*1111
N3*STREET ADDRESS
N4*CITY*NC*27344
N1*BS*THAT COMPANY*92*2222
N3*STREET
N4*CITT*NC*27607
ITD*ZZ*3*2**15
DTM*011*080206
IT1**160*EA*3.78**VC*42367
PID*F****PRODUCT
TDS*60480*60480*60480*60480
CTT*1
SE*15*11039
GE*1*11039
IEA*1*000011253
```

Listing 13-2 contains a sample EDIFACT purchase order, an ORDERS message. The ORDERS message is the equivalent to an X12 850 transaction.

Listing 13-2. *An EDIFACT ORDERS Sample*

```
UNA:+.?
UNB+UNOA:1+AAAAAA BBBBBB:ZZ+1111111111:12+2222222:1131+887++ORDERS++1++1
UNH+00000108323976+ORDERS:D:97A:UN
BGM+220+20050825+2
DTM+79:20050311:102
DTM+17:000000:402
FTX+ADU+++L
NAD+BY+123456
NAD+SU+3477889900
RFF+AIS:E113
TDT+30+++6
TOD++PC+:::N
LOC+18+MO2
LOC+25+US
LIN+00001++02K6651:BP::92
QTY+21:1:EA
TDT+30++++VEND:172
UNS+S
UNT+45+00000108323976
UNZ+1+887
```

There are more similarities between these two standards than are obvious from viewing the samples purchase orders in Listings 13-1 and 13-2. The differences between the two standards also have very little impact on how you will construct your maps. You will see how similar the two standards are as we break them down in the following discussion.

Examining a Simple X12 Data Element

The X12 data element defines a specific business object. Name, Address, Purchase Order Number, Identification Number, Currency, and Due Date are a few examples. Every X12 data element has a minimum of six associated properties, with a seventh that may appear once the data element has been assigned to a segment:

- *Dictionary ID*: The four-digit number used to identify the element
- *Description*: The short name for the element
- *Purpose*: The basic use for the element
- *Type*: The data type of the element
- *Minimum Length*: The minimum number of characters for the element
- *Maximum Length*: The maximum number of characters for the element
- *Requirement*: Defines whether the element is mandatory, optional, or conditional, and appears only when the element is in a segment

There are seven types of X12 data elements:

- *AN*: The Alphanumeric Character element includes any letter or number and several punctuation symbols from the standard ASCII character set. Unprintable characters are not part of the alphanumeric character set. Here's an example alphanumeric element descriptor: *127 Reference Identification AN 1/30*

- *ID*: ID Code elements are a specific subset of alphanumeric data. Each type of ID element has a code table of associated values. Here's an example ID line:
  374 Date/Time Qualifier ID 3/3

  EDI translation software validates the code sent in any element with an ID type to ensure that the code is included in the set of valid values. Not all ID element types have predefined code look-up tables. In such cases, the implementation guide should be used to indicate which codes are valid. In 4010, element 374 has an associated list of 1,112 codes that describe types of dates. Here are three example codes for that element:

  - 001: Cancel After Date
  - 002: Delivery Requested Date
  - 003: Invoice Date

- *Nx*: In the Numeric Integer element, the "x" represents the number of implied decimals. Integers may be negative if the minimum length of the element permits, and negative integers will be indicated by a separate leading sign. Here's an Nx example:
  610 Amount N2 1/15

- *R*: A Real Number element's value may or may not include a sign or decimal, and here's a Real Number example from the manual: *649 Multiplier R 1/10*

- *DT*: Date elements are always expressed without punctuation, either as CCYYMMDD or YYMMDD. In X12 translations, DT element types will be validated as correctly formatted dates. Here is an example Date element descriptor:
  370 Terms discount Due Date DT 8/8

- *TM*: Time elements are also expressed without punctuation, in 24-hour format with leading zeros. In X12 translations, TM element types will be validated as correctly formatted times. Here is an example Time element descriptor: *337 Time TM 4/8*

- *B*: Binary elements contain binary data. They are seldom used, because they can contain compiled code including viruses. They are also, as you might find with CAD drawing files, extremely large, thus the cost of transfer through a value-added network can be prohibitive.

Using Simple EDIFACT Data Elements

Like the X12 data element, the EDIFACT data element contains one piece of information. It also shares most of the same properties:

- *Code Number*: The four-digit code number that identifies the element
- *Name*: The name of the element
- *Type*: The data type of the element

- *Minimum Length*: The minimum number of characters for the element

- *Maximum Length*: The maximum number of characters for the element

- *Requirement*: Defines whether the element is mandatory, optional, or conditional and appears only when the element is in a segment

A significant difference between elements in X12 and in EDIFACT is in the types of elements that may exist. You saw that X12 defined seven specific types of elements. EDIFACT allows only three types of elements:

- *n*: Numeric elements may contain only digits, a decimal point, and a minus sign. When a decimal point exists, there must be at least one digit before and after the decimal point.

- *a*: Alphabetic elements may contain only alphabetic characters and embedded blanks. Leading spaces must be preserved.

- *an*: Alphanumeric elements may contain both alphabetic and numeric characters.

The fact that EDIFACT specifies only these three types of elements changes some behaviors as well. For example, all numbers may be real in EDIFACT. In X12, you must be more careful to ensure that a number be in the correct format. Also, in EDIFACT all dates and times are treated as strings, thus they are not validated to a specific format by the EDI engine.

Using Composite X12 Elements

A composite element is an organized collection of data elements such as medical diagnostic codes or measurements. The Dictionary ID for a composite element is a "C" followed by a three-digit sequence number. A composite element might be a string with the same element repeated several times, or it might be a set of different elements.

The composite element that is most used in X12 is C001, Composite Unit of Measure, which contains the 15 data elements shown in Table 13-1.

Table 13-1. *X12 Composite Element C001, Composite Unit of Measure*

Pos	ID	Name	M/O	Type	Min/Max
01	355	Unit or Basis for Measurement Code	M	ID	2/2
02	1018	Exponent	O	R	1/15
03	649	Multiplier	O	R	1/10
04	355	Unit or Basis for Measurement Code	O	ID	2/2
05	1018	Exponent	O	R	1/15
06	649	Multiplier	O	R	1/10
07	355	Unit or Basis for Measurement Code	O	ID	2/2
08	1018	Exponent	O	R	1/15
09	649	Multiplier	O	R	1/10
10	355	Unit or Basis for Measurement Code	O	ID	2/2
11	1018	Exponent	O	R	1/15

Continued

Table 13-1. *Continued*

Pos	ID	Name	M/O	Type	Min/Max
12	649	Multiplier	O	R	1/10
13	355	Unit or Basis for Measurement Code	O	ID	2/2
14	1018	Exponent	O	R	1/15
15	649	Multiplier	O	R	1/10

Note The tables in this chapter are excerpts from standards manuals and specifications. As such, we have retained as much of the original formatting as possible, including the use of abbreviations in the headers. Thus the header for a particular column may change from table to table even though the contents of the column are of the same type.

Individual elements in a composite element add the Requirement property just as they do when assigned to a segment. Composite elements are more common in EDIFACT messages than in X12 messages.

Using Composite EDIFACT Elements

EDIFACT makes much more extensive use of composite elements, instead of relying on multiple segment definitions to contain the same data as does X12. A perfect example is the EDIFACT NAD, or Name and Address, segment. All the information for the address can be contained in a single segment. In X12, a group of four segments is needed to contain the same information. The 04B standard has almost 200 composite element definitions; X12 4010 has only 28. Table 13-2 shows a simple EDIFACT composite element.

Table 13-2. *EDIFACT Composite Element C507, DATE/TIME PERIOD*

Num	Name	M/O Type	Len
2005	DATE/TIME/PERIOD FUNCTION CODE QUALIFIER	M	an..3
2380	DATE/TIME/PERIOD	C	an..35
2379	DATE/TIME/PERIOD FORMAT QUALIFIER	C	an..3

Like X12, EDIFACT elements in a composite gain the Mandatory/Optional/Conditional property just as if they were in a segment.

Creating X12 Segments

A version of the X12 standards contains many segments. Release 4010 defines 1,132 segments. A segment, the EDI equivalent of a record in a flat file, is composed of a group of data elements that are related to one another in some business sense. For example, the segment N4,

Geographic Location, contains data elements that relate in some way to a geographic location. Let's look at the data elements that form the N4 segment as shown in Table 13-3.

Table 13-3. *Definition of the N4 Segment*

Pos	No	Description	M/O	Type	Min/Max
01	19	City Name	O	AN	2/30
02	156	State or Province Code	O	ID	2/2
03	116	Postal Code	O	ID	3/15
04	26	Country Code	O	ID	2/3
05	309	Location Qualifier	X	ID	1/2
06	310	Location Identifier	O	AN	1/30

■**Caution** One feature unique to segments is the use of an "X" in the M/O, or Mandatory/Optional, field for elements. Data elements in a segment may have a conditional relationship with other data elements in the segment. These rules are not enforced in BizTalk unless the value for X12Condition_Check in the schema is set to Yes.

As Table 13-3 shows, the N4 segment can have as many as six or as few as one data element. Even with all elements shown as optional, there must be at least one data element present in order for the segment to be sent. The N4, like all X12 segments, has several general characteristics:

- A two- or-three digit alphanumeric tag, beginning with a letter, to identify the segment
- A specific business definition to define the business use of the segment
- One or more data elements in a defined sequence
- A delimiter
- Empty trailing data elements and separators are dropped
- At least one element in a segment that contains data if the segment is to be transmitted
- A segment delimiter to terminate the segment that must be a different character than the element separator

This is a typical N4 segment: N4*Raleigh*NC*27607*USA~. You should notice that the fifth and sixth data elements are missing and that the asterisks that would normally be used to separate them from each other and from the fourth element have been dropped. If we remove the state code, NC, we get N4*Raleigh**27607*USA~. Now, you see that the second data element is empty but the separators remain.

Note Examples of segments in this material use the asterisk as the element delimiter. In X12 transactions, the asterisk is probably the most commonly used delimiter. Others that are often used are the pipe (|) or the tilde (~).

Referring to a data element by the segment tag and the positional location of the element in the segment is common practice. In the N4 segment, the element City would be referred to as the N401.

Creating EDIFACT Segments

EDIFACT segments are also logical groupings of business-related data items. EDIFACT has two kinds of segments, service and generic segments. Service segments are analogous to X12 interchange, group, and transaction enveloping segments and are discussed in the next section with them. General characteristics of EDIFACT segments follow:

- A three-character alphanumeric code is used to identify the segment.

- A description defines the contents of the segment.

- A segment contains one or more data elements in a defined sequence.

- A delimiter is used to separate the elements. In EDIFACT, the delimiter is usually a plus sign (+) for elements and a colon (:) for subelements.

- Empty trailing data elements and separators are dropped.

- A segment terminator, different from the element delimiter, terminates the segment. In EDIFACT the standard segment terminator is a single-quote, (').

Tip EDIFACT provides a standard release character to allow use of the plus sign and the colon in general text. The release character is the question mark (?). For example 10?+5=15 is interpreted as 10 + 5 = 15. A question mark is signified by ??.

A typical EDIFACT segment would appear as LIN+00001++02K6651:BP::92'. Note that this segment shows three elements and four subelements. The second element is empty as denoted by the two consecutive plus signs. The third subelement is empty as denoted by the two consecutive colons.

Exploring X12 Segment Syntax Rules and Mapping

X12 segments have an additional type of validation in the form of syntax rules, for which there is no equivalent in EDIFACT. These syntax rules place restrictions, beyond those described in the element definitions, on how the elements within an EDI segment may be used. The rules also introduce a wrinkle to mapping that is not often encountered when mapping other transaction types.

■**Caution** Segment syntax rules are not active by default in the BizTalk R2 schemas. They are activated by setting the annotation `X12ConditionDesignator_Check` in a schema to `Yes`. Many trading partners will require that the segment syntax rules in your outbound transactions be validated before they are sent.

X12 segment syntax rules provide for several types of enforceable relationships between conditional elements in a segment. The stipulation of a conditional element requirement means that there is a syntactical relationship between that element and some other element in the same segment. There are five types of syntactical relationships:

- *Required*: At least one of the data elements noted must be used. In segment N1, the notation R0203 means that either element N102 or N103 is required.

- *Paired*: If any of the noted data elements are present, all must be present. In segment N1, the notation P0304 means that if either element N103 or N104 is present, the other must also be present.

- *Exclusion*: No more than one data element in the list may be used. In segment TD3, the notation E0110 means that if either element TD301 or TD310 is present then the other must not be present.

- *Conditional*: Both noted data elements must be present. In segment PO1, the notation C0504 means that if the P0105 element is present then the PO104 must also be present.

- *List Conditional*: If the first data element is present, at least one of the other elements listed must be present. In segment SAC, the notation L130204 means that if the SAC13 element is present then either the SAC02 or SAC04 must also be present.

Understanding these syntax rules is especially important for mapping when using the default BizTalk schemas without activating the checking, because you must enforce the rules in your map.

Understanding X12 Transactions

Each X12 transaction relates to a single type of business document such as a purchase order or an invoice. X12 transactions are identified by a three-digit numeric code. These codes are maintained from one release of the standards to the next, thus a purchase order will always have the same identifier. We often refer to the type of transaction by the identifier. For example, we refer to a purchase order as an 850.

Tables

The definition of a transaction contains a list of the segments used, the order in which the segments must appear, and how the segments are repeated or grouped. X12 transactions generally have a three-part structure. Each part is referred to as a table.

- *Header table*: Segments and groups of segments whose contents relate to the entire transaction are in the header table, for example, the purchase order number in an 850 transaction.

- *Detail table*: Segments that relate to the business object focal to the transaction. For example, the focus of an 850 is the line items, so line item information is found in the detail table. Segments in the detail are often repetitive, or looping, with the contents in each repetition relating to a different instance of the business object.

- *Summary table*: Segments that contain summary information such as line counts and hash totals that relate to the entire transaction. The total monetary value of the purchase order is an example.

Segments within each table are organized into a specific sequence following these general rules:

- A segment has a positional indicator consisting of a three-digit number that relates its position in the transaction. The first segment has 010, the next 020, and so forth. When an error occurs, an error message might use the number to indicate in which segment the error occurred.

- A segment may be mandatory or optional. There are no conditional segments.

- A segment may repeat up to a specified maximum number of iterations.

- Segments may be grouped. Groups may repeat, up to a specified maximum number of iterations. A group of segments may be defined, or nested, within another group. We refer to groups as loops.

Loops

There are two different types of loops in X12 transactions, bounded and unbounded loops. Bounded loops begin with a specific loop control segment and end with a specific loop control segment. Listing 13-3 has two iterations of a bounded loop that begin with the loop control LS segment and end with the loop control LE segment.

Listing 13-3. *A Bounded Loop*

```
LS*01
    LDT*AE*17*DA
    REF*CR*8331
LE*01
LS*02
    QTY*EA*100
    MSG*THIS IS TOTAL QTY
LE*02
```

A bounded loop is used when none of the segments in a group is mandatory. Parsers cannot identify the start or end of a loop that has no mandatory segment, so the start and end are marked by the loop start (LS) and loop end (LE) segments.

Unbounded loops are triggered by the presence of the first segment in the looping group and terminated by the presence of a segment that is not in the group. The name and address loop, also called the N1 loop, is a common loop. The N1 segment indicates the beginning of a name and address loop. An N1 loop with four iterations is in Listing 13-4.

Listing 13-4. *An Unbounded Loop*

```
N1*ST*JIM DAWSON
   N4*SILER CITY*NC
N1*SF*JOHN WAINWRIGHT
   N4*RALEIGH*NC
N1*RT*SSPS
N1*BT*SSPS
```

Two of the loops in Listing 13-4 contain only the N1 segment; two contain a child N4 segment as well. A recurrence of the N1 before a segment not allowed in the loop indicates a repetition of the loop. Encountering a segment not allowed in the loop terminates the looping.

As you might expect, loops may contain other loops. Listing 13-5 shows three LIN loops, two of which contain an N1 loop. We refer to these N1 loops as children of the LIN loop, or as nested loops.

Listing 13-5. *A Nested N1 Loop*

```
LIN**MG*AEAS001-04
  UIT*EA*22.85
LIN**MG*AEAS001-04
  N1*ST*JIM DAWSON
     N4*SILER CITY*NC
LIN**MG*AHMC002-02
  UIT*EA*36.6
  N1*SF*JOHN WAINWRIGHT
     N4*RALEIGH*NC
```

Transaction Structure

The grouping arrangements that we have just examined, tables and loops, define the overall structure of an X12 transaction. Table 13-4 contains the structure for a sample 4010 purchase order acknowledgment (855). Not all of the segments are shown, as you can tell by the sequence numbers.

Table 13-4. *Sample Purchase Order Acknowledgment (855)*

No.	ID	Name Description	Req	Max. Use	Repeat
Heading					
020	BAK	Beginning Segment for Purchase Order Acknowledgment	M	1	
150	DTM	Date/Time Reference	O	10	
		LOOP ID - N1			200
300	N1	Name	O	1	
320	N3	Address Information	O	2	
330	N4	Geographic Location	O	1	

Continued

Table 13-4. *Continued*

No.	ID	Name Description	Req	Max. Use	Repeat
Detail					
		LOOP ID - PO1			10,0000
010	PO1	Baseline Item Data	O	1	
		LOOP ID – ACK			104
270	ACK	Line Item Acknowledgment	O	1	
Summary					
		LOOP ID – CTT			1
010	CTT	Transaction Totals	O	1	

The structure depicted in Table 13-4 is what you might find in an implementation guide from a trading partner. The trading partner is including only those segments of interest to him.

Understanding EDIFACT Transactions

The structure of an EDIFACT message is very similar to an X12 transaction. Like X12, an EDIFACT message represents a single business document. Each EDIFACT message is identified by a six-character name. While we call an X12 purchase order an 850 transaction, we refer to an EDIFACT purchase order as an ORDERS message.

Areas

An EDIFACT message is made of three areas:

- *Header*: The header contains information that pertains to the entire business document.

- *Detail*: The detail section contains information that pertains to the primary business object.

- *Summary*: The summary contains totals and/or control information.

As you see, the three areas of the EDIFACT message are the same as the three tables of the X12 transaction, right down to the type of content.

Transaction Structure

Segments in each area are organized according to specifications presented in the area definitions. Here are the specifications:

- *Position*: The position is a four-digit number that indicates order of the segment in the message.

- *Requirements Designator*: Mandatory means that the segment must appear. Conditional means that the segment may be used but is not required. The Conditional designator is equivalent to the X12 Optional designator.

- *Repetition*: This specifies how many times the segment may appear.

- *Segment Group*: Groupings of segments that may repeat as a group are defined as Segment Group 1, Segment Group 2, and so on. Segment groups are the equivalent of X12 loops. Like X12 loops, segment groups may be nested.

Segment groups, which we also refer to as loops, behave like the unbounded loops of X12. The first segment in the group is mandatory and indicates the beginning of the loop. The occurrence of a segment not in the group ends the loop. The recurrence of the first segment of the loop before a segment not in the loop is encountered begins a new iteration of the loop. Table 13-5 depicts a sample structure for an EDIFACT ORDERS message as you might find in a client's specification.

Table 13-5. *Sample ORDERS Message*

TAG	NAME	S	REPT	S	REPT
Header Section					
BGM	Beginning of message	M	1		
DTM	Date/time/period	M	35		
	Segment Group 2	C			99
NAD	Name and address	M	1		
LOC	Place/location identification			C	99
Detail Section					
	Segment Group 29	C			200,000
LIN	Line item	M	1		
IMD	Item description	C	99		
QTY	Quantity	C	99		
	Segment Group 33	C			25
PRI	Price details	M	1		
Summary Section					
UNS	Section control	M	1		

Exploring X12 Interchanges

To this point, we've focused on the data portion of an X12 transaction. Every X12 transaction is part of an X12 interchange, which is a hierarchical grouping of one or more transactions. The data portion of the transaction is the inner block of the hierarchy.

ST and SE

Two segments surround each data portion. These are the ST (Transaction Set Header) and SE (Transaction Set Trailer) segments. An example is in Listing 13-6.

Listing 13-6. *ST and SE Segments*

```
ST*855*0001
...
SE*21*0001
```

The ST segment in Listing 13-6 states that the data enclosed between itself and the next SE segment pertains to a purchase order acknowledgment. You know this because the ST01 contains the value 855, which is the X12 transaction designator for a purchase order acknowledgment. The ST02 contains the Transaction Set control number, in this case the value 00001. This number tells you that this transaction is first in the block of transactions at this level of the hierarchy. The value would be incremented for each additional message at this level.

The SE segment in Listing 13-6 terminates the current transaction data set. SE01, here with the value 21, says that there should be 21 segments in this transaction, including the ST and SE segments. SE02, with the value 0001, tells you that this SE segment should be the first SE segment encountered after the ST segment with the ST02 value of 0001.

GS and GE

One or more transactions, as denoted by the ST and SE segments, become part of the next higher level hierarchy, the group. A group is denoted by the segments GS (Functional Group Header) and GE (Functional Group Trailer). Listing 13-7 presents an X12 Group containing two 855 transactions.

Listing 13-7. *Group Segments*

```
GS*PO*SENDERID*RECEIVERID*20080825*0521*000000001*X*004010
ST*855*0001
...
SE*19*0001
ST*855*0002
...
SE*22*0002
GE*2*000000001
```

The GS segment presents information about the group. A group allows transactions within an interchange to be addressed to different receivers. A group consists of the following elements:

- *GS01*: This is the Functional Identifier Code used to indicate the type of transactions in this group. A group contains related transactions, such as purchase orders and purchase order acknowledgments. You would not expect to find an 856, Advance Ship Notice, in the same group as these transactions. The value PO states that the transactions contained in this group relate to purchase orders.

- *GS02*: This is the Application Sender's Code, a value that identifies the sender of the group.

- *GS03*: The Application Receiver's Code indicates the party to whom the group is being sent.

- *GS04*: The Date is the date the group was formed.

- *GS05*: The Time is the time the group was formed.

- *GS06*: The Group Control Number works the same way as the Transaction Control number.

- *GS07*: The Responsible Agency Code identifies the standard under which these transactions were formed. The value X indicates X12.

- *GS08*: The Version/Release/Industry Identifier Code is a code that specifies the version and release of the transactions in the group. The value 004010 tells you that this group contains X12 release 4010 transactions.

The GE segment terminates the group. The GE01 contains the number of transactions (ST to SE blocks) in the group; the GE02 contains the control number that must match the control number in the paired GS segment.

ISA and IEA

The top level of the hierarchy is the interchange. An X12 interchange can contain one or more groups of transactions. The interchange is formed by an ISA (Interchange Control Header) segment and an IEA (Interchange Control Trailer) segment. Listing 13-8 shows an interchange with two groups.

Listing 13-8. *Interchange Segments*

```
ISA*00* . . . . . . . . . . . *00* . . . . . . . . . . . *ZZ*1234567890 . . . . . *01*
          190450551 . . . . . . *030214*1251*U*00401*000000001*0*P*>~
GS*PO*SENDERID*RECEIVERID*20080825*0521*000000001*X*004010
ST*855*0001
...
SE*19*0001
ST*855*0002
...
SE*22*0002
GE*2*000000001
GS*PO*SENDERID*RECEIVERID*20080825*0521*000000002*X*004010
ST*855*0001
...
SE*19*0001
GE*1*000000002
IEA*1*0000000501~
```

Tip The ISA segment is the only fixed-length segment in X12. The separators in inbound X12 transactions are specified in the ISA. The element separator is always found in byte 4, the sub-element separator in byte 105, and the segment separator in byte 106. Technically, the segment separator is actually the one or two characters from byte 106 to the beginning of the next segment, which must be the GS segment. This is because most translators allow for a carriage return/line feed (CR/LF) to trail the segment terminator (or for either the CR or LF to be the segment terminator and the other to follow).

Our ISA segment in Listing 13-8 contains the following:

- *ISA*: These characters identify the start of an X12 interchange.

- *Byte 4*: This contains the element separator that will be used throughout the interchange.

- *ISA01*: The Authorization Information Qualifier is invariably the value 00.

- *ISA02*: The Authorization Information field is seldom used. You will see ten blanks in this field.

- *ISA03*: The Security Information Qualifier is invariably the value 00.

- *ISA04*: The Security Information element is seldom used. You will see ten blanks in this field.

- *ISA05*: The Interchange ID Qualifier value tells you from what code list the ISA06 is derived. In our segment, the value ZZ means Mutually Determined (generated by the two trading partners).

- *ISA06*: The Interchange Receiver ID contains the value that identifies the sending party.

- *ISA07*: Here is another Interchange ID Qualifier. This value tells you from what code list the ISA08 is derived. In our segment, the value 01 means the ISA08 element is a DUNS number.

- *ISA08*: The Interchange Receiver ID contains the value that identifies the receiving party.

- *ISA09*: The Interchange Date provides the date the interchange was created.

- *ISA10*: The Interchange Time provides the time the interchange was created.

- *ISA11*: This is the Interchange Control Standards Identifier. The value U in our ISA indicates that we are using the U.S. EDI Community of ASC X12, TDCC, and UCS.

- *ISA12*: This is Interchange Control Version Number. The value 00401 indicates that the transaction groups in this interchange all contain transactions from Version 4010.

- *ISA13*: The Interchange Control Number is used to ensure that interchanges are received in the correct order. If you receive interchange 0000012 followed by interchange 0000014, interchange 0000013 may have gotten lost.

- *ISA14*: The Acknowledgement Requested flag indicates whether or not the sender desires that you return a 997 transaction to acknowledge receipt of the transactions in this interchange.

- *ISA15*: The Usage Indicator flag indicates the purpose of this interchange: test, production, or information.

- *ISA16*: The Component Element Separator is byte 105, now used to specify the separator that is used in any component elements in the interchange.

- *Byte 106*: This is the location of the segment terminator. Segments might also have one or two more characters following them. Following characters can be either or both the carriage return and line feed. A carriage return or line feed character can also be the segment terminator.

Caution The ISA12 element has fallen into disuse over the years, and many parties do not update their software when they change the versions of their transactions. You may receive interchanges where the ISA12 specifies that the version is 3010, but the groups specify 4050, for example. The transactions would be version 4050 in this case. Certain EDI engines struggle when the ISA12 contains a version number that does not match the transactions.

This very brief review of the ISA, GS, ST, SE, GE, and IEA segments provides the basics necessary for you to understand the concept of an X12 interchange. Years ago, interchanges with multiple groups, each with multiple transactions, were very common. Today, the majority of our clients send one transaction per group and one group per interchange. Even though there is only one transaction in an interchange, the rules governing these six segments are still enforced, and you must be aware of them.

Exploring EDIFACT Interchanges

The architecture of the EDIFACT interchange is similar to X12 in that there are enveloping segments at the interchange, group, and message level. The interpretation and rules surrounding the EDIFACT interchange architecture differ considerably from X12, though, as you will see. EDIFACT requires two levels of enveloping and allows one optional level:

- *Interchange*: The EDIFACT interchange begins with a UNB segment and terminates with a UNZ segment.

- *Message*: Each message begins with a UNH segment and terminates with a UNT segment.

- *Group*: This level allows you to group together like messages within an interchange and to route messages within an interchange to different departments. Consisting of the UNG/UNE pair, this level is optional in the EDIFACT standards.

Caution Although the UNG/UNE group is optional in the standards, use of the UNG/UNE is mandatory in interchanges going to or from North America.

UNH and UNT

The message-level envelope consists of the UNH and UNT segments.

An example of the message-level segments is shown in Listing 13-9. The UNH segment is more complex than the equivalent X12 ST:

- *0062*: The Message Reference Number is unique within a group and identifies the message within that group. This is a mandatory element.

- *S009*: The Message Identifier is a mandatory composite element, with seven subelements that identify the message type, version, release, controlling agency, responsible association, code list directory version, and message type subfunction. As you can see in Listing 13-9, the last three subelements are optional.

- *0068*: The optional Common Access Reference Number element provides a means for tracking a series of messages and ensuring that a business transaction is completed. For example, the business process might require four messages: ORDERS, DESADV, INVOIC, and REMADV. By putting the same Common Reference Number in all four messages, the parties can ensure that the entire business process completes.

- *S010*: Status of the Transfer is an optional, composite element with two subelements. This element allows the parties to assign sequence numbers to messages relating to the same business transaction.

- *S016*: Message Subset Identification is an optional, composite element with four subelements. If the message is a subset, this element contains the identifier, version, release, and source of that subset.

- *S017*: Message Implementation Guideline Identification is another optional, composite element with four subelements. It provides a means to identify the details of the implementation guide used to create the message.

- *S018*: Scenario Identification is an optional, composite element with four subelements that identify a scenario.

Listing 13-9. *UNH and UNT Segments*

```
UNH+00000108323976+ORDERS:D:97A:UN
......
UNZ+1+887
```

The UNT segment, shown in Listing 13-9, is the message-terminating segment that pairs with the UNH. The UNT, which is formed by two data elements, contains the information necessary to make sure that the message is intact.

- *Number of Segments*: This is the number of segments in the message including the UNH and UNT segments.

- *Message Reference Number*: This number should be the same as the message reference number in the paired UNH segment.

Messages may be grouped by message function. Grouping is optional except for messages flowing to or from North America, in which case grouping is required. Functional groups are formed using the UNG and UNE segments. The UNG segment that specifies the beginning of a group has seven data elements.

- *0038*: The required Message Group Identification element specifies the type of messages that make up the group.

- *S006*: Application Sender Identification is a required, two-subelement composite element that contains the identification code qualifier and the identification code for the sender of the group.

- *S007*: Application Recipient Identification is a required, two-subelement composite element that contains the identification code qualifier and the identification code for the receiver of the group.

- *S004*: This is the Date and Time of Preparation element. Date and time subelements form this mandatory composite element that indicates the date and time the group was created.

- *0048*: The mandatory Group Reference Number, assigned by the sender, must be unique for groups within the interchange.

- *0051*: The optional, coded Controlling Agency element identifies the controlling agency under which the group was formed.

- *S008*: The mandatory Message Version composite element has three subelements that specify the version and release used to format the group.

- *0058*: Application Password is an optional element that may be used for security.

UNG and UNE

The UNG segment begins the group and is paired with an UNE segment that ends the group. Listing 13-10 contains a group with two messages.

Listing 13-10. *EDIFACT Group*

```
UNG+ORDERS+SENDER:01+ RECEIVER+20080904:1213+1+UN+D:05B'
UNH
...
UNT
UNH
...
UNT
UNE+2+1'
```

The UNE segment that ends a group contains two elements that provide the means to ensure that the group is intact.

- *Group Control Count*: This is the number of messages in the group.

- *Group Reference Number*: This number must match the group reference number in the paired UNG.

Of course, there may be more than one group in an interchange, which is the top level of the EDIFACT hierarchy.

UNA, UNB, and UNZ

The UNA, UNB, and UNZ segments are used to create the interchange.

Note The UNA segment is optional, thus the interchange may be fully formed using the UNB and UNZ segments, which are both mandatory. The UNA segment is required only when the character set used in the interchange is not the default character set as defined for the version.

The optional UNA segment is used to specify the character set used in the interchange when not using the default. It contains six elements, each of which specifies a separator or terminator used in the interchange.

- *Component Data Element Separator*: The character used to separate subelements

- *Data Element Separator*: The character used to separate elements

- *Decimal Mark*: The character used for decimal notation

- *Release Character*: The character used as a release character

- *Repetition Separator*: The character used for repetition separation

- *Segment Terminator*: The character that indicates the end of a segment

The UNB segment that starts the interchange consists of ten elements, including those that identify the sender and receiver of the interchange:

- *S001*: The Syntax Identifier is a mandatory composite element made of four subelements; the syntax identifier specifies the syntax and version information for the interchange.

- *S002*: This is the Interchange Sender. Four subelements form this mandatory element that identifies the sender of the interchange.

- *S003*: The Interchange Recipient is a mandatory composite element formed by four subelements. It identifies the receiver of the interchange.

- *S004*: Date and Time of Preparation is a mandatory composite element containing two subelements that indicate the date and time that the interchange was created.

- *0020*: The mandatory Interchange Control Reference element contains the control number that identifies the interchange.

- *S005*: The optional Recipient Reference/Password Details composite element is made up of two subelements that contain security information.

- *0026*: The optional Application Reference element specifies the type of message in the interchange if the interchange contains only one type. It may be used by the receiver to route the interchange to the correct application.

- *0029*: The optional Processing Priority Code element allows interchanges to be assigned priorities for processing.

- *0031*: Acknowledgment Request, another optional element, indicates whether or not an acknowledgment is wanted by the sender.

- *0032*: The Interchange Agreement Identifier element identifies any underlying agreements that control the exchange of data.

- *0035*: The optional Test Indicator element indicates if the message is a test or production message.

Listing 13-11 shows an interchange enveloping the group from Listing 13-10. It includes a sample UNA segment.

Listing 13-11. *EDIFACT Interchange*

```
UNA:+.?*'
UNB+UNOC:4+SENDER:01+RECEIVER:14+20080904:1200+
                              123455678+++++EANCOMREF 52'
UNG+ORDERS+SENDER:01+RECEIVER+20080904:1213+1+UN+D:05B'
UNH
...
UNT
UNH
...
UNT
UNE+2+1'
UNZ+1+123456789'
```

The UNZ segment terminates the interchange and contains two elements:

- *Interchange Control Count*: This is the number of messages in the interchange if there are no functional groups. If there are functional groups, this is the number of groups.

- *Interchange Control Reference*: This number must match the interchange control reference number found in the paired UNB.

As with the X12 interchange discussion, this review of the segments that are used to create the enveloping for EDIFACT messages is very brief and intended to provide only the basics necessary for you to understand the concept.

Next, let's look at an example that illustrates some of the differences between EDIFACT and X12.

Illustrating the Differences Between X12 and EDIFACT

Finally, let's look at how the two standards present a common set of information, such as name and address information, a block of data common to all EDI transactions. Listing 13-12 is the information we wish to insert into our EDI message.

Listing 13-12. *Name and Address Information*

```
Type Partner:  Bill To (BT)
Second Star Professional Services, LLC
Attn: John Wainwright
7008 Robbie Drive
Raleigh, NC  27607  USA
```

In an X12 message, it would take a group of four segments to encode all of this information, as shown in Listing 13-13.

Listing 13-13. *Name and Address Information in X12*

```
N1*BT*Second Star Professional Services, LLC
N3*Attn: John Wainwright*7008 Robbie Drive
N4*Raleigh*NC*27607*USA
```

Notice that there is only one separator, the asterisk, and that the segment terminator is CR/LF. Listing 13-14 shows that EDIFACT uses a single segment for the same information.

Listing 13-14. *Name and Address Information in EDIFACT*

```
NAD+BT++Second Star Professional Services, LLC:Attn?: John Wainwright+
        7008 Robbie Drive ++Raleigh+NC+55343+US
```

Here, you see that instead of breaking the data into segments, EDIFACT uses composite elements so that all the data can fit in one segment. Remember that the use of composite elements, high in EDIFACT and very low in X12, is one of the primary differences between the two.

Summary

This chapter barely scratched the surface of EDI but should suffice to help you understand the basic characteristics of transactions, interchanges, groups, segments, and so forth. Once you begin mapping EDI documents, you may find that you need to dig even deeper into the subject. Fortunately, the remainder of Part 4 of this book starts you down that path by examining BizTalk mapping difficulties that you may encounter in trying to map to or from an EDI schema.

The next four chapters all focus on EDI mapping with BizTalk and become increasingly technical in content. The first brings looping into the EDI arena, where business requirements often force you to create unusual looping structures. EDI code pairs are discussed next. Code pairs, while not unique to EDI, certainly are made more complex by X12 in that their positions are often free-floating within records. The X12 SDQ segment, which introduces a new kind of paired object whose interpretation varies based on qualifiers in other segments is next. Then, finally, we encounter the big bugaboo, the HL loop. The HL loop is another X12 construct where the interpretation of the data at any given point must be inferred from several data items in another segment.

Although these next four chapters address EDI mapping specifically, the techniques that appear in the examples can certainly be of value in non-EDI mapping.

■■■

CHAPTER 14

Exploring EDI Looping

Mapping to or from EDI schemas brings new twists. Not only do you have to work through the kind of problems that you saw in the general mapping chapters but now you have to deal with the specific syntax conditions that the EDI standards bring to the table. On top of that, you must manipulate your maps to accommodate sometimes-quirky business rules.

The last chapter introduced you to the structure and syntax of EDI documents. This chapter begins the EDI mapping discussion right where we left off in the general looping discussion—with EDI looping problems. Every EDI schema has segments that loop; most have groups and nested groups that all loop. You can expect to encounter looping in every map that involves EDI transactions.

Adding to the complexity of handling looping in EDI is that you will almost always find that the structure of your non-EDI schema does not match well with the structure of your EDI schema. You can expect to encounter many instances of one-to-many and many-to-one looping requirements. This chapter presents some common EDI looping issues that you will encounter.

Note This is the first of four chapters that discuss the mapping of EDI structures with BizTalk. The examples in these chapters are discussed using EDI terms and phrases, thus you are expected to have some familiarity with EDI. The previous chapter provided a high-level overview of EDI. The methods used in the maps in these EDI chapters are adaptable to non-EDI mapping, just as we use many of the techniques discussed in the non-EDI chapters to do EDI maps.

Looping from EDI to an Application

The common looping problems in EDI mapping can be illustrated using the name and address loop. Since almost every X12 or EDIFACT message has one or more of these loops, the name and address loop is a natural choice for use in examples. The X12 name and address loop is the N1 loop; the EDIFACT counterpart is the NAD loop.

Figure 14-1 shows the BizTalk schema structure for the EDIFACT NAD loop; Figure 14-2 shows the corresponding N1 loop structure. We will focus on the NAD segment in the NAD loop and on the N1, N2, N3, and N4 segments in the N1 loop.

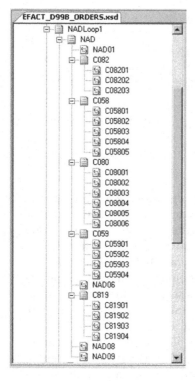

Figure 14-1. *EDIFACT name and address (NAD) loop structure*

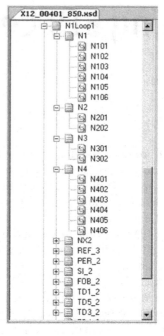

Figure 14-2. *X12 name and address (N1) loop structure*

The NAD loop has fewer segments than the N1 and the actual address information is contained in a single segment instead of four segments. Also, the NAD segment uses composite elements. While both the NAD and the N1 segments may occur as stand-alone segments in a loop, more often than not, the loop will also contain other segments. For example, the X12 version 4010 N1 loop has 14 other segments that may appear with the N1 segment.

■**Note** The examples in this section use EDI terminology. If you have difficulty following the discussion, you should read Chapter 13.

Our first examples use the application file schema shown in Figure 14-3. The Address loop, highlighted in the figure, contains the name and address nodes with which we will work.

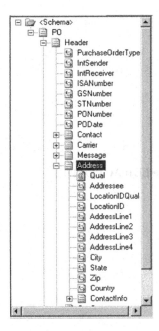

Figure 14-3. *Application file schema*

Here are the data files that we use for the EDI-to-application mapping examples.
Listing 14-1 is the X12 source file.

Listing 14-1. *X12 4010 850 (Purchase Order) Data*

```
ST*850*0001
BEG*00*SA*BTB281155**20081105
CUR*ZZ*USD
PER*BD*MAPPER JOE*TE*617-555-1234
FOB*PP
DTM*002*20090311
TD5****M*BEST WAY
N9*LI*TEXT
MSG*THIS IS A TEST FOR EDI
MSG*THIS IS NOT AN ORDER
MSG*THIS IS A TEST ONLY
  N1*SE*SECOND STAR PROFESSIONAL SERVICES*1*114718214 - 1st N1 Loop
    N2*EDUCATION SERVICES
    N3*7008 ROBBIE DRIVE
    N4*RALEIGH*NC*27607*US
  N1*SF*PACKAGE EXPRESS   - 2nd N1 Loop
    N3*557 SOME STREET
    N4*CARY*NC*27511*US
  N1*ST*BIG TECHNICAL BOOKSHOP - 3rd N1 Loop
    N3*532 ARESENAL ROAD
    N3*REECEIVING DOCK A
```

```
   N4*WATERTOWN*MA*16016*US
  N1*BT*BIG BOOK EMPIRE   - 4th N1 Loop
    N2*ATTN ACCOUNTS PAYABLE
    N3*1058 DEAD END ST.
    N4*BOSTON*MA*16016*US
PO1*0001*100*EA*49.95*PE*IB*978-1-4302-1857-9
PID*F****PRO MAPPING FOR BIZTALK 2009
CTT*1
SE*30*0001
```

The X12 850 example has four N1 loops. Listing 14-2 contains the EDIFACT ORDERS source data, which has four NAD loops.

Listing 14-2. *EDIFACT E99B ORDERS (Purchase Order) Example Data*

```
UNH+00000108323976+ORDERS:D:99B:UN'
BGM+220+BTB281155+9'
DTM+74:20090311:102'
FTX+PUR+++MAPPER JOE'
FTX+ORI+++617-555-1234'
RFF+ADJ:SECONDSTAR'
RFF+ON:BTB281155'
RFF+ACF:SECOND STAR'
RFF+ACF:SSPS TRAINING DIVISION'
  NAD+SE+114718214::16+SECOND STAR PROFESSIONAL SERVICES:ATTN
         JIM DAWSON++7008 ROBBIE DRIVE+RALEIGH+NC+27607+US' - 1st NAD Loop
  NAD+SF++PACKAGE EXPRESS++557 SOME STREET+CARY+NC+
         27511+US' - 2nd NAD Loop
  NAD+ST++BIG TECHNICAL BOOKSHOP++532 ARESENAL RD.::::RECEIVING
         DOCK A+WATERTOWN+MA+16016+US' - 3rd NAD Loop
  NAD+BT++BIG BOOK EMPIRE+ATTN ACCOUNTS PAYABLE+1058 DEAD END
          ST.+BOSTON+MA+16016+US' - 4th NAD Loop
CUX+6:USD'
TDT+30+++18:BEST WAY'
TOD++PC'
LIN+0001++978-1-4302-1857-9:IB'
IMD+F++:::PRO MAPPING FOR BIZTALK 2009'
QTY+21:100:EA'
UNS+S'UNS+S
```

■**Caution** All of our EDI examples contain a carriage return and line feed at the end of each segment to make the data easier to read. EDIFACT messages do not normally have the carriage return and line feed, and X12 transactions frequently do not.

Exploring the X12-to-Application Solution

One common requirement in EDI mapping is that you must selectively retrieve data from several different instances of a source address loop. As a rule, you will find that you can do this using standard functoids. In this example, we only need the Bill-To address and the Ship-To address information. We can't be sure, however, that they are the only addresses in the source.

Tip Don't fall into the trap of expecting to receive only the data shown in your trading partner's implementation guide. First, in our experience, the majority of implementation guides are out of date and inaccurate. Second, implementation guides often show only the data that will be mapped and do not show the data that will be transmitted. For example, the guide may show only the Bill-To and Ship-To address loops but many more types actually are sent. Always plan on sifting out the data you need, as we do in this example.

This example maps the inbound X12 data from Listing 14-1 to the AddressInfo node in our target application file. We will only map the loops where the N101 value is equal to ST or BT. In a mapping specification, this might be expressed in pseudo code in a mapping specification as AddressInfo = N1Loop [N101 = "ST" or N101 = "BT"].

We also have the requirement to combine the N102 and N201 data into one string. That rule would be Addressee = N1Loop [N102 + " " + N201]. The map is shown in Figure 14-4.

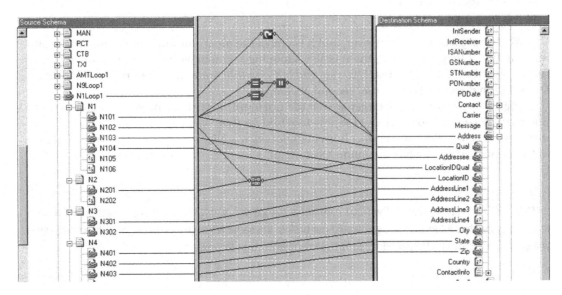

Figure 14-4. *Address loop using functoids*

As Figure 14-4 shows, all of the data is mapped using direct links from the source node to the target node except for the N102 and N201, which pass through a String Concatenate functoid. We control which source loops are output using the logical functoid chain of two Equal functoids and a Logical OR functoid.

The top Equal functoid tests to see if the N101 node value is ST; the bottom Equal functoid tests to see if the N101 node value is BT. The results are fed into the Logical OR functoid, which outputs true when either Equal functoid finds a match. The result is that the target address node will receive data and be output only when the source N101 node contains either ST or BT.

The Looping functoid forces the mapping engine to cycle through all of the N1Loop1 nodes. The output from the map is in Listing 14-3. As you can see, only the two desired addresses have been output.

Listing 14-3. *Output of Address Loop Using a Functoids Map*

```
<ns0:Address Qual="ST">
  <ns0:Addressee>BIG TECHNICAL BOOKSHOP  </ns0:Addressee>
  <ns0:AddressLine1>532 ARESENAL RD.</ns0:AddressLine1>
  <ns0:City>WATERTOWN</ns0:City>
  <ns0:State>MA</ns0:State>
  <ns0:Zip>16016</ns0:Zip>
</ns0:Address>
<ns0:Address Qual="BT">
  <ns0:Addressee>BIG BOOK EMPIRE  ATTN ACCOUNTS PAYABLE</ns0:Addressee>
  <ns0:AddressLine1>1058 DEAD END ST.</ns0:AddressLine1>
  <ns0:City>BOSTON</ns0:City>
  <ns0:State>MA</ns0:State>
  <ns0:Zip>16016</ns0:Zip>
</ns0:Address>
```

We do have a problem, however, and it is one of the most common that mappers encounter with the N1 loop. The N3 segment is also a looping segment with a maximum of two. In our source data the Ship-To address has a second N3 loop that contains a loading dock address. Our solution does not capture that second N3 loop.

The address nodes in the target are flat (do not loop), so we have no corresponding target node to which we could connect a looping functoid for this. We need some other way to loop through the source data and extract both instances of the N3. Our solution is a simple inline XSLT script. Listing 14-4 has the inline XSLT script.

Note Within the N3 segment, the N301 element is mandatory, and N302 is optional. Logic would dictate that if you have two address units, you would put both in the same N3 segment. In practice, however, you will often see the two units split between two N3 segments as in this example.

Listing 14-4. *Inline XSLT Script for the N3 Loop*

```
<!--Each of the next four variable nodes collects one of the four values from
<!-the N3 loop and concatenates the value with a pipe character.  -->
  <xsl:variable name = "N301a">
    <xsl:if test="./*[local-name()='N3'][1]/*[local-name()='N301'] != '' ">
      <xsl:value-of select="concat
```

```
                  ( ./*[local-name()='N3'][1]/*[local-name()='N301'] , '|')"/>
        </xsl:if>
    </xsl:variable>
    <xsl:variable name = "N302a">
        <xsl:if test="./*[local-name()='N3'][1]/*[local-name()='N302'] != '' ">
            <xsl:value-of select="concat
                    ( ./*[local-name()='N3'][1]/*[local-name()='N302'] , '|')"/>
        </xsl:if>
    </xsl:variable>
    <xsl:variable name = "N301b">
        <xsl:if test="./*[local-name()='N3'][2]/*[local-name()='N301'] != '' ">
            <xsl:value-of select="concat
                    ( ./*[local-name()='N3'][2]/*[local-name()='N301'] , '|')"/>
        </xsl:if>
    </xsl:variable>
    <xsl:variable name = "N302b">
        <xsl:if test="./*[local-name()='N3'][2]/*[local-name()='N302'] != '' ">
            <xsl:value-of select="concat
                    ( ./*[local-name()='N3'][2]/*[local-name()='N302'] , '|')"/>
        </xsl:if>
    </xsl:variable>

<!--Next all the collect values are concatenated -->
<---together to form one pipe-delimited string -->
    <xsl:variable name="AddrString1" select="concat($N301a, $N302a, $N301b, $N302b)"/>

<!-- If the string has data, remove the first address and write to AddressLine1-->
    <xsl:if test="$AddrString1 != '' ">
        <AddressLine1>
          <xsl:value-of select="substring-before($AddrString1, '|' )"/>
        </AddressLine1>
    </xsl:if>

<!--  Remove the first address from the string and see if there is a second -->
<!--  address. If there is, then output the second address to AddressLine2.  -->
<!--  Then repeat for the third and fourth fields -->
    <xsl:variable name="AddrString2" select="substring-after($AddrString1, '|') "/>
    <xsl:if test="$AddrString2 != '' ">
        <AddressLine2>
          <xsl:value-of select="substring-before($AddrString2, '|' )"/>
        </AddressLine2>
    </xsl:if>
    <xsl:variable name="AddrString3" select="substring-after($AddrString2, '|' )"/>
    <xsl:if test="$AddrString3 != '' ">
        <AddressLine3>
          <xsl:value-of select="substring-before($AddrString3, '|' )"/>
        </AddressLine3>
```

```
    </xsl:if>
    <xsl:variable name="AddrString4" select="substring-after($AddrString3, '|' )"/>
    <xsl:if test="$AddrString4 != '' ">
        <AddressLine4>
          <xsl:value-of select="substring-before($AddrString4, '|' )"/>
        </AddressLine4>
    </xsl:if>
```

Figure 14-5 shows the map adjusted to use the inline XSLT script, which is in the Scripting functoid.

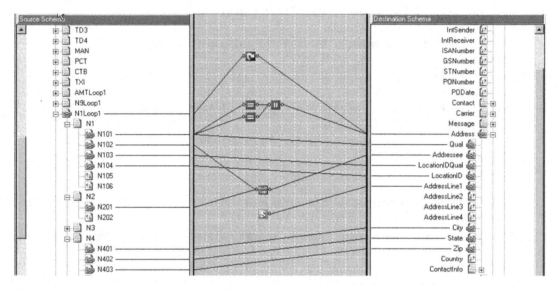

Figure 14-5. *Address loop using functoids and inline XSLT*

The output is in Listing 14-5. Notice that the receiving dock information is now in the Ship-To address data.

Listing 14-5. *Output of the Address Loop Using Functoids and Inline XSLT Script Map*

```
<ns0:Address Qual="ST">
  <ns0:Addressee>BIG TECHNICAL BOOKSHOP</ns0:Addressee>
  <AddressLine1>532 ARESENAL RD.</AddressLine1>
  <AddressLine2>RECEIVING DOCK A</AddressLine2>
  <ns0:City>WATERTOWN</ns0:City>
  <ns0:State>MA</ns0:State>
  <ns0:Zip>16016</ns0:Zip>
</ns0:Address>
<ns0:Address Qual="BT">
  <ns0:Addressee>BIG BOOK EMPIRE ATTN ACCOUNTS PAYABLE</ns0:Addressee>
  <AddressLine1>1058 DEAD END ST.</AddressLine1>
  <ns0:City>BOSTON</ns0:City>
  <ns0:State>MA</ns0:State>
```

```
<ns0:Zip>16016</ns0:Zip>
</ns0:Address>
```

There are several other ways that we could solve the N3 problem in this case, of course, including using an array or hash table. The nice thing about the inline XSLT script is that you can quickly alter it to fit a different application file by changing the node names in the script. Thus maps for the same inbound 850 can quickly be altered to handle different application file structures.

Exploring the EDIFACT-to-Application Solution

Now, let's look at the same mapping requirement applied to an EDIFACT ORDERS message. Remember that the address information in the NAD segment is in a series of composite elements instead of separate segments. Also, realize that the NAD segment has more data elements than you typically see in the N1 loop, so you must be careful to select the correct source nodes. Here is the map in Figure 14-6.

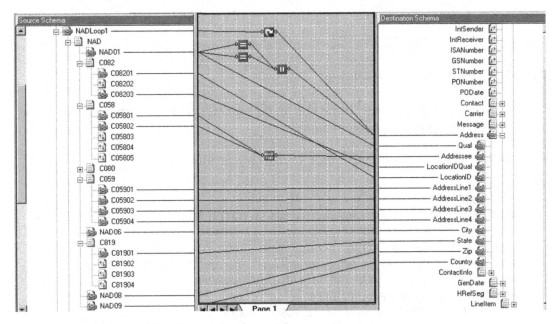

Figure 14-6. *EDIFACT Address loop using functoids*

Handling the possibility of four address nodes is easier here because all four are in one composite element, not in a loop. Notice that you could output AddressLine1 and AddressLine4 nodes without outputting an AddressLine2 or AddressLine3 node. That might be a problem if your client wants the four address fields in the target output in order, for example, when you have data in the first and fourth source node and you want to output the data in the target AddressLine1 and AddressLine2 nodes. In that case, you would turn to an inline XSLT script just as we did with the X12 map. The output of this map would be no different than for the X12 map.

Looping from an Application to EDI

Next, we flip the direction of flow and look at examples where we map from application schemas to EDI schemas. We'll use the schema shown in Figure 14-7. The figure is split into two parts, the first showing that the source document may have as many as five address nodes; the second showing the data that an address node may contain.

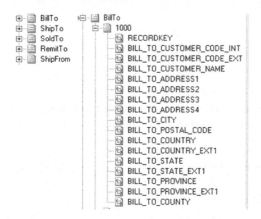

Figure 14-7. *Application schema structure*

We use the source data from Listing 14-6 for the next set of examples. There are four separate nodes that contain address information.

Listing 14-6. *Source Data for the Application-to-EDI Loop Solution*

```
<BillTo xmlns="">
  <_x0031_000>
    <RECORDKEY>114718214SSPS 13886839 1000ADBT1</RECORDKEY>
    <BILL_TO_CUSTOMER_CODE_INT>5553215</BILL_TO_CUSTOMER_CODE_INT>
    <BILL_TO_CUSTOMER_CODE_EXT>0012</BILL_TO_CUSTOMER_CODE_EXT>
    <BILL_TO_CUSTOMER_NAME>BIG BOOK EMPIRE</BILL_TO_CUSTOMER_NAME>
    <BILL_TO_ADDRESS1>1058 DEAD END ST.</BILL_TO_ADDRESS1>
    <BILL_TO_CITY>BOSTON</BILL_TO_CITY>
    <BILL_TO_POSTAL_CODE>16016</BILL_TO_POSTAL_CODE>
    <BILL_TO_COUNTRY>US</BILL_TO_COUNTRY>
    <BILL_TO_STATE>MA</BILL_TO_STATE>
    <BILL_TO_COUNTY />
  </_x0031_000>
</BillTo>
<ShipTo xmlns="">
  <_x0031_100>
```

```
    <RECORDKEY>114718214SSPS 13886839 1100ADST1</RECORDKEY>
    <SHIP_TO_CUSTOMER_CODE_INT>170</SHIP_TO_CUSTOMER_CODE_INT>
    <SHIP_TO_CUSTOMER_CODE_EXT />
    <SHIP_TO_CUSTOMER_NAME>BIG BOOKSHOP</SHIP_TO_CUSTOMER_NAME>
    <SHIP_TO_ADDRESS1>532 ARESENAL RD.</SHIP_TO_ADDRESS1>
    <SHIP_TO_ADDRESS2>REECEIVING DOCK A</SHIP_TO_ADDRESS2>
    <SHIP_TO_ADDRESS3 />
    <SHIP_TO_ADDRESS4 />
    <SHIP_TO_CITY>WATERTOWN</SHIP_TO_CITY>
    <SHIP_TO_POSTAL_CODE>16016</SHIP_TO_POSTAL_CODE>
    <SHIP_TO_COUNTRY>US</SHIP_TO_COUNTRY>
    <SHIP_TO_STATE>MA</SHIP_TO_STATE>
  </_x0031_100>
</ShipTo>
<RemitTo xmlns="">
  <_x0031_300>
    <RECORDKEY>114718214SSPS 13886839 1300ADRE1</RECORDKEY>
    <REMIT_TO_CODE_INT>114718214</REMIT_TO_CODE_INT>
    <REMIT_TO_CUSTOMER_NAME>SECOND STAR</REMIT_TO_CUSTOMER_NAME>
    <REMIT_TO_ADDRESS1>7008 ROBBIE DRIVE</REMIT_TO_ADDRESS1>
    <REMIT_TO_CITY>RALEIGH</REMIT_TO_CITY>
    <REMIT_TO_POSTAL_CODE>27607</REMIT_TO_POSTAL_CODE>
    <REMIT_TO_COUNTRY_EXT1>US</REMIT_TO_COUNTRY_EXT1>
    <REMIT_TO_STATE>NC</REMIT_TO_STATE>
  </_x0031_300>
</RemitTo>
<ShipFrom xmlns="">
  <_x0031_400>
    <RECORDKEY>114718214SSPS 13886839 1400SFSF1</RECORDKEY>
    <SHIP_FROM_CODE_INT>SSPSI</SHIP_FROM_CODE_INT>
  </_x0031_400>
</ShipFrom>
```

Our first map moves two of the four address nodes to a target NAD segment. The map is in Figure 14-8, and we won't even attempt to walk through it functoid by functoid. Note, first of all, that we barely got the functoids needed to map two nodes on the same mapping grid. Of course, if this were a map for a client, we would place the stand-alone portions for each address on separate grid pages.

The looping functoid, barely visible at the top of the grid, drives one instance of the NAD node for each source address node that is linked to the functoid. The Logical String/Value Mapping functoid pairs, as usual, ensure that the target node is only output when there is data to place in it. Imagine how the map would loop with all four address nodes being mapped, and how much effort would be involved to modify the map. Now look at the map in Figure 14-9.

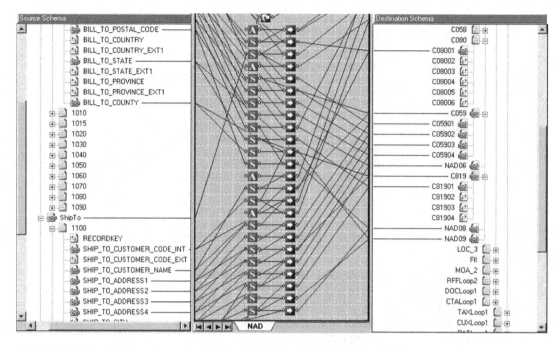

Figure 14-8. *Two addresses mapped to the NAD segment using functoids*

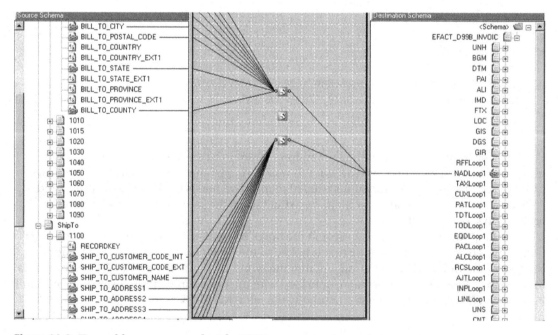

Figure 14-9. *Two addresses mapped to the NAD segment using scripts*

Not only is this map less cluttered, the maintenance is easier for two reasons. First, the separation of the source data links from the different address nodes is cleaner. Second, the same script is used to build the NADLoop1 node, so changes to how that node is built need only be made once. Let's see how the three scripts, one per Scripting functoid, work. The script for the Bill-To address is in Listing 14-7.

Listing 14-7. *Script for the Bill-To Address Node*

```
<!--*******************************************************
Gathers output data for an NAD Bill-To Address
*********************************************************-->
<xsl:template name="BuildN1BT">
<-- These parameters are filled with the data from the source -->
<---Bill-To address node -->
  <xsl:param name="Name"/>
  <xsl:param name="IDCode"/>
  <xsl:param name="Address1"/>
  <xsl:param name="Address2"/>
  <xsl:param name="Address3"/>
  <xsl:param name="Address4"/>
  <xsl:param name="City"/>
  <xsl:param name="State"/>
  <xsl:param name="Zip"/>
  <xsl:param name="Country"/>
<-- Check the name to see if it is there.  If it is, call the XSLT template in -->
<-- the free-floating Scripting functoid to build the target NAD.  Pass the   -->
<-- parameters just received to the called template -->
  <xsl:if test="$Name != '' ">
    <xsl:call-template name="BuildNADLoop">
      <xsl:with-param name="Qual" select=" 'BT' "/>
      <xsl:with-param name="Name" select="$Name"/>
      <xsl:with-param name="IDQual" select=" '' "/>
      <xsl:with-param name="IDCode" select=" '' "/>
      <xsl:with-param name="Address1" select="$Address1"/>
      <xsl:with-param name="Address2" select="$Address2"/>
      <xsl:with-param name="Address3" select="$Address3"/>
      <xsl:with-param name="Address4" select="$Address4"/>
      <xsl:with-param name="City" select="$City"/>
      <xsl:with-param name="State" select="$State"/>
      <xsl:with-param name="Zip" select="$Zip"/>
      <xsl:with-param name="Country" select="$Country"/>
    </xsl:call-template>
  </xsl:if>
</xsl:template>
```

Our script for the Ship-To address (the bottom Scripting functoid) is the same as for the Bill-To address, with the obvious exception that the hard-coded parameter Qual is ST instead of BT, so we won't display it. Note that the two do not have to be the same—you might not want to output some of the optional nodes in one or the other. The nice thing is that you can customize what data is output to the NAD segment for each address type.

The XSLT template that is called by the other two scripts lies in the middle, free-floating Scripting functoid. The script is in Listing 14-8. There are no new XLST constructs in the code, so we don't provide comments.

Listing 14-8. *Script Called to Output the NAD*

```
<--_Creates an output NAD Loop -->
<--*****************************************************-->
<xsl:template name="BuildNADLoop">
  <xsl:param name="Qual"/>
  <xsl:param name="Name"/>
  <xsl:param name="IDQual"/>
  <xsl:param name="IDCode"/>
  <xsl:param name="Address1"/>
  <xsl:param name="Address2"/>
  <xsl:param name="Address3"/>
  <xsl:param name="Address4"/>
  <xsl:param name="City"/>
  <xsl:param name="State"/>
  <xsl:param name="Zip"/>
  <xsl:param name="Country"/>

  <xsl:if test="$Name != ''  ">
    <xsl:element name = "ns0:NADLoop1">
      <xsl:element name="ns0:NAD">
        <xsl:element name="NAD01"><xsl:value-of select="$Qual"/></xsl:element>

        <xsl:if test="$IDCode != '' and $IDQual != ''  ">
          <xsl:element name="ns0:C082">
            <xsl:element name="C08201">
              <xsl:value-of select="$IDCode"/>
            </xsl:element>
            <xsl:element name="C08203">
              <xsl:value-of select="$IDQual"/>
            </xsl:element>
          </xsl:element>
        </xsl:if>

        <xsl:if test="$Name != '' ">
          <xsl:element name="ns0:C080">
            <xsl:element name="C08001">
              <xsl:value-of select="$Name"/>
            </xsl:element>
          </xsl:element>
        </xsl:if>
```

```
        <xsl:if test="$Address1 != '' ">
          <xsl:element name="ns0:C059">
            <xsl:element name="C05901">
              <xsl:value-of select="$Address1"/>
            </xsl:element>
            <xsl:if test="$Address2 != '' ">
              <xsl:element name="C05902">
                <xsl:value-of select="$Address2"/>
              </xsl:element>
            </xsl:if>
            <xsl:if test="$Address3 != '' ">
              <xsl:element name="C05903">
                <xsl:value-of select="$Address3"/>
              </xsl:element>
            </xsl:if>
            <xsl:if test="$Address4 != '' ">
              <xsl:element name="C05904">
                <xsl:value-of select="$Address4"/>
              </xsl:element>
            </xsl:if>
          </xsl:element>
        </xsl:if>

        <xsl:if test="$City != '' ">
          <xsl:element name="NAD06"><xsl:value-of select="$City"/></xsl:element>
        </xsl:if>

        <xsl:if test="$State != '' ">
          <xsl:element name="ns0:C819">
            <xsl:element name="C81901"><xsl:value-of select="$State"/></xsl:element>
          </xsl:element>
        </xsl:if>

        <xsl:if test="$Zip != '' ">
          <xsl:element name="NAD08"><xsl:value-of select="$Zip"/></xsl:element>
        </xsl:if>

        <xsl:if test="$Country != '' ">
          <xsl:element name="NAD09"><xsl:value-of select="$Country"/></xsl:element>
        </xsl:if>
      </xsl:element>
    </xsl:element>
  </xsl:if>
</xsl:template>
```

As you see, for each target node, the script simply checks to see if the parameter has data, and if it does, outputs that node. Thus if you want the address3 (target node C05903) and address4 (target node C05904) output, you pass the values to the script. If you do not want them output, you pass no values to the script. This is the feature that allows you to customize the output in the individual address scripts.

Summary

This chapter discussed looping issues that you encounter when working with EDI transactions. For the most part, the problems are not different than would be encountered outside of EDI. You are forcing looping of output nodes, blocking output of empty nodes, limiting the number of output loops, and so on—all things we discussed in earlier chapters.

The syntax rules imposed by EDI standards and the hidden business rules are two contributing factors that make mapping to and from EDI looping structures different from general mapping of loops. A third factor is that EDI loops are often nested with business definitions defining the looping structure. You'll see the most difficult of those constructs in Chapter 17 when we examine the HL loop.

Next, though, we will move to EDI code pairs, in particular X12 code pairs. Code pairs run rampant throughout X12 transaction structures, and mapping them presents some interesting issues.

CHAPTER 15

■ ■ ■

Processing EDI Code Pairs

Code pairs are one EDI message structure that requires special discussion in regards to mapping. This construct is very prevalent in EDI, because the message structures have been designed to be highly flexible. The code pair consists of a qualifier and one or more data nodes. The qualifier describes the meaning of the data node or nodes. Some data elements have hundreds of possible meanings. This chapter examines some of the ways that code pairs affect mapping.

Introducing EDI Code Pairs

The X12 version 4010 element 374, Date/Time Qualifier, lists 1,114 possible values—more than a thousand different types of dates can be sent. Imagine the size of your data element repository if you had to define an individual date element for each type of date. Listing 15-1 shows an excerpt from the code list for element 373.

Listing 15-1. *Excerpt from the Code List for the Date/Time Qualifier*

```
002     Delivery Requested
003     Invoice
004     Purchase Order
005     Sailing
006     Sold
007     Effective
008     Purchase Order Received
009     Process
010     Requested Ship
011     Shipped
012     Terms Discount Due
```

Instead of defining over a thousand different date elements, the use of the code pair 374 Date/Time Qualifier and 373 Date means that we can define a date using two elements. For example, the segment DTM*011*20081015 means "Shipped on October 15, 2008". The savings in number of elements is actually over two thousand, since the meaning of the time element, 337 Time, is also derived from the Date/Time Qualifier. Thus the segment DTM*011*20081015*2130 means "Shipped on October15, 2008, at 9:30 p.m.". EDIFACT also makes use of code pairs. The EDIFACT segment DTM+10:200812031113 means "Requested ship date and time is December 3, 2008, at 11:13 a.m.".

Tip In X12, when code pairs are used, the document specification always contains a syntax note in the description of the particular EDI segment, indicating that if either of the two elements is present then the other element must also be present.

As you see, there is a definite benefit to using code pairs. But code pairs also cause some interesting side effects in the BizTalk mapper. First, as we cautioned earlier, segment syntax rules are not enforced by default in the BizTalk EDI schemas. You must manually modify each schema to activate the syntax rules for that schema. Thus, out of the box, the BizTalk mapping engine does not check to see if both elements of a code pair are present when one is present. You must put the check into your map.

Another side effect of code pairs is particular to X12. Some segments allow for ten or more code pairs in sequence without defining the sequence. Elements 6–25 of the 4010 IT1 segment are code pairs, with each pair being defined as Product/Service ID Qualifier and Product/Service ID. When there is a series of code pairs such as this, X12 provides no syntax rule for ordering the data. Thus if your trading partner sends 10 code pairs in the IT1, your map might need to check every pair for every one of the 10 codes, because there are hundreds of permutations for the possible order of codes.

Handling ID Codes in X12 REF and EDIFACT RFF Segments

The REF segment and its EDIFACT counterpart the RFF segment both contain reference information. These, along with the DTM segments in both standards, are some of the most-often used segments that contain code pairs. The first data element of both the REF and the DTM segments is an ID Code Qualifier that defines the context of the other elements in the rest of the segment.

Looking for Specific Code Pairs in an X12-to-Application Map

When the source is an X12 message, the data often contains multiple occurrences of the REF segment. Each occurrence will contain a different code qualifier. Listing 15-2 shows an excerpt from an X12 850 Purchase Order transaction that contains three REF segments.

Listing 15-2. *Excerpt from X12 850 Containing Three REF Segments*

```
ST*850*0001
BEG*00*SA*BTB281155**20081105
CUR*ZZ*USD
REF*CT*0061375
REF*IL*20080701A
```

```
REF*CO*BTB281155
PER*BD*MAPPER JOE*TE*617-555-1234
FOB*PP
DTM*002*20090311
TD5****M*BEST WAY
```

We extract two of these reference numbers in the map in Figure 15-1, the customer order number (CO) and the contract number (CT).

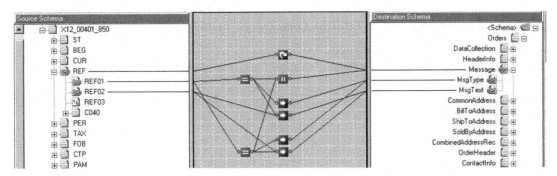

Figure 15-1. *Map to extract REF CO and CT values*

There are four operations in the map:

- The Looping functoid forces the target Message node to loop once for each source REF node.

- The two Equal functoids and the Logical OR functoid form a chain that limits output of the Message node to when the REF01 node value equals either CO or CT.

- The top Equal functoid and top two Value Mapping functoids pass the source values through when the source REF01 value equals CO, converting the CO to CON.

- The bottom Equal functoid and bottom two Value Mapping functoids pass the source values through when the source REF01 value equals CT, converting the CT to CPT.

The output is in Listing 15-3.

Listing 15-3. *Output of the Map to Extract REF CO and CT Values*

```
<Message>
  <MsgType>CON</MsgType>
  <MsgText>0061375</MsgText>
</Message>
<Message>
  <MsgType>CPO</MsgType>
  <MsgText>BTB281155</MsgText>
</Message>
```

Looking for Specific Code Pairs in an EDIFACT-to-Application Map

Mapping an EDIFACT message structure with these types of code qualifiers is no different than mapping with X12. The only difference between the EDIFACT RFF segment and the X12 REF segment is that the code pair in a RFF segment is in a composite element instead of two separate elements. Listing 15-4 shows three RFF segments in an excerpt from an ORDERS message. The codes are ADJ, ON, and BC.

Listing 15-4. *Excerpt from EDIFACT ORDER Containing Three RFF Segments*

```
UNH+00000108323976+ORDERS:D:99B:UN'
BGM+220+BTB281155+9'
DTM+74:20090311:102'
FTX+PUR+++MAPPER JOE'
FTX+ORI+++617-555-1234'
RFF+ADJ:SECONDSTAR'
RFF+ON:BTB281155'
RFF+BC:0061375
```

As Figure 15-2 shows, the mapping structure for outputting target data based on two of the RFF code values is exactly the same as for the X12 REF segment. This map would output the RFF segment data where the C50601 contained either ON or BC.

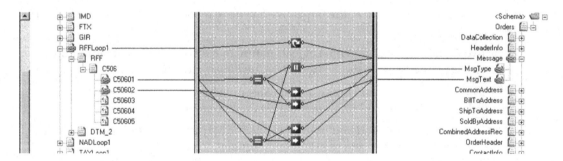

Figure 15-2. *Map to extract RFF ON and BC values*

As you can imagine, if you have more than two or three values to select in either of the previous maps, your mapping grid rapidly fills up with functoids. Also, since X12 and EDIFACT messages both contain multiple REF/RFF loops, you might need to select the values to output in one Message loop from more than one source loop. As the extractions become more numerous or more complicated you should turn to scripts.

Using a Script to Select Specific Code Pairs from One REF or RFF Loop

As long as the source of the reference numbers is within one REF or RFF loop, the map in Figure 15-3 can be used.

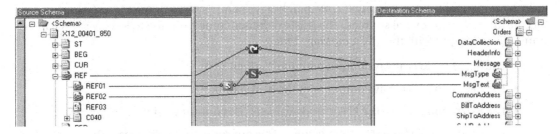

Figure 15-3. *Map using a script to collect specific code pairs*

The script in Listing 15-5 performs double duty. First, it controls the output of the Message segment by only outputting a string when a match is found. Second, it converts the input code into the desired output code when a match is found, and outputs the code to the MsgType node. The REF02 node can be linked directly to the MsgText node, since the link will only fire if the Message segment is output. The same map structure and script could easily be adjusted for use with the RFF segment.

Listing 15-5. *Script for Collecting Specific Code Pairs*

```
public string GetREF(string IDQual)
{
  string retval = "";
// Use a Switch statement to find the input value and select the correct output
  switch (IDQual)
  {
//  If the input value is "CO" return "CPO"
    case "CO":
      retval = "CPO";
      break;
//  If the input value is "CT" return "CON"
    case "CT":
      retval = "CON";
      break;
//  If the input value is neither "CT" nor "CO", return an empty string
    default :
      retval = "";
      break;
  }
  return retval;
}
```

Using a Recursive XSLT Call Template to Process Code Pairs

Sometimes, the code pair problem is on the target side. Often, you must collect values from a variety of source document numbers and reference numbers and build a code pair output loop. In our example here, the target code pair MsgType and MsgText in the Message loop must be constructed from several sources. The MsgText values come from the following source locations and are output with the given message types:

- The BEG03 node is always output with the MsgType CPO.
- The BEG05 node is always output with the MsgType POD.
- The REF02 node where the REF01 node value is CT is output with the MsgType CON.
- The CUR02 node where the CUR01 value is ZZ is output with the MsgType CUR.
- The DTM02 node where the DTM01 value is 002 is output with the MsgType RSD.
- The DTM02 node where the DTM01 value is 038 is output with the MsgType SNL.

The only thing we know for sure about the source is that the two BEG nodes, which are mandatory, will be present and hold data. The REF, CUR, and DTM segments, though, are all optional. Of course, even if one or more of any of these segments are present, they may not have the code values that we desire. Thus we can expect to output between two and six Message segments.

We also know that we cannot use the Looping functoid to force the looping of the Message segment, since we would have to use four different source nodes to drive the looping. As you know from earlier looping discussions, the compiler has difficulty untangling such looping constructs. The map is shown in Figure 15-4.

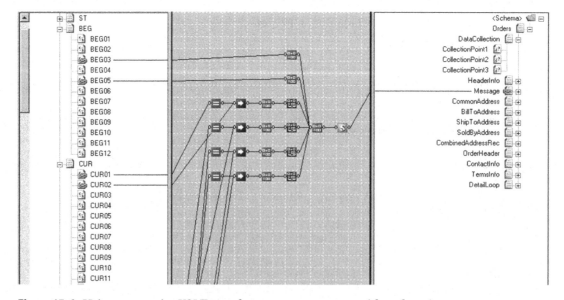

Figure 15-4. *Using a recursive XSLT template to process a map with code pairs*

The map uses a functoid construct that you've seen before, in Chapter 12's Figure 12-3. We discussed the process in detail there. The four Equal/Value Mapping/String Concatenate/Cumulative Concatenate functoid chains each pull all the data from one looping source location and build a pipe-delimited string. The top two stand-alone String Concatenate functoids build pipe-delimited strings from BEG03 and BEG05. The right-most String Concatenate joins all six strings into one.

The Scripting functoid contains the inline XSLT Call Template that creates and outputs the target Message, MsgType, and MsgText nodes. The script is in Listing 15-6.

Listing 15-6. *Script for Using a Recursive Call to Process a Map with Code Pairs*

```
<!-- Build the Message loop from a delimited string-->
 <xsl:template name="PutMessage">
    <xsl:param name="inString"/>
<!-- If inString is empty, exit the processing loop-->
    <xsl:if test="$inString != '' ">
<!-- Extract the leading code/value pair from the pipe-delimited input string -->
        <xsl:variable name="Next1">
            <xsl:value-of select="substring-before($inString, '|')"/>
        </xsl:variable>
<!-- Extract the code  into variable $Qual from $Next1-->
        <xsl:variable name="Qual">
            <xsl:value-of select="substring-before($Next1, '~')"/>
        </xsl:variable>
<!-- Extract the value into variable $Text from $Next1-->
        <xsl:variable name="Text">
            <xsl:value-of select="substring-after($Next1, '~')"/>
        </xsl:variable>
<!-- Build the output Message, MsgType, and MsgText nodes from current variables-->
        <xsl:if test=" $Qual != '' and $Text != '' ">
            <xsl:element name="Message">
                <xsl:element name="MsgType">
                    <xsl:value-of select="$Qual"/>
                </xsl:element>
                <xsl:element name="MsgText">
                    <xsl:value-of select="$Text"/>
                </xsl:element>
            </xsl:element>
        </xsl:if>

<!-- Call the template again, removing the leading set of code/value -->
        <xsl:call-template name="PutMessage">
            <xsl:with-param name="inString" select=
                "substring-after($inString, '| )"/>
        </xsl:call-template>
    </xsl:if>
</xsl:template>
```

As long as there is data left in the input string, the script calls itself, each time outputting another Message segment. Our source file is too long to include, but Listing 15-7 contains the pipe-delimited string that is received by the script. The string has only five of the code pairs, since the source data has only one of the two desired DTM segments.

Listing 15-7. *Pipe-Delimited Input String*

```
CPO~BTB281155|POD~20081105|CUR~USD|CON~0061375|RSD~20090311|
```

The output of the map is in Listing 15-8. The correct values from the source code values are in the MsgText nodes, and the converted codes are in the MsgType nodes.

Listing 15-8. *Output of the Recursive XSLT Call Template to Process the Map with Code Pairs*

```
<Message>
  <MsgType>CPO</MsgType>
  <MsgText>BTB281155</MsgText>
</Message>
<Message>
  <MsgType>POD</MsgType>
  <MsgText>20081105</MsgText>
</Message>
<Message>
  <MsgType>CUR</MsgType>
  <MsgText>USD</MsgText>
</Message>
<Message>
  <MsgType>CON</MsgType>
  <MsgText>0061375</MsgText>
</Message>
<Message>
  <MsgType>RSD</MsgType>
  <MsgText>20090311</MsgText>
</Message>
```

The recursive XSLT script solution works best when you work with only a few code pairs. Since you are building a pipe-delimited string, though, the string may become large and unwieldy if many source code pair nodes or many business rules impact the mapping. As you add additional functoid chains to handle the new nodes, not only will the mapping grid get more cluttered but the efficiency of your map may be affected as well.

Using Nested XSLT Call Templates to Process Code Pairs

This solution works well in any case but is most valuable when the code pair extractions involve many source nodes and/or the rules for processing the code pair data are complex. In this solution, we pass the extracted code pairs to the primary XSLT call template as separate input variables. The same six code pairs must be output to the target Message node with this map as in the previous example.

In this case, we know what each input variable is: a purchase order number from the BEG01, purchase order date from the BEG03, currency from the CUR, contract number from the REF, and schedule date and cancel dates from the DTM. Since we know this, we do not need to pull the codes into the scripts. The map is in Figure 15-5.

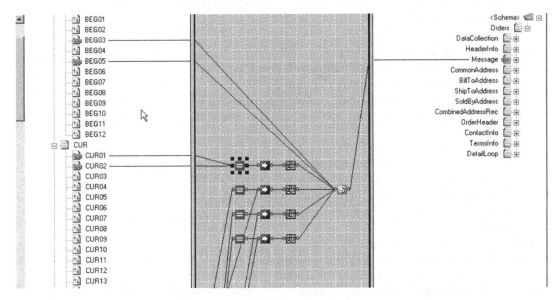

Figure 15-5. *Using nested XSLT call templates to process a map with code pairs*

This map performs the same as the previous map, but the grid is much less cluttered. The script for the XSLT call template is in Listing 15-9.

Listing 15-9. *Script for Using Nested XSLT Call Templates to Process a Map with Code Pairs*

```
<xsl:template name="PutMessage">
<-- First declare the six variables that will hold the input values -->
  <xsl:param name="PONumber"/>
  <xsl:param name="PODate"/>
  <xsl:param name="Currency"/>
  <xsl:param name="Contract"/>
  <xsl:param name="ScheduleDate"/>
  <xsl:param name="CancelDate"/>
<-- Begin with the PO Number.  First check to see if a PO number was received -->
<-- If one was, then pass the code value "PON" and the PONumber value -->
<-- to the BuildMessageSegment call-template at the end of this script -->
  <xsl:if test="$PONumber != '' ">
    <xsl:call-template name="BuildMessageSegment">
        <xsl:with-param name="Qual" select=" 'PON' "/>
        <xsl:with-param name="Text" select="$PONumber"/>
    </xsl:call-template>
  </xsl:if>
```

```
    </xsl:if>
<-- Now do the same thing for  each of the other five parameters, one at a time -->
<-- When all five have been completed, exit the script -->
  <xsl:if test="$PODate != '' ">
    <xsl:call-template name="BuildMessageSegment">
        <xsl:with-param name="Qual" select=" 'POD' " />
        <xsl:with-param name="Text" select="translate($PODate,'-','')"/>
    </xsl:call-template>
  </xsl:if>
  <xsl:if test="$Contract != '' ">
    <xsl:call-template name="BuildMessageSegment">
        <xsl:with-param name="Qual" select=" 'CON' " />
        <xsl:with-param name="Text" select="$Contract"/>
    </xsl:call-template>
  </xsl:if>
  <xsl:if test="$Currency != '' ">
    <xsl:call-template name="BuildMessageSegment">
        <xsl:with-param name="Qual" select=" 'CUR' " />
        <xsl:with-param name="Text" select="$Currency"/>
    </xsl:call-template>
  </xsl:if>
  <xsl:if test="$ScheduleDate != '' ">
    <xsl:call-template name="BuildMessageSegment">
        <xsl:with-param name="Qual" select=" 'SSD' " />
        <xsl:with-param name="Text" select="$ScheduleDate"/>
    </xsl:call-template>
  </xsl:if>
  <xsl:if test="$CancelDate != '' ">
    <xsl:call-template name="BuildMessageSegment">
        <xsl:with-param name="Qual" select=" 'RSD' " />
        <xsl:with-param name="Text" select="$CancelDate"/>
    </xsl:call-template>
  </xsl:if>
</xsl:template>
<-- Here is the call-template that is called from the above template -->
<-- once for each of the six input values received by the above template. -->
<xsl:template name="BuildMessageSegment">
  <xsl:param name="Qual"/>
  <xsl:param name="Text"/>
<-- Test to make sure you have both input values, just for safety -->
    <xsl:if test="$Qual != '' and $Text != '' ">
<-- Write out the Message node -->
        <xsl:element name="Message">
<-- Write out the MsgType node -->
            <xsl:element name="MsgType">
                <xsl:value-of select="$Qual"/>
            </xsl:element>
```

```
<-- Write out the MsgText node -->
        <xsl:element name="MsgText">
            <xsl:value-of select="$Text"/>
        </xsl:element>
    </xsl:element>
</xsl:if>
```

Tip If you use the method in Listing 15-9, you can also build separate scripts within the template to evaluate different types of source data. You could, for example, build a separate script for handling the dates.

Multiple Code Pair Positions in a Single Segment

We mentioned this special headache—many code pairs in a single segment without a defined order—earlier in the chapter. One example of this situation occurs with the PO1 segment. The PO1 segment allows ten consecutive code pairs, all with the same list of acceptable codes. From the perspective of the X12 standards, the two PO1 segments in Listing 15-10 both are identical.

Listing 15-10. *Two PO1 Segments*

```
PO1*003*168*EA*14.34*LE*IN*626848879*UP*824686905967*VN*10596***IZ*0084
PO1*003*168*EA*14.34*LE*UP*824686905967*VN*10596***IZ*0084*IN*626848879
```

The PO101 to PO105 portions are truly identical. The remainder of each segment contains four codes (IN, UP, VN, and IZ), each with its corresponding value. The values are the same in both segments. There are 477 possible codes that can be placed in each of the 10 code pairs in the PO1. As the two PO1 segments in the listing show, nothing in the standards defines any order in which the codes must appear. In fact, notice that you can even have empty code pair elements between data-filled code pairs.

When processing inbound PO1 segments, the issue is finding the right code pair for each application data element that needs a specific value, such as pulling the vendor number (VN) and putting it in the correct target node. On the outbound side, the problem is finding the next empty PO1 code pair into which you can put the vendor number. We once saw a map where the mapping grid was solid black, as the mapper had tried to account for all the possibilities on one map page. There were thousands of links and functoids.

Tip In practice, make sure that you and your trading partner define specific positions in a segment for each code pair if at all possible. Mapping is much easier if you know the vendor code VC will be in the PO108 than it will be if you have to check all ten code pair positions to find it. The first thing you should do when planning your map is to check your partner's implementation guide to see if they specify in which positions they desire each code pair.

Handling Multiple Code Pairs in an Inbound Segment with C#

A simple solution to this problem is to use a hash table, using the code as the key. Although the standards do not prevent you from using the same code twice in the same segment, doing so makes no sense, as you could not tell which code pair was correct. Thus we can safely assume that every code in the segment will be different and can be used as the hash table key. The map is shown in Figure 15-6.

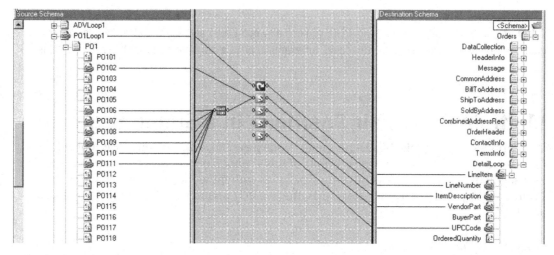

Figure 15-6. *A map using a hash table for code-pair parsing*

■**Caution**   Notice that the data collection functoid (top Scripting functoid) in Figure 15-6 is attached to the LineNumber node on the target side. You are used to seeing it attached to a data collection node or other node near the start of the map. In this case, we must gather and output the data specific to each pass of the LineItem node. The codes will repeat in each PO1 segment, so each one must be processed individually. Remember that the data collection functoid will not work if attached to the LineItem node, since child nodes are processed before their parent node.

Listing 15-11 contains the script that we use to extract the PO1 code pairs and store them into the hash table.

Listing 15-11. *Script to Collect the Code Pairs into a Hash Table*

```
// Define the hash table as a global variable
public System.Collections.Hashtable PO1Table = new System.Collections.Hashtable();

// Accept the string of all code pair information from the PO1 segment
// Also accept the PO102 value for output to the LineNumber node
public string LoadPO1Table(string inQty, string inPairs)
{
```

```
  string pairs = inPairs;
  string pair = "";
// Empty the hash table each time to avoid having residual values
  PO1Table.Clear();
// pairs contains a copy of the input string.  If there is still data in the string
// continue processing through the while loop
  while (pairs != "")
  {
// Break off the first code pair, separate the code and the value
    int delimpos = pairs.IndexOf("|",0);
    pair = pairs.Substring(0,delimpos);// isolates the first pair from the string
    pairs = pairs.Remove(0,delimpos + 1); // removes that pair from the string
    string pairQual = pair.Substring(0,pair.IndexOf("~",0));
    string pairVal = pair.Substring(pair.IndexOf("~",0)+ 1);
// Check to see if a code pair was found, and if so put them into the hash table
    if (pairVal != "" && pairQual != "")
    {
      PO1Table[pairQual] = pairVal; // then write the value to the hash table
    }
  }
//  Output the Line Number
  return inQty;
}
```

Since we are using the target LineNumber node as the data collection node, we also are using the script to accept the source value from the PO102 node and output that value to the target LineNumber node. Thus the script is doing double duty.

We then use a different Scripting functoid to extract each value from the hash table and output it to the target. We can use the same script in each of these by having the script accept the desired code value as input into the functoid Configure Functoid Inputs pane. The script is in Listing 15-12.

Listing 15-12. *Script to Extract the Value from the Hash Table and Output It to the Target*

```
public string ReturnPO1Pair(string inQual)
{
  string retval = "";
  if (PO1Table.ContainsKey(inQual)
    retval = PO1Table[inQual].ToString();
 return retval;
}
```

Remember, you only need the full script for the first extract. The second and subsequent extracts only need the `public string ReturnPO1Pair(string inQual) {}` line. If we put the value VN into the script's Configure Functoid Inputs pane, we would output the value 10596 from either PO1 line in Listing 15-10. The location of the code pair VN 10596 would not factor into the extraction.

Handling Multiple Code Pairs in an Inbound Segment with XSLT

We can eliminate the need to process each PO1-to-LineItem line separately by using an inline XSLT script. The script uses XPATH queries, which search the child nodes of the PO1 segment for the node that contains the requested code. When the correct node is located, the value associated with that node is extracted.

We use an inline XSLT script because it requires no inputs. The context node for the XPATH query is the source PO1Loop1 node currently being processed. You remember that the context node is the node designated as the origin node for the XPATH queries. The code fragment for extracting one value from all of the PO1 code pairs is in Listing 15-13.

Listing 15-13. *XPATH Query to Extract the Value of a Specified Code Pair*

```
<xsl:for-each select="./s0:PO1/child::*[text()='VN']">
  <xsl:variable name="VendNum" select="./following-sibling::*[1]" />
  <ItemDescription><xsl:value-of select="$VendNum" /></ItemDescription>
</xsl:for-each>
```

This code fragment does the same as our previous example, returning the value 10596 from either PO1 line in Listing 15-10. The map for this single extraction is in Figure 15-7.

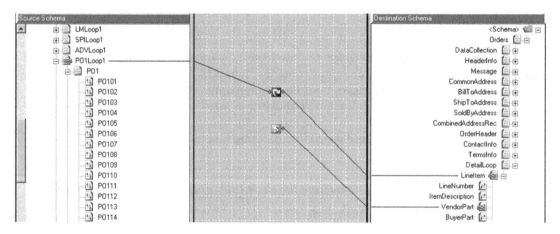

Figure 15-7. *Handling multiple code pairs in an inbound segment with XSLTMap*

Creating Code Pairs in EDI Output

As we mentioned at the beginning of this chapter, you can rest assured that there is usually a syntax rule of some sort associated with any code pair you build in an EDI target document. Such a rule may not be obvious, especially with BizTalk maps, because the rules are not enforced unless you manually activate them. Both elements will show as optional, and there will be nothing to indicate that you must not populate one without populating the other. You have to enforce the syntax rules yourself.

The construct for outputting code pairs when the target for each pair is defined is one you've seen many times before. Figure 15-8 shows the line item number (code IB) being output to the IT106/IT107 code pair.

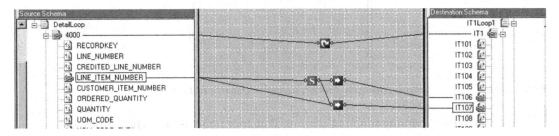

Figure 15-8. *Outputting a code pair to SpecificTarget nodes*

When the target nodes are not defined, there is more than one code pair to be output, and your trading partner does not want open elements between code pairs, you must find a way to move code pairs up in the segment as they are output. Suppose we are to output two code pairs, a line item number and a lot number, into the IT1 segment. We must put them in the IT106–IT107 and IT108–IT109 pairs when both are present. When only one pair is present, we must put that one into IT106–IT107. We cannot put one in the IT108–IT109 pair and leave IT106–IT107 empty. Listing 15-14 shows the possibilities.

Listing 15-14. *IT1 Segments That Are and Are Not Acceptable*

```
IT1*1*2*3*4*5*code*value*code*value - acceptable
IT1*1*2*3*4*5*code*value             - acceptable
IT1*1*2*3*4*5*6*7*code*value         - not acceptable
```

Naturally, we turn to a script. We will use one script and a counter to output all four values in whichever sequence is necessary. The map is in Figure 15-9.

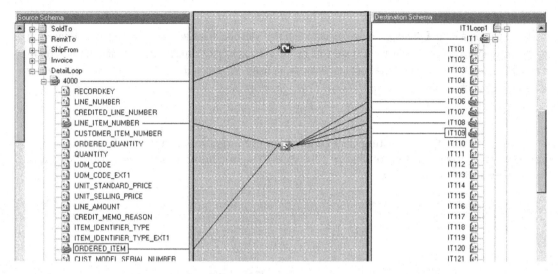

Figure 15-9. *A map to output code pairs when target nodes are not specific*

Notice that one Scripting functoid outputs to all four target nodes. The script is in Listing 15-15.

Listing 15-15. *Script to Output Code Pairs When Target Nodes Are Not Specific*

```
// Declare a counter to keep track of what position you are in the output
// Must be initialized to zero
  int counter = 0;

// Accept both the line number and the lot number as input on each pass
public string ControlCodePairOutput(string linnum, string lotnum)
  {
// Output the line number code if this is first pass and you have a line number
  if (counter == 0 & linnum != "")
  {
  counter++;
  return "IB";
  }
// Output the line number if this is second pass and you have a line number
  if (counter == 1 & linnum != "")
  {
  counter++;
  return linnum;
  }
// Output the lot number code if this is first pass and you have a lot number (means
// you had no line number), or if this is the third pass and you have a lot number
// (means you had a line number and have already output it)
  if (counter == 0 | counter == 2 & lotnum != "")
  {
```

```
  counter++;
  return "LT";
  }
// Output the lot number if this is second pass and you have a lot number (means
// you had no line number), or if this is the fourth pass and you have a lot number
// (means you had a line number and have already output it)

  if (counter == 1 | counter == 4 & lotnum != "")
  {
   counter = 0;
   return lotnum;
  }
// None of above conditions were met so you are done.  Reset the counter for the
// next IT1 segment
  counter = 0;
  return "";
  }
```

This example does not show blocking of the IT1 segment or blocking of either of the four target nodes. We can use a Logical String functoid to block the output of the IT1 segment, but we need to initialize the counter to minus one if we do so. Remember that the link to the IT1 node would activate the script, so we would need the counter set to not output data. We can use Logical String/Value Mapping functoid pairs to control the output of the four target nodes. With the exception of manipulating the counter, these are standard segment and element blocking procedures we have used many times in earlier examples.

Summary

This chapter addressed issues that you may encounter when working with EDI code pairs, especially in X12 transactions. For the most part, these are simple examples, because each code pair has a specific meaning. The most difficult problems are extracting specific values from a source EDI file and outputting codes and values to loosely defined target nodes in a target EDI file. These problems pale in comparison to another type of code pair usage—the SDQ segment.

In the SDQ segment, up to ten code pairs may be present. One classic example of SDQ code-pair content is store numbers where each SDQ contains references to multiple stores. There may be several SDQ segments, so the number of stores may be 30, 40, 50, or more. Each line item may contain an SDQ loop, so the same stores may appear under multiple line items. And you must reorder the data so that the data is sorted by store number with a loop of line items beneath each store. This level of complexity is why our next chapter is devoted entirely to unraveling the code pairs in SDQ segments.

CHAPTER 16

■■■

Unraveling the SDQ Segment

We discussed code pairs in the last chapter. Now, we focus on a different kind of pair, those found in the SDQ segment. The pairs in the SDQ are not qualifier/value code pairs like those you just saw, but are value/value pairs. The first node in the pair contains a location; the second node in the pair contains a quantity. The location and quantity are for a line item, usually indicating a store and the quantity of the line item for that store. The same store may appear in every iteration of a line item loop, and the most common mapping requirement is that the data be rearranged from line-item–centric to store-centric. This chapter discusses such a rearrangement.

Exploring the SDQ Segment

A common usage of the SDQ appears in Listing 16-1. The listing shows two instances of an LIN loop. The LIN segment contains two items, 0633928 and 0633929. Each LIN segment contains three ZA segments, each of which indicates the type of SDQ data (QA is on-hand; OP is on-order; QS is sold).

Each ZA segment then contains one or more SDQ segments. The SDQ segments contain the code pairs for location/quantity. The location 147 has 13 on-hand and 12 sold items for item 0633928 and 11 sold items for item 0633929.

Listing 16-1. *The SDQ Segment in Use*

```
LIN*1*SK*0633928
  ZA*QA
    SDQ*EA*92*0018*1*0035*1*0081*1*0082*1*0083*1*0084*1*0085*1*0086*1*0087*1*0088*1
    SDQ*EA*92*147*13*151*14*152*15*154*12*157*10*160*14*161*11*162*16*163*7*164*14
  ZA*QP
    SDQ*EA*92*0018*2*0035*1*0081*1*0082*1*0083*1*0084*1*0085*1*0086*1*0087*1*0088*1
    SDQ*EA*92*207*1*211*1*217*1*227*2*234*1*244*1*251*1*254*2*262*3*264*1
  ZA*QS
    SDQ*EA*92*0018*3*0035*1*0081*1*0081*1*0081*1*0081*1*0081*1*0081*1*0081*1*0081*1
    SDQ*EA*92*147*12*151*16*152*13*154*9*157*12*160*11*161*10*162*9*163*10*164*11
LIN*2*SK*0633929
  ZA*QS
    SDQ*EA*92*101*1*107*2*121*3*127*4*132*5*133*6*134*7*139*8*141*9*0018*4
    SDQ*EA*92*147*11*151*12*152*13*154*14*157*15*160*16*161*17*162*18*163*19*164*20
```

```
ZA*QA
  SDQ*EA*92*107*1*133*1*144*1*154*2*0018*5*174*1*190*1*197*1*201*1*204*1
  SDQ*EA*92*207*1*211*1*217*1*227*2*234*1*244*1*251*1*254*2*262*3*264*1
ZA*QP
  SDQ*EA*92*101*11*107*10*121*12*127*16*132*12*133*11*0018*6*139*12*141*12*144*11
```

The SDQ example in Listing 16-1 is from an X12 852 (Stock Status Report) transaction, which is the transaction on which we focus our examples in this chapter. The 852 reports stock status (e.g., on-hand, on-order, back ordered, and sold) by location (e.g., store and warehouse) for each item in inventory. We look at two SDQ mapping examples in this chapter, one mapping from an 852 and the other mapping to an 852. We will focus on location 0018 (bold text in Listing 16-1).

Mapping Inbound SDQ Data

Our first example addresses one of the most common transformations that occur with SDQ segments: the data is sorted by line item in the source but must be sorted by location in the target. In essence, changing the sort order in this way requires turning the data inside out. The source file that we use is the 852 transaction that contains the LIN, ZA, and SDQ segment data from Listing 16-1. The desired target structure, shown for location 0018, is shown in the output in Listing 16-2.

Listing 16-2. *Excerpt from the Map Output Showing the Desired Structure*

```
<Location>
  <LocationID>0018</LocationID>
    <LineItem>
      <ItemNumber>0633928</ItemNumber>
      <QtyAvailable>1</QtyAvailable>
      <QtyOnOrder>2</QtyOnOrder>
      <QtySold>3</QtySold>
    </LineItem>
    <LineItem>
      <ItemNumber>0633929</ItemNumber>
      <QtyAvailable>5</QtyAvailable>
      <QtyOnOrder>6</QtyOnOrder>
      <QtySold>4</QtySold>
    </LineItem>
</Location>
```

As Listing 16-2 shows, the data is now sorted by location, with each line item and its quantities shown under the location. This excerpt contains the output for our focus location, 0018. Each unique location number in the source produces one Location loop in the target with all the associated line numbers with the quantity information.

Many EDI translators have difficulty performing this type of data reorganization without pre- or post-processing the data. The process would be very difficult, if not impossible, to do in one BizTalk map using only functoids. Fortunately, the BizTalk engine allows multiple types of scripting to enable us to handle this problem in a single map.

We solve this problem by first mining the source data to gather the data into hash tables. Next, we create an XSLT Call Template that will process each location number in the list. Finally, we have the XSLT Call Template call an external C# script to process the locations and quantities. This solution contains nothing that has not been discussed before; the difficulty is visualizing the solution when faced with the problem. Let's walk through the process step by step, following the incremental testing methodology.

Gathering the Data

The first step we take is to gather all the SDQ data using the map in Figure 16-1. We need to gather the line item number from each LIN03, the quantity-type code from each ZA01, and all the location/quantity pairs from each SDQ segment.

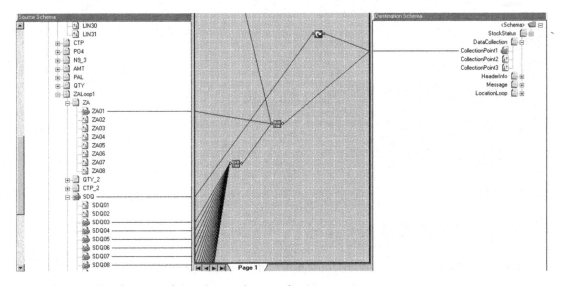

Figure 16-1. *A map for our inbound SDQ data-gathering test*

The looping functoid forces the CollectionPoint1 node to loop once for every instance of the SDQ segment. The lower, left-hand String Concatenation functoid pulls all the location/ quantity pairs from each SDQ segment. The upper, right-hand String Concatenate functoid is part of the incremental testing, gathering all three pieces of data—the item number, the quantity-type code, and each SDQ string—into a string. We do not block the output of the strings to the CollectionPoint1 node at this time, because we want to look at the gathered data to make sure we are getting what we expect. Listing 16-3 contains an example of the strings created for the first two SDQ segments.

Listing 16-3. *Incremental Testing Data Strings Output by the Inbound SDQ Data-Gathering Test Map*

```
<CollectionPoint1>0633928:QA:0018~1|0035~1|0081~1|0082~1|0083~1|0084~1|0085~1
                   |0086~1|0087~1|0088~1|</CollectionPoint1>
<CollectionPoint1>0633928:QA:147~13|151~14|152~15|154~12|157~10|160~14|161~11
                   |162~16|163~7|164~14|</CollectionPoint1>
```

The first value is the line item number from the current LIN03. The second value is the quantity type code from the current ZA01, and the rest of the values are the location/quantity pairs. We get 11 strings, one for each SDQ segment. We compare the values in the strings against the input data (see Listing 16-1) and see that the output is correct. We also examine the separators (colon, tilde, and pipe characters) to make sure the string is formatted correctly.

Since there are many inputs to the first String Concatenate functoid, knowing the order of the inputs is critical should the output string be incorrect. We make checking this easy by labeling the links from the source nodes to the functoid, as mentioned in the basic mapping chapters. A portion of our Configure Functoid Inputs pane is shown in Figure 16-2.

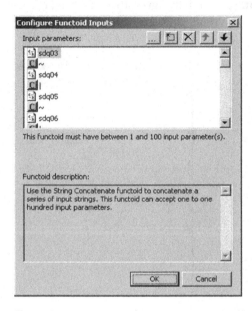

Figure 16-2. *Inputs to the String Concatenate functoid showing link labels*

Now that we have verified that the data is being extracted correctly, we can move to the next step, which is extracting the data from the strings and storing it into hash tables.

Sorting and Storing the Data into Hash Tables

Since this step requires scripting, we replace the second String Concatenate functoid with a Scripting functoid, as shown in Figure 16-3.

We continue to leave the CollectionPoint1 node unblocked so that we can output values from the Scripting functoid. Doing so allows us to selectively output information during the script's execution for debugging purposes. The script, displayed in Listing 16-4, includes some alternate return statements that we used to check the operation.

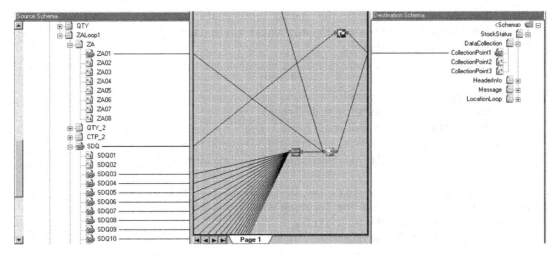

Figure 16-3. *Our next step in the map for inbound SDQ: adding a script to store data in hash tables*

■**Tip** Scripts of this nature are best developed and tested in the development studio, which provides syntax checking and allows you to run data through the script while using watch points to examine the impact of each line of code. This increases, but does not assure, the chances that your script will run correctly in your map.

Listing 16-4. *Script to Put Gathered Data into Hash Tables*

```
// Declare global hashtables, one for the locations and one for the quantities
   System.Collections.Hashtable LocationTable =
               new System.Collections.Hashtable();
   System.Collections.Hashtable QuantityTable =
               new System.Collections.Hashtable();
// Receive the LIN03, the ZA01, and the output from String Concatenate functoid
   public string ExtractSDQPairs(string inItem, string inZA01, string inPairs)
   {
     string retval = "";
     string pairs = inPairs;
     string singlePair = "";
     double locQty = 0;
     string locKey = "";
     string locKey1 = "";
```

```
// Parse through each string from the String Concatenate functoid,
// picking off each location-quantity pair until there is no
// data left in the input string.
   while (pairs != "")
   {
      int delimpos = pairs.IndexOf("|",0);
      singlePair = pairs.Substring(0,delimpos);
      pairs = pairs.Remove(0,delimpos + 1);
      string pairLoc = singlePair.Substring(0,singlePair.IndexOf("~",0));
      string pairQty = singlePair.Substring(singlePair.IndexOf("~",0)+ 1);

// For each location/quantity pair, add to or update the LocationTable
// and the QuantityTable.  Pad the location with zeros to ensure each
// number has the same length as a string
      if (pairQty != "" && pairLoc != "")
      {
         pairLoc = pairLoc.PadLeft(4, Convert.ToChar("0"));
         locKey = pairLoc;
         LocationTable[locKey] = locKey;
         locQty = Convert.ToDouble(pairQty);
         double tableQty = 0;
         locKey1 = pairLoc + ":" + inItem + ":" + inZA01;

// Write or update the Location:item:QtyType by adding the pair qty
// to any existing quantity
         if (QuantityTable.ContainsKey(locKey1))
                 tableQty = Convert.ToDouble(QuantityTable[locKey1]);
         locQty = locQty + tableQty;
         QuantityTable[locKey1] = locQty.ToString();
      }
   }
   return "";
// Here are some alternate return values that allow verification
// of what is being loaded into a table and that show the locKey values
// These are useful for debugging in the map.  To use one, comment out
// the return above and then uncomment the one you want to use
//   return LocationTable[locKey].ToString();
//   return locKey1 + ":" +  QuantityTable[locKey1].ToString();
//   return locKey1;

   }
```

If we use the alternate return statement return locKey1 + ":" + QuantityTable[locKey1].
ToString();, we get the output shown in Listing 16-5. Of course, the output for each string is
only the last location/quantity value, since the script does not return until the last pair is processed. Still, this output is sufficient for us to determine that the data is being stored into the
quantity table correctly.

Listing 16-5. *Output of Our Quantity Table Data*

```
<DataCollection>
    <CollectionPoint1>0088:0633928:QA:1</CollectionPoint1>
    <CollectionPoint1>0164:0633928:QA:14</CollectionPoint1>
    <CollectionPoint1>0088:0633928:QP:1</CollectionPoint1>
    <CollectionPoint1>0264:0633928:QP:1</CollectionPoint1>
    <CollectionPoint1>0081:0633928:QS:8</CollectionPoint1>
    <CollectionPoint1>0164:0633928:QS:11</CollectionPoint1>
    <CollectionPoint1>0144:0633929:QS:10</CollectionPoint1>
    <CollectionPoint1>0164:0633929:QS:20</CollectionPoint1>
    <CollectionPoint1>0204:0633929:QA:1</CollectionPoint1>
    <CollectionPoint1>0264:0633929:QA:1</CollectionPoint1>
    <CollectionPoint1>0144:0633929:QP:11</CollectionPoint1>
</DataCollection>
```

Once we verify that the script is working correctly, we no longer need to output the DataCollection node. The next map will block that node from being created.

Retrieving the Locations for Output

Now that we have all the data stored in hash tables, we move to the script that loops through the locations and extracts them. These locations are the keys to the hash tables. The values are moved to an array list, sorted, pulled from the array list, and placed in a delimited string. The script is in Listing 16-6.

Listing 16-6. *Extracting Locations and Building a Delimited String*

```
public string ReturnLocString()
{
// Create an array list
   System.Collections.ArrayList IDList = new System.Collections.ArrayList();
// Call the sub-function below to get the keys from the location hash table
// Then sort the list of keys
   IDList = GetKeys(LocationTable);
   IDList.Sort();
// Go through the array an build a delimited string containing all the keys
   string delimitedData = "";
   foreach (string strData in IDList)
   {
     if (strData != "") delimitedData += strData + "|";
   }
   return "";
// Debug return statement that will output the delimited string for checking
//   return delimitedData;
}
```

```
// Function called from above to fill the array with keys from the hashtable
public ArrayList GetKeys(Hashtable table)
{
    return new ArrayList(table.Keys);
}
```

Note Remember that XSLT Call Templates accept each input parameter only once. If you need to pass them multiples of a parameter, such as we do with the locations, all the instances must be passed as one. Thus we put the locations into a delimited string like that shown in Listing 16-6 so they can be passed to the XSLT Call Template as a single parameter later.

Since we are doing incremental testing, before we move on, we comment out the normal return and activate the debug return in the script. Then we test the map, which now looks like Figure 16-4.

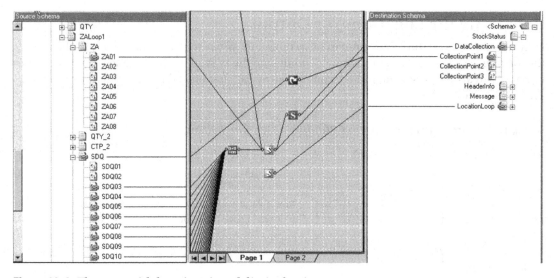

Figure 16-4. *The map with locations in a delimited string*

The output of our debug `return` statement is in Listing 16-7. As you see, the string contains a sorted list of the unique locations that were present in the source data. This is the output that we desired, so we can move forward.

Listing 16-7. *Delimited String of Values*

```
<LocationLoop>0018|0035|0081|0082|0083|0084|0085|0086|0087|0088|0101|0107|0121|
0127|0132|0133|0134|0139|0141|0144|0147|0151|0152|0154|0157|0160|0161|0162|0163|
0164|0174|0190|0197|0201|0204|0207|0211|0217|0227|0234|0244|0251|0254|0262|0264|
</LocationLoop>
```

If you also want to check the extraction of values from the quantity hash table, copy the script from Listing 16-6. You'll need to change the name of the script and replace two lines. Replace the following line

```
IDList = GetKeys(LocationTable);
```

with this one

```
IDList = GetKeys(QuantityTable);
```

Also replace this line

```
delimitedData += strData + "|";
```

with

```
string strQty = QuantityTable[strData].ToString();
delimitedData += strData + "~" + strQty +   "|";
```

The new script will output the entire string of data from the quantity hash table in the format 0018:0633928:QA~1|0018:0633928:QP~2|. The string will be around 1,900 characters in length for this source data.

Outputting the Locations

Now that we are satisfied that we can build the input strings for the XSLT Call Template correctly, we can begin building an XSLT Call Template that will loop through the locations and output one LocationLoop node containing one LocationID node for each location in the string. We add one Scripting functoid to the map, as shown in Figure 16-5.

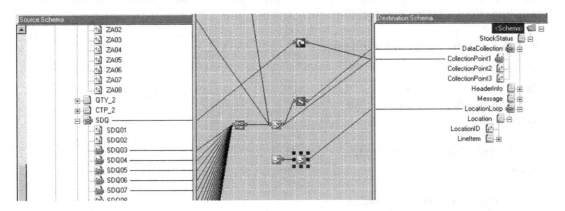

Figure 16-5. *Amending our map to output locations*

Our script to output the location information is in Listing 16-8. Notice that the script is recursive, calling itself continually until the entire input string is consumed.

Listing 16-8. *Code to Output Location Information*

```
<xsl:template name="CreateLocation">
<!-- inString is the delimited string of all locations-->
   <xsl:param name="inString"/>
<!--If the input string has no value, end the execution of the template -->
   <xsl:if test="$inString != '' ">
<!--Extract the Location ID from the string, store it in $LocID, -->
<!-- and write it to the document -->
        <xsl:variable name="LocID"  select="substring-before($inString, '|' )"/>
        <xsl:if test="$LocID != '' ">
            <xsl:element name="Location">
                <xsl:element name="LocationID">
                  <xsl:value-of select="$LocID"/>
                </xsl:element>
            </xsl:element>
        </xsl:if>
<!-- Call the template again after removing the used location from the input -->
        <xsl:call-template name="CreateLocation">
            <xsl:with-param name="inString" select=
                                        "substring-after($inString, '|' )"/>
        </xsl:call-template>
    </xsl:if>
</xsl:template>
```

We test the map and get the output shown in Listing 16-9. This output is the first piece of the solution. We now have one Location node loop for each unique location in the source data. The listing shows the first four location loops that are output.

Listing 16-9. *Output Location Information*

```
<StockStatus>
 <Location>
    <LocationID>0018</LocationID>
  </Location>
 <Location>
    <LocationID>0035</LocationID>
  </Location>
  <Location>
    <LocationID>0081</LocationID>
  </Location>
 <Location>
    <LocationID>0082</LocationID>
  </Location>
```

We now have the output for each location. We must add the output for the item numbers and the quantities.

Adding the Item Numbers and Quantity Information to the Output

The final piece to the puzzle is outputting the LineItem nodes for each location, and within each of those nodes, the ItemNumber, QtyAvailable, QtyOnOrder, and QtySold nodes. We need to modify the script in Listing 16-8 to output these nodes, and we need to add a script to retrieve the information. The key for the hash table containing this information is Location:Item:Quantity. The script to retrieve quantities is in Listing 16-10.

Listing 16-10. *Script to Retrieve the Quantities*

```
// Input the location number, the item number, and the quantity type code
  public string ReturnQty(string inLoc, string inItem, string inCode)
  {
  string localQty ="";
// Form the key from the input values
    string locKey = inLoc + ":" + inItem + ":" + inCode;
// Look up the quantity and return it
    if (QuantityTable.ContainsKey(locKey)) localQty =
                              QuantityTable[locKey].ToString();
  return localQty;
}
```

Next, we modify our previous script by adding an inner for-each loop to cycle through all the line items and, for each one, call the script in Listing 16-10 to get the three quantities. The new code will output the line item information. Listing 16-11 is the script from Listing 16-8 with the new code added.

Listing 16-11. *Script to Output All Location, Line Item, and Quantity Information*

```
<xsl:template name="CreateLocation">
  <xsl:param name="inString"/>
  <xsl:if test="$inString != '' ">
  <xsl:variable name="LocID"select="substring-before($inString, '|' )"/>
  <xsl:if test="$LocID != '' ">
    <xsl:element name="Location">
      <xsl:element name="LocationID"><xsl:value-of select="$LocID"/></xsl:element>
<!-- Code added to loop through the line items -->
        <xsl:for-each select="//so:LIN">
            <xsl:variable name="ItemID">
              <xsl:value-of select="LIN03"/>
            </xsl:variable>
<-- Call the C# script "ReturnQty" to get each quantity into a variable-->
            <xsl:variable name="QtyOnHand"
                    select="userCSharp:ReturnQty($LocID, $ItemID, 'QA' )"/>
            <xsl:variable name="QtyOnOrder"
                    select="userCSharp:ReturnQty($LocID, $ItemID, 'QP' )"/>
            <xsl:variable name="QtySold"
                    select="userCSharp:ReturnQty($LocID, $ItemID, 'QS' )"/>
```

```
<!--Then output the quantities
        <xsl:if test="$QtyOnHand != '' or $QtyOnOrder != '' or $QtySold != '' ">
                <LineItem>
                        <ItemNumber>
                                <xsl:value-of select="$ItemID"/>
                            </ItemNumber>
                        <QtyAvailable>
                                <xsl:value-of select="$QtyOnHand"/>
                            </QtyAvailable>
                        <QtyOnOrder>
                                <xsl:value-of select="$QtyOnOrder"/>
                            </QtyOnOrder>
                        <QtySold>
                                <xsl:value-of select="$QtySold"/>
                            </QtySold>
                    </LineItem>
            </xsl:if>
        </xsl:for-each>
<!-- End of code added to loop through the line items -->
    </xsl:element>
  </xsl:if>
<!-- Call the template again-->
  <xsl:call-template name="CreateLocation">
     <xsl:with-param name="inString" select="substring-after($inString, '|' )"/>
  </xsl:call-template>
</xsl:if>
</xsl:template>
```

Once everything is in place, the map looks like Figure 16-6. We've added one new Scripting functoid, the one that is unattached, to hold the ReturnQty C# script.

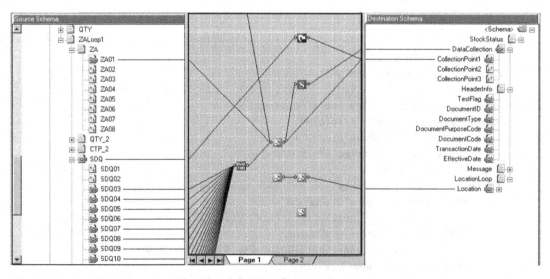

Figure 16-6. *Our final map for processing the SDQ segment*

An excerpt from the output of the map is in Listing 16-12. Notice that our focus location, location 0018, correctly contains two line items and the correct quantities for each.

Listing 16-12. *Output Excerpt from Our Final Map for Processing the SDQ Segment*

```
<LocationLoop>
 <Location>
    <LocationID>0018</LocationID>
    <LineItem>
      <ItemNumber>0633928</ItemNumber>
      <QtyAvailable>1</QtyAvailable>
      <QtyOnOrder>2</QtyOnOrder>
      <QtySold>3</QtySold>
    </LineItem>
    <LineItem>
      <ItemNumber>0633929</ItemNumber>
      <QtyAvailable>5</QtyAvailable>
      <QtyOnOrder>6</QtyOnOrder>
      <QtySold>4</QtySold>
    </LineItem>
  </Location>
  <Location>
    <LocationID>0035</LocationID>
    <LineItem>
      <ItemNumber>0633928</ItemNumber>
      <QtyAvailable>1</QtyAvailable>
      <QtyOnOrder>1</QtyOnOrder>
      <QtySold>1</QtySold>
    </LineItem>
  </Location>
```

Note To keep the script easier to read, we did not suppress individual quantity fields if they had no quantity. In a production script, we might need to do so, or we might need to insert a zero.

Considering the Decisions in This Map

Of course, with a map such as this, there are many ways that could be used to accumulate, reorganize, and output the data. Here are some thoughts on why we handled the example as we did:

- *Hash table*: We used hash tables, as opposed to arrays, because in this case, we were able to look up keyed items much easier. Even the compound key (location, item, and type) for the quantity data was easy to handle. Using hash tables kept us from having to spend time designing the arrays and the code to search those arrays.

- *Delimited strings*: We like delimited strings as input to XSLT scripts when we know the approximate volume of data is not going to cause the strings to become so large as to affect performance, as might happen if the trading partner had 1,000 locations, 5,000 items, and 5 different types of quantities.

Mapping Outbound SDQ Data

Now, let's flip the previous example and map the data from the application file to an X12 Stock Status transaction. We use the same file formats, and the output from our previous map as the input to this map. To visualize what the map must accomplish, look at Listings 16-1 and 16-2. This map must take the data from the structure in Listing 16-2 and convert it into the structure of Listing 16-1.

Collecting the Item and Quantity Information

Although similar in methodology to the script we used in the first example to gather data, our script in this example differs slightly in technique. We use fixed-length strings instead of delimited strings. The script that we use to load data into the hash tables is in Listing 16-13.

Listing 16-13. *Loading the Hash Tables*

```
// Declare the hash tables
  System.Collections.Hashtable ItemTable = new System.Collections.Hashtable();
  System.Collections.Hashtable QuantityTable = new System.Collections.Hashtable();
// Input the item number, location, and three quantities
  public string ExtractSDQPairs(string inItem, string inLoc, string inQA,
                                                 string inQP, string inQS)

  {
    string typeKey = "";
    string locString = "";
// Put the item number into its hash tablel with itself as the key
    ItemTable[inItem] = inItem;
// For each quantity type that has an input value, create a key (item number plus
// colon plus the quantity type code).  Create a string containing all the
// location/quantity values for the current item number/quantity location/quantity
// value code.  Make each fixed length.
    if (inQA != "")
    {
        typeKey = inItem + ":QA";
        if (QuantityTable.ContainsKey(typeKey))
        }
            locString = QuantityTable[typeKey].ToString();
        }
        QuantityTable[typeKey] = locString + inLoc.PadLeft(4, Convert.ToChar("0")) +
                                    inQA.PadLeft(6, Convert.ToChar("0"));
        locString = "";
    }
```

```
    if (inQO != "")
    {
        typeKey = inItem + ":QP";
        if (QuantityTable.ContainsKey(typeKey))
        }
            locString = QuantityTable[typeKey].ToString();
        }
        QuantityTable[typeKey] = locString + inLoc.PadLeft(4, Convert.ToChar("0")) +
                                 inQP.PadLeft(6, Convert.ToChar("0"));
        locString = "";
    }
    if (inQS != "")
    {
        typeKey = inItem + ":QS";
        if (QuantityTable.ContainsKey(typeKey))
        }
            locString = QuantityTable[typeKey].ToString();
        }
        QuantityTable[typeKey] = locString + inLoc.PadLeft(4, Convert.ToChar("0")) +
                                 inQS.PadLeft(6, Convert.ToChar("0"));
        locString = "";
    }
  return "";
// Alternate return values for debugging
//    return ItemTable[inItem].ToString();
//    return typeKey + ":" + QuantityTable[typeKey].ToString();
}
```

At this point, the map looks like Figure 16-7. We are using the XPO node as the data-collection node, because that node is optional and is not to be output. In this map, we do not block the output, because we want our debug process to output data to the XPO1. Once we move to the next step, we will block output of the XPO node with a Logical String functoid.

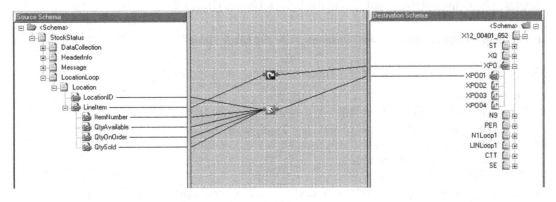

Figure 16-7. *Gathering the data*

We want to check to make sure the data is being put into the hash table correctly, so we use the debug return statement `return typeKey + ":" + QuantityTable[typeKey].ToString()`. A sample from the debug output is in Listing 16-14. The excerpt shows three passes through the gathering of data and the creation of the string for the line item number/quantity type pair `0633928:QS`. Each pass appends another location/quantity pair to the string. Notice that there are no delimiters separating the location/quantity pairs, as they are fixed length.

Listing 16-14. *Output of the Debug Operation for Gathering the Data*

```
<ns0:XPO>
  <XPO01>0633928:QS:0018000001</XPO01>
</ns0:XPO>
<ns0:XPO>
  <XPO01>0633928:QS:00180000010035000001</XPO01>
</ns0:XPO>
<ns0:XPO>
  <XPO01>0633928:QS:001800000100350000010081000008</XPO01>
</ns0:XPO>
```

■ **Caution** When you create debugging statements, you must make sure they will work with your data. In this script, for example, if you specify a key in the return statement, such as `0633928:QA`, you will get an error if there is no data in the hash table for that key.

Retrieving Item Numbers from the Hash Table

Our next step is to retrieve the item numbers from their hash table and build the delimited string that we will pass to the XSLT Call Template. This script, shown in Listing 16-15, is cloned from the script in Listing 16-6 that performed the same function for the first example of the chapter. The names of the script and of the hash table are changed.

Listing 16-15. *Script to Extract Item Numbers from the Hash Table*

```
public string ReturnItemString()
{
// Create an array list
  System.Collections.ArrayList IDList = new System.Collections.ArrayList();
// Call the sub-function below to get the keys from the location hash table
// Then sort the list of keys
  IDList = GetKeys(LocationTable);
  IDList.Sort();
// Go through the array an build a delimited string containing all the keys
·  string delimitedData = "";
  foreach (string strData in IDList)
  {
```

```
    if (strData != "") delimitedData += strData + "|";
  }
    return "";
// Debug return statement that will output the delimited string for checking
//  return delimitedData;
}
//  Function called from above to fill the array with keys from the hashtable
public ArrayList GetKeys(Hashtable table)
{
  return new ArrayList(table.Keys);
}
```

With this script in place, the map looks like Figure 16-8. We add the Scripting functoid linked to the LINLoop1 node. With output validation off, we can send our debug output to that node even though the node is a record, not an element.

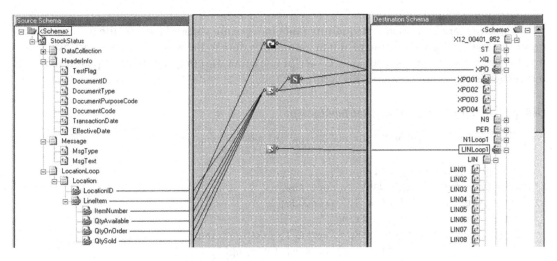

Figure 16-8. *A map with a script to extract a list of item numbers*

The output from this map, when we use the debug return statement return delimited-Data;, looks like Listing 16-16. Since we have only two line items in the source data, we easily confirm that this output is correct.

Listing 16-16. *Debug Output of a Line-Item String*

```
<nsO:LINLoop1>0633928|0633929|</nsO:LINLoop1>
```

Building the LIN and ZA Loops

Now, we want to make sure that we can output the line items and the quantity codes correctly. The first step in this process is to build the means to output a line number to the LIN01 node. We consider that the item numbers, quantity types, locations, and quantities will all be output using an XSLT Call Template. We know that we can only modify the value of a variable in an

XSLT Call Template by calling the template again and passing it a new value for the variable. We also know that our XSLT Call Template will be recursive, calling itself repeatedly until there is no more data. This means that we can build a C# script that can be called to provide a new input value each time the XSLT routine is called. We use this means to build a line number counter. The C# script is in Listing 16-17.

Listing 16-17. *Line Item Counter Script*

```
//Declare a global variable,
  int LineCounter = 0;
// Increment and return the line count
  public string ReturnLineID()
  {
    LineCounter += 1;
    return LineCounter.ToString();
  }
```

Since we stored our location/quantity pairs in separate strings keyed by the item number/ quantity type, we have the same problem getting this data to the XSLT Call Template as in the previous example. We must provide a C# script to extract the correct string and pass it to the template. Listing 16-18 contains this script.

Listing 16-18. *Location/Quantity Retrieval Script*

```
  public string ReturnLocQtyString(string inItem, string inCode)
  {
    string LocQtyString ="";
// Build the item number/quantity code key
    string itemKey = inItem + ":" + inCode;
// Extract  the appropriate string
    if (QuantityTable.ContainsKey(itemKey)) LocQtyString =
                   QuantityTable[itemKey].ToString();
    return LocQtyString;
}
```

With these scripts in place, we construct the first-level call template, which receives as input a delimited string containing all the item numbers. For each item number processed, the script creates a LINLoop1 node and a LIN node. The LIN node contains the LIN01 (line number from the line item counter script), LIN02 (code qualifier SK), and LIN03 (item number).

After the LIN node is created, the script will generate a ZALoop1 loop with a ZA node for each quantity type for which a location/quantity string is received (see Listing 16-18). Since we are doing incremental testing, we will not break the string apart but will output the entire string. This will make it possible to validate that we have the LINLoop1, LIN, ZALoop1, and ZA values correct. The script is in Listing 16-19.

Listing 16-19. *Output of the Line Number, Item Number, and Quantity Type*

```
<xsl:template name="CreateLINLoop">
<!-- Receive as input the delimited string containing a list of item numbers -->
  <xsl:param name="inString"/>
<!-- If there is no string just exit. -->
  <xsl:if test="$inString != '' ">
<!-- Get the first item number -->
    <xsl:variable name="Item"  select="substring-before($inString, '|' )"/>
<!-- If there is no item number we're done -->
    <xsl:if test="$Item != '' ">

<!-- Output the LINLoop1 node and the LIN node.  Call the C# routine -->
<!-- ReturnLineID to get the LIN01 line number -->
      <xsl:element name="LINLoop1">
        <xsl:element name="LIN">
          <xsl:element name="LIN01
            xsl:value-of select="userCSharp:ReturnLineID()"/>
          </xsl:element>
          <xsl:element name="LIN02">SK</xsl:element>
          <xsl:element name=" LIN03"><xsl:value-of select="$Item"/></xsl:element>
        </xsl:element>

<!-- Call the C# routine ReturnLocQtyString to get the location quantity string -->
<!-- for quantity type "QA" -->
        <xsl:variable name="QAString" select=
                              "userCSharp:ReturnLocQtyString($Item, 'QA' )"/>
<!-- If there is no string, go on to the next quantity type -->
        <xsl:if test="$QAString != '' ">
<!-- Output a ZALoop1 node for  the quantity type QA -->
          <xsl:element name="ZALoop1">
            <xsl:element name="ZA">
              <xsl:element name="ZA01">QA</xsl:element>

<!-- Here we output the full location/quantity string so we can debug the other  -->
<!-- portions of the script. -->
              <xsl:element name="itemString">
                <xsl:value-of select="$QAString"/>
              </xsl:element>
            </xsl:element>
          </xsl:element>
        </xsl:if>

<!--Repeat the ZALoo1 node process for quantity type "QP" -->
        <xsl:variable name="QPString" select=
                              "userCSharp:ReturnLocQtyString($Item, 'QP' )"/>
        <xsl:if test="$QPString != '' ">
          <xsl:element name="ZALoop1">
```

```
                <xsl:element name="ZA">
                   <xsl:element name="ZA01">QP</xsl:element>
                   <xsl:element name="itemString">
                      <xsl:value-of select="$QPString"/>
                   </xsl:element>

                </xsl:element>
             </xsl:element>
          </xsl:if>
<!-- Create the ZA loop for quantity type "QS" -->
          <xsl:variable name="QSString" select=
                              "userCSharp:ReturnLocQtyString($Item, 'QS' )"/>
          <xsl:if test="$QSString != '' ">
             <xsl:element name="ZALoop1">
                <xsl:element name="ZA">
                   <xsl:element name="ZA01">QS</xsl:element>
                   <xsl:element name="itemString"><xsl:value-of
                                 select="$QSString"/></xsl:element>
                </xsl:element>
             </xsl:element>
            </xsl:if>
          </xsl:element>
          </xsl:if>

<!--Make the template recursive by getting the next item number from the -->
<!--item number string and calling the template again-->
       <xsl:call-template name="CreateLINLoop">
          <xsl:with-param name="inString" select="substring-after($inString, '|' )"/>
       </xsl:call-template>
     </xsl:if>
</xsl:template>
```

Figure 16-9 contains the map for outputting the line item number, location, and quantity type information.

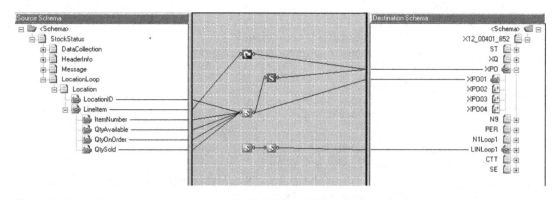

Figure 16-9. *An incremental test map to check LIN and ZA output*

Listing 16-20 contains an excerpt of the output of the map shown in Figure 16-9.

Listing 16-20. *Output from the Incremental Test Map to Check LIN and ZA Output*

```
<LINLoop1>
  <LIN>
    <LIN01>1</LIN01>
    <LIN02>SK</LIN02>
    <LIN03>0633928</LIN03>
  </LIN>
  <ZALoop1>
    <ZA>
      <ZA01>QA</ZA01>
      <itemString>0018000001003500000100810000010082000001008300000l
        0084000001008500000100860000010087000001008800000l014700001301
        51000014015200001501540000120157000010016000001401610000110162
        00001601630000070164000014
      </itemString>
    </ZA>
  </ZALoop1>
  <ZALoop1>
    <ZA>
      <ZA01>QP</ZA01>
      <itemString>0018000002003500000100810000010082000001008300000l
        0084000001008500000100860000010087000001008800000l020700000102
        11000001021700000102270000020234000001024400000102510000010254
        00000202620000030264000001
      </itemString>
    </ZA>
  </ZALoop1>
```

This excerpt shows that we are correctly producing the nodes and that we are filling them with the correct data. Remember that we are ignoring the data in the <itemString> nodes, since those nodes are just holding places for the location/quantity data. Our interests in this output are the LINLoop1, LIN, LIN01, LIN02, LIN03, ZALoop1, and ZA01 nodes. We are checking to make sure they contain the correct data.

Adding the SDQ Node to the ZALoop1 Nodes

The first thing we must do is to replace the following debugging code

```
<xsl:element name="itemString"><xsl:value-of select="$QPString"/></xsl:element>
```

that is found in the main script shown in Listing 16-19. We replace each occurrence of this line with the lines shown in Listing 16-21.

Listing 16-21. *Replacement Lines for Main Script*

```
<xsl:call-template name="ParseSDQString">
<xsl:with-param name="typeString" select="$QSString"/>
</xsl:call-template>
```

Now, instead of outputting the whole line in a temporary node, we will output one
SDQ segment for each group of ten or fewer location/quantity pairs per quantity type. The
ParseSDQString call template that is called by the new lines is shown here in Listing 16-22.

Listing 16-22. *ParseSDQString Call Template*

```
<xsl:template name="ParseSDQString">
  <xsl:param name="typeString"/>
  <xsl:if test="$typeString != '' ">
    <xsl:variable name="SDQString"  select="substring($typeString,1,100)"/>
    <xsl:if test="$SDQString != '' ">
      <xsl:element name="SDQString">
        <xsl:value-of select="$SDQString"/>
      </xsl:element-->
      <xsl:call-template name="BuildSDQ">
        <xsl:with-param name="SDQString" select="$SDQString"/>
      </xsl:call-template>
    </xsl:if>
<!-- Call the template again -->
  <xsl:call-template name="ParseSDQString">
    <xsl:with-param name="typeString" select="substring($typeString, 101)"/>
    </xsl:call-template>
  </xsl:if>
</xsl:template>
```

The ParseSDQString template takes the full string received from the CreateLINLoop template and breaks it into 100-byte chunks, which equates to 10 pairs of location/quantity data.
If there are fewer than 100 bytes in the string, no breaking is needed. Each chunk is passed to a
third XSLT template, shown in Listing 16-23. We have removed some of the code from the listing to save space.

Listing 16-23. *Building the SDQ Segment (Finally)*

```
<xsl:template name="BuildSDQ">
  <xsl:param name="SDQString"/>
  <xsl:if test="$SDQString != '' ">
<!-- Output the SDQ segment node and the SDQ01 and SDQ02 nodes -->
    <xsl:element name="SDQ">
      <xsl:element name="SDQ01">EA</xsl:element>
      <xsl:element name="SDQ02">92</xsl:element>
<!-- Get the first location and quantity from the string -->
      <xsl:variable name="SDQ03" select="substring($SDQString,1,10)"/>
```

```xsl
<!-- If there is a location, output the SDQ03 and SDQ04 nodes -->
    <xsl:if test="$SDQ03 != '' ">
      <xsl:element name="SDQ03">
        <xsl:value-of select="substring($SDQ03,1,4)"/>
      </xsl:element>
      <xsl:element name="SDQ04">
        <xsl:value-of select="substring($SDQ03,5,10)"/>
      </xsl:element>
    </xsl:if>
<!-- Now get the second location and quantity from the string -->
    <xsl:variable name="SDQ05" select="substring($SDQString,11,10)"/>
    <xsl:if test="$SDQ05 != '' ">
      <xsl:element name="SDQ05">
        <xsl:value-of select="substring($SDQ05,1,4)"/>
      </xsl:element>
      <xsl:element name="SDQ06">
        <xsl:value-of select="substring($SDQ05,5,6)"/>
      </xsl:element>
    </xsl:if>
...
Repeat this process for each of the last eight location/quantity pairs in the SDQ
...
    </xsl:element>
  </xsl:if>
</xsl:template>
```

The map with all three scripts is in Figure 16-10. The second and third scripts are in the two free-floating Scripting functoids.

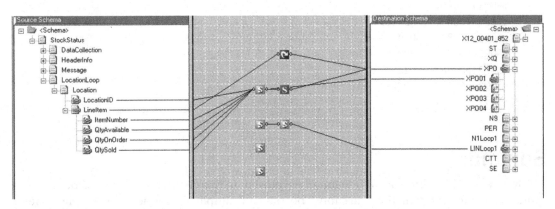

Figure 16-10. *Our final map for building the SDQ segment*

An excerpt of the output of the final map is in Listing 16-24; it depicts one SDQ node.

Listing 16-24. *Output of the Final Map for Building the SDQ Segment*

```
<LINLoop1>
  <LIN>
    <LIN01>1</LIN01>
    <LIN02>SK</LIN02>
    <LIN03>0633928</LIN03>
  </LIN>
  <ZALoop1>
    <ZA>
      <ZA01>QA</ZA01>
    <SDQ>
      <SDQ01>EA</SDQ01>
      <SDQ02>92</SDQ02>
      <SDQ03>0018</SDQ03>
      <SDQ04>000001</SDQ04>
      <SDQ05>0035</SDQ05>
      <SDQ06>000001</SDQ06>
      <SDQ07>0081</SDQ07>
      <SDQ08>000001</SDQ08>
      <SDQ09>0082</SDQ09>
      <SDQ10>000001</SDQ10>
      <SDQ11>0083</SDQ11>
      <SDQ12>000001</SDQ12>
      <SDQ13>0084</SDQ13>
      <SDQ14>000001</SDQ14>
      <SDQ15>0085</SDQ15>
      <SDQ16>000001</SDQ16>
      <SDQ17>0086</SDQ17>
      <SDQ18>000001</SDQ18>
      <SDQ19>0087</SDQ19>
      <SDQ20>000001</SDQ20>
      <SDQ21>0088</SDQ21>
      <SDQ22>000001</SDQ22>
    </SDQ>
```

Summary

The methods of handling the SDQ segment we present in this chapter are complex, but the requirements for handling the data cannot be met with simple techniques. We include some of the steps that we would follow using our incremental testing methodology to demonstrate both how incremental testing works and how it helps. The SDQ segment in this chapter and the HL loop in the next chapter are two challenges that cannot be met without visualizing the process and planning the approach.

Next, we move on to the HL loop, which over the years has been the one mapping exercise that has brought the most calls for help to us. We focus on this loop as used in the X12 856 Advanced Ship Notice, because that transaction is involved in most of those calls for help.

CHAPTER 17

■ ■ ■

Taming the Dreaded 856 ASN HL Loop

Perhaps the most difficult of all mapping problems is the HL loop in the X12 856 Advanced Ship Notice (ASN). Many, if not most, mapping engines designed for EDI transactions do not handle the HL loop well. In this chapter, we present example methods for mapping inbound and outbound HL loops, but there are many permutations of the HL loop structure. You should not expect the methods used in these examples to fit all HL loops. Instead, you should consider these methods to provide theoretical approaches that you may examine when tackling your HL loop issues.

Exploring the HL Loop

Why is the HL loop so difficult? Let's first examine the loop. A typical HL loop definition contains an HL segment followed by 1 to 31 additional segments. Seven of those are child loops, which together contain an additional 27 segments. Every one of those fifty-plus segments can appear in every HL loop and can have a different context in each occurrence. How is that possible?

The data in an HL loop is given context by the contents of the HL segment. For example, the interpretation of a date with the code Departed in a DTM segment varies depending on the contents of the HL segment. That date could be the shipment departed date, the pallet departed date, or a package departed date. You cannot tell which type date it is by looking at the DTM segment alone; you must examine the HL segment to make the determination. Why is this?

Note You may have encountered transactions where the trading parties have defined a specific HL loop structure so that the context of the data can be determined by the order in which the HL loops arrive. Thus the first DTM would pertain to the shipment, the second to the order, and all following to the line items, for example. This discussion, for the most part, addresses those HL loops where the order of the data is not set.

The HL loop is designed to allow you to replicate the packing hierarchy of a shipment in the 856 ASN. Visualize a railroad freight car. The freight car is a container. Now, put two boxes in the freight car, and you have two containers inside one container. Next, put two boxes in each of those boxes. This gives you seven containers. One of those boxes contains widgets. How do we convey in an 856 ASN message to our trading partner not only that there are widgets in one of these boxes but also indicate which set of boxes must be opened to get to the widgets?

We do so by using the HL loop structure, with the HL segment as the key. We know that we have eight items (railroad car, order, two big boxes, and four little boxes). We need an HL loop to describe each item, so we need eight HL loops. Each HL loop begins with an HL segment, and each HL segment contains an identifier. The identifier, which goes in the HL01, is the means of specifying the object contained in the HL loop. Listing 17-1 shows the eight HL segments with only their identifiers present.

Listing 17-1. *Eight HL Segments with HL01 Identifiers*

```
HL*1
HL*2
HL*3
HL*4
HL*5
HL*6
HL*7
HL*8
```

Next, we define the hierarchy for the shipment using two elements to do so: a type in the HL03 and a parent identifier in the HL02. Listing 17-2 shows the HL segments with those two elements defined. The comments are indented to show the packaging.

Listing 17-2. *Eight HL Segments with Identifiers, Parent Identifiers, and Types*

```
HL*1*0*S   // the railroad car
HL*2*1*O    // the order
HL*3*2*P      // the first big box
HL*4*3*I        // the first little box
HL*4*3*I        // the second little box
HL*6*1*P      // the second big box
HL*7*6*I        // the third little box
HL*8*6*I        // the fourth little box
```

The railroad car has 0 in its HL02. Since there is no HL01 with the identifier 0, the railroad car must be the top of the hierarchy. The HL02 for the order is 1, the value of the shipment HL01. This indicates that the order is inside the railroad car. The first big box has 2 in its HL02. Since 2 is the identifier for the order, the first big box must be inside the order. The first little box has 3 in its HL02. Since 3 is the identifier for the first big box, the first little box must be inside the first big box, and so forth.

We have also assigned each HL loop a type in the HL03. In Listing 17-2, the railroad car has been assigned S, for "shipment." The order is type O; the big boxes are type P for "package," and the little boxes are I for "items." In X12 4010, there are 170 different codes that can be assigned in the HL03, thus even if you only used each qualifier once, you could conceivably have a shipment of boxes nested 170 deep.

One of the frustrating things about the HL structure is this extreme degree of flexibility. You can look at Listing 17-2 and derive the packing by the order of the HL segments plus the type. The shipment is first a railroad car, then an order, then a package, then items until the next package, then items. But there is nothing that says we have to use this structure. Just for grins, look at Listing 17-3, which contains exactly the same information. Which little box goes in which big box? You can tell only by examining the HL01 and HL02 data of the segments.

Listing 17-3. *Eight HL Segments with Identifiers, Parent Identifiers, and Types—Again*

```
HL*1*0*S      // the railroad car
HL*2*1*O      // the order
HL*3*1*P      // the first big box
HL*4*1*P      // the second big box
HL*5*2*I       // the first little box
HL*6*2*I       // the second little box
HL*7*3*I       // the third little box
HL*8*3*I       // the fourth little box
```

These HL segments define the hierarchy of the shipment in a manner that allows us to find any box we want without randomly opening boxes. They also give context to the segments following them in their loop. Look at the MAN segments in Listing 17-4. Without the HL03, we have no way of determining what these boxes are, other than looking at the HL03 data. The HL03 data tells us that the big boxes are packages and the little boxes are line items.

Listing 17-4. *Seven HL Segments with Content Identifiers*

```
HL*1*0*S // The railroad car.  The value SEAU1234567 is the car number
    TD3*RR*SEAU*1234567
HL*2*1*O // The order number for all the contents of this shipment
    PRF*
HL*3*2*P      // The first big box, with the UPC number BIGBOX1
    MAN*UC*BIGBOX1
HL*4*3*I          // The first little box, with UPC number LITTLEBOX1
    MAN*UC*LITTLEBOX1
HL*5*3*I          // The second little box, with UPC number LITTLEBOX2
    MAN*UC*LITTLEBOX2
HL*6*2*P  // The second big box, with the UPC number BIGBOX1
    MAN*UC*BIGBOX2
HL*7*6*I          // The third little box, with UPC number LITTLEBOX3
    MAN*UC*LITTLEBOX3
HL*8*6*I          // The fourth little box, with UPC number LITTLEBOX4
    MAN*UC*LITTLEBOX4
```

We also added segments to provide the container identification. Now, the loop tells us not only us how things are packaged but also the UPC number of each entity. Now, we can find a package if we know the UPC number. To get to LITTLEBOX3, we know we must open the railroad car SEAU1234567 and the box BIGBOX2. We don't actually open the order, since that is a logical container rather than a physical container. But we do know that we should see LITTLEBOX3 as a line item on the order document.

Caution Don't be fooled by the ease with which you can use the package name to look at this shipment and determine which package goes where. Instead of BIGBOX and LITTLEBOX, the UPC codes would normally be unintelligible without a bar code reader. We've used names in this example to help you visualize the structure and the movement of the objects when mapped.

The first problem with mapping HL loops is that the map must unravel the hierarchy of the contents by interpreting the values in the HL segment. The second difficulty with the HL loop is that, while the data in the loop is hierarchical, the loop is not. Unless we design the application schema ourselves, we find that we are in a multiloop–to–single-loop or single-loop–to–multiloop situation. As you saw in the looping chapters, both these situations increase the complexity of the map.

The structure of this file inverts the hierarchy by making the line item the top level. Since the line item might be contained in more than one package, we need a package loop under the item. Consider mapping the structure in Listing 17-4 to or from the format shown in Listing 17-5.

Listing 17-5. *Application File Structure*

```
ITEMLoop
  ITEMID
  ORDERNUM
  RAILROADCARID
  PACKLoop
    PACKID
```

The third difficulty with the HL loop is that the same segments may be used at different levels. In Listing 17-4, for example, the MAN segment appears in both the P and the I loops and does not appear in the S or O loops. The mapping engine, being totally unaware that these are different types of loops, has difficulty establishing when to create a MAN segment on the output side and from which MAN segment to pull data on the input side. You must manually insert map logic to control the use of each segment in every HL loop.

Note If you are not totally confused about the HL loop at this point, we are a heck of a lot better at explaining it than we think we are. If you are totally confused, you have just joined the largest club there is of folks that do EDI mapping—of which we were charter members, by the way.

Planning to Map the HL Loop

Whether the HL loop is in the source or the target document, the single most important step is to plan your approach. Handling the HL loop is one exercise that requires careful planning before you begin the map. Here are some thoughts on planning:

- *Be prepared*: Know your source and target schemas in detail, particularly the looping.

- *Address looping first*: Always address the looping first. You must ensure that you produce at least enough target loops to hold the data.

- *Perform incremental testing*: Test after every step. Ensure that a change does not affect the looping and does not affect completed mapping.

- *Use scripts*: Don't expect to get the map done without scripts. The standard functoids, other than the scripting functoid, have limited use other than to support your scripts.

- *Know your business requirements*: Determine the business requirements on which the structure of the HL loop for your map is based. These requirements often affect the interpretation of the contents of the HL loop in ways that are not apparent in the data.

Tip When you find yourself mapping HL loops, you can rest assured that you're not in Kansas any more. The scripted examples that follow contain complex logic, and understanding how the examples work is made more difficult because you must also be familiar with where the scripts are placed in a map and how the relationships among them are intertwined.

Mapping an Inbound 856

Now, we will look at two examples of unraveling an inbound 856 ASN. The annotated source data that will be used for the examples is in Listing 17-6.

Listing 17-6. *Example Source Data for Mapping an Inbound 856 ASN*

```
<HLLoop1>  First HL loop, the shipment loop
  <HL><HL01>1</HL01><HL02>0</HL02><HL03>S</HL03></HL>
  <TD3><TD301>RR</TD301><TD302>SEAU</TD302><TD303>1234567</TD303>  </TD3>
</HLLoop1>
<HLLoop1>  Second HL loop, the order loop
  <HL><HL01>2</HL01><HL02>1</HL02><HL03>O</HL03>  </HL>
  <PRF><PRF01>PO111111</PRF01>  </PRF>
</HLLoop1>
<HLLoop1>  Third HL loop, the first package loop
  <HL><HL01>3</HL01><HL02>2</HL02><HL03>P</HL03>  </HL>
  <MAN><MAN01>UC</MAN01><MAN02>PACKAGE1</MAN02>  </MAN>
</HLLoop1>
<HLLoop1>  Fourth HL loop, the first item loop
  <HL><HL01>4</HL01><HL02>3</HL02><O3>I</HL03>  </HL>
```

```
    <MAN><MAN01>UC</MAN01><MAN02>ITEM_1</MAN02>  </MAN>
  </HLLoop1>
  <HLLoop1> Fifth HL loop, the second item loop
    <HL><HL01>5</HL01><HL02>3</HL02><HL03>I</HL03>  </HL>
    <MAN><MAN01>UC</MAN01><MAN02>ITEM_2</MAN02>  </MAN>
  </HLLoop1>
  <HLLoop1> Sixth HL loop, the second package loop
    <HL><HL01>6</HL01><HL02>2</HL02><HL03>P</HL03>  </HL>
    <MAN><MAN01>UC</MAN01><MAN02>PACKAGE2</MAN02>  </MAN>
  </HLLoop1>
  <HLLoop1> Seventh HL loop, the third item loop
    <HL><HL01>7</HL01><HL02>6</HL02><HL03>I</HL03>  </HL>
    <MAN><MAN01>UC</MAN01><MAN02>ITEM_1</MAN02>  </MAN>
  </HLLoop1>
  <HLLoop1> Eighth HL loop, the fourth item loop
    <HL><HL01>8</HL01><HL02>6</HL02><HL03>I</HL03>  </HL>
    <MAN><MAN01>UC</MAN01><MAN02>ITEM_3</MAN02>  </MAN>
  </HLLoop1>
```

There are eight HL loops in this ASN: one shipment, one order, two packages, and four line items. Each package contains two line items. Note that one line item, ITEM_1, is in both packages. Note also that the MAN segment is used in both the package and line item loops to contain the identifying number. This is an intentional construct to illustrate the common problem of the same segment appearing at multiple levels. Listing 17-7 shows the desired output of our map.

Listing 17-7. *Target Data for Mapping an Inbound 856 ASN*

```
<ItemLoop> First item with both packages in which it is contained
  <ItemID>ITEM_1</ItemID>
  <OrderNum>PO111111</OrderNum>
  <RailRoadCar>SEAU1234567</RailRoadCar>
  <PackLoop>
      <PackID>PACKAGE2</PackID>
  </PackLoop>
  <PackLoop>
      <PackID>PACKAGE1</PackID>
  </PackLoop>
</ItemLoop>
<ItemLoop> Second item with its package
  <ItemID>ITEM_2</ItemID>
  <OrderNum>PO111111</OrderNum>
  <RailRoadCar>SEAU1234567</RailRoadCar>
  <PackLoop>
      <PackID>PACKAGE1</PackID>
  </PackLoop>
```

```
</ItemLoop>
<ItemLoop> Third item with its package
  <ItemID>ITEM_3</ItemID>
  <OrderNum>PO111111</OrderNum>
  <RailRoadCar>SEAU1234567</RailRoadCar>
  <PackLoop>
      <PackID>PACKAGE2</PackID>
  </PackLoop>
</ItemLoop>
```

We produce only three output loops, one for each unique item. The structure of the output requires that we invert the item/package hierarchy by putting the packages inside the line loops. We solve three major problems in this map:

- We generate exactly the correct number of ItemLoop nodes, one for each unique item in the 856 ASN, as determined by evaluating the item numbers in the MAN02 nodes inside the item loops.

- We determine which packages belong in which line items. As we process each item, we must find the package that contains that item in the source and reverse that hierarchy in the target.

- We force the PackLoop node to repeat inside the ItemLoop node once for each package that contains the item associated with that ItemLoop.

The completed map is shown in Figure 17-1.

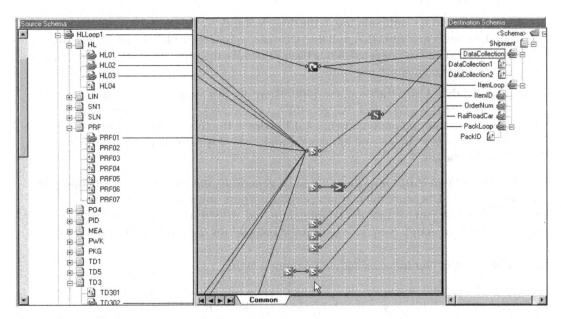

Figure 17-1. *Completed inbound 856 ASN example map*

Let's walk through the map as the mapping engine would, by traversing the target schema:

1. The first link is the link from the Looping functoid to the `DataCollection` node. Since the source is the `HLLoop1` node and there are eight of those in the source, this link forces eight evaluations of the input.

2. The second link is the input to the `DataCollection` node. The Scripting functoid will pull data from the seven source nodes (`HL01`, `HL02`, `HL03`, `PRF01`, `TD302`, `TD303`, and `MAN02`) eight times—once for each pass through the `HLLoop1` node. The data will be gathered into global variables but no `DataCollection` node will be output due to the Logical String functoid.

3. The third link is from the Looping functoid to the `ItemLoop` node. This link drives eight iterations of the `ItemLoop`, more than the three we know that we need.

4. The fourth link is from the Greater Than functoid to the `ItemLoop` node. The Scripting functoid in this link retrieves the value from a counter and passes that value to the Greater Than functoid. The counter begins set to the number of item loops found in the source and is decremented on each pass through the output. Since there were only three items, only three `ItemLoop`s are allowed to be created, and this is exactly the number we need.

5. The fifth link is to the `ItemID` node. The Scripting functoid on this link retrieves the next item number from a hash table and outputs that number to the target node. The script also obtains a list of the packages in which the line item is contained and puts that list in a global variable.

6. The sixth and seventh links are to the `OrderNum` and the `RailRoadCar` nodes respectively; both connect to scripts that pull the necessary values from global variables created when the data was collected. Since both values are the same for every output loop, there is no magic involved.

7. The eighth link is to the `PackLoop` node. There are two Scripting functoids on this link. The first (left) is a C# script that gets the list of the packages for this item from the global variable and passes it to the XSLT script in the second Scripting functoid. The XSLT script is recursive and iterates through the list, creating a package loop for each entry in the list.

The key problem in this map turns out to be generating the package loop. A Looping functoid cannot be used, because the mapping engine outputs only one package loop per item loop no matter how you connect the Looping functoid. After much gnashing of teeth, we cave in and use the XSLT script. Now, let's look at the code for the map, shown in Listing 17-8.

Listing 17-8. *Code for Our Inbound 856 ASN Example Map*

```
// The first script
// Creates a hash table keyed by item numbers (MAN02 from I loops)
// Values in table will be parent package HL01
  public System.Collections.Hashtable items =
                     new System.Collections.Hashtable();
  public string order_number = "";        // storage for the order number
```

```csharp
  public string railcar_number = "";      // storage for the railroad car num
  public int number_of_lineitems = 0;     // number of line item loops
  public string last_package = "";        // the HL01 from the last package loop
  public string item_package = "";        // item number being output


  public void Globals (int hl01, int hl02, string hl03, string prf01, string td302,
                  string td303, string man02)
  {
// When HL loop is item loop store the parent HL01 into local variable
// packages, then add that package to the string of packages in which
// this line item is contained.  Put the results into the hash table.
// Increment the number of line items found.
  if (hl03 == "I")
  {
    string packages = last_package;
    if (items.ContainsKey(man02))
      {
        packages = last_package + items[man02].ToString();
      }
    items[man02] = packages;
    number_of_lineitems = items.Count;
    return;
  }
// When HL loop is package loop, update  last_package with the new HL01
  if (hl03 == "P")
  {
    last_package = hl01 + "|";
    return;
  }
// When the HL loop is order loop, store the order number
  if (hl03 == "O")
  {
    order_number = prf01;
    return;
  }
// When the HL loop is shipment, store the railroad car number
  if (hl03 == "S") railcar_number = td302 + td303;
  return;
}


// The second script
// Controls the generation of the item loop by outputting
// the value from the number of items counter.  The counter is also
// decremented each time the script is called
public int ControlItemLoop ()
{
return number_of_lineitems--;
}
```

// The third script

```
// Serves a dual purpose pulling both the items and the packages from the tables
  public string PutItemNumber ()
  {
// Pull a list of remaining keys from the hash table
    string itemnumbers = "";
    foreach (string itemkey in items.Keys)
                itemnumbers = itemnumbers + itemkey + "|";
// Get the next key (item number) from the list
    int pipe = itemnumbers.IndexOf("|");
    string currentitem = itemnumbers.Substring(0,pipe);
// Get the list of packages that contain this item from the hash table
    item_package = items[currentitem].ToString();
// Delete the entry for this item from the hash table
    items.Remove(currentitem);
// Output the item number
    return currentitem;
}
```

// The fourth script
// Outputs the order number

```
  public string PutOrderNum ()
  {
    return order_number;
  }
```

// The fifth script

```
// Outputs the rail car number
  public string PutRailCar ()
  {
    return railcar_number;
  }
```

// The sixth script

```
// Gets the list of packages created by the third script
// and passes it to the seventh script
  public string GetPackageList()
  {
    return item_package;
  }
```

// The seventh script

```
// Builds and outputs the package loop.  It does so
// by using XPATH lookups, searching first for the source HL loop with
// an HL01 value equal to the value retrieved from the package list,
// then retrieving the MAN02 from that loop.
  <!-- Processes inbound HL Pack Loops -->
```

```
<xsl:template name="BuildPack">
  <xsl:param name="HL01String"/>
  <xsl:variable name="CurrentHL01" select="substring-before($HL01String,'|') "/>
  <xsl:if test="$CurrentHL01 != '' ">
    <xsl:for-each select="//s0:HLLoop1[s0:HL/HL03 = 'P' and
                          s0:HL/HL01 = $CurrentHL01 ]">
      <xsl:element name="PackLoop">
      <xsl:element name="PackID">
         <xsl:value-of select="s0:MAN/MAN02"/>
      </xsl:element>
      </xsl:element>
    </xsl:for-each><!-- end of Item for Loop-->
    <xsl:call-template name="BuildPack">
      <xsl:with-param name="HL01String"
                      select="substring-after($HL01String, '|') "/>
    </xsl:call-template>
  </xsl:if>
</xsl:template>
```

Unfortunately, we could not generate the output file without resorting to XSLT, because we could not force the package looping. We would likely have decided to output the entire map using XSLT in that case. Why? Here is the XSLT code required to duplicate the preceding map, shown in Listing 17-9.

Listing 17-9. *XSLT Code for an Inbound 856 ASN Example Map*

```
<!-- ********************************************************************
Processes inbound HL Loops for AdvancedShipNotice Application file
Line 02 captures the current TD502/03 Railcar number
Line 03 captures the current PRF01 Order Number
******************************************************************** -->
01  <xsl:template name="BuildASN">
02    <xsl:variable name="RailRoadCar"
              select="concat(//s0:TD3/TD302,//s0:TD3/TD303 )"/>
03    <xsl:variable name="OrderNum" select="//s0:PRF/PRF01"/>
<!-- ********************************************************************
Line 04 create a node set of unique part numbers from the MAN segments
  of the HL*I loop
Line 05 captures the ItemID from the MAN02 child of the current
  context node
******************************************************************** -->
04    <xsl:for-each select="//s0:HLLoop1[s0:HL/HL03='I']
              /s0:MAN[not(MAN02=preceding::s0:MAN/MAN02)]"> .
05      <xsl:variable name="ItemID" select="MAN02"/>
06      <xsl:element name="ItemLoop">
07        <xsl:element name="ItemID">
              <xsl:value-of select="$ItemID"/></xsl:element>
08        <xsl:element name="OrderNum">
```

```
                   <xsl:value-of select="$OrderNum"/></xsl:element>
09          <xsl:element name="RailRoadCar">
                   <xsl:value-of select="$RailRoadCar"/></xsl:element>
<!-- *********************************************************************
Line 10 creates a node set of all HL*I loops where the MAN is equal
            to the current $ItemID.
Line 11 captures the current HLO2 parent value.
Line 14 captures the MANO2 value for the HLloop whose HLO1 = current HLO2 parent,
        and where the HLO3 = "P"
********************************************************************* -->
10          <xsl:for-each select="//sO:HLLoop1[sO:HL/HLO3='I' and
                                 sO:MAN/MANO2 = $ItemID]">
11            <xsl:variable name="HLPack" select="sO:HL/HLO2"/>
12            <xsl:element name="PackLoop">
13             <xsl:element name="PackID">
14               <xsl:value-of select="//sO:HLLoop1[sO:HL/HLO1=$HLPack and
                        sO:HL/HLO3='P' ]/sO:MAN/MANO2"/>
15             </xsl:element>
16            </xsl:element>
17          </xsl:for-each>
18        </xsl:element>
19      </xsl:for-each>
20  </xsl:template>
```

The entire map can be done in 20 lines of XSLT code, which makes XSLT scripting a much more efficient method for creating complex 856 ASN maps. However, using XSLT does require specific expertise that may not be available on the user staff; in which case, using XSLT makes maintenance more difficult. For that reason, some staffs will prefer the first map since the use of XSLT is minimized. The XSLT map is shown in Figure 17-2.

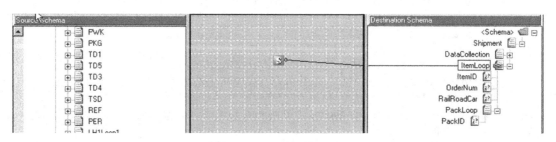

Figure 17-2. *XSLT map for our inbound 856 ASN example*

Mapping an Outbound 856 ASN

Mapping the outbound ASN is typically a bit more complicated than mapping the inbound version, because you are faced with the always-difficult problem of mapping data from many different loops into a single HL loop. And that problem is complicated by the fact that you will more than likely have to generate at least three, and probably four, different types of HL loops, each with its own specific segment content. Finally, you've got the additional problem of getting the HL02 parent value stated correctly.

For an example of outbound mapping, let's turn the map around, mapping from the application file format shown in Listing 17-5 to the 856 ASN. We use the output data from our last example (Listing 17-7) as the source data for this map. The expected HL loop structure to be output by this map is shown in Listing 17-10.

Listing 17-10. *HL Loop Output for Outbound 856 ASN Map*

```
<HLLoop1>
    <HL><HL01>1</HL01><HL02>0</HL02><HL03>S</HL03></HL>
    <TD3><TD302>SEAU</TD302><TD303>1234567</TD303></TD3>
</HLLoop1>
<HLLoop1>
    <HL><HL01>2</HL01><HL02>1</HL02><HL03>O</HL03></HL>
    <PRF><PRF01>PO111111</PRF01></PRF>
</HLLoop1>
<HLLoop1>
<HL>
    <HL01>3</HL01><HL02>2</HL02><HL03>P</HL03></HL>
    <MAN><MAN02>PACKAGE2</MAN02></MAN>
</HLLoop1>
<HLLoop1>
    <HL><HL01>4</HL01><HL02>3</HL02><HL03>I</HL03></HL>
    <MAN><MAN02>ITEM_1</MAN02></MAN>
</HLLoop1>
<HLLoop1>
    <HL><HL01>5</HL01><HL02>3</HL02><HL03>I</HL03></HL>
    <MAN><MAN02>ITEM_3</MAN02></MAN>
</HLLoop1>
<HLLoop1>
    <HL><HL01>6</HL01><HL02>2</HL02><HL03>P</HL03></HL>
    <MAN><MAN02>PACKAGE1</MAN02></MAN>
</HLLoop1>
<HLLoop1>
    <HL><HL01>7</HL01><HL02>6</HL02><HL03>I</HL03></HL>
    <MAN><MAN02>ITEM_1</MAN02></MAN>
</HLLoop1>
<HLLoop1>
    <HL><HL01>8</HL01><HL02>6</HL02><HL03>I</HL03></HL>
    <MAN><MAN02>ITEM_2</MAN02></MAN>
</HLLoop1>
```

The output replicates the original 856 ASN data shown in Listing 17-6 with one exception: the order of the packages and items is different. This difference is apparent only because of the names we have assigned these objects. The items are children of the correct packages, so the revised order is of no consequence. The map that produces this output is shown in Figure 17-3.

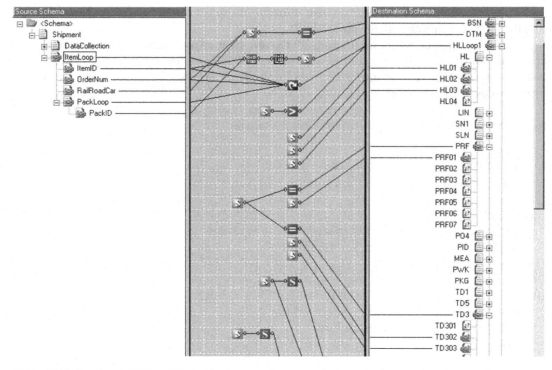

Figure 17-3. *Outbound 856 ASN map*

Mapping an outbound HL loop presents a different set of problems than did the inbound map. The key elements that we must handle follow:

- Ensure that sufficient HL loops are generated to hold all the objects.
- Infer the contents to put into the HL02 parent and the HL03 type nodes.
- Manually control the output of the HL segment contents.
- Control segment output so that segments are output only in the correct instances of the HL loop.

We again attack the problems with incremental testing. We know that producing the correct structure is the first problem to solve, so we add the Looping functoid and test different links to see how many HL loops are produced. We know that we need at least one loop for each package, one for each item, one for the order, and one for the shipment. Looking at the source data tells us that we should produce at least eight loops with that data. The four input links shown in the map produce 13 HL loops, more than we need, so we will accept that structure.

Since the key to the 856 ASN is the HL loop, the next issue we address is the HL segment. We first set up the HL01 structure using the scripts shown in Listing 17-11.

Listing 17-11. *Scripts for the HL01 Element*

Script 1
```
// Outputs the HL01 element
public int PutHLO1()
{
return hl01;
}
```

Script2
```
// Outputs the V1Loop1
public string IncrementHLO1()
{
hl01++;
return "";
}
```

Script 1 outputs the current value of the global variable hl01 to the HL01 node. On the first pass that value is 1. Script 2 increments the value of the hl01 variable. Script 2 is linked to the V1Loop1 node (off the mapping grid in Figure 17-3). We chose the V1Loop1 node, since it is the last node in the HL loop, thus all of our mapping activity occurs before the V1Loop1 node.

Since the value of the hl01 variable remains the same through the entire HL loop, we can use it to control the number of HL loops we create, to block the output of segments that do not belong in the current loop, and to select data from the hash tables for output.

We use a Scripting functoid and a Greater Than functoid attached to the HLLoop1 node to control the number of HL loops created. The script for this is shown in Listing 17-12.

Listing 17-12. *Controlling the Number of HL Loops Output*

```
public int ControlHLLoop()
{
return totalhl - hl01;
}
```

The current value of hl01 is compared to the contents of another global variable, totalhl. During the collection of data, we count the number of packages and the number of items, and then add two to that count to get the total number of objects to be output. Our source data will produce the value eight (two packages plus four items plus one shipment plus one order).

We add a Scripting functoid linked to the BSN node to hold our global variables, hl01 and totalhl. With hl01 initialized to 1 and totalhl set to 8, we test the map and find that this structure limits the number of HL loops created to eight. Our control method works, so we can set the totalhl variable to 0; it will be incremented as the data is read.

The next issue is the key issue for this map: how do we figure out the type of HL loop (HL03) and the parent ID for the HL02? We know the first three because they are predetermined. The shipment (HL03 equals S) will always be first and have an HL02 value of 0. The order (HL03 equals O) will always be second and have an HL02 value of 1. The third will always be a package (HL03 equals P) and have an HL02 value of 2. After that, we cannot be sure whether the next loop is a package or an item loop.

We decide the only way to determine the structure is to examine the input data as we collect it. We create global variables to hold the data and to define the output structure. We add these to the same Scripting functoid in which we defined the `hl01` and `totalhl` variables. The finished script is shown in Listing 17-13.

Listing 17-13. *Scripting Functoid with Global Variables*

```
// HL01 value and corresponding HL03 value
public System.Collections.Hashtable hl03list =
       new System.Collections.Hashtable();
// Link the HL03 to the object id
public System.Collections.Hashtable id =
       new System.Collections.Hashtable();

public int hl01 = 1;          // output value for next HL01
public string hl03 = "S";     // output value for next HL03
public int totalhl = 0;       // number of HL loops to output
public int lastpkg = 3;       // HL01 value of last package output

public string td302 = "";     // Value to output in the td302
public string td303 = "";     // Value to output in the td303
public string ordernum = "";  // Value to output in the PRF01

public int controlbsn = 0;    // Flag to control BSN output

// Also gather variables that are output in the S and O loops.
public int DeclareGlobals(string rail, string order)
{
td302 = rail.Substring(0,4);
int length = rail.Length;
td303 = rail.Substring(4, length-4);
ordernum = order;
return controlbsn++;
}
```

Note that the script also gathers the values from the source data for the shipment segment TD3 and the order segment PRF. This setup helps simplify the next script. We need three functoids to collect the item and package data: a String Concatenate functoid, a Cumulative Concatenate functoid, and a Scripting functoid. They are the second row of functoids in the map, connected to the DTM node in the output document.

The order of the links to the String Concatenate functoid is important, since the order in which the objects arrive in the Scripting functoid is critical. The PackID node must be the first input to the String Concatenate functoid, the ItemID node must be the third, and the pipe character must be the second and fourth. The result is a string of package/item pairs as shown in Listing 17-14.

Listing 17-14. *String Passed to the Data-Gathering Script*

```
PACKAGE2|ITEM_1|PACKAGE1|ITEM_1|PACKAGE1|ITEM_2|PACKAGE2|ITEM_3|
```

The content of this string (the identification information for each object) is sufficient for us to determine the type of each HL loop and the parent ID for each loop using the script in Listing 17-15. The script picks off the first package/item pair from the string and adds the package to the id hash table. At the same time, it builds an entry in the HL03 hash table indicating what type of loop it will be. Both tables are keyed by the HL01 index. The script will then search the string for any additional pairs with the current package ID. As the inner loop processes subsequent pairs, it removes them from the string. The outer loop continues to loop through the string, storing a package and all the items associated with that package, until there are no more packages.

Listing 17-15. *Script to Fill Global Variables Using Object Identifiers*

```
public void CreateGlobals(string list)
  {
 // internal variables
  int hl03 = 1;
  int index = 0;
  int endindex = 0;
  int length = 0;
  string package = "";
  string item = "";
  string prelist = "";
  string postlist = "";
  string copylist = "";
// put the shipment and order into the hl type table
  hl03list.Add(hl03++, "S");
  hl03list.Add(hl03++, "O");
// Do as long as there is data in the input string
  while (list.IndexOf("|") > 0)
    {
// The first item in the string is always a package.  Get the package ID from
// the string and then clip that field value from the string
    index = list.IndexOf("|");
    length = list.Length;
    package = list.Substring(0, index);
    list = list.Substring(index + 1, length - index - 1);
// If the ID table already contains this package, we are done.
// Otherwise add the package to the tables, then get the paired item
// and add it to the tables
    while (!id.ContainsValue(package))
      {
      hl03list.Add(hl03, "P");
      id.Add(hl03++, package);
      index = list.IndexOf("|");
      length = list.Length;
      item = list.Substring(0, index);
      list = list.Substring(index + 1, length - index - 1);
      hl03list.Add(hl03, "I");
```

```
      id.Add(hl03++, item);
// As long as the package ID  can be found in the string, continue to extract it
// and its paired item, and put them in the tables
    while (list.IndexOf(package) > -1)
    {
     copylist = list;
     index = copylist.IndexOf(package);
     length = copylist.Length;
     prelist = copylist.Substring(0, index);
     copylist = copylist.Substring(index, length - index);
     index = copylist.IndexOf("|");
     length = copylist.Length;
     copylist = copylist.Substring(index+1, length - index - 1);
     index = copylist.IndexOf("|");
     length = copylist.Length;
     item = copylist.Substring(0, index);
     copylist = copylist.Substring(index + 1, length - index - 1);
     list = prelist + copylist;
     hl03list.Add(hl03, "I");
     id.Add(hl03++, item);
    }
   }
  }
// Keep track of how many entries we make into the tables for use in controlling
// output later
totalhl = hl03;
 }
```

When the script completes, we have a totalhl count and two tables filled with data. Both are keyed by the HL01 value. The hl03list table contains the HL03 value to be output with each HL01 node:

[1]"S" [2]"O" [3]"P" [4]"I" [5]"I" [6]"P" [7]"I" [8]"I"

The id table contains the object ID for each item:

[3]"Package2" [4]"Item1" [5]"Item3" [6]"Package1" [7]"Item1" [8]"Item3"

The [1] and [2] entries are not needed, since we stored the shipment and order data in regular global variables in the script shown in Listing 17-13.

This map only contains data for one node in each HL loop. Normally, each loop would have many nodes and segments. The same mechanism would work for that additional data. We would just add additional hash tables as needed.

Since we use the hl01 value as the key to the tables, and we already have the hl01 value being output, we are ready to begin building the output side of the map. We begin by completing the HL segment using the scripts shown in Listing 17-16.

Listing 17-16. *Completing the HL Segment*

Script 1
```
public int PutHL02 ()
{
int hl02 = 0;

hl03 = hl03list[hl01].ToString();

if (hl03 == "I") hl02 = lastpkg;
else if (hl03 == "O") hl02 = 1;
else if (hl03 == "P")
{
 hl02 = 2;
 lastpkg = hl01;
}
return hl02;
}
```

Script 2
```
public string PutHL03 ()
{
return hl03;
}
```

The first script initialized the hl02 value to 0, which is the value to be output if the current HL type is S. It then gets the current HL type from the table using the HL01 value as the index and puts it into the global variable hl03. The hl02 value is adjusted based on the contents of the current HL type: if the HL type is S, O, or P, the HL02 value is hard-coded. When we encounter an HL with a type P, we will also store the current HL01 value in the lastpkg variable for use as the parent ID for the line items that are in this package. Finally, the hl02 value is passed to the HL02 node. The second script simply outputs the value of the global hl03 value as set in the first script. Remember that we are testing the map after each step to make sure it is working.

The remainder of the map consists of two types of mechanisms. The first controls the output of the data nodes (PRF, TD3, and MAN). The MAN node is controlled by our old standby, the Logical String functoid. We control the PRF and TD3 nodes by obtaining the current HL type and testing that type with an Equals functoid. Remember that data for the PRF and TD3 nodes comes from global variables that always have data, so we can't use the Logical String functoid for them.

The scripts for the remainder of the map are shown in Listing 17-17.

Listing 17-17. *Scripts to Output the Data*

Script 1
```
// Get the current HL03 value for testing with Logical String functoids that
// control the PRF and TD3 segment output
public string ControlSegments ()
```

```
{
return hl03;
}
```

Script 2

```
// Get the PRF01 value from the global variable and output it
public string PutPRF01()
{
return ordernum;
}
```

Script 3

```
// Get the TD302 value and output it
public string PutTD302()
{
return td302;
}
```

Script 4

```
// Get the TD303 value and output it
public string PutTD303()
{
return td303;
}
```

Script 5

```
// Get the MAN02 value and output it
public string PutMAN02()
{
if (hl03 == "P" | hl03 == "I") return id[hl01].ToString();
return "";
}
```

Building the ASN with an XSLT Script

In the inbound example, we were able to duplicate the inbound mapping effort very simply with about 20 lines of code. That is not the case for the outbound XSLT script. We still have to extract the correct data for each type of HL looping, and we will still have the problem of determining and outputting the correct HL01, HL02, and HL03 values. The handling of counters is best done in a C# script external to and called by the XSLT script. The C# script is shown in Listing 17-18, and the XSLT script is in Listing 17-19.

The HL01 is easy; we just initialize the value and increment the value for each HL loop. We store the HL01 value in variables that tell us the ID for the last of each type of object we output. For example, when we output a package type loop, we store the HL01 in the variable for the last package output. Then, as we loop through the items, we can assign the value from that variable as the HL02 (parent ID) for the item.

Listing 17-18. *C# Script for Processing HL01 and HL02 Code Values*

```
int HL01 = 0;      // This is HL01 value for the current HL loop
int ShipHL = 0;    // This is Hl01 value for the last shipment output
int OrdrHL = 0;    // This is Hl01 value for the last order output
int PackHL = 0;    // This is Hl01 value for the last pack output
int ItemHL = 0;    // This is Hl01 value for the last item output
```

First Function
```
// This function increments the hl01 value and then stores the value into the
// appropriate "last" object variable.  It returns the current value of hl01 to the
// XSLT script.
public string ReturnHL01(string LevelCode )
{
    HL01 += 1;
    if (LevelCode == "S")
        ShipHL = HL01;
    if (LevelCode == "O")
        OrdrHL = HL01;
    if (LevelCode == "I")
        ItemHL = HL01;
    return HL01.ToString();
}
```
Second Function
```
// This function returns the
public string ReturnHL02(string LevelCode )
{
    int retlevel = 0;
    if (LevelCode == "S")
        retlevel = ShipHL;
    if (LevelCode == "O")
        retlevel = OrdrHL;
    if (LevelCode == "I")
        retlevel = ItemHL;
    return retlevel.ToString();
}
```

Listing 17-19. *XSLT Code for an Outbound 856 ASN Example Map*

```
<xsl:template name="BuildASN">
<!-- =============================================
Create an HL Ship Loop
============================================= -->
 <xsl:element name="HL_S">
<!-- =============================================
Build TD3 for Shipment here
============================================= -->
   <xsl:variable name="TD302" select="substring(//RailRoadCar,1,4)"/>
```

```
 <xsl:variable name="TD303" select="substring(//RailRoadCar,5)"/>
 <xsl:if test="$TD302 != '' and $TD303 != '' ">
  <xsl:element name="ns0:TD3">
    <xsl:element name="TD302"><xsl:value-of select="$TD302"/></xsl:element>
    <xsl:element name="TD303"><xsl:value-of select="$TD303"/></xsl:element>
  </xsl:element>
 </xsl:if>
</xsl:element><!-- end of HL Ship Loop-->
<!-- ==========================================
Create one HL Order Loop
========================================== -->
 <xsl:element name="ns0:HLLoop1">
  <xsl:element name="ns0:HL">
   <xsl:element name="HL01">
    <xsl:value-of select="userCSharp:ReturnHL01('O')"/>
   </xsl:element>
   <xsl:element name="HL02">
    <xsl:value-of select="userCSharp:ReturnHL02('S')"/>
   </xsl:element>
   <xsl:element name="HL03">O</xsl:element>
  </xsl:element>
<!-- ==========================================
Create the PRF segment for the Order Loop here
========================================== -->
  <xsl:element name="ns0:PRF">
   <xsl:element name="PRF01"><xsl:value-of select="//OrderNum"/></xsl:element>
  </xsl:element>
 </xsl:element><!-- end of HL Order Loop -->
<!-- ==========================================
Create an HL Pack loop for each unique instance of the Pack ID
========================================== -->
<xsl:for-each select="//ItemLoop/PackLoop
                      [not( PackID=preceding::PackLoop/PackID )]/PackID">
  <xsl:variable name="PackID" select="."/>
  <xsl:element name="ns0:HLLoop1">
   <xsl:element name="ns0:HL">
    <xsl:element name="HL01">
     <xsl:value-of select="userCSharp:ReturnHL01('P')"/>
    </xsl:element>
    <xsl:element name="HL02">
     <xsl:value-of select="userCSharp:ReturnHL02('O')"/>
    </xsl:element>
    <xsl:element name="HL03">P</xsl:element>
   </xsl:element>
<!-- ==========================================
Create the MAN segment for the Pack loop using the $PackID
For the current instance of the HL Loop
```

```
=========================================== -->
    <xsl:element name="ns0:MAN">
     <xsl:element name="MAN02">UC</xsl:element>
     <xsl:element name="MAN03"><xsl:value-of select="$PackID"/></xsl:element>
    </xsl:element>
   </xsl:element><!-- end of HL Pack Loop -->
 <!-- Create an HL Item Loop for each item that contains the current $PackID-->
 <!-- ===========================================
 Create an HL Item loop for each ItemLoop/Item found in the data
 That contains a PackLoop/PackID child equal to the current
 $PackID
 =========================================== -->
    <xsl:for-each select="//ItemLoop[PackLoop/PackID = $PackID ]">
     <xsl:element name="ns0:HLLoop1">
      <xsl:element name="ns0:HL">
       <xsl:element name="HL01">
        <xsl:value-of select="userCSharp:ReturnHL01('I')"/>
       </xsl:element>
       <xsl:element name="HL02">
        <xsl:value-of select="userCSharp:ReturnHL02('P')"/>
       </xsl:element>
       <xsl:element name="HL03">I</xsl:element>
      </xsl:element>
 <!-- insert MAN segment here -->
 <!-- ===========================================
 Create the MAN segment for the Item loop using the current ItemID value
 =========================================== -->
      <xsl:element name="ns0:MAN">
       <xsl:element name="MAN02">UC</xsl:element>
       <xsl:element name="MAN02">
        <xsl:value-of select="ItemID"/>
       </xsl:element>
      </xsl:element>
     </xsl:element><!-- end of Item HL Loop -->
    </xsl:for-each><!-- end of Item For Loop -->
   </xsl:for-each><!-- end of Pack for Loop-->
  </xsl:template>
```

Creating the Simple Outbound 856 ASN

Fortunately, most 856 ASN structures are not as complicated as the previous example. Perhaps the most common is the HL loop structure Shipment, Order, Item (SOI), where the number of items may be more than one (as in SOIIIII) but there can be only one shipment and one order loop. This structure is seen so often because many applications have trouble generating files with nested loops, just like many EDI mapping engines do. So let's end this chapter with some hope that your next 856 ASN map will be more like this example.

We decided to include this discussion because most of the 856 ASN questions that we receive are related to simple outbound 856 ASN transactions. The two questions most asked follow:

- How do I generate the correct values for HL01, HL02, and HL03?

- How do I make the data segments appear in the correct loops?

Although these questions are applicable to the example we just presented, there are so many other aspects to that complicated problem that we felt that we should provide an example that stressed answering just these two questions.

We will use the input file shown in Listing 17-20. The input file contains one shipment, one order, and two line items. Because, as you know from the mapping specifications, the 856 ASN will always consist of one shipment loop, one order loop, and one or more item loops, the 856 ASN formed from this input should be of the structure SOII.

Listing 17-20. *Input Data for a Simple Outbound 856 ASN Map*

```
<AdvancedShipNotice>
  <Shipment>
    <ShipmentPurposeCode>00</ShipmentPurposeCode>
    <ShipmentID>907161318</ShipmentID>
    <ShipmentDate>20081104</ShipmentDate>
    <ShipmentTime>1634</ShipmentTime>
    <PONumber>BTB281155</PONumber>
    <PODate>20081102</PODate>
    <Item>
      <ItemLineNo>0001</ItemLineNo>
      <PartNumber>978-1-4302-1857-9</PartNumber>
      <QuantityShipped>100</QuantityShipped>
    </Item>
    <Item>
      <ItemLineNo>0002</ItemLineNo>
      <PartNumber>1857-9-TRG</PartNumber>
      <QuantityShipped>200</QuantityShipped>
    </Item>
  </Shipment>
</AdvancedShipNotice>
```

The output from the map is shown in Listing 17-21. Notice the HL segments and the values in the elements of those segments. The HL01 elements contain the correct sequencing of the HL loops (1, 2, 3, and 4). The HL02 elements point to the correct parents (none for the shipment HL, 1 for the order HL, and 2 for each item HL). The HL03 elements correctly identify the type of loop (S, O, I, and I). The data segments appear only in the proper loops.

Listing 17-21. *Output Data for the Simple Outbound 856 ASN Map*

```
ST*856*0001
BSN*00*907161318*20081104*1634
HL*1**S                              < Start of Shipment Loop
```

```
    DTM*011*20081104
HL*2*1*O                        < Start of Order Loop
    PRF*BTB281155
HL*3*2*I                        < Start of First Item Loop
    LIN*0001*VP*978-1-4302-1857-9
    SN1*0001*100*EA
HL*4*2*I                        < Start of Second Item Loop
    LIN*0002*VP*1857-9-TRG
    SN1*0002*200*EA
CTT*4
SE*14*0001
```

Figures 17-4, 17-5, and 17-6 show the three pages from the map that we created to generate this output. Figure 17-4 has four direct links that output the BSN01, BSN02, BSN03, and BSN04 nodes. The BSN node appears before the HL loops. The Looping functoid in Figure 17-4 generates the correct amount of HL loops in the output; we know we need one shipment loop, one order loop, and one item loop for each item. The looping structure in this map will output exactly the correct number of loops. Three Scripting functoids generate the values that are output in the HL01, HL02, and HL03 elements. We'll see those scripts after we discuss the figures.

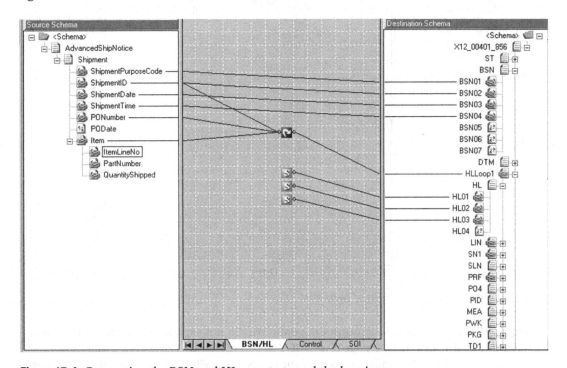

Figure 17-4. *Generating the BSN and HL segments and the looping*

Figure 17-5 shows the page of the map that contains the functoids that control the output of the nodes. We want the LIN and SN1 nodes in the item loop, the PRF node only in the order loop, and the DTM_2 node only in the shipment loop. The Scripting functoid returns the current value of the HL01 node, from which we can deduce the type of segment. This value is passed to the Equal and Greater Than functoids, which return true or false as appropriate. The three conditions evaluate as follows:

- *Greater Than functoid*: This controls the output of the LIN and SN1 nodes to when the current HL01 value is greater than 2. The first item loop will always be the third loop.

- *Top Equals functoid*: This controls the output of the PRF nodes to when the current HL01 value is exactly 2. The order loop will always be the second loop.

- *Bottom Equals functoid*: This controls the output of the DTM_2 nodes to when the current HL01 value is exactly 1. The shipment loop will always be the first loop.

There is a fourth link from the Scripting functoid going to a segment that is off the page. That link goes to the CTT01 element, which should contain the total number of HL loops in the transaction. Since that link is executed after all the HL loops have been completed, the value will be correct. In this case, that value will be four.

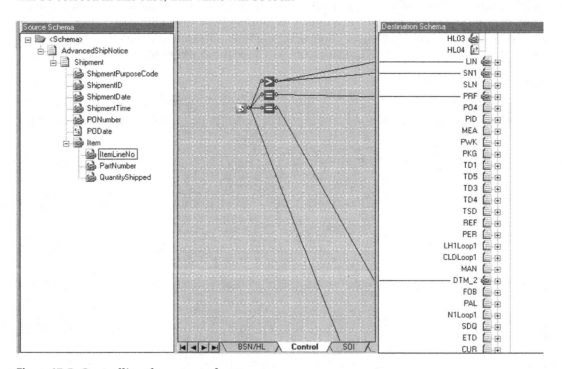

Figure 17-5. *Controlling the output of segments*

Figure 17-6 shows the links to output the data. We did not expand the output nodes, since they would not all appear on the page if we did. You can see by the dotted lines that the shipment date goes to the DTM_2 node, the PO number goes to the PRF node, and the item data goes to the LIN and SN1 nodes. The three Uppercase functoids output constant values as needed.

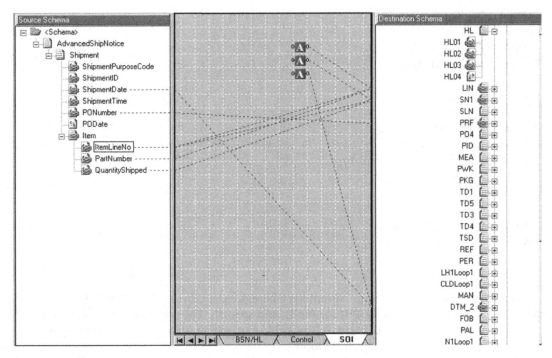

Figure 17-6. *Outputting the data*

The key to this map is in the scripts that determine the output for the HL segment, as noted in the discussion on Figure 17-4. Listing 17-22 shows those scripts.

Listing 17-22. *Scripts for the HL Segment*

```
// Code for the HL01
// Initializes the hl01 variable to the Shipment loop value
// minus one.  Each time the script is executed, the variable
// is incremented before being output.  This means the value
// will be for the current HL01 throughout each loop.  Returns
// the current value of hl01.

int hl01 = 0;

public int PutHL01 ()
{
return ++hl01;
}


// Code for the HL02
// Determines the parent of the current HL segment using the
// hl01 variable.  Returns the parent.
```

```
public string PutHL02 ()
{
if (hl01 > 2) return "2";
else if (hl01 == 1) return "";
return "1";
}


// Code for the HL03
// Determines the type of the current HL segment using the
// hl01 variable.  Returns the type.

public string PutHL03 ()
{
if (hl01 > 2) return "I";
else if (hl01 == 1) return "S";
return "O";
}
```

This method will work for most situations where the structure of the 856 ASN being created is fixed, such as SOIOIOI, SOPIIII, SOTPIII, and so forth. The scripts must be altered, of course. In each of these types of cases, it is possible to mathematically determine the type of each HL loop and the parent of each HL loop.

The XSLT version of this map is shown in Figure 17-7. The direct links output the BSN segment just as in the standard map. Two scripting functoids are used to generate the HL loop and the CTT01 value.

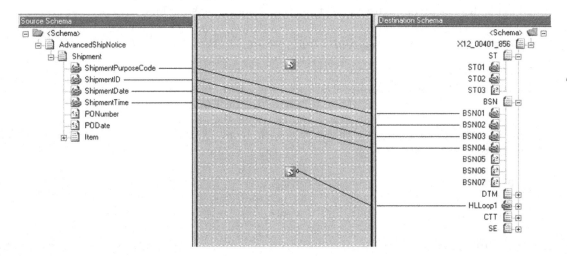

Figure 17-7. *XSLT version of the simple outbound 856 ASN map*

The scripts from the Scripting functoids are shown in Listing 17-23. Both C# and XSLT scripts are needed.

Listing 17-23. *Scripts for the XSLT Version of the Simple Outbound 856 ASN Map*

```
// The top scripting functoid contains the global variables and
// the C# scripts that are called to return the HL element values.

int HL01 = 0;
int ShipHL = 0;
int OrdrHL = 0;
int PackHL = 0;
int ItemHL = 0;

public string ReturnHL01(string LevelCode )
{
  HL01 += 1;
  if (LevelCode == "S")
    ShipHL = HL01;
  if (LevelCode == "O")
    OrdrHL = HL01;
  if (LevelCode == "P")
    PackHL = HL01;
  if (LevelCode == "I")
    ItemHL = HL01;
  return HL01.ToString();
}

public string ReturnHL02(string LevelCode )
{
  int retlevel = 0;
  if (LevelCode == "S")
    retlevel = ShipHL;
  if (LevelCode == "O")
    retlevel = OrdrHL;
  if (LevelCode == "P")
    retlevel = PackHL;
  if (LevelCode == "I")
    retlevel = ItemHL;
  return retlevel.ToString();
}

public string GetHL01()
{
  return HL01.ToString();
}


<!-- The XSLT Script builds the HL loop and the CTT segment --!>
<xsl:template name="BuildFullASN">
<!-- *****************************************************************
```

```
      Create an HL loop here for the Shipment
      ************************************************************************** -->
<xsl:for-each select="//Shipment">
  <xsl:element name="ns0:HLLoop1">
    <xsl:call-template name="BuildHL">
      <xsl:with-param name="HL02" select=" '' " />
      <xsl:with-param name="HL03" select=" 'S' " />
    </xsl:call-template>
    <xsl:element name="ns0:DTM_2">
      <xsl:element name="DTM01">011</xsl:element>
      <xsl:element name="DTM02">
        <xsl:value-of select="//ShipmentDate"/>
      </xsl:element>
    </xsl:element>
  </xsl:element><!-- end of HL Loop for Shipment -->


<!-- **********************************************************************
      Create an HL loop here for each Order in the source Document
      ************************************************************************** -->
  <xsl:element name="ns0:HLLoop1">
    <xsl:call-template name="BuildHL">
      <xsl:with-param name="HL02" select=" 'S' " />
      <xsl:with-param name="HL03" select=" 'O' " />
    </xsl:call-template>
    <xsl:element name="ns0:PRF">
      <xsl:element name="PRF01">
        <xsl:value-of select="./PONumber"/>
      </xsl:element>
    </xsl:element>
  </xsl:element><!-- end of HL Loop for Order-->


<!-- **********************************************************************
      Create an HL loop here for each Item
      ************************************************************************** -->
  <xsl:for-each select="./Item">
    <xsl:element name="ns0:HLLoop1">
      <xsl:call-template name="BuildHL">
        <xsl:with-param name="HL02" select=" 'O' " />
        <xsl:with-param name="HL03" select=" 'I' " />
      </xsl:call-template>
      <xsl:element name="ns0:LIN">
        <xsl:element name="LIN01">
          <xsl:value-of select="ItemLineNo"/>
        </xsl:element>
        <xsl:element name="LIN02">VP</xsl:element>
        <xsl:element name="LIN03">
          <xsl:value-of select="PartNumber"/>
```

```xml
        </xsl:element>
      </xsl:element>
      <xsl:element name="ns0:SN1">
        <xsl:element name="SN101">
          <xsl:value-of select="ItemLineNo"/>
        </xsl:element>
        <xsl:element name="SN102">
          <xsl:value-of select="QuantityShipped"/>
        </xsl:element>
        <xsl:element name="SN103">EA</xsl:element>
      </xsl:element>
    </xsl:element><!-- end of HLLoop for Item -->
  </xsl:for-each><!-- end of for-each for Item -->
</xsl:for-each><!-- end of for-each for Shipment -->

<!-- **********************************************************************
    Build the CTT Segment
    ****************************************************************** -->
  <xsl:element name="ns0:CTT">
    <xsl:element name="CTT01">
      <xsl:value-of select="userCSharp:GetHL01()"/>
    </xsl:element>
  </xsl:element>
</xsl:template>


<!-- **********************************************************************
    Build the HL Segment
    ****************************************************************** -->
<xsl:template name="BuildHL">
  <xsl:param name="HL02"/>
  <xsl:param name="HL03"/>
  <xsl:element name="ns0:HL">
    <xsl:element name="HL01">
      <xsl:value-of select="userCSharp:ReturnHL01($HL03)"/>
    </xsl:element>
    <xsl:if test="$HL02 != '' ">
      <xsl:element name="HL02">
        <xsl:value-of select="userCSharp:ReturnHL02($HL02)"/>
      </xsl:element>
    </xsl:if>
    <xsl:element name="HL03">
      <xsl:value-of select="$HL03"/>
    </xsl:element>
  </xsl:element>
</xsl:template>
```

Summary

Whether you choose XSLT, C#, or another of the scripting options, you will not succeed in mapping an HL loop without understanding the base functionality of the loop and without knowing the business processes that drive the structure of the loop in your map. Since the business processes differ from one organization to the next, you must make analyzing them a standard step in your preparation for completing an 856 ASN map.

We would like to tell you that, once you learn how to create one 856 ASN map, you are home free, but the fact is that almost every 856 ASN is different in some way. You can expect a new challenge each time you encounter one. Just remember that the underlying structure is always the same no matter what the HL hierarchy is or what segments are present in each HL loop.

This chapter is the last of the "EDI Mapping with BizTalk" part of this book, but could have just as easily been placed in the next part, "Advanced Techniques." In that part, we first look at examples of building custom functoids and custom assemblies and then move on to examples such as using a map to generate multiple output files for one input file, code to reformat an inbound file to make mapping easier, and a custom pipeline component to manipulate the EDI envelope.

PART 5

■ ■ ■

Advanced Techniques

CHAPTER 18

■ ■ ■

Building Custom Assemblies and Functoids

In the preceding chapters, you've seen many examples of using custom scripting to solve mapping problems. Sometimes, the most effective use of scripting is not in the map. This is particularly true when a script is one that is reusable without modification. In this chapter, we examine the building of custom external assemblies and custom functoids. One example of an external assembly, used for universal date conversions, was presented in Chapter 3. We expand that assembly here by adding some utility functions that are handy for mapping. Once that is complete, we'll build a custom functoid that contains the same functions.

This chapter covers advanced mapping topics and requires familiarity with .NET coding and testing procedures. It contains an overview of the techniques with the expectation that you either have, or will obtain, the necessary proficiency in .NET development. The examples are in C#, but that is a matter of our own preference and not a requirement for doing external assemblies or custom functoids. Since the object that will actually be used by the map is a compiled object, the code may be developed using the .NET programming language you prefer.

Note If you are new to .NET development, we strongly recommend that you consult one of the many excellent references available on .NET development in either C# or VB.

Deciding to Use a Custom Assembly or Custom Functoid

When you create many maps, you become aware that there exist actions that are common to most, if not all, maps. You find yourself maintaining a code library containing snippets of code that you copy and paste into many of your maps. Such a snippet, when it can be condensed into a function, is a good candidate for inclusion in a custom functoid or a custom assembly. Thus a primary reason to use a custom assembly or custom functoid is to obtain reusability with minimal effort.

Reusability also decreases maintenance of maps, because changes only need to be made in one place. If a custom functoid is used in 50 maps, you may have to rebuild and redeploy all 50 maps, but you won't have to search each map for the Scripting functoid that contains the script in order to make the change. If you use a custom assembly, you only have to build and redeploy that assembly.

Controlling changes is another reason to go this route. When you add a script to a library and make it available to many others, the different copies of the script tend to mutate until there are multiple copies, often with different names and with slight modifications. After all, who can resist making one little change that improves the code? Or what if someone doesn't like the name? In a large project with many maps and mappers, this kind of proliferation of a script is inevitable. You can control the code by using an external assembly or a custom functoid and ensuring that the object is used when its purpose fits the need.

Also, a custom assembly can possess multiple functions. Adding new functions is easy, and the new functions become available to all maps as soon as the updated assembly is built and deployed. By carefully organizing your custom functions into different assemblies, you can create a library of objects that, once added as a reference to a project, become immediately available for use.

Creating an External Assembly for Date Conversion Functions

You saw in Chapter 3 that creating an external assembly is more difficult than using a Scripting functoid. For this example, we are going take the existing external assembly built in Chapter 3 and add two additional date functions. Since we covered the steps in detail in Chapter 3, the purpose here is to refresh your memory by having you review those steps in adding additional functions to your assembly. We will add these two functions:

- Convert a calendar date to its ordinal format.
- Convert an ordinal date back to its corresponding Gregorian format.

These two functions are worthwhile additions to a general utility for handling dates because there are no readily available methods or properties for accomplishing them. We first build the code for these functions in a console application where we can test the script. When we have them working we add them to the SSPS_CommonFunctions project that holds the assembly from Chapter 3. The script for the Gregorian date to ordinal date is in Listing 18-1. We use the try/catch method so that errors do not cause a failure but simply return an error string.

Listing 18-1. *Converting a Gregorian Date to an Ordinal Date*

```
/* -------------------------------------------
Convert a standard windows format date to an ordinal date
format (yyyyddd)
------------------------------------------- */
01  public string GregToOrdinal(string inVar, string inFmt)
02  {
03      string returnDate = "";
```

```
04      try
05      {
06          DateTime testDate = DateTime.ParseExact(inVar, inFmt, null);
07          returnDate = testDate.Year.ToString() +
                        testDate.DayOfYear.ToString("000") ;
08      }
09      catch
10      {
11          returnDate = "INVALID";
12      }
13      return returnDate;
14  } // end of GregToOrdinal()
```

The code for the ordinal date to Gregorian date conversion is in Listing 18-2. This code is more complex as we must account for leap years.

Listing 18-2. *Converting an Ordinal Date to a Gregorian Date*

```
/* -----------------------------------------
Convert an ordinal date format (yyyyddd) to any standard
windows format
-------------------------------------- */
01  public string OrdinalToGreg(string inDate, string outFmt)
02  {
03      int year = Convert.ToInt32(inDate.Substring(0,4));
04      int day = Convert.ToInt32(inDate.Substring(4,3));
05      int month = 0;
06      int dayOfMonth = 0;
07      int div = 4;
/* -----------------------------------------
The LeapArray in line 08 and DateArray in line 99 contain
an entry for the last day of the month represented by the
subscript for that entry.
-------------------------------------- */
08      int[] LeapArray = new int[13] {
            0,31,60,91,121,152,182,213,244,274,305,335,366};
09      int[] DateArray = new int[13] {
            0,31,59,90,120,151,181,212,243,273,304,334,365};
/* -----------------------------------------
Lines 10 - 13: The LeapArray will be used if the date is evenly
divisible by 4.  For extreme date ranges, you should add a check
to see if the Year is divisible by 400.
-------------------------------------- */
10      if ( (year % div ) == 0)
11      {
12          LeapArray.CopyTo( DateArray, 0 );
13      }
/* -----------------------------------------
```

```
Loop through the array to find the month and day-of-month.
If the current day of the year is greater than the month-ending
day of the current array value, and it is equal to or less than
the month-ending day of the next array value, set the month
equal to the next index value, and the day equal to the day -
the current month-end value.
---------------------------------------- */
14      for (int i = 0;i < 13;i ++)
15      {
16          if (day > DateArray[i] && day <= DateArray[i + 1])
17          {
18              month = i+1;
19              dayOfMonth = day - DateArray[i];
20              break;
21          }
22      }
/* ----------------------------------------
Format the output to a standard MM/dd/yyyy format and
Return it in the output format specified in the outFmt value.
---------------------------------------- */
23      string outDate = month.ToString("00") + "/"
                        + dayOfMonth.ToString("00") + "/"
                        + year.ToString("0000");
24      return DateTime.ParseExact
            (outDate,"MM/dd/yyyy",null).ToString(outFmt);
25  } // end of OrdinalToGreg
```

We add these functions into the class object that we built in Chapter 3 by cutting the code from our test bed and pasting it into the original module. We then rebuild the assembly and deploy it to the global assembly cache (GAC). Complete this step, reviewing the process in Chapter 3 if necessary.

Once the assembly is in the GAC, add a reference to the DLL to any project containing a map that needs to call one of the functions. Once the reference is there, both new functions are available in the Configure Script window of a Scripting functoid.

Building a Custom Functoid

Building a custom functoid is an advanced topic. There are many steps involved in the process. Existing documentation on the process is uneven—very complete on some parts of the process and curiously absent on others. This leaves you on your own in a situation where a minor mistake results in a very frustrating experience. In this discussion, we break the process into steps. There is not sufficient space to provide a detailed discussion, so our goal is to provide you with a roadmap that you can follow.

Establishing a Common Terminology

We need to ensure that we are all on the same page as to the meaning of the terms that are critical to the discussion, so we begin with a brief glossary of terms, using our descriptions of those terms.

- *Class library*: The class library is the object you create to contain the code for defining the various custom functoids. The class object is the top of the code hierarchy and is the object that is built and deployed (the `.dll`). In our example, the class library is `SSPS.CustomFunctoids.dll`.

- *Functoid class*: This is the public class inside the class library that contains the code necessary to implement a functoid. We have three functoid classes: `DateTimeConversion`, `ConvertToOrdinal`, and `ConvertToGreg`. Each contains the resource file, the external properties of the functoid, and the function for that class.

- *Function*: This is the code that performs a date conversion. There is one function for each of the functoid classes noted previously: `FormatDateTime()`, `GregToOrdinal()`, and `OrdinalToGreg()`.

- *Resource file*: This file contains the structure information for the functoid, including the bitmap for the functoid icon, the external functoid name, the tooltips, and the description.

- *Connection type*: This defines the types of nodes (e.g., `All`, `AllExceptRecord`, `Element`, and `Field`) that can be linked to the functoid.

Note Consistent naming conventions make dealing with many separate elements easier. Keep this in mind anytime you are working with code.

Laying Out the Approach

Here are the steps that we follow to create a custom functoid:

1. Build the information worksheet.
2. Create the class library project.
3. Create a strong-named key file.
4. Set up the application values in project properties.
5. Set up the class library resource file.
6. Add the bitmap for the functoid.
7. Add resource references to the project.
8. Add the code for the functoid.
9. Build and deploy the class library.
10. Add the functoid to the toolbar.

11. Test the new functoid in a map.

12. Add additional functoids.

Building the Functoid Worksheet

The first thing we do is to construct a short worksheet that specifies the information that we need for each functoid. Building this worksheet helps ensure that naming conventions are consistent for all of the custom functoids that will be placed in this class library. Table 18-1 shows the worksheet for the first functoid, DateTimeConversion.

Table 18-1. *Functoid Worksheet for DateTimeConversion*

Object	Value
Class Library	
Namespace	SSPS.CustomFunctoids
Assembly name	SSPS.CustomFunctoids
Resource file name	SSPS_CustomFunctoidsResources
Strong-named key	SSPS_CustomFunctoids.snk
Functoid Class	
Functoid name	DateTimeConversion
External ID number	10000
External name reference	FMT_DATE_NAME
External name value	"Custom Date Conversion"
External description reference	FMT_DATE_DESC
External description	"Converts a valid date from one format to another. This functoid requires 3 inputs: first, the date; second the input date format; third the output date format."
External tooltip reference	FMT_DATE_TOOLTIP
External tooltip value	"Converts a date from one format to another"
External bitmap reference	FMT_DATE_BITMAP
External bitmap path	C:\ProMapping\SampleMaps\SSPS_CustomFunctoids
Output connection type	AllExceptRecord
Input connection type 1	All
Input connection type 2	All
Input connection type 3	All
Function	
Function name	FormatDateTime

Creating the Class Library Project

Next, we create a project named SSPS_CustomFunctoids using the Windows Class Library template in the development studio, as shown in Figure 18-1.

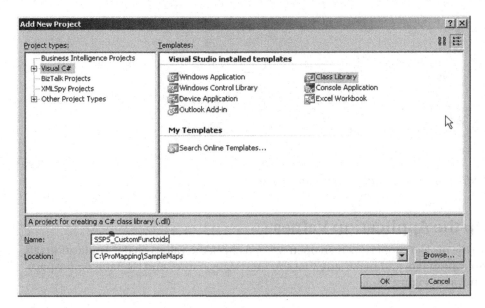

Figure 18-1. *Creating the class library project*

Caution We skip some of the basic steps relating to opening windows and other common development studio activities. Our explanation of Figure 18-1, for example, skips stating how to get to the Add New Project window. If you need to review any of the development studio steps, please consult Chapter 3.

Creating a Strong-Named Key File

We next create a strong-named key so that we can deploy the assembly into the GAC. We name the key SSPS_CustomFunctoid.snk and add it to the project, as shown in Figure 18-2.

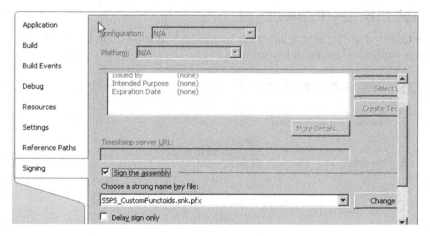

Figure 18-2. *Adding the strong-named key to the assembly*

Setting Up the Application Values

While we have the project property screen open, we can check the values on the Application tab. Select the Application tab, and make sure that the "Assembly name" and "Default namespace" fields are as shown in Figure 18-3.

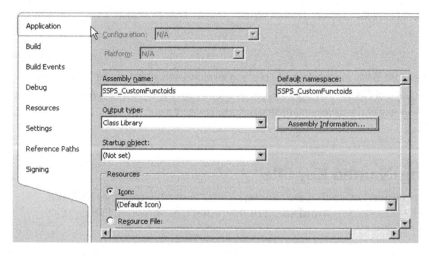

Figure 18-3. *Checking the Application tab values*

Click the Assembly Information button to verify that the assembly information is correct using the dialog shown in Figure 18-4.

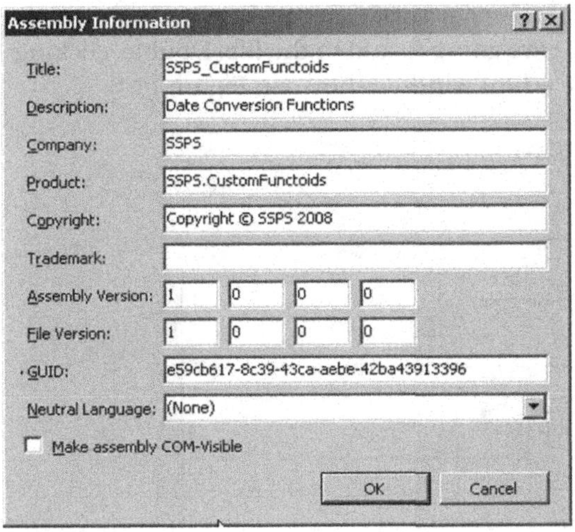

Figure 18-4. *Checking the Assembly Information values*

Setting Up the Functoid Resource File

The resource file contains important pieces of information such as the name, description, and icon for your functoid. Create a reference file adding a new item to the project to get the window shown in Figure 18-5.

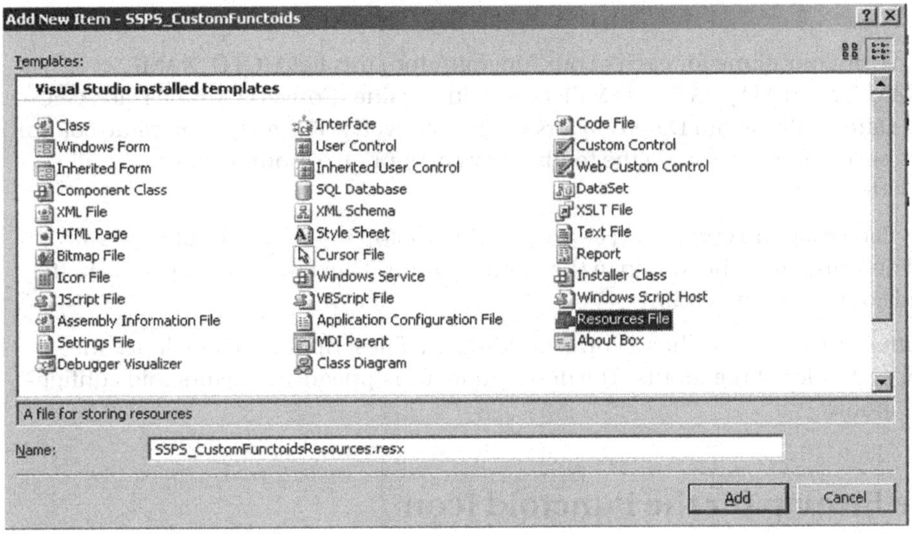

Figure 18-5. *Adding a new resources file to the project*

We've created a resources file named `SSPS_CustomFunctoidsResources.resx`, which will contain four elements for each of the functions we are going to add to the file. Double-clicking the `.resx` file in the project brings up the resource editor window shown in Figure 18-6.

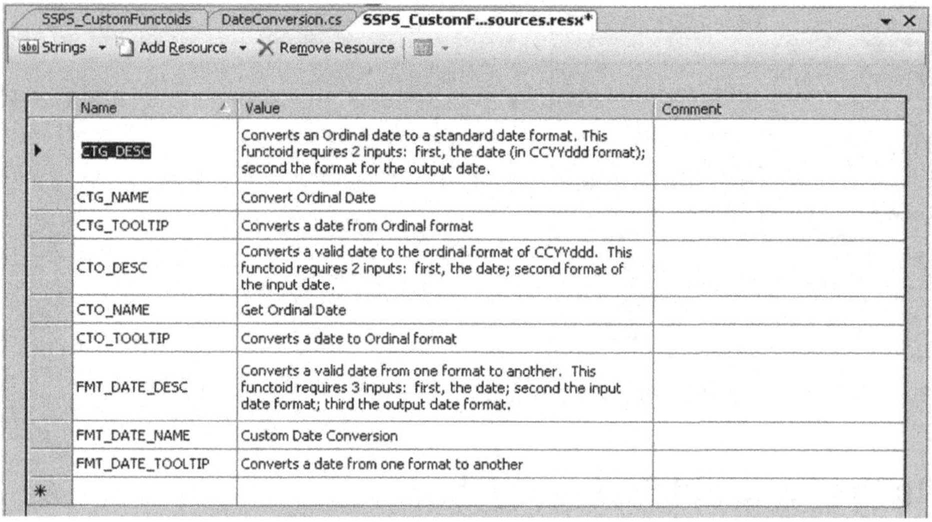
SSPS_CustomFunctoids
DateConversion.cs
SSPS_CustomF...sources.resx*
Strings
Add Resource
Remove Resource
Name
Value
Comment
CTG_DESC
Converts an Ordinal date to a standard date format. This functoid requires 2 inputs: first, the date (in CCYYddd format); second the format for the output date.
CTG_NAME
Convert Ordinal Date
CTG_TOOLTIP
Converts a date from Ordinal format
CTO_DESC
Converts a valid date to the ordinal format of CCYYddd. This functoid requires 2 inputs: first, the date; second format of the input date.
CTO_NAME
Get Ordinal Date
CTO_TOOLTIP
Converts a date to Ordinal format
FMT_DATE_DESC
Converts a valid date from one format to another. This functoid requires 3 inputs: first, the date; second the input date format; third the output date format.
FMT_DATE_NAME
Custom Date Conversion
FMT_DATE_TOOLTIP
Converts a date from one format to another

Figure 18-6. *The resource editor window*

We need three entries for each of the three functions we are going to add to the resource file:

- *Name*: We put our name for each of our functoids into this field (CTG_NAME, CTO_NAME, and FMT_DATE_NAME) along with a value (Convert Ordinal Date, Get Ordinal Date, and Custom Date Conversion, respectively). The text in the value column appears next to the functoid in the toolbox. By convention, resource names are all capital letters.
- *Tooltip*: Each functoid entry has a corresponding tooltip in the Name column with the text description of the tooltip in the Value column. The description appears in the functoid configuration window.
- *Description*: Each functoid has a corresponding brief description that includes the number and order of the inputs. The description also appears in the functoid configuration window.

Adding the Bitmap for the Functoid Icon

We switch to the Images screen via the drop-down next to Strings to bring up an image field where we can create and add an 8×8 bitmap for each of our functoids. Figure 18-7 shows our three bitmaps.

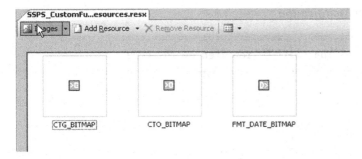

Figure 18-7. *Adding bitmaps in the Images window*

If you have any difficulties referencing the bitmap as an external file, you can use the built-in image tool to create your bitmap. In this case, if you have an external bitmap file that you want to use, select Add Existing File from the Add Resource drop-down to add the file. Then make the bitmap persistence property "Embedded in .resx," as shown in Figure 18-8.

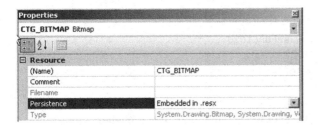

Figure 18-8. *Changing the bitmap to be Embedded in .resx*

Adding Resources to the Project

We add these two references to our project before we begin building the class object.

- `C:\WINDOWS\Microsoft.NET\Framework\v2.0.50727\System.Drawing.dll`
- `<BizTalk base directory>\Developer Tools\Microsoft.BizTalk.BaseFunctoids.dll`

Adding Code to the Class Library Object

Now that all of the external props are in place, we can complete the class object code. We prefer not to create the entire object from scratch, thus we use a working example, such as the custom functoid model found in the BizTalk SDK. This is the easiest method to ensure you get all the various bits into place. We've added some comments to that skeleton to provide some more direction as to what we have to add and/or modify (see Listing 18-3).

We use the code from `CustomFunctoid.cs` to replace the code found in the `SSPS_CustomFunctoids.cs` module that was generated when we created our project. We also rename the module `DateConversion.cs`. We then modify the code to meet the needs of our first functoid, the date conversion routine.

Listing 18-3. *DateConversion.cs After Modification*

```
/* ------------------------------------------------------------------
Lines 1 - 8 add specific resources that will be required by the code
------------------------------------------------------------------ */
01   using System;
02   using System.Drawing;
03   using System.Resources;
04   using Microsoft.BizTalk.BaseFunctoids;
05   using System.Reflection;
06   using System.Text;
07   using System.Collections;
08   using System.Globalization;
/* ------------------------------------------------------------------
Line 9 contains the class namespace.  This name MUST be the same as the
namespace you place in the resource file.
------------------------------------------------------------------ */
09   namespace SSPS.CustomFunctoids
10   {
11     public class DateTimeConversion : BaseFunctoid
12     {
13       public DateTimeConversion() : base()
14       {
/* ------------------------------------------------------------------
Line 15 contains assembly ID.  Microsoft recommends that you use a number
greater than 6000.  If you clone the code from another assembly, be sure to
remember to change this value.
------------------------------------------------------------------ */
15          this.ID = 10000;
/* ------------------------------------------------------------------
Line 16 sets the reference to the resource file we constructed in step 4.  Note
that you MUST use the Assembly name that you entered in the Assembly
properties of the project.  This reference also contains the exact resource file
name that you created when building the resource file.  We stress the
importance of getting these names exact because if you are copying existing
code, it is very easy to forget to change one of these names.
------------------------------------------------------------------ */
16      SetupResourceAssembly("SSPS.CustomFunctoids.SSPS_CustomFunctoidsResources"
                ,Assembly.GetExecutingAssembly());
/* ------------------------------------------------------------------
Lines 17 - 20 set the reference names to the three strings and the bitmap
 icon entered into the resource file.  Once again, getting the capitalized
name exactly correct will ensure that the code can access the correct
element of the resources file.
------------------------------------------------------------------ */
17          SetName("FMT_DATE_NAME");
18          SetTooltip("FMT_DATE_TOOLTIP");
19          SetDescription("FMT_DATE_DESC");
```

```
20              SetBitmap("FMT_DATE_BITMAP");
/* ------------------------------------------------------------------
Lines 21 - 22 set the minimum and maximum number of input parameters.
------------------------------------------------------------------ */
21              this.SetMinParams(3);
22              this.SetMaxParams(3);
/* ------------------------------------------------------------------
Line 23 sets the function name that needs to be called when this
functoid is invoked
------------------------------------------------------------------ */
23              SetExternalFunctionName(GetType().Assembly.FullName,
                   "SSPS.CustomFunctoids. ? DateTimeConversion", "FormatDateTime");
/* ------------------------------------------------------------------
Line 24 sets the Toolbox category where the functoid will be placed.
------------------------------------------------------------------ */
24              this.Category = FunctoidCategory.DateTime;
/* ------------------------------------------------------------------
Line 25 sets the  function name that needs to be called when this
Functoid is invoked
------------------------------------------------------------------ */
25              this.OutputConnectionType = ConnectionType.AllExceptRecord;
/* ------------------------------------------------------------------
Lines 26 - 29 set a connection type for each of the inputs.  Since
they are not identified, we do so by adding the input type as a comment.
------------------------------------------------------------------ */
26          AddInputConnectionType(ConnectionType.All); //first input
27          AddInputConnectionType(ConnectionType.All); //second input
28          AddInputConnectionType(ConnectionType.All); //third input
29      } // end of DateTimeConversion function
/* ------------------------------------------------------------------
Lines 30 - 46 present the code you have developed for the specific
function named in line 23.
------------------------------------------------------------------ */
30      // Convert one standard date format to another standard date format
31      public string FormatDateTime(string inVar, string inFmt, string outFmt)
32      {
33          string outDate = "";
34          try
35          {
36              outDate = DateTime.ParseExact(inVar, inFmt, null).ToString(outFmt);
37          }
38          catch
39          {
40              outDate = "INVALID";
41          }
42          return outDate;
43      } // end of FormatDateTime function
```

```
44
45    } // end of DateTimeConversion class
46  }
```

Here are three things to remember about the process:

- The easiest way to test functoid code is to insert the code into a console application function in the development studio workbench.

- You will often create new functoids from the code of old ones. When you do so, remember to change the function and variable names. A main impediment to building a new functoid from an old functoid is bits of the old code hanging around.

- If you test your code in a console application, the object will be a public static object. Be sure to remove the keyword static before placing your code into the class library.

Building and Deploying the Class Library Object

We next build and deploy the code so that we can use the functoid in the mapping editor. Once we get a clean build, we follow these two steps to deploy the functoid:

1. Place a copy of the .dll that is created by building the code into the mapper extensions directory, <BizTalk home>\Developer Tools\Mapper Extensions.

2. Install the assembly in the GAC.

Tip When you are reinstalling an assembly, we recommend that you first delete any copy of the same version of the assembly that is already in the GAC. Sometimes, though rarely, we have found that the newer edition fails to overwrite the old edition.

Adding the Functoid to the Toolbar

Open the Choose Toolbox Items window by right-clicking the toolbox and selecting Choose Items. Click the Functoids tab to get a list of available functoids, as shown in Figure 18-9.

If the assembly is deployed to the GAC and added to the Mapper Extension folder, the Custom Date Conversion functoid should appear in the list. If it is not in the list, we add it by browsing to the Mapper Extensions folder and selecting the DLL. Once the file appears in the window, we make sure the box is checked to ensure that the functoid appears in the toolbox.

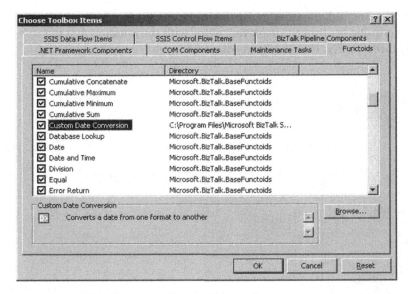

Figure 18-9. *The Choose Toolbox Items window*

Testing the Functoid

The last step in our process is adding the functoid to a map and verifying that it works as expected. We tested the functoid in one of our sample maps from Chapter 17 by passing the BSN03 date element through the functoid before passing it to the target. The map is shown in Figure 18-10.

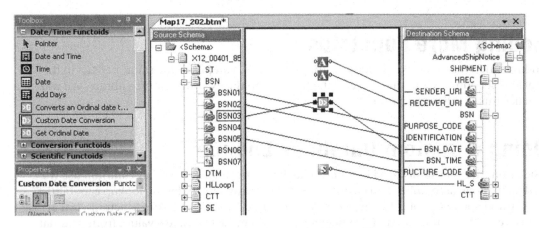

Figure 18-10. *The map with the Custom Date Conversion functoid*

When we double-click the functoid, the Configure Functoid Inputs screen opens, and we see that the functoid description is properly displayed, along with the notation that the functoid must have exactly three inputs. The Configure Functoid Inputs screen is shown in Figure 18-11.

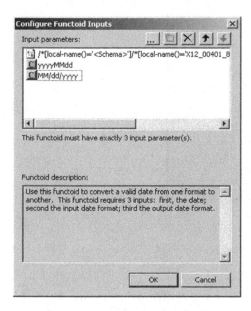

Figure 18-11. *The Configure Functoid Inputs window*

We test the map and ensure that the output is correct.

Adding More Functoids

Adding functions to the class library is straightforward. You follow the same steps as in the previous sections, except that you add the functoid to the existing resource library. We will practice this in the next section.

Doing a Custom Database Lookup

Aside from the commonly used functions like date conversions, the other common use we find for external assemblies and custom functoids is providing database lookup capabilities. We showed you in Chapter 10 how to use the standard Database Lookup functoids, but at the same time, we noted that, if you needed to return more than a few values from your database table, you should consider using an external assembly or a custom functoid. Building a database lookup differs only in minor ways from the class objects we've created for the date conversion routines.

Note We present the solution here as a custom functoid, but building an external assembly to accomplish the lookup would use the same code. The custom functoid provides more in the way of self-documentation, but the external assembly is easier to deploy.

We used the same database table for this example as we used in Chapter 10. We accept a customer ID number as input and return four fields from the table. Rather than create a new class library, we are going to add the required code to our existing custom functoid solution containing the data conversion routines.

Even though our functoid is going to be built into the existing class library, we still construct a worksheet as we did in our first step for the date conversion functoid. We also use a copy of the date conversion code for the first part of the function class object, making the necessary changes to fit it to our new function. The new code is shown in Listing 18-4.

Listing 18-4. *The Initial Code for Our Database Lookup Function*

```
/* --------------------------------------------------------------------
Line 09:  We've added one additional project resource here, to allow access to
 the method to access the system configuration file where
we are placing our connection string.
--------------------------------------------------------------------*/
01   using System;
02   using System.Drawing;
03   using System.Resources;
04   using Microsoft.BizTalk.BaseFunctoids;
05   using System.Reflection;
06   using System.Text;
07   using System.Collections;
08   using System.Globalization;
09   using System.Configuration;
/* --------------------------------------------------------------------
Declare the class name.   It must be the same as the assembly name
in the project property
--------------------------------------------------------------------*/
10   namespace SSPS. CustomFunctoids
11   {
12    public class GetExternalCustomerID: BaseFunctoid
13    {
14        public  GetExternalCustomerID ()
15            : base()
16        {
17          this.ID = 9000;
18          SetupResourceAssembly("SSPS.CustomFunctoids. ?
              SSPS_CustomFunctoidsResources",Assembly.GetExecutingAssembly());
19          SetName("CUSTURI_NAME");
20          SetTooltip("CUSTURI_TOOLTIP");
```

```
21          SetDescription("CUSTURI_DESC");
22          SetBitmap("CUSTURI_BITMAP");
23          this.SetMinParams(1);
24          this.SetMaxParams(1);
25          SetExternalFunctionName(GetType().Assembly.FullName, ?
                    "SSPS. CustomFunctoids.GetExternalCustomerID", " GetCustURI ");
26          this.Category = FunctoidCategory.Conversion;
27          this.OutputConnectionType = ConnectionType.All;
28          AddInputConnectionType(ConnectionType.All); //first input
29       } // End of GetExternalCustomer function
/* -------------------------------------------------------------------------
The called function will be inserted here.
-------------------------------------------------------------------------*/
30   } // end of SSPS.SQLFunctions class
```

Next, we add a function for returning the information. There are four actions the function must execute:

1. Determine a connect string. We want this code to be independent of database names, server names, and so on, so we have the code obtain the database connect string from an external source. In this case, we will use a configuration file.

2. Establish a connection to the database and table.

3. Build and execute an SQL query command to retrieve the required fields from the table.

4. Format the returned data in a manner useful to the map; this example returns a delimited string containing the lookup value and the four variables retrieved from the table.

■**Caution** Remember to add a reference to your functoid project for the System.Configuration.dll, which is located in C:\WINDOWS\Microsoft.NET\Framework\<version number>. The version number will depend on the edition of BizTalk that you are using.

Listing 18-5 contains the remainder of the code with the function that will be executed when the functoid is invoked.

Listing 18-5. *Operational Code for the Database Lookup Functoid*

```
/* -------------------------------------------------------------------------
This function will return a delimited string containing each of the 4
elements we wish to return from the lookup of the customer ID.
-------------------------------------------------------------------------*/
31 public string GetCustURI (string custID)
32 {
33  string connectString = System.Configuration.ConfigurationSettings. ?
                    AppSettings.Get("MapBookConnectString");
```

```
34  string retval = "No Address";
35  string queryString = "Select custLastName, custFirstName, custCity, ?
                   custURI from CustAddress where LocationID = '" + custID + "'";
36  System.Data.SqlClient.SqlConnection MapBook = ?
                   new System.Data.SqlClient.SqlConnection(connectString);
37  System.Data.SqlClient.SqlCommand custQuery = ?
                   new System.Data.SqlClient.SqlCommand(queryString, MapBook);
38  try
39  {
40   MapBook.Open();
41   System.Data.SqlClient.SqlDataReader GetAddress = custQuery.ExecuteReader();
42   while (GetAddress.Read())
43   {
44    string custLast = GetAddress.GetValue(0).ToString();
45    string custFirst = GetAddress.GetValue(1).ToString();
46    string custCity = GetAddress.GetValue(2).ToString();
47    string custURI = GetAddress.GetValue(3).ToString();
48    retval = custID + "|" + custLast.Trim() + "|" +
                   custFirst.Trim() + "|" + custCity.Trim() + "|" + custURI.Trim();
49   }
50  }
51  catch (System.Data.SqlClient.SqlException ex)
52  {
53   return ex.ToString();
54  }
55  finally
56  {
57   MapBook.Close();
58  }
59    return retval;
60 } // End of ExternalCustID function
61} // End of GetExternalCustomer Class
```

Once the module is tested and we have incorporated it into the code for the class library, we follow the same steps as before to build and deploy the assembly.

Caution When the assembly is redeployed, you must restart the development studio in order to rebuild the cache. Otherwise, you may not be able to see the new functoid and will not be able to add it to the toolbox.

We add a database connection string to the BizTalk or system configuration file C:\WINDOWS\Microsoft.NET\Framework\<version number>\CONFIG, inserting an appSettings node right after the configSections end tag as shown in Listing 18-6.

Listing 18-6. *Inserted appSettings Node*

```
<appSettings>
    <add key="MapBookConnectString" value="Data Source=SSPS;?
                    Initial Catalog=Promapping;Trusted_Connection=Yes;" />
</appSettings>
```

We add the custom functoid to the toolbox and then to a map for a testing. The map is shown in Figure 18-12.

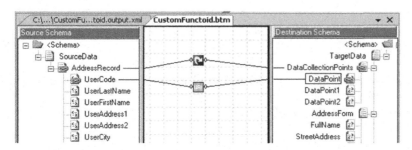

Figure 18-12. *A map with the Database Lookup functoid*

The map uses the UserCode value as the lookup key and returns the data in a pipe-delimited string, which can be parsed to determine the four values.

Summary

Building external assemblies and custom functoids definitely requires experience with .NET programming. You can succeed best by working through the processes in small steps. Many wonder what external assembly and custom functoid creation have to do with mapping. We hope that we've shown that these two tools provide mechanisms that facilitate both the creation of large numbers of maps that share common functions and the maintenance of those maps.

In our final chapter, which we call "Topics from the Fringe," we discuss some of the more unusual solutions that we have created for our clients. Solutions addressed include modifying EDI enveloping using a custom pipeline component, how to build a stand-alone XSLT map outside the map editor, and how to break up large strings using the Table Looping functoid. While you may not encounter these same problems, we believe that some of these techniques might help you visualize solutions to other difficult problems. The chapter also contains an overview of testing custom scripts in the development studio, a subject far too broad for detailed discussion in this book.

CHAPTER 19

■ ■ ■

Examples from the Fringe

We built several hundred BizTalk maps in the last several years, completing nearly all of them using the techniques that we introduced in the previous chapters. Some presented mapping problems that could only be overcome with solutions that were unusual and often unique to that situation. Almost all of these unusual problems resulted from business requirements that imposed processes for which the mapping engine was not suited.

These types of problems frequently cannot be solved within the mapping environment as discussed to this point in this book. They often involve construction of custom pipelines, orchestrations, or pre- and post-processing library objects. The discussions assume that you are familiar with such subjects. If you are not, you should consult *Pro BizTalk 2006* by George Dunphy and Ahmed Metwally (Apress, 2006) and *BizTalk 2006 Recipes: A Problem-Solution Approach* by Mark Beckner, Ben Goeltz, Brandon Gross, Brennan O'Reilly, Stephen Roger, Mark Smith, and Alexander West (Apress, 2006), or consult the equivalent books for your version of BizTalk.

We look at several of these problems and their solutions in this chapter. We chose these particular cases because they are more likely to be encountered than others and, frankly, because space limitations precluded inclusion of some of our favorites. Thus this chapter discusses an eclectic set of problems. Hopefully, even if you never encounter one of them, the techniques that we discuss will prove helpful to you in other cases.

Note The discussions in this chapter are high level, presenting techniques for solving problems rather than detailed reviews as in previous chapters.

Modifying Outbound EDI Envelope Data

Sometimes, you must access the EDI envelope segments (ISA, GS, ST, SE, GE, IEA) of an outbound transaction after the EDI interchange has been created. When an outbound EDI transaction is built by a BizTalk map, only the data segments are created. The envelope segments are built by the EDI pipeline component on the BizTalk send port.

The contents of the envelope segments are determined by the sending and receiving party setups in the BizTalk Administration Console. These contents are based on promoted data or data in the message context file. In short, envelope segments cannot be accessed from within the map. The envelope segments can be modified only after they are created by the EDI send pipeline. In other words, the envelope segments must be intercepted and modified at some point after the transaction passes through the pipeline. In the example here, the ISA15 element, which contains the Test/Production flag, must be modified.

A custom pipeline is our solution to this problem. The standard send pipeline contains three modules: the PreAssemble module, the Assemble module, and the Encode module. The EDI message generation in the standard EDI send pipeline takes place using the EDI Assembler component in the assemble stage.

Since the encode stage occurs after the assemble stage, we can add a component to the encode stage. Then, we can intercept and modify the EDI transaction before it leaves the pipeline. This solution has three requirements:

- The application data must allow inference of whether the transaction is a production or a test transaction so that routing can be determined.

- A promotion property schema must be created that promotes the data field that contains the test/production indicator.

- A custom pipeline encoding component must be built that can read and write a flat file stream.

Creating the Custom Pipeline Component

A discussion of the details of how to build a custom pipeline component is beyond the scope of this book. Excellent discussions of the various elements of pipeline interfaces are presented in Chapter 3 of *BizTalk 2006 Recipes* and Chapters 4 and 5 of *ProBizTalk 2006*. Also, the BizTalk SDK contains an example of an encoding module for a pipeline that can be adapted. Although all of the code for this example is available in the download for this chapter, only the code for the IComponent interface and the function that it calls (where the actual envelope modification takes place) is included in this chapter. Listing 19-1 contains the IComponent code.

Listing 19-1. *IComponent Function of the Encoding Module*

```
/* ------------------------------------------------------------------------
IComponent function of the Encoding module.  Receives the flat file (inmsg), calls
the function ReformatEnvelope, receives the modified file back from the function,
and returns the file to the calling object.
-----------------------------------------------------------------------*/
01 #region IComponent
02 public IBaseMessage Execute(IPipelineContext pc, IBaseMessage inmsg)
03 {
04   try
05   {
06     Stream s = ReformatEnvelope(inmsg.BodyPart.Data);
07     s.Position = 0;
08     inmsg.BodyPart.Data = s;
09     return inmsg;
10   }
11   catch (Exception ex)
```

```
12   {
13     throw new ApplicationException(string.Format
         ("The {0} ReformatEnvelope Encoder encountered an error. ",
                 this.GetType().ToString()), ex);
14   }
15 }
16 #endregion
```

The IComponent method accepts the pipeline context and the message from the pipeline and passes the body part of the message stream to the function that will modify the contents. Line 07 of the code rewinds the stream that is returned, moving the file pointer back to the start of the file. Line 08 assigns the stream back to the body part of the message, and line 09 returns the stream to the pipeline.

Listing 19-2 shows the ReformatEnvelope function that performs the modification to the stream.

Listing 19-2. *ReformatEnvelope Function*

```
/* --------------------------------------------------------------------------
Function to update the prod/test flag of an EDI envelope
--------------------------------------------------------------------------*/
01   public Stream ReformatEnvelope(Stream inStream)
02   {
03       MemoryStream ms = new MemoryStream();
04       StreamWriter sw = new StreamWriter(ms);
05       StreamReader sr = new StreamReader(inStream);
06       int bufferSize = 1024;
07       char[] buffer = new char[bufferSize];
08       int sizeRead = 0;
/* --------------------------------------------------------------------------
Read one block of the input stream into the buffer and replace
The prod/test flag value with a "T"
--------------------------------------------------------------------------*/
09       if ((sizeRead = sr.Read(buffer, 0, bufferSize)) != 0)
10       {
11           buffer[102] = Convert.ToChar("T");
12           sw.Write(buffer, 0, sizeRead);
13       }
/* --------------------------------------------------------------------------
Read the balance of the file into the buffer with no modification
--------------------------------------------------------------------------*/
14       while ((sizeRead = sr.Read(buffer, 0, bufferSize)) != 0)
15       {
16           sw.Write(buffer, 0, sizeRead);
17       }
18       sr.Close();
19       sw.Flush();
/* --------------------------------------------------------------------------
```

```
   Rewind the stream and return it to the calling function
   ----------------------------------------------------------------------*/
20      ms.Seek(0, SeekOrigin.Begin);
21      return ms;
22   }
```

The function reads the input stream and changes byte 102 (the Test/Production flag) to T. Since that byte is in the first block read, the remainder of the stream is read and written without modification. When the entire stream has been read, the stream point is reset to the start of the stream and the stream returned to the calling object.

■**Note** If the file being streamed is large, increase the buffer size for smoother processing. Also note that the large message transformation capabilities of BizTalk 2006, 2006 R2, and 2009 buffer large messages to the file system. By default, a large message is defined as one greater than 1MB in size. As with large message transportation, a performance degradation can be expected compared to performing this example in a memory stream.

We build a console application in the development studio to test the component. The application opens a file, calls the ReformatEnvelope function and writes the output to a new file. Testing in this way allows us to step through the code in the debugger and see exactly what happens. Listing 19-3 shows the code for the console application.

Listing 19-3. *The Console Application for Testing ReformatEnvelope*

```
01   using System;
02   using System.IO;
03   using System.Collections;
04
05   using SSPS.BizTalk.PipelineComponents;
06
07   namespace PipelineComponentTestAp
08   {
20     class PipelineFunctionTestor
10     {
11       [STAThread]
12       static void Main(string[] args)
13       {
/* --------------------------------------------------------------
   Open an external EDI file as a FileStream
   ----------------------------------------------------------------------*/
14           FileStream inputStream = new FileStream(@"C:\ProMapping\SampleMaps
                   \Chapter_19\Data\EDI_Message.edi", FileMode.Open);
15           SSPS.BizTalk.PipelineComponents.SSPS.BizTalk.PipelineComponents
                   .X12EnvelopeEncoder ReformatEnvelope
                   = new SSPS.BizTalk.PipelineComponents.SSPS.
```

```
                  BizTalk.PipelineComponents.ReformatEnvelope();
/* --------------------------------------------------------------------------
Pass the stream to the reformatting function and receive
The updated file stream returned from the function
--------------------------------------------------------------------------*/
16        Stream newMessage = updateEnvelope.ReformatEnvelope(inputStream);
17        newMessage.Position = 0;
18
19        StreamWriter sw = new StreamWriter(@"C:\ProMapping\SampleMaps
                  \Chapter_19\Data\EDI_Message.new.edi", false);
20        StreamReader sr = new StreamReader(newMessage);
/* --------------------------------------------------------------------------
Write the new stream to the file system
--------------------------------------------------------------------------*/
21        sw.Write(sr.ReadToEnd());
22        sw.Flush();
23        sr.Close();
24        sw.Close();
25        Console.ReadLine();
26     }
27   } // end of class
28 } // end of namespace
```

This solution is specific to a particular EDI problem, but the technique can be applied to many other situations where contents of a transaction must be modified before or after passing through one or more maps.

Building BizTalk Maps Outside the Map Editor

There is not much left in the mapping grid when we use extensive XSLT in our maps, either in call templates or in inline code. Our XSLT version of the inbound 856 ASN in Chapter 17 has only two items on the grid, the Scripting functoid containing the XSLT code and the link from that functoid to the output schema.

Only a few, quick modifications are required to replace those two items with an XSLT file that is called from the properties of the mapping grid. If you have reached the point in mapping where you might prefer XSLT maps to traditional functoid-based maps, consider building the entire map in an XSLT external file. This example shows how to implement such a map.

Deciding to Use an XSLT File As Your Map

There are several reasons why this approach might be a good choice:

- *Ease of testing large scripts*: If a map requires a lot of scripting, you create and test the scripts outside the map, then migrate the script into a Scripting functoid and test it in the map. You must continue this process of moving code back and forth as you correct or update the code. While this process is not burdensome with short scripts, when maps require extensive scripting, you gain an advantage by creating the entire map in one script and testing in the map editor.

- *Ease of maintenance*: One of the most difficult tasks in mapping is modifying a map
  created by someone else. For that matter, going back to modify a map *you* created six
  months ago can be difficult. Modifying the code in an extended XSLT map may be
  faster than modifying a large chain of functoids or modifying two or more scripts that
  interact. In the latter case, you have to copy the applicable scripts into a text editor
  where you can review them together or into the development studio for testing.

- *Development time*: The fact that you can develop the entire map in one file, without
  dragging and dropping links and opening and closing functoids and testing piecemeal
  scripts means less time spent in development. By developing a library of XSLT excerpts,
  you further reduce that time. In X12 maps, for example, we don't have to build many
  N1 loops or fill the contents of HL segments, because we have generic library templates
  that we just copy into the script.

- *Documentation*: Documenting BizTalk maps is a challenge, since the contents of the
  generated map file can be pretty daunting for someone not used to reading XPATH
  references. While it is possible to provide at least some documentation in the labels of
  functoids and tags, these are not visible without clicking the object in the map. There
  is also no way to comment on a group of functoids. We use external documents, such
  as Word documents, into which we copy scripts as well as enter comments on how the
  maps work. Adding comments to an external XSLT map is easy and ensures that both
  the code and the comments can be reviewed together.

Creating an External XSLT Map

We use the script that we created for the inbound 856 ASN sample discussed in Chapter 17 as
the base for our example. The script is shown in Listing 19-4.

Listing 19-4. *The Script for the XSLT Template Used in the Unbound 856 Map Scripting Functoid*

```
<!-- **********************************************************************
Processes inbound HL Loops for AdvancedShipNotice Application file
********************************************************************** -->
01 <xsl:template name="BuildASN">
02  <xsl:variable name="RailRoadCar"
      select="concat(//so:TD3/TD302,//so:TD3/TD303 )"/>
03  <xsl:variable name="OrderNum" select="//so:PRF/PRF01"/>
04  <xsl:for-each select="//so:HLLoop1[so:HL/HL03='I']
          /so:MAN[not(MAN02=preceding::so:MAN/MAN02)]">
05   <xsl:variable name="ItemID" select="MAN02"/>
06   <xsl:element name="ItemLoop">
07    <xsl:element name="ItemID">
08     <xsl:value-of select="$ItemID"/>
20    </xsl:element>
10    <xsl:element name="OrderNum">
11     <xsl:value-of select="$OrderNum"/>
12    </xsl:element>
13    <xsl:element name="RailRoadCar">
```

```
14      <xsl:value-of select="$RailRoadCar"/>
15      </xsl:element>
16      <xsl:for-each select="//s0:HLLoop1
                  [s0:HL/HL03='I' and s0:MAN/MAN02 = $ItemID]">
17       <xsl:variable name="HLPack" select="s0:HL/HL02"/>
18       <xsl:element name="PackLoop">
19        <xsl:element name="PackID">
20         <xsl:value-of select="//s0:HLLoop1
                                  [s0:HL/HL01=$HLPack and
                          s0:HL/HL03='P' ]/s0:MAN/MAN02"/>
21        </xsl:element>
22       </xsl:element>
23      </xsl:for-each>
24     </xsl:element>
25    </xsl:for-each>
26 </xsl:template>
```

This script uses a call template format without input parameters, so very little modification is needed to convert it into an external XSLT file to be used as a map. Listing 19-5 contains the converted script.

Listing 19-5. *The Script for the External XSLT Map*

```
<!-- ***********************************************************************
Processes inbound HL Loops for AdvancedShipNotice Application file
*********************************************************************** -->
<xsl:stylesheet xmlns:xsl="http://www.w3.org/1999/XSL/Transform"
   xmlns:msxsl="urn:schemas-microsoft-com:xslt"
   xmlns:s0="http://schemas.microsoft.com/BizTalk/EDI/X12/2006"
   xmlns:ns0="http://Chapter_17.FlatFileSchema1"
   xmlns:var="urn:var" xmlns:userCSharp="urn:user"
       exclude-result-prefixes="msxsl var userCSharp" version="1.0">
 <xsl:output method="xml" indent="yes" omit-xml-declaration="yes"/>
 <xsl:template match="/">
   <xsl:element name="ns0:Shipment">

      <!--insert lines 02 through 25 of the original script seen
      In Listing 19-4--!>

   </xsl:element>
  </xsl:template>
</xsl:stylesheet>
```

Only a few modifications were required to convert the script:

- We remove the template name node and enclose the remaining lines inside a stylesheet tag that contains namespace declarations for the source and target document schemas. The namespace declarations give us a shortened prefix by which to refer to the nodes in the input and output schemas.

- We add an output declaration to specify output parameters.
- We add a `match` attribute to tell the style sheet to begin reading the source document at the root node.
- We add an element node to output the root tag of the target document.

Implementing the External XSLT File As a Map

We create a BizTalk map project and select the source and target schemas in the new map window, just as with any other BizTalk map. BizTalk will add the schemas and open the map for editing. The empty map grid appears, but instead of connecting links and adding functoids, we simply right-click the grid and select Properties, as shown in Figure 19-1.

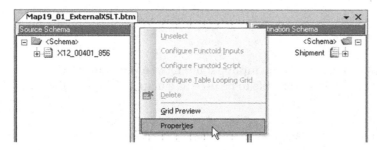

Figure 19-1. *Opening the map's Grid Properties window*

The Grid Properties window is shown in Figure 19-2. Select the Custom XSL Path property, click the ellipses, and browse to our XSLT map file.

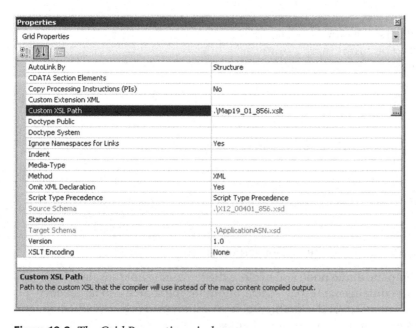

Figure 19-2. *The Grid Properties window*

Once we select the file, we close the properties window. Now, we are ready to treat this map just like any other map. We open the map properties, set the input and output file types and names, and turn validations on or off as required. We test the map by right-clicking the map name in the project and selecting test map. As we test the map, we modify the XSLT file as needed. We use incremental testing here as well, by building a small part of the map, testing it, and opening the XSLT file to add another piece of the map.

Accessing C# Scripts in a Stand-Alone XSLT Map

Of course, we may need to access C# functions from a XSLT map, just as we do from XSLT templates in regular maps. The process is simple. We manually add a CDATA section with the C# script to the end of the XSLT, just as the mapping engine does when a Scripting functoid is added to the grid of a standard map. We add the code fragment shown in Listing 19-6 to the XSLT file that we developed in Listing 19-5.

Listing 19-6. *CDATA Section to Add to the XSLT Map*

```
<!-- ***********************************************************************
Adding a CDATA section to your stand-alone XSLT map
*********************************************************************** -->
<xsl:stylesheet xmlns:xsl="http://www.w3.org/1999/XSL/Transform"
    xmlns:msxsl="urn:schemas-microsoft-com:xslt"
    xmlns:s0="http://schemas.microsoft.com/BizTalk/EDI/X12/2006"
    xmlns:ns0="http://Chapter_17.FlatFileSchema1"
    xmlns:var="urn:var"
    xmlns:userCSharp="urn:user"
    exclude-result-prefixes="msxsl var userCSharp" version="1.0">
 <xsl:output method="xml" indent="yes" omit-xml-declaration="yes"/>
 <xsl:template match="/">
  <xsl:element name="ns0:Shipment">

        <!-- code here from lines 02 through 25 of the original script -->

  </xsl:element>
 </xsl:template>

<msxsl:script language="C#" implements-prefix="userCSharp">

<![CDATA[]]>
/* -----------------------------------------------------------
Manually add CDATA section above and then C# code
functions here
----------------------------------------------------- */
public string GetCurrentDate()
{
```

```
    DateTime dt = DateTime.Now;
    return dt.ToString("yyyy-MM-dd");
}
</msxsl:script>
</xsl:stylesheet>
```

Any other C# scripts we need are also placed in this CDATA section. The C# scripts are accessed by the XSLT map in the same way as they would be accessed from an inline XSLT call template in a regular map.

Calling Other XSLT Templates From a Stand-Alone XSLT Map

XSLT templates can be used in a stand-alone map exactly as in a regular map. In fact, creating your XSLT map by using XSLT templates allows you to separate processes within your map. They may reduce the amount of code needed; they certainly increase the ease with which code can be added from script libraries.

■**Caution** When designing a call template for a stand-alone XSLT map, remember that if you are going to access data directly from the source document, you'll need to keep track of the context node for your relative XPATH expressions.

Building Dynamic Tag Names in Your XML Output

Sometimes, the output schema node tag names contain a sequence number. We encounter this problem when converting maps created with the Mercator mapping tool to BizTalk, since the Mercator output files have sequenced nodes.

■**Note** Mercator was the EDI software from TSI International, a major player in the EDI arena for many years. For a few years, Mercator was marketed by Ascential as DataStage TX. IBM bought the software and released it as the IBM WebSphere Transformation Extender (WTX), a universal data transformation and validation engine.

The problem in replicating this behavior with BizTalk is that the number of output nodes needed is not known when the map runs. Fortunately, solving the problem is not difficult. When writing the XSLT code to output the element name, use this format:

```
<xsl:element name="{concat('ROW', position())}">
```

This code creates the nodes ROW1, ROW2, ROW3, and so forth by concatenating the literal ROW with the number returned from the XSLT position() function.

Caution The problem with the concatenation approach is that you must have an output node defined in the schema for each of the ROW tags created unless you set Validate TestMap Output to False. This is not desirable from our best practices point of view, since we like to have our maps validate before certifying them as complete, but we bend the rules in this case.

Breaking Up Large Strings Using Table Looping

We covered some methods of breaking up large strings in Chapter 14, but one method we didn't discuss was the use of the Table Looping and Table Extractor functoids. We don't use these functoids, because it is easier for us to write a script to do the same thing. Still, since the use of these two functoids is often unclear, we feel that we should provide an example of their use.

Our example maps strings from an input file to an output file, where each source string may be up to 264 bytes long, but each target string cannot exceed 66 bytes. Listing 19-7 shows the input data.

Listing 19-7. *Source Data for the Table Looping and Table Extractor Functoids Map*

```
<ns0:N9>
 <N901>ZZ</ N901 >
 <N902 >TextMesssage Follows</N902>
 <ns0:MSG>
   <MSG01>THIS IS A TEST FOR THE N9 MSG TEXT ELEMENT WHICH  CAN
       BE UP TO 264 BYTES LONG.  IT MUST BE BROKEN UP INTO
       SMALLER FIELDS OF NO MORE THAN 66 BYTES.</MSG01>
 </ns0:MSG>
 <ns0:MSG>
  <MSG01>THIS IS THE SECOND OCCURRENCE OF THE MESSAGE TEXT
       FIELD.  ALL OCCURRENCES OF THIS MESSAGE MUST BE
       PARSED INTO 66-BYTE FIELDS</MSG01>
 </ns0:MSG>
 <ns0:MSG>
  <MSG01>IN SOME CASES THE TEXT SHOULD BE CONCATENATED
       TOGETHER BEFORE BREAKING IT UP.  IN OTHERS EACH
       MESSAGE LINE SHOULD BE TREATED SEPARATELY.</MSG01>
 </ns0:MSG>
</N9>
```

We must map this data into a looping output node that looks like that shown in Listing 19-8, which shows the first two output lines of text.

Listing 19-8. *Output Format for the Table Looping and Table Extractor Functoids Map*

```
Message>
 < MsgText >
  THIS IS A TEST FOR THE N9 MSG TEXT ELEMENT WHICH CAN BE UP TO 264
 </ MsgText >
</Message>
<Message>
 <MsgText>
  BYTES LONG. IT MUST BE BROKEN UP INTO SMALLER FIELDS OF NO MORE T
 </MsgText>
</Message>
```

The Table Looping functoid extracts the data from the source node and places the data into a table. The Table Extractor functoid iterates across a specific column of the table and extracts the data therein. In our example, we use the String Extract functoid to break the large MSG01 strings into smaller strings of no more than 66 bytes. These smaller strings are passed to the Table Load functoid, which places each string into column 1 of the table. The Table Extractor functoid then removes each string and puts it into the MsgText field. Figure 19-3 shows the map.

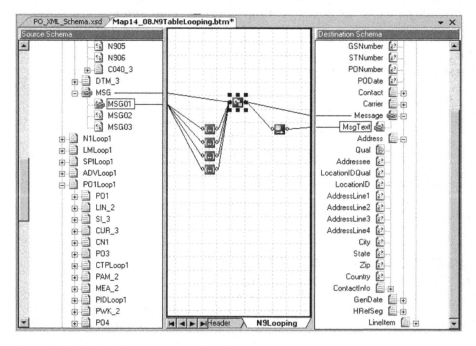

Figure 19-3. *The Table Looping and Table Extractor map*

The Table Looping functoid has a minimum of three inputs and a single output, as described here:

- The single output connects the functoid to the node with which you wish to associate the table. Here, that node is the Message node, which contains the MsgText node where we will output the data.

- The first input connects the node through which we will iterate and collect data. The MSG segment is the node in this case, since we want to collect the data from each instance of MSG01.

- The second input is not visible on the mapping grid, as it is placed directly in the Configure Functoids Input window of the functoid. The value is the number of columns to be in the table. In this case, we set the value to 1, since we only need one.

- The remaining inputs in this example are the four strings produced by the four String Extract functoids. The order in which these links are attached to the Table Looping functoid is not important, because the order in which they will be inserted into the table is determined when the table is configured.

The Configure Functoids Input window for the Table Looping functoid in this map is shown in Figure 19-4.

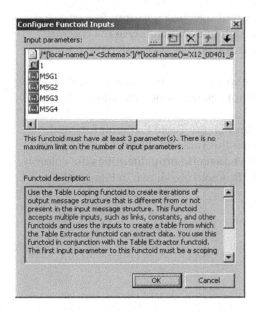

Figure 19-4. *The Configure Functoids Input window for Table Looping functoid*

We've labeled the links from the String Extract functoids to the Table Looping functoid for clarity. Once the inputs are in place, we can configure the Table Looping grid. We open the window by right-clicking the functoid and selecting that option or by selecting that option in the functoid properties. The window is shown in Figure 19-5.

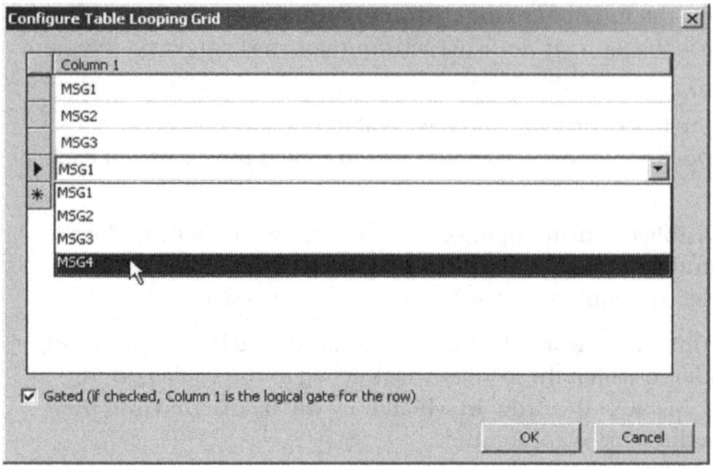

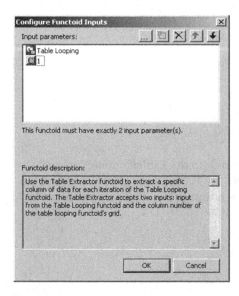

Figure 19-5. *The Configure Table Looping Grid window*

The inputs to the table are added by clicking a row and selecting the input from the drop-down list that appears. We have four inputs, and we assign one to each row in the column. Since we want to control the order in which the text is extracted, we also assign them in the same order as they were extracted from the source.

The Gated check box in the lower left corner of the window tells the extractor to skip any row where the first column is empty. In our case, an empty column one indicates no data, so we definitely want to bypass that source node.

You define what data is retrieved from the table through the Table Extractor functoid. That functoid requires two inputs. The first is a link from the Table Looping functoid, which identifies the table from which data is to be extracted. The second input identifies the column number for the data. The inputs to our Table Extractor functoid are shown in Figure 19-6.

Figure 19-6. *Inputs for the Table Extractor functoid*

When we test the map using the source data from Listing 19-7, we get the output shown in Listing 19-9.

Listing 19-9. *Output of the Table Looping and Table Extractor Map*

```
<Message>
 < MsgText >
  THIS IS A TEST FOR THE N9 MSG TEXT ELEMENT WHICH CAN BE UP TO 264
 </ MsgText >
</Message>
<Message>
 <MsgText>
  BYTES LONG. IT MUST BE BROKEN UP INTO SMALLER FIELDS OF NO MORE T
 </MsgText>
</Message>
<Message>
 <MsgText>HAN 45 BYTES.</MsgText>
</Message>
<Message>
 <MsgText>
  THIS IS THE SECOND OCCURRENCE OF THE MESSAGE TEXT FIELD. ALL OCCU
 </MsgText>
</Message>
<Message>
 <MsgText>
  RRENCES OF THIS MESSAGE MUST BE PARSED INTO 40-BYTE FIELDS
 </MsgText>
</Message>
<Message>
 <MsgText>
  IN SOME CASES THE TEXT SHOULD BE CONCATENATED TOGETHER BEFORE BREA
 </MsgText>
</Message>
<Message>
 <MsgText>
  KING IT UP. IN OTHERS EACH MESSAGE LINE COULD BE TREATED SEPARATE
 </MsgText>
</Message>
<Message>
 <MsgText>LY.</MsgText>
</Message>
```

We could eliminate the looping of the Message node by moving the link from the Table Looping functoid to the MsgText node.

Reformatting Source Files for Easier Mapping

There are times when the schema structures of the source document and the destination document are so different that handling the transformation in a map is more trouble than it is worth. We don't recommend preprocessing a source file before passing it to the map, but twice in the past we've done so ourselves. An example of this is worth presenting.

Naturally, our example deals with the 856 ASN. We faced a situation where the clients had designed their application schema with fully nested HL loops, as shown in the data file in Listing 19-10.

Listing 19-10. *A Client Data File for an ASN*

```
<EliteASN>
 <ASNHeader />
  <BOL>
   <BSN BSN01="00" BSN02="07438" BSN03="2006-05-18" BSN04="00:00" />
    <HLLoopShipment>
     <HL_S HL01="1" HL03="S" />
     <TD1_S TD101="CTN25" TD102="94" TD106="G" TD107="804.824" TD108="LB" />
     <TD5_S TD501="B" TD502="2" TD503="AVRT" TD504="G" TD505="MOTOR CO" />
     <REF_S REF01="BM" REF02="07438770021167515" />
     <N1Loop_S>
      <N1_S N101="SF" N103_1="1" N104_1="234" N103_91="91" N104_91="" />
     </N1Loop_S>
     <N1Loop_S>
      <N1_S N101="ST" N103_1="1" N104_1="" N103_91="91" N104_91="345" />
      <N3_S N301="11000 MY STREET" N302="" />
      <N4_S N401="MY TOWN" N402="KY" N403="40299" N404="US" />
     </N1Loop_S>
     <HLLoopOrder>
      <HL1_O HL01="1" HL02="2" HL03="O" />
      <PRF_O PRF01="0049733306" />
      <REF_O REF01="IV" REF02="" />
      <N1Loop_O>
        <N1_O N101="BY" N102="MY TOWN" N103="92" N104="0025" />
      </N1Loop_O>
      <HLLoopTare>
       <HLLoopPack>
        <HL1_P HL01="3" HL02="1" HL03="P" />
        <PO4_P PO405="LB" PO406="9.86" />
        <HLLoopItem>
         <HL1_I HL01="4" HL02="3" HL03="I" />
         <LIN_I CB_LIN02="CB" UP_LIN02="UP" UP_LIN03="743877010047" />
         <SN1_I SN102="12" SN103="EA" SN105="48" SN106="EA" />
        </HLLoopItem>
       </HLLoopPack>
       <HLLoopPack>
        <HL1_P HL01="5" HL02="1" HL03="P" />
```

```
            <PO4_P PO405="LB" PO406="9.86" />
            <HLLoopItem>
             <HL1_I HL01="6" HL02="5" HL03="I" />
             <LIN_I CB_LIN02="CB" CB_LIN02="UP" UP_LIN03="743877010047" />
             <SN1_I SN102="12" SN103="EA" SN105="48" SN106="EA" />
            </HLLoopItem>
          </HLLoopPack>
        </HLLoopTare>
      </HLLoopOrder>
    </HLLoopShipment>
   <CTT CTT01="193" />
 </BOL>
</EliteASN>
```

The original file from which the data in Listing 19-10 was extracted was over 1,100 lines long. This excerpt has been altered to fit page width as well. The loops in this file are nested six levels deep: BOL, Shipment, Order, Tare, Pack, and Item. Mapping this data to an outbound 856 ASN requires mapping these six levels into a single level HL loop. Many of the segments of the HL loop are used in more than one of the levels, making control of output very difficult. But, unlike many application files, this one contains the hierarchy information for the HL segment built in, so we don't have to worry about inferring that data.

We decided that, since we could not alter the input format received from the application, we would design our own source schema and modify the data to fit that schema. The script to modify the file is shown in Listing 19-11.

Listing 19-11. *Restructuring the Application Input File Format from Listing 19-10*

```csharp
using System;
using System.IO;
using System.Xml;

namespace sspsi.APPS
{
[Serializable]

 public class Reformat856
 {

  public static void Main()
  {
   // The debug code in this script, when activated, allows you
   // to accept the source document from a file and write the output
   // to a file
   // Debuggin code start
   //XmlDocument a = new XmlDocument();
   //a.PreserveWhitespace = true;
   //a.Load("Z:\\z_temp\\original.856.xml");
   //Reformat(a);
```

```
 //  Debugging code end
 //return;
 }

 static public XmlDocument Reformat(XmlDocument _asn)
 {
 //Debugging Code Start
 //string outputfile = "Z:\\z_temp\\asn_out.xml";
 //FileStream fileout = new FileStream(outputfile, FileMode.Create,
        FileAccess.Write);
 //StreamWriter writefileln = new StreamWriter(fileout);
 //Debugging Code End

 string line;
 int writeflag = 1;

 MemoryStream read = new MemoryStream();
 _asn.PreserveWhitespace = true;
 _asn.Save(read);
 read.Position = 0;

 MemoryStream _asnout = new MemoryStream();

 StreamReader readln = new StreamReader(read);
 StreamWriter writeln = new StreamWriter(_asnout);

 while (readln.Peek() != -1)
 {
  //=====================================================================
  line = readln.ReadLine();
  if (line.IndexOf("<EliteASN") != -1) line = line.Replace
       ("<EliteASN", "<EliteASN_Map") + "\r" + "\n";
  if (line.IndexOf("</EliteASN>") != -1) line = "</EliteASN_Map>" + "\r" + "\n";
  if (line.IndexOf("<HLLoopShipment>") != -1) line = "<Loop>";
  if (line.IndexOf("<HLLoopOrder>") != -1) line = "</Loop>" + "\r" +
       "\n" + "<Loop>";
  if (line.IndexOf("<HLLoopPack>") != -1) line = "</Loop>" + "\r" +
       "\n" + "<Loop>";
  if (line.IndexOf("<HLLoopItem>") != -1) line = "</Loop>" + "\r" +
       "\n" + "<Loop>";
  if (line.IndexOf("<CTT") != -1) line = "</Loop>" + "\r" + "\n" + line;
  if (line.IndexOf("<HL_S") != -1) line = line.Replace("_S", "");
  if (line.IndexOf("TD1_S") != -1) line = line.Replace("_S", "");
  if (line.IndexOf("TD5_S") != -1) line = line.Replace("_S", "");
  if (line.IndexOf("N1Loop_S") != -1) line = line.Replace("_S", "");
  if (line.IndexOf("N1_S") != -1) line = line.Replace("_S", "");
  if (line.IndexOf("N3_S") != -1) line = line.Replace("_S", "");
  if (line.IndexOf("N4_S") != -1) line = line.Replace("_S", "");
```

```csharp
            if (line.IndexOf("<REF_S") != -1) line = line.Replace("_S", "");
            if (line.IndexOf("<DTM_S") != -1) line = line.Replace("_S", "");
            if (line.IndexOf("<HL1_O") != -1) line = line.Replace("1_O", "");
            if (line.IndexOf("PRF_O") != -1) line = line.Replace("_O", "");
            if (line.IndexOf("TD1_O") != -1) line = line.Replace("_O", "");
            if (line.IndexOf("<REF_O") != -1) line = line.Replace("_O", "");
            if (line.IndexOf("N1Loop_O") != -1) line = line.Replace("_O", "");
            if (line.IndexOf("N1_O") != -1) line = line.Replace("_O", "");
            if (line.IndexOf("N3_O") != -1) line = line.Replace("_O", "");
            if (line.IndexOf("N4_O") != -1) line = line.Replace("_O", "");
            if (line.IndexOf("<HL1_P") != -1) line = line.Replace("1_P", "");
            if (line.IndexOf("PO4_P") != -1) line = line.Replace("_P", "");
            if (line.IndexOf("MAN_P") != -1) line = line.Replace("_P", "");
            if (line.IndexOf("<HL1_I") != -1) line = line.Replace("1_I", "");
            if (line.IndexOf("LIN_I") != -1) line = line.Replace("_I", "");
            if (line.IndexOf("SN1_I") != -1) line = line.Replace("_I", "");
            if (line.IndexOf("PO4_I") != -1) line = line.Replace("_I", "");
            if (line.IndexOf("TD5_I") != -1) line = line.Replace("_I", "");

            if (line.IndexOf("</HLLoopShipment>") != -1) writeflag = 0;
            if (line.IndexOf("</HLLoopOrder>") != -1) writeflag = 0;
            if (line.IndexOf("<HLLoopTare>") != -1) writeflag = 0;
            if (line.IndexOf("</HLLoopPack>") != -1) writeflag = 0;
            if (line.IndexOf("</HLLoopItem>") != -1) writeflag = 0;
            if (line.IndexOf("</HLLoopTare>") != -1) writeflag = 0;

            //Debugging Code Begins
            //if (writeflag == 1) writefileln.Write(line + "\r\n");
            //End Debugging Code

            if (writeflag == 1) writeln.Write(line + "\r\n");

            //Debugging Code Starts
            //writefileln.Flush();
            //Debugging Code Ends

            writeln.Flush();
            writeflag = 1;
        }

        _asnout.Seek(0, SeekOrigin.Begin);

        XmlDocument retdoc = new XmlDocument();
        retdoc.Load(_asnout);
        return retdoc;
    }
  }
}
```

Fundamentally, all this script does is convert the names of the Shipment, Order, Tare, Pack and Item loop nodes found in the application file to the name Loop, essentially flattening those loops. Since the first record in each loop contains the information needed to map the HL01 segment, this converts the source format into a replica of the target format, and mapping can be accomplished by dragging and dropping links. The output is in Listing 19-12.

Listing 19-12. *Reformatted Source Document*

```
<EliteASN_Map>
<ASNHeader />
<BOL>
 <BSN BSN01="00" BSN02="07438" BSN03="2006-05-18" BSN04="00:00" />
 <Loop>
  <HL HL01="1" HL03="S" />
  <TD1 TD101="CTN25" TD102="94" TD106="G" TD107="804.824" TD108="LB" />
  <TD5 TD501="B" TD502="2" TD503="AVRT" TD504="G" TD505="MOTOR CO" />
  <REF REF01="BM" REF02="07438770021167515" />
  <N1Loop>
   <N1 N101="SF" N103_1="1" N104_1="234" N103_91="91" N104_91="" />
  </N1Loop>
  <N1Loop>
   <N1 N101="ST" N103_1="1" N104_1="" N103_91="91" N104_91="345" />
   <N3 N301="11000 MY STREET" N302="" />
   <N4 N401="MY TOWN" N402="KY" N403="40299" N404="US" />
  </N1Loop>
 </Loop>
 <Loop>
  <HL HL01="1" HL02="2" HL03="O" />
  <PRF PRF01="0049733306" />
  <REF REF01="IV" REF02="" />
  <N1Loop>
   <N1 N101="BY" N102="MY TOWN" N103="92" N104="0025" />
  </N1Loop>
 </Loop>
 <Loop>
  <HL HL01="3" HL02="1" HL03="P" />
  <PO4 PO405="LB" PO406="9.86" />
 </Loop>
 <Loop>
  <HL HL01="4" HL02="3" HL03="I" />
  <LIN CB_LIN02="CB" UP_LIN02="UP" UP_LIN03="743877010047" />
  <SN1 SN102="12" SN103="EA" SN105="48" SN106="EA" />
 </Loop>
 <Loop>
  <HL HL01="5" HL02="1" HL03="P" />
  <PO4 PO405="LB" PO406="9.86" />
 </Loop>
 <Loop>
```

```
 <HL HL01="6" HL02="5" HL03="I" />
 <LIN CB_LIN02="CB" CB_LIN03="" UP_LIN02="UP" UP_LIN03="743877010047" />
 <SN1 SN102="12" SN103="EA" SN105="48" SN106="EA" />
 </Loop>
 <CTT CTT01="193" />
 </BOL>
 </EliteASN_Map>
```

This example provides a template for use in developing similar routines to massage data before or after mapping. The concept of manipulating the data structure to make processing simpler is the focus, not the specifics of this script. When you start struggling with a map, let your imagination soar.

Testing C# and VB Scripts

Chapter 4 covered testing maps and alluded to the need for scripts to be tested in the development studio. The art of testing code alone could be a sizable discussion. The subject of developing and testing code in Visual Studio would be a tome. We felt that this topic was worth at least an overview of those parts of the development studio debugger that we use most often. If you are familiar with using the development studio to develop and test code, you won't find anything new. If you are not, you will at least be able to recognize some of the capabilities that are available.

A BizTalk map is the worst place to test scripts. A simple typographical error, such as omitting a semicolon or misspelling a variable name, can cost a lot of time, since you have to manually go through the script to find the error. When the script executes but outputs erroneous data, you must add debugging code to the script to pin down where the error occurs. Fortunately the development studio provides you with a test bed for testing scripts.

Setting Up a Test Project

First, we create a new C# project and solution in the development studio. We do this in the same manner as we did with our map projects, except that we select a different project type and template, as shown in Figure 19-7. We select the template Console Application, because this template allows us not only to test entirely within the development studio but also to use a console application to test the script.

■**Note** The new C# project could be created as part of your existing BizTalk solution, but when you try to compile your script in the BizTalk project, scripts in other projects also build unless you manually disable those projects. This is particularly frustrating when there are overlapping object names and so forth.

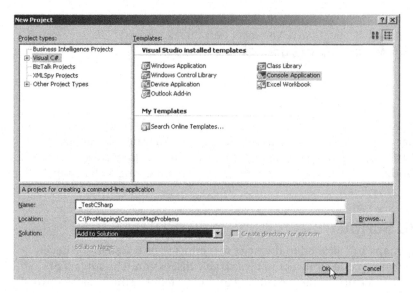

Figure 19-7. *Creating a C# solution and project*

The new application will contain a default code module named Program.cs. We rename the module to a more useful name, in this case CSharpTestBed.cs. Open the code module just as you would a map or schema. The code window for the new application is shown in Figure 19-8.

```
CSharpTestBed.cs*

ConsoleApplication1.Program                                    Main(string[] args)

using System;
using System.Collections.Generic;
using System.Text;

namespace ConsoleApplication1
{
    class Program
    {
        static void Main(string[] args)
        {
        }
    }
}
```

Figure 19-8. *The code window for a new application*

The default code is the starting point for development of an application. Note that there are only three using statements. If your code requires access to other objects you will need to add them here.

Creating Test Code

In this example, we develop a function that accepts a string value, pads it to a specified length, and returns the modified string. The function requires two inputs, the string to be padded and an integer indicating the desired length of the returned string. The script is in Listing 19-13.

Listing 19-13. *Script Used in the Test Example*

```
// padding a text string
public string PadText(string inText, int padLen)
{
 return inText.PadRight(padLen, Convert.ToChar("."));
}
```

We type this code into the code window, inside the brackets for the `class` object and outside the brackets of the `Main` function. We could put the code for multiple functions in the same location if, for example, we had a chain of functoids that called each other. Figure 19-9 shows the code window with our function added.

Note The code window provides some syntax checking as code is entered and substantial syntax checking when code is built. Drop-downs also appear to assist you in using standard functions.

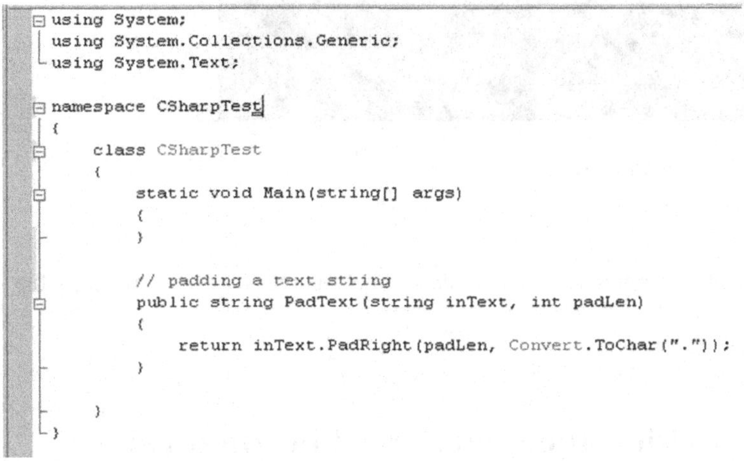

```
using System;
using System.Collections.Generic;
using System.Text;

namespace CSharpTest
{
    class CSharpTest
    {
        static void Main(string[] args)
        {
        }

        // padding a text string
        public string PadText(string inText, int padLen)
        {
            return inText.PadRight(padLen, Convert.ToChar("."));
        }
    }
}
```

Figure 19-9. *The code window with the function to be tested*

Using a Console Window to View the Function's Returned Value

Our next step depends on whether or not we wish to view the output data from our function in a console window. Using the console window provides a quick and easy method of checking the output. When we desire to use a console window for output, we insert the code shown in Listing 19-14 between the brackets of the main function.

Listing 19-14. *The Code to Output the Return Value to a Console Window*

```
Console.WriteLine(PadText("TEXT", 10));
Console.ReadLine();
```

The `Console.WriteLine` method opens a DOS window and writes the value returned from the `PadText` function into that window (see Figure 19-10). The `Console.ReadLine` function holds the DOS window open so that you can view the returned value. Press any key to close the window. Figure 19-10 shows the DOS window.

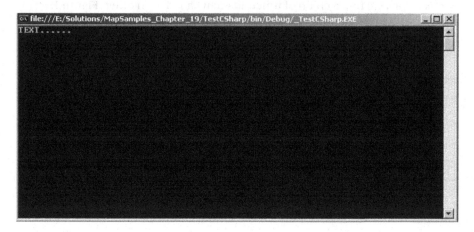

Figure 19-10. *Console window showing padded text*

■ **Caution** Remember that public objects referenced in the code window must be `static`. In this case, the PadText functoid must be `static`.

Using Function Calls to View the Function's Returned Value

If you do not desire to use a console window, you can replace the code in Listing 19-14 with the code in Listing 19-15.

Listing 19-15. *Calling Your Function Without Producing a Console Window*

```
PadText("TEXT", 10);
PadText("", 10);
PadText("TEXT", 48);
```

Here, we can call the `PadText` functoid three times and examine the output each time. Viewing the output is not as easy as with the console window, however. To use this method, you must understand the basics of using the development studio debugger. Figure 19-11 shows the results of this test as seen in the development studio.

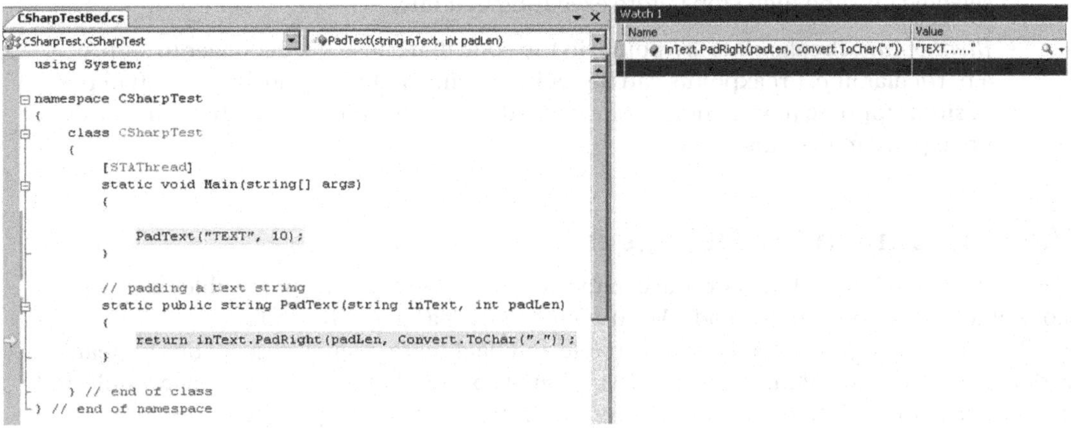

Figure 19-11. *The development studio with results of testing without a console window*

We used two capabilities of the development studio in this test. The first was the capability to select a specific line in the code and have the function stop running at that line. The second was the ability to assign a value to be watched in real-time. That value, shown in the right-hand pane, is the contents of `inText.PadRight(padLen, Convert.ToChar("."))`. That value in this case is `TEXT......`, the same value that we saw in the console window.

Now, let's examine some of the features of the development studio, including those we just used.

Running and Continuing the Debugger

We can start the debugger in one of several ways:

- *Use Start*: The green arrow icon on the toolbar and in the Debug drop-down starts the debugger and causes the code to execute.

- *Press F11*: This key, called Step Into, causes the debugger to execute one line at a time and follows the execution down into subfunctions.

- *Press F10*: This key, called Step Over, causes the debugger to execute one line at a time but does not follow the execution down into subfunctions.

We use the same three mechanisms to continue, or restart, the debugger once debugging has stopped inside the code, but the Start icon changes to a Continue icon.

Stopping the Debugger

To stop and exit a debugging session, use the blue square icon on the tool bar or in the Debug drop-down. This fully terminates the debugger. Often, stopping the debugger at a specific point in the code without stepping line-by-line to that point is necessary. We use two primary methods to stop at a particular point:

- *Run to cursor*: Right-clicking a line in the code brings up a selection menu that has this option. Selecting this option causes the debugger to execute all the code before the selected line and then stop before executing that line.

- *Breakpoints*: Breakpoints are points in the code that cause the debugger to stop at a particular line. Breakpoints can be set by clicking in the gray area to the left of the desired stopping point. They can be cleared by clicking the red ball that indicates a breakpoint in the same area.

Viewing Data in the Debugger

The main value of the debugger is the capability to view the contents of variables and expressions at different points in the code. We use mouse-over and watch windows.

When the mouse is moved over a variable and held there, a small pop-up box appears with the current value of that variable, assuming of course, that the variable is accessible and has a value at that point in the code. Figure 19-12 shows one of the pop-up boxes.

```
// padding a text string
static public string PadText(string inText, int padLen)
{
    return inText.PadRight(padLen, Convert.ToChar("."));
                            ♦ padLen  10
}

// end of class
```

Figure 19-12. *Debugging pop-up window*

Another alternative is to use watch windows. Right-clicking a variable or expression in the code window with the debugger running brings up a menu that allows the item to be added to a watch window. The value in the window changes as the item is affected by the code. Figure 19-13 shows a watch window for our code.

Watch 1			
Name	Value	Type	
● inText	"TEXT"	string	
● padLen	10	int	
● inText.PadRight(padLen, Convert.ToChar("."))	"TEXT......"	string	

Figure 19-13. *A watch window for our code*

We hardly touch the richness and depth of the development studio debugger in this section, but the pieces we mention are the keys to beginning to use it. There are a number of books on .NET debugging that may help expand your understanding of the subject.

Summary

This chapter presented solutions to a few oddball situations that we have encountered over the years. These are only a few of a number that we could include, and we had to leave many out because the solutions were so weird that we couldn't figure out what we did. Such oddball problems are often triggered by the business processes for which the mapping is created. Also, migrating old formats directly to BizTalk schemas without allowing changes, insisting that BizTalk produce multiple files from one input file, and refusing to modify a flag that causes incorrect EDI behavior are all situations that often create the need for fringe solutions such as the ones in this chapter.

Mapping in a BizTalk implementation cannot be isolated from other aspects of a BizTalk implementation. BizTalk developers find themselves faced with understanding business processes and data conversion issues related to the implementation that lie outside their normal experience. EDI mappers become BizTalk EDI mappers by virtue of their organizations changing from traditional EDI engines to BizTalk and in the process discover that they must become familiar with Visual Studio, scripting, configuring ports and trading partners, and so on. The secret to becoming a successful BizTalk mapper is to understand that the mapping engine is a critical part of BizTalk Server. Dedicating time to understanding the mapping engine and how it may be applied to a specific situation is as critical as learning any other aspect of BizTalk. Unfortunately, many folks' efforts to do just that have been derailed by the lack of documentation and instructional material on the subject. We hope that this book has helped you fill that knowledge gap.

Index

    exception to exception map, 54
    exception to the exception map with Equal
        Functoid, 56
    exception to the rule map
        code generated for, 52–53
        output of, 52
        scripts for, 51
    extending numbers, 138
    external assemblies, format date function
        code for, 78
    external XSLT map, 419
    extracting
        eight characters from within string, 160
        first forty characters from string, 160
        from beginning and end of string, 160
        left eight characters from string, 159
        locations and building delimited string,
            341
        part of date, 173
        REF CO and CT values, output of map
            for, 319
        right eight characters from string, 159
    Figure 5-2 map, output of, 117
    flat file
        calling function from listing 10-9, 212
        data for hash table, 209
        example of, 204
        extracting data from array, 215, 216
        extracting records from hash table and
            placing in array, 210–211
        extracting value from array, 211
        loading data into hash table, 206–207
        looking up one value in, 204–205
        multiple value lookup map, output
            from, 212
        records for retrieving multiple values,
            209
        revised, with no keys, 213
        unkeyed, loading into array, 213–214
    Format8Date script, 68–70
    formatting zero, 138
    Generated Instance excerpt, 100
    global variables
        declaring, and returning counter, 190
        for hash table, adding, 193
    hash tables
        collecting code pairs into, 328
        extracting value from and outputting it
            to target, 329
        getting value from, 207

        loading data into, 348–349
        retrieving item numbers from, 350–351
    HelloWorldInput.xml file, 16–17
    HelloWorld map
        custom script from, 44
        FullName node, original script to form
            and output, 62, 83
        internal variables, 38
        XSL code for, 34–36
        XSLT map, code generated for, 89–90
    HL segments
        with content identifiers, 361
        with HL01 identifiers, 360
        with identifiers, parent identifiers, and
            types, 360
        with identifiers, parent identifiers, and
            types—again, 361
    IComponent function of encoding mod-
        ule, 414
    if/else condition
        C# version, 124
        XSLT version, 124
    If-Exists
        C# version, 116
        XSLT version, 119
    if statement, splitting, 148
    inbound 856 ASN
        code for example map, 366–369
        source data for mapping, 363
        target data for mapping, 364
        XSLT code for example map, 369–370
    incremental testing data strings output by
        inbound SDQ data-gathering, 337
    InvoiceDueDate, 181
    LineCounter, outputting, 145
    line item container, checking, 194
    line items, counting, 144
    loading container numbers into hash
        table, 194
    LogicalIsString function exposed, 42
    Logical Numeric functoid
        C# code for, 133
        code generated for, 132
    Logical OR functoid for single return
        value, 126
    looping, many-to-one, 247, 248
    Looping functoid
        code generated by map with, 233
        using to determine looping structure,
            110

You Need the Companion eBook

Your purchase of this book entitles you to buy the companion PDF-version eBook for only $10. Take the weightless companion with you anywhere.

We believe this Apress title will prove so indispensable that you'll want to carry it with you everywhere, which is why we are offering the companion eBook (in PDF format) for $10 to customers who purchase this book now. Convenient and fully searchable, the PDF version of any content-rich, page-heavy Apress book makes a valuable addition to your programming library. You can easily find and copy code—or perform examples by quickly toggling between instructions and the application. Even simultaneously tackling a donut, diet soda, and complex code becomes simplified with hands-free eBooks!

Once you purchase your book, getting the $10 companion eBook is simple:

❶ Visit **www.apress.com/promo/tendollars/**.

❷ Complete a basic registration form to receive a randomly generated question about this title.

❸ Answer the question correctly in 60 seconds, and you will receive a promotional code to redeem for the $10.00 eBook.

THE EXPERT'S VOICE™

2855 TELEGRAPH AVENUE | SUITE 600 | BERKELEY, CA 94705

Offer valid through 9/09.